Gladstone Centenary Essays

To the memory of Colin Matthew
1941–1999
Gladstone scholar

Gladstone Centenary Essays

Edited by

David Bebbington and

Roger Swift

LIVERPOOL UNIVERSITY PRESS

First published 2000 by
Liverpool University Press
4 Cambridge Street
Liverpool
L69 7ZU

British Library Cataloguing-in-Publication Data
A British Library CIP record is available

ISBN 0 85323 925 8 cased
    0 85323 935 5 paperback

Typeset by Northern Phototypesetting Co. Ltd, Bolton
Printed in Great Britain by Bell and Bain Ltd, Glasgow

Contents

Contributors

David Bebbington is a Professor of History at the University of Stirling. His publications include *The Nonconformist Conscience* (1982), *Evangelicalism in Modern Britain* (1989), *Victorian Nonconformity* (1992) and *Holiness in Nineteenth-Century England* (2000) as well as *William Ewart Gladstone: Faith and Politics in Victorian Britain* (1994). He is one of the editors of the present volume.

Eugenio Biagini is a University Lecturer in Modern British History and a Fellow and Director of Studies in History at Robinson College, Cambridge. His publications include *Liberty, Retrenchment and Reform: Popular Liberalism in the Age of Gladstone* (1992), *Citizenship and Community* (1996) and *Gladstone* (2000).

Clyde Binfield is Professor Associate in History at the University of Sheffield. His publications include *George Williams and the YMCA* (1973), *So Down To Prayers: Studies in English Nonconformity, 1780–1920* (1977) and *Pastors and People: The Biography of a Baptist Church* (1984); he has also co-edited *The History of the City of Sheffield, 1843–1993* (3 vols, 1993) and *Mesters to Masters: A History of the Cutlers' Company of Hallamshire* (1997).

D. George Boyce is a Professor in the Department of Politics, University of Wales, Swansea. His publications include *Nationalism in Ireland* (3rd edition, 1996), *The Irish Question and British Politics, 1868–1996* (new and revised edition, 1996) and (edited with Alan O'Day) *Parnell in Perspective* (1991).

David Brooks is a Lecturer in History at Queen Mary and Westfield College, University of London. His publications include *The Destruction of Lord Rosebery* (1987) and *The Age of Upheaval: Edwardian Politics, 1899–1914* (1995).

Stewart J. Brown is Professor of Ecclesiastical History at the University of Edinburgh. His publications include *Thomas Chalmers and the Godly Commonwealth in Scotland* (1982) – awarded the Saltaire Society History Prize – *Scotland in the Age of the Disruption* (edited with Michael Fry, 1993), *William Robertson and the Expansion of Empire* (1997), *Piety and Power in Ireland, 1760–1960* (edited with D. W. Miller, 2000) and a number of articles and contributed book chapters. He has been co-editor of the *Scottish Historical Review* since 1993.

Eric J. Evans is Professor of Social History at the University of Lancaster. His publications include *The Forging of the Modern State, 1783–1870* (2nd ed., 1996), *The Great Reform Act of 1832* (2nd ed., 1994)), *Political Parties in Britain, 1783–1867* (1985), *Britain before the Reform Act: Politics and Society, 1815–32* (1989) and *Sir Robert Peel: Statesmanship, Power and Party* (1991). He is co-editor of the Lancaster Pamphlets series.

Anthony Howe is Senior Lecturer in International History at the London School of Economics. His publications include *The Cotton Masters, 1830–1860* (1984) and *Free Trade and Liberal England, 1846–1946* (1997). He has written widely on nineteenth-century economic policy and on aspects of the cultural and political formation of the Victorian middle classes.

Alan O'Day is a Senior Lecturer in History at the University of North London. His publications include *The English Face of Irish Nationalism* (1977), *Parnell and the First Irish Home Rule Episode* (1985) and *Irish Home Rule, 1867–1921* (1999), and he has also edited *A Survey of the Irish in England (1872)* (1990) and (with George Boyce) *Parnell in Perspective* (1991).

Jonathan Parry is a University Lecturer in Modern British History at Cambridge University and a Fellow and Director of Studies in History at Pembroke College. He has written *Democracy and Religion: Gladstone and the Liberal Party, 1867–1875* (1986) and *The Rise and Fall of Liberal Government in Victorian Britain* (1993).

Roland Quinault is a Reader in History at the University of North London. He was Honorary Secretary of the Royal Historical Society from 1990 until 1998. He has published many studies on British political and social history, including several on parliamentary reform. Most recently, he has co-edited *Anglo-American Attitudes: from Revolution to Partnership* (2000). He is currently writing a book on Prime Ministers and democracy.

Roger Swift is Professor of Victorian Studies at Chester College. His publications include *Police Reform in Early Victorian York, 1835–1856* (1988) and *Victorian Chester: Essays in Social History, 1830–1900* (1996), and he has co-edited (with Sheridan Gilley) *The Irish in the Victorian City* (1985), *The Irish in Britain, 1815–1939* (1989) and *The Irish in Victorian Britain: The Local Dimension* (1999). He is one of the editors of the present volume.

Chris Wrigley is Professor of Modern History at Nottingham University. He was President of the Historical Association from 1996 to 1999. His publications include *David Lloyd George and the British Labour Movement* (1976), *Lloyd George and the Challenge of Labour* (1990), *Arthur Henderson* (1990) and *Lloyd George* (1992). He has also edited a three-volume history of British industrial relations and several collections of A. J. P. Taylor's essays.

List of Illustrations

6, 7, 8, 9, 10, 12, 20, 21 and 23 are reproduced
with permission of Punch Ltd.

Preface

As this volume was in press, news came of the death of Professor Colin Matthew on 29 October 1999. His unexpected passing at the age of only 58 created a sense of shock in the scholarly community, especially amongst those who have taken an interest in the life of W. E. Gladstone. From its inception, Colin gave tremendous support to the project of holding an international conference to mark the centenary of the death of Gladstone. He participated in the conference at Chester, delivering, as the introduction below mentions, the opening public lecture. Colin was the obvious choice of speaker for the occasion because of his unparalleled expertise on the statesman. His first book, published in 1973, had described Gladstone as 'for so long the unifier and inspirer of the Liberal party' and for the next two decades he was occupied with explaining how that came to be.[1] Already Lecturer in Gladstone Studies at Christ Church, Oxford, Colin ran a seminar at Oxford on features of the statesman's career, produced articles on aspects of his activities and prepared the material that was to emerge in the two volumes which he described as his 'extended biographical essay' on Gladstone in 1986 and 1995.

The biographical study was based on the introductions to the successive volumes of Gladstone's diaries that Matthew edited. The series of diaries, inaugurated in 1968 by M. R. D. Foot, included two volumes edited by Foot and Matthew in 1974 and then a further ten volumes issued by Matthew alone from 1978 to 1994. This massive enterprise was on any estimate a triumph of perseverance, but it was far more. The introductions reinterpreted Gladstone's achievement by integrating the private with the public life of the statesman, so showing how the personal preoccupations – with Christian reunion, for example – impinged on his conduct in national and international affairs. The footnotes in the diaries, copious but always unfussy, drew attention to the unpublished memoranda in the British Library whose significance Matthew fully appreciated. In later volumes some of them were published in the text of the diaries, together with selected correspondence and notes on cabinet meetings that greatly enhance the value of the edition. Colin was probably proudest of volume 14, the last to be issued. It contains three indexes: to the 20,000 or so individuals named in the diaries; to the roughly 21,000 books and articles that Gladstone recorded reading; and to the subjects mentioned in the printed material, including (a typical Matthew touch) topics ranging from card games to God. The index, let alone the remaining volumes of the edition, will forever remain an invaluable resource for the historian of the Victorian era. The successful publication of the diaries earned Matthew deserved recognition – a Fellowship of the British Academy in 1991 and a personal Professorship of Modern History at Oxford in the following year. It also brought him his next vast responsibility, the editing of *The New Dictionary of National Biography*, which he had taken more than half way to completion by the time of his untimely death. Colin Matthew was an immensely productive scholar; he was also, as many of the contributors to this book have cause to testify, an extremely generous one. All Gladstone specialists are greatly in his debt.

David Bebbington
University of Stirling

Roger Swift
Chester College

Note

1   H. C. G. Matthew, *The Liberal Imperialists: The Ideas and Politics of a Post-Gladstonian Elite*, Oxford, Oxford UP, 1973, p. vii.

Acknowledgements

This collection of essays arises from some of the papers delivered at the Gladstone Centenary International Conference held at Chester College in July 1998, which brought together almost one hundred scholars from Britain, Europe, North America, Australia and Japan in commemoration of the centenary of the death of William Ewart Gladstone. The conference represented a joint initiative between St Deiniol's Library, Hawarden, and the Centre for Victorian Studies at Chester College, and its success, of which the present volume is, we trust, an appropriate testament, owes much to the support and encouragement provided by several individuals and institutions. In particular, we wish to express our gratitude to Sir William Gladstone, the great-grandson of the Prime Minister, for his kindness and generosity in helping to make the conference possible; to the Reverend Peter Francis, Warden and Chief Librarian of St Deiniol's Library; and to Professor Michael Wheeler and the Trustees of St Deiniol's Library for their endorsement and help. We are also indebted to the Royal Historical Society and Primary Source Media for co-sponsoring the conference. We also gratefully acknowledge the help of Sir William Gladstone, of the staff of St Deiniol's Library, Hawarden, and of the Flintshire Record Office in the preparation of the illustrations for this volume. Thanks are due to each of them and also to the following for permission to reproduce illustrations: the Mary Evans Picture Library and the University of Edinburgh Library. Our greatest debt, however, is to the contributors themselves for providing new insights into the life, both public and private, of the 'Grand Old Man'.

Abbreviations

The following abbreviations are used in the notes:

GD *The Gladstone Diaries*, 14 vols, Oxford, Clarendon Press, 1968–94, ed. M. R. D. Foot [vols 1–2]; ed. M. R. D. Foot and H. C. G. Matthew [vols 3–4]; ed. H. C. G. Matthew [vols 5–14]. Diary entries are indicated by date only. Inserted material is indicated by volume and page number.
GP Gladstone Papers, British Library, Add. MS(S).

Introduction

David Bebbington

The centenary of the death of W. E. Gladstone in 1998 was marked in several ways. On 18 May 1998, the eve of the precise anniversary, the University of Oxford, which he represented in parliament from 1847 to 1865, held a service of commemoration at the University Church of St Mary the Virgin. Lord Runcie, the former Archbishop of Canterbury, preached a sermon that soon appeared under the title 'God's Politician'.[1] On the following day a sequence of events took place at Westminster. An exhibition was opened in Westminster Hall by Lord Jenkins, recently Gladstone's biographer; evensong, incorporating Gladstone's own hymn 'O Lead My Blindness by the Hand', was sung in Westminster Abbey; wreaths were laid by junior members of the Gladstone family on the grave and by the statue in the abbey; and another was placed by the Speaker of the House of Commons on the spot where Gladstone's body had lain in state in Westminster Hall. A reception followed at the National Liberal Club. Church, state and university, the institutions that Gladstone served, had not forgotten him.

Nor had historians. From 5 to 8 July there was held at Chester College a Gladstone Centenary International Conference, attracting almost one hundred people. The occasion included visits to Hawarden Castle, Gladstone's home from 1851 onwards, and to St Deiniol's Library in the same village, the residential library that Gladstone established with the gift of the bulk of his own books. After the conference the annual Founder's Day gathering associated with the library took place: Lord Habgood, the former Archbishop of York, preached in Hawarden Church and Lord Jenkins delivered the Founder's Day address. Sir William Gladstone, the Prime Minister's great-grandson, was the after-dinner speaker during the conference. But the chief activity of the conference was listening to academic papers. Twenty-seven were given on various aspects of the statesman, the first being a public lecture by Professor Colin Matthew on 'Gladstone: The Man through his Diaries'. Many of these papers are due to be published by St Deiniol's Library itself; others are collected in the present volume, published by the university press of the city where Gladstone was born. They represent some of the estimates of the statesman current among historians a century after his death.

In the intervening hundred years the scholarship relating to Gladstone has fallen into a number of categories. It will be useful to review that literature here to provide a context for the papers in this volume. First, there was the material published by those who wished to keep the statesman's memory green. Pride of place must go to the three-volume biography composed by Gladstone's former cabinet colleague, John Morley. Massive, leisurely and authoritative, it was a huge achievement – all the greater since it appeared a mere five years after its subject's death.[2] It inevitably breathes a spirit of devotion to the lost leader. The chapter in the first volume on 'Characteristics', for example, concludes with celebration of 'a personality so vigorous, intrepid, confident, and capable as his'. Yet the biography is far less hagiographical than might be assumed. The same chapter is studded with criticisms of its subject, often veiled or oblique but criticisms none the less. 'Whether', he reflects, 'Mr Gladstone ever became what is called a good judge of men it would be hard to say.'[3] The statement is tentative, noncommittal, but its implication, pointing to one of Gladstone's greatest deficiencies, is clear enough. Similar techniques repeatedly qualify the praise poured on the Liberal leader. If Gladstone was eulogised, he was also viewed with the critical eye that we know Morley trained on the leader during his lifetime. The biography remains a rich repository of judicious perspectives on the statesman as well as the basic source of information about his career.

Other similar appraisals, scholarly but dedicated to the promotion of Gladstonian ideals in the twentieth century, followed in the track marked out by Morley. A few of them can be singled out as instances. Paul Knaplund wrote on foreign affairs in 1927 and 1935, wishing to commend the pursuit of peace, the defence of small nations and the emerging ideal of the Commonwealth.[4] F. W. Hirst, who had assisted Morley with the biography of the Liberal leader, published a book on *Gladstone as Financier and Economist* in 1931, the fateful year when global economic conditions drove Britain to abandon free trade. As the introduction by Gladstone's son Henry makes plain, Hirst's purpose was to commend the principle of retrenchment as the lodestar of government policy.[5] In a collection of essays for the Liberal luminary Gilbert Murray issued in 1936, J. L. Hammond described Gladstone as possessing a 'League of Nations mind'. His contemporary purpose, the shoring up of the declining international peace-keeping body, could hardly have been more explicit.[6] The culmination of the tradition of works celebrating Gladstone's legacy came in 1938 with *Gladstone and the Irish Nation*, again by Hammond, a special correspondent of the *Manchester Guardian*. Near the conclusion Hammond claimed that his hero was 'a most ardent democrat because he believed that free discussion and self-government were essential to man's dignity and self-respect'.[7] Though containing a germ of truth, the anachronism of the judgement illustrates the unavoidable weakness of this early body of literature.

In another sense, however, Hammond's book inaugurated the era of detailed research on Gladstone. He examined the Gladstone papers on issues relating to Ireland with care and discrimination – though the debt to that source is obscured by the paucity of references, a consequence of the fact that the papers were still unfoliated when Hammond worked on them. In 1963 M. R. D. Foot, who had completed Hammond's unfinished biography of Gladstone in the 'Teach Yourself History' series, judged *Gladstone and the Irish Nation* to be 'the most formidable and incisive piece of original research yet published on the history of England or Ireland in the second half of the nineteenth century'.[8] But other works of significant scholarship had already appeared. Apart from Sir Philip Magnus-Allcroft's biography of 1954, which was immensely readable and brought out the risibility of some of Gladstone's traits,[9] there appeared in 1952 a scrupulously prepared edition of the correspondence of Gladstone with Lord Granville, his cabinet trouble-shooter as well as Foreign Secretary from 1870, covering in two volumes the years from 1868 to 1876. A decade later Agatha Ramm, their editor, added two more volumes, taking the coverage down to 1886.[10] The process that, in the concluding session of the Chester conference, Professor Walter Arnstein described as 'the transition from the memoir to the monograph' was completed by the publication, in 1963, of R. T. Shannon's *Gladstone and the Bulgarian Agitation, 1876*. Shannon drew fully for the first time on the entire range of available evidence in analysing an episode in Gladstone's career.[11] Another followed shortly afterwards in Professor Arnstein's own *The Bradlaugh Case* (1965).[12] The inauguration of the publication of the statesman's diaries in 1968, initially under the editorship of M. R. D. Foot, showed that Gladstone studies had come of age.[13]

In the mature era of the scrutiny of Gladstone since the 1960s, there have been several distinct approaches to the subject. One, showing least interest in the detail of Gladstone's career but nevertheless acknowledging his importance, has been the perspective associated with analysis of the nineteenth century in terms of class and economic interest. Usually but by no means always left-wing or even *marxisant* in orientation, historians of this school have commonly mentioned Gladstone as an obstacle to the progress of labour in the political sphere. Thus in a paper revised in 1963 E. J. Hobsbawm wrote that the Liberal party might have succeeded in gaining the allegiance of the workers 'but for the reluctance of older politicians like Gladstone and of certain groups of businessmen in the party to pay the necessary price in "government interference"'.[14] An instance of this body of writing that recognises that Gladstonian Liberalism did actually rouse the enthusiasm of working-class leaders was Royden Harrison's *Before the Socialists* (1965).[15] But this school of historiography, if operating on premises moulded by Marx, could contend that the Liberal allegiance of the working people was a form of false consciousness. Material interests were the ultimate reality; ideas were the chaff of politics, tossed in the air to blur the vision of the people. The notion that Gladstone was repressing the working classes, for whom he had no sympathy, might have been severely dented by Michael Barker's *Gladstone and Radicalism* (1975),[16] but it still lives on in many popular understandings of the Victorian period.

The 'high politics' school of historians, usually of right-wing opinions, reacted against this reading of the epoch. Like their opponents, they deprecated ideas, holding that Gladstone may have expressed an elaborate body of thought but that his political actions were shaped by the constraints of tactical manoeuvre. Hence, like other politicians, he was constantly prepared to shift his ground and so was inconsistent over time. But, unlike those historians who analysed the period in terms of economic interests, they concentrated attention on the few individuals near the centre of public life. Only this small group mattered in the exercise of power. Consequently the high politics analysts paid extensive consideration to Gladstone, who for so long was at the heart of the fray at Westminster. Believing in the power of narrative to illuminate the predominant motive of ambition, they chronicled Gladstone's doings at several periods – during the reform controversies of the 1860s, in John Vincent's *The Formation of the Liberal Party* (1966) and in Maurice Cowling's *1867* (1967); during the gestation of the next Reform Act, in Andrew Jones's *The Politics of Reform, 1884* (1972); and, most fully, during the emergence of home rule in 1885–86, in A. B. Cooke and John Vincent's *The Governing Passion* (1974).[17] The charge of inconsistency is brilliantly developed in John Vincent's 'Gladstone and Ireland' (1977), targeting Hammond's eulogistic treatment of the statesman's Irish policy, an article which concludes with the paradox that the only pattern of achievement reveals Gladstone as 'the most masterly upholder of Unionism since Pitt'.[18] The approach of this school of historians has been most directly criticised in the thorough statistical study of the home rule crisis by W. C. Lubenow (1988). Ideology, he shows, did influence MPs: consistency mattered to them, and politics was not just a quest for power.[19] The pains taken by Gladstone to justify his change of course on Irish disestablishment in his 'Chapter of Autobiography' (1868) go a long way towards making the same point.[20] It is hard to suppose that ideas were really so remote from Gladstone's political activities as the high politics school believes.

A further distinct perspective on Gladstone's politics has been offered by two other historians whose sympathies are with the older Liberal tradition of the nineteenth century. T. A. Jenkins argued in a book on the Whigs between 1874 and 1886 that Gladstone gave too little scope to the skills of Hartington, Granville and their landed colleagues.[21] Jonathan Parry, in a work on Gladstone's first administration and another on the Liberal style of government, contended that the statesman introduced an alien Peelite impatience with leisurely parliamentary decision-making that destabilised Liberalism.[22] By contrast with the two previous schools of thought, the clash of ideas is central to Parry's analysis. Both writers are critical of the interpretation of D. A. Hamer that Gladstone was able to keep the Whig and Radical wings of the party together by means of adroit and authoritative management.[23] Home rule, which on Hamer's account was a masterly project for welding his forces into unity, was in reality a disaster for the party.

This point of view is represented in the present volume by Jonathan Parry's own contribution on some of the difficulties of the first administration. Gladstone's arbitrary manner of leadership is also held responsible in David Brooks's paper for many of the problems of the fourth administration.

Much recent study has been directed, with a varying but substantial degree of sympathy, to understanding Gladstone's position on major questions rather than taking issue with it. Olive Anderson, in her examination of Crimean War finances, established that the statesman's policies were far less determined by the dictates of laissez-faire than Hirst had supposed.[24] Deryck Schreuder has greatly illuminated Gladstone's attitude to overseas affairs.[25] Derek Beales, whose expertise in the field of Gladstone's stance on foreign affairs went back to his study of Anglo-Italian relations in 1961, subsequently proposed in a suggestive review that Gladstone was far more proactive in his first administration than others have believed.[26] His Irish policy has been scrutinised with particular care: David Steele analysed his first Land Act of 1870, Margaret O'Callaghan the circumstances of the second in 1881 and Alan Warren the genesis of home rule.[27] James Loughlin has examined the attitude of the Liberal leader to Ulster,[28] though part of his thesis, that Gladstone neglected the significance of Unionism, is challenged in this volume by George Boyce.

There have also been important overall interpretations of Gladstone. The outstanding achievement is the synthesis created by the editor of most of the statesman's diaries, Colin Matthew. His introductions have been brought together in a biography that will long stand as the benchmark for other Gladstone studies.[29] It shows a remarkable skill in drawing connections between apparently disparate aspects of his subject's career. The identification, for example, of a crisis in Gladstone's life around 1850 precipitated by sexual temptation, bereavement, the drawing away of friends to Rome, family debt and the disintegration of the Conservative party transformed our understanding of the man. Earlier articles also made a particular impact because of their linking of what had previously been treated separately: fiscal and franchise policies in one article, ecclesiastical and Bulgarian enthusiasms in another.[30] The first biography by another hand to draw on the full range of diaries was that by Roy Jenkins, who could consequently integrate the private with the public life to a greater degree than previous writers. Himself a former Chancellor of the Exchequer, Jenkins was able to portray the achievements of his subject in the fiscal sphere with special authority.[31] Even more recently there has appeared an attempt to deploy psychology to understand Gladstone's life. T. L. Crosby suggested that a stress and coping model helps explain the statesman's mingling of angry outbursts with stern self-discipline.[32] Although it would be hard to say how far this analysis advances our understanding of the man, it has the undoubted merit of – once more – trying to see Gladstone whole.

What was the chief influence on Gladstone's career? Several authors, following remarks by Gladstone himself, have identified Sir Robert Peel as a decisive mentor. Peel the pragmatic strategist depicted by Norman Gash and Peel the committed ideologue portrayed by Boyd Hilton have both been seen as shaping the young man brought into his cabinet by the Conservative Prime Minister in 1843.[33] Gladstone the Peelite has been documented by J. B. Conacher,[34] and his debt to Peel is explored in this volume by Eric Evans. It is a fundamental premise of the interpretations of a number of recent scholars that there is a continuity in Gladstone's subsequent career deriving from his maintenance of a Peelite stance – defending traditional institutions by making ample concessions through decisive executive action. This esti-mate is a salient feature of Parry's analysis, but it is also a central contention in Richard Shannon's biography.[35] The continuity, though it is not traced explicitly to Peel, is reasserted in the present collection by Roland Quinault's study of Gladstone's attitude to parliamentary reform. Others, however, have discerned sharper discontinuities because of subsequent influences. Thus David Steele has argued for a rich legacy from Palmerston to Gladstone, proposing that the older statesman was far more progressive than has been supposed and that Gladstone learned even the technique of provincial speak-ing tours from him.[36] In this volume Anthony Howe puts forward the case for recognising Richard Cobden as another formative influence. A measure of discontinuity is also implicit in the analysis of Eugenio Biagini, who has seen Gladstone as sharing his mature outlook in essentials with John Stuart Mill.[37] Biagini nevertheless argues in this collection for the enduring signifi-cance of Edmund Burke, an earlier mentor than Peel, on Gladstone's atti-tudes to empire during his second administration.

Other very early influences on Gladstone came from his home. Sidney Checkland brought out in his study of the family background the powerful personality of the statesman's father, the self-made millionaire Sir John Glad-stone.[38] Equally, however, Checkland showed that Gladstone's mother, Anne, exerted an influence over her son by introducing him to Evangelical religion. The first stages of Gladstone's subsequent religious pilgrimage are traced in books by Perry Butler and Peter Jagger.[39] The importance of reli-gion to Gladstone emerges in the present book in, among other places, the essay by Stewart Brown on his relations with Thomas Chalmers, the Evan-gelical leader in the Church of Scotland.

Gladstone's own legacy to later generations has not yet been systemati-cally researched. Here, however, his reputation in the Liberal party of the early twentieth century is examined by Chris Wrigley. His image in Irish his-torical studies is the theme of Alan O'Day's contribution. Clyde Binfield explores the subsequent ramifications of the family in his paper, which also looks at his contemporary reputation among Nonconformists. So a begin-ning has been made in this volume in tracing how the image of Gladstone – surely one of the most potent ever generated in politics – was sustained and put to use in the years after his death.

The cultural dimensions of Gladstone studies have produced some valuable work. Frank Turner's book *The Greek Heritage in Victorian Britain* contains a penetrating account of Gladstone's views on the significance of Homer in politics as well as religion.[40] Sir Hugh Lloyd-Jones has also written on Gladstone's Homeric concerns,[41] and in this volume there is a study of the theme by David Bebbington. Sir Owen Chadwick has written on Gladstone's appreciation of Dante,[42] and Marcia Pointon on his taste and patronage in art.[43] The essays in the second volume of Founder's Day addresses from St Deiniol's Library include further items in this category.[44] It was suggested at the Chester conference that, because of the record of Gladstone's cultural interests now available in the diaries, this field is likely to be more fully cultivated in the future. It may well be that the development of interest in cultural history *per se*, seconded by the rise of postmodernism in historical work,[45] may tend in the same direction.

It certainly seems just to expect a growth of Gladstone studies in the future. It is true that the later nineteenth century has not been the most widely explored period of British history in the recent past; nor has high politics commanded as much attention as many other themes. Yet the Grand Old Man exercises a perennial fascination, as the success of Roy Jenkins's biography illustrates. Gladstone touched life at too many points for him ever to fall out of scholarly fashion. The centrality of the man in Victorian Britain, together with his ascendancy in politics and his versatility in so many other areas, means that insofar as Victorian studies flourish, so will scholarship on Gladstone.

Notes

1 *The Spectator*, 23 May 1998, pp. 14–15.
2 M. R. D. Foot, 'Morley's Gladstone: A Reappraisal', *Bulletin of the John Rylands Library*, Vol. 51, 1969, pp. 368–80.
3 J. Morley, *The Life of William Ewart Gladstone*, London, Macmillan, 1903, vol. 1, pp. 218, 197.
4 P. Knaplund, *Gladstone and Britain's Imperial Policy*, London, Allen & Unwin, 1927; P. Knaplund, *Gladstone's Foreign Policy*, New York, 1935. Cf. D. M. Schreuder, 'The Making of Mr Gladstone's Posthumous Career: The Role of Morley and Knaplund as "Monumental Masons", 1903–27', in *The Gladstonian Turn of Mind*, ed. B. L. Kinzer, Toronto, University of Toronto Press, 1985, pp. 197–243.
5 H. N. Gladstone in F. W. Hirst, *Gladstone as Financier and Economist*, London, Ernest Benn, 1931, p. xx.
6 J. L. Hammond, 'Gladstone and the League of Nations Mind', in *Essays in Honour of Gilbert Murray*, ed. J. A. K. Thomson and A. J. Toynbee, London, Allen & Unwin, 1936, pp. 95–118.
7 J. L. Hammond, *Gladstone and the Irish Nation*, London, Longmans Green, 1938, p. 720.
8 Foot in rev. edn of ibid., London, Frank Cass, 1964, p. xxi.
9 P. Magnus (Magnus-Allcroft), *Gladstone*, London, John Murray, 1954.

10 A. Ramm (ed.), *The Political Correspondence of Mr Gladstone and Lord Granville, 1868–1876*, Camden Third Series, vols 81 and 82, London, Royal Historical Society, 1952. A. Ramm (ed.), *The Political Correspondence of Mr Gladstone and Lord Granville, 1876–1886*, Oxford, Clarendon Press, 1962.

11 R. T. Shannon, *Gladstone and the Bulgarian Agitation, 1876*, London, Thomas Nelson & Sons, 1963.

12 W. L. Arnstein, *The Bradlaugh Case: Atheism, Sex and Politics among the Late Victorians*, Oxford, Oxford UP, 1965.

13 M. R. D. Foot and H. C. G. Matthew (eds), *The Gladstone Diaries*, 14 vols, Oxford, Clarendon Press, 1968–94.

14 E. J. Hobsbawm, 'Trends in the British Labour Movement since 1850', *Labouring Men: Studies in the History of Labour*, London, Weidenfeld & Nicolson, 1964, p. 338.

15 R. Harrison, *Before the Socialists: Studies in Labour and Politics, 1861–1881*, London, Routledge & Kegan Paul, 1965.

16 M. Barker, *Gladstone and Radicalism: The Reconstruction of Liberal Policy in Britain, 1885–1894*, Hassocks, Sussex, Harvester Press, 1975.

17 J. Vincent, *The Formation of the Liberal Party, 1857–1868*, London, Constable, 1966; M. Cowling, *1867: Disraeli, Gladstone and Revolution: The Passing of the Second Reform Bill*, Cambridge, Cambridge UP, 1967; A. Jones, *The Politics of Reform, 1884*, Cambridge, Cambridge UP, 1972; A. B. Cooke and J. R. Vincent, *The Governing Passion: Cabinet Government and Party Politics in Britain, 1885–86*, Brighton, Harvester Press, 1974.

18 J. Vincent, 'Gladstone and Ireland', *Proceedings of the British Academy*, Vol. 63, 1977, p. 232.

19 W. C. Lubenow, *Parliamentary Politics and the Home Rule Crisis: The British House of Commons in 1886*, Oxford, Clarendon Press, 1988.

20 W. E. Gladstone, 'A Chapter of Autobiography', *Gleanings of Past Years, 1843–79*, 7 vols, London, John Murray, 1879, vol. 7.

21 T. A. Jenkins, *Gladstone, Whiggery and the Liberal Party, 1874–1886*, Oxford, Clarendon Press, 1988.

22 J. P. Parry, *Democracy and Religion: Gladstone and the Liberal Party, 1867–1875*, Cambridge, Cambridge UP, 1986; J. P. Parry, *The Rise and Fall of Liberal Government in Victorian Britain*, New Haven, Connecticut, Yale UP, 1993.

23 D. A. Hamer, *Liberal Politics in the Age of Gladstone and Rosebery: A Study in Leadership and Policy*, Oxford, Clarendon Press, 1972.

24 O. Anderson, *A Liberal State at War: English Politics and Economics during the Crimean War*, London, Macmillan, 1967.

25 D. M. Schreuder, *Gladstone and Kruger: Liberal Government and Colonial 'Home Rule', 1880–85*, London, Routledge & Kegan Paul, 1969; D. M. Schreuder, 'Gladstone and Italian Unification: The Making of a Liberal?', *English Historical Review*, Vol. 85, 1970, pp. 475–501; D. M. Schreuder, 'Gladstone as "Trouble-Maker": Liberal Foreign Policy and the German Annexation of Alsace-Lorraine, 1870–1871', *Journal of British Studies*, Vol. 17, 1978, pp. 106–35.

26 D. Beales, *England and Italy, 1859–60*, London, Nelson, 1961; D. Beales, 'Gladstone and his First Ministry', *Historical Journal*, Vol. 26, 1983, pp. 987–98.

27 E. D. Steele, *Irish Land and British Politics: Tenant Right and Nationality, 1865–1870*, Cambridge, Cambridge UP, 1974; M. O'Callaghan, *British High Politics and a Nationalist Ireland: Criminality, Land and the Law under Forster and Balfour*, Cork,

Cork UP, 1994; A. Warren, 'Gladstone, Land and Social Reconstruction in Ireland, 1881–87', *Parliamentary History*, Vol. 2, 1983, pp. 153–73.

28 J. Loughlin, *Gladstone, Home Rule and the Ulster Question, 1882–93*, Dublin, Gill & Macmillan, 1986.

29 H. C. G. Matthew, *Gladstone, 1809–1898*, Oxford, Clarendon Press, 1997. This is a revised version of what had originally appeared as two volumes in 1986 and 1995.

30 H. C. G. Matthew, 'Disraeli, Gladstone and the Politics of Mid-Victorian Budgets', *Historical Journal*, Vol. 22, 1979, pp. 615–43; H. C. G. Matthew, 'Gladstone, Vaticanism and the Question of the East', in *Religious Motivation: Biographical and Sociological Problems for the Church Historian*, ed. D. Baker (Studies in Church History, vol. 15), Oxford, Basil Blackwell, 1978, pp. 417–42.

31 R. Jenkins, *Gladstone*, London, Macmillan, 1995.

32 T. L. Crosby, *The Two Mr Gladstones: A Study in Psychology and History*, New Haven, Connecticut, Yale UP, 1997.

33 N. Gash, *Sir Robert Peel: The Life of Sir Robert Peel after 1830*, London, Longman, 1972; B. Hilton, 'Peel: A Reappraisal', *Historical Journal*, Vol. 22, 1979, pp. 585–614; B. Hilton, *The Age of Atonement: The Influence of Evangelicalism on Economic and Social Thought, 1785–1865*, Oxford, Clarendon Press, 1988, chap.9.

34 J. B. Conacher, *The Aberdeen Coalition, 1852–1855: A Study in Mid-Nineteenth-Century Party Politics*, Cambridge, Cambridge UP, 1968; J. B. Conacher, *The Peelites and the Party System, 1846–52*, Newton Abbot, David & Charles, 1972.

35 R. Shannon, *Gladstone*, 2 vols, London, Hamish Hamilton, 1982, and Allen Lane, 1999.

36 E. D. Steele, *Palmerston and Liberalism, 1855–1865*, Cambridge, Cambridge UP, 1991.

37 E. F. Biagini, *Liberty, Retrenchment and Reform: Popular Liberalism in the Age of Gladstone, 1860–1880*, Cambridge, Cambridge UP, 1992.

38 S. G. Checkland, *The Gladstones: A Family Biography, 1764–1851*, Cambridge, Cambridge UP, 1971.

39 P. Butler, *Gladstone: Church, State and Tractarianism: A Study of his Religious Ideas and Attitudes, 1809–1859*, Oxford, Clarendon Press, 1982; P. J. Jagger, *Gladstone: The Making of a Christian Politician: The Personal Religious Life and Development of William Ewart Gladstone, 1809–1832*, Allison Park, Pennsylvania, Pickwick Publications, 1991.

40 F. M. Turner, *The Greek Heritage in Victorian Britain*, New Haven, Connecticut, Yale UP, 1981, chaps 4 and 5.

41 H. Lloyd-Jones, 'Gladstone on Homer' *The Times Literary Supplement*, 3 January 1975, pp. 15–17 (reprinted in his *Blood for the Ghosts*, London, Duckworth, 1982).

42 O. Chadwick, 'Young Gladstone and Italy', *Journal of Ecclesiastical History*, Vol. 30, 1979, pp. 243–59 (reprinted in P. J. Jagger (ed.), *Gladstone, Politics and Religion*, London, Macmillan, 1985).

43 M. Pointon, 'Gladstone as Art Patron and Collector', *Victorian Studies*, Vol. 19, 1975, pp. 73–98.

44 P. J. Jagger (ed.), *Gladstone*, London, Hambledon Press, 1998.

45 A start has been made in P.Joyce, *Democratic Subjects: The Self and the Social in Nineteenth-Century England*, Cambridge, Cambridge UP, 1994, chaps 15–17.

Gladstone, Chalmers and the Disruption of the Church of Scotland

Stewart J. Brown

1 Thomas Chalmers, calotype by David Octavius Hill, c. 1844

I

IN April and May 1838, the 28-year-old William Ewart Gladstone attended a series of lectures on the establishment and extension of national churches delivered in London by the celebrated Scottish Presbyterian divine, Thomas Chalmers. The rooms at Hanover Square were 'crowded to suffocation' with fashionable audiences, including Anglican bishops and leading politicians. Chalmers's aim in the lectures was to inspire co-ordinated political action for the defence and extension of the established churches in both England and Scotland. Gladstone attended the lectures both as a politician who shared Chalmers's commitment to the idea of a national church, and as a friend and admirer of the Scottish divine. However, he came away from the lectures convinced they were fundamentally unsound. He conveyed his misgivings to his friend, Henry Manning, on 14 May 1838: 'Such a jumble of church, unchurch, and anti-church principles as that excellent and eloquent man Dr Chalmers has given us in his recent lectures, no human being ever heard.' Chalmers, Gladstone insisted, had no real understanding of the visible church, nor any idea of the true relationship of church and state. 'He flogged', Gladstone continued to Manning, 'the apostolical succession grievously, seven bishops sitting below him: London, Winchester, Chester, Oxford, Llandaff, Gloucester, Exeter, and the Duke of Cambridge incessantly bobbing assent.' Stung into action, Gladstone began writing his own book on the relations of church and state, a subject that had been ripening in his mind for some months. He completed the first draft of his book on 23 July 1838, and published the work by the end of the year.[1]

Gladstone's *The State in its Relations with the Church* reflected the acute religious tensions of the 1830s, as Dissenters, Radicals and Roman Catholics pressed for an end to the connection of church and state in the United Kingdom, and the established churches struggled to redefine their role in the radically new social and political order that had emerged with the passing of Catholic Emancipation and the Reform Act. The book provided an intelligent defence of the exclusive claims of Anglicanism to state support in an increasingly pluralistic society. It also questioned the claims of the Presbyterian establishment in Scotland to state support, and in so doing it marked the end of his close association with Chalmers, a man whom Gladstone would later describe as 'that noble-hearted man ... the flower and cream of Presbyterianism'.[2] During the mid-1830s, the young Anglican politician and the middle-aged Scottish Presbyterian clergyman had been friends and political allies. Chalmers had been arguably Britain's leading intellectual advocate of the establishment principle, a clergyman and university professor whose numerous publications argued for the necessity of an established church for social cohesion and harmony. Gladstone had been the rising hope of the Anglican establishment in parliament, a man who had entered politics with the professed aim of advancing church interests. Chalmers had viewed

Gladstone as the leading parliamentary supporter of his plans for the co-ordinated defence and extension of the established churches throughout the United Kingdom. Gladstone had advised Chalmers's efforts to secure a parliamentary grant for church building in the Church of Scotland, and served as Chalmers's main channel of communication with the Conservative party leader, Sir Robert Peel. The two men had shared a vision of the Christian commonwealth, based upon the organisation of the whole of society into closely-knit parish communities within the established churches. Their break in 1838 brought an end to their promising co-operation for the achievement of the Christian commonwealth in the United Kingdom. It also contributed to the growing estrangement between the Church of Scotland and the British parliamentary state that would culminate in the break up of the Scottish church in 1843, the most important event in the history of nineteenth-century Scotland.[3]

II

The connection between Chalmers and the Gladstone family began in June 1817, when Chalmers, returning from the triumphant visit to London that had established his reputation as perhaps the foremost preacher in the British Isles, stayed for three days in Liverpool with his fellow Lowland Scot, the Evangelical merchant Sir John Gladstone.[4] 'What a treat we had', Mrs Gladstone wrote to her son Thomas on 12 June 1817, 'in hearing Dr Chalmers preach and having him under our roof. Your father says his delight was beyond expression.'[5] Chalmers, for his part, informed a friend on 18 June that he 'was greatly delighted with the Gladstones'.[6] Chalmers was at that time minister of a crowded urban parish in Glasgow, and was developing new methods of ministry aimed at reviving the parish system in the urban environment. Convinced of the need for additional churches in the rapidly growing towns and cities of industrialising Britain, he had been greatly impressed with Gladstone's achievement in building, at private expense, two new churches in Liverpool. On his return to Glasgow, Chalmers tried to stimulate private church-building on Gladstone's model in the established Church of Scotland.[7] The following year, when parliament provided a grant of £1,000,000 to the Church of England for church-building, Chalmers asked Gladstone to use his influence with his friend, the liberal Tory, George Canning, to gain parliamentary support for a church-building grant of £100,000 for the Scottish establishment. Gladstone approached Canning, and also members of the Evangelical 'Clapham Sect', William Wilberforce, Charles Grant and Thomas Babington – though in the event, the Church of Scotland did not receive the parliamentary grant.[8] Three years later, in the first volume of his influential *Christian and Civic Economy of Large Towns*, Chalmers wrote warmly of Gladstone as a 'patriotic and enlightened gentleman' who had demonstrated 'philanthropy and

public spirit' through his church extension work in Liverpool.[9] This account
brought John Gladstone a modest national reputation as a philanthropist.[10]
In 1825, Gladstone asked Chalmers's advice when his wife wished to erect
a chapel-of-ease in her native town of Dingwall, in Ross-shire.[11] Gladstone
and Chalmers were drawn together by a shared Evangelical piety, interest
in political economy, and practical philanthropic commitment. Both men
worked to increase the influence of the established churches of England and
Scotland through an extension of the parish system; for both, the differences
between the episcopal Church of England and Presbyterian Church of Scotland were relatively unimportant. Gladstone had been born and raised
within the Church of Scotland, and although now an Anglican, respected
both national churches. Chalmers seemed almost to prefer the Church of
England to his own church. 'I am compelled to regard it', he wrote to John
Gladstone of the Church of England in 1821, '[as] by far the most effective
instrument of Christian good that is now in operation in our land.'[12]

William Gladstone no doubt encountered Chalmers's name from childhood. He recorded in his diary reading Chalmers's popular *Astronomical
Discourses* in 1826 and hearing Chalmers speak in the General Assembly of
the Church of Scotland in May 1828.[13] He heard Chalmers preach in England on two occasions in 1830, and was impressed by both Chalmers's 'judicious and sober manner' and his 'lofty principles and piety'.[14] Chalmers had
by now left the parish ministry for an academic career, and in 1828 he
became professor of theology at the University of Edinburgh. As a professor,
he advocated urban church extension through a growing body of writings
– arguing that only the revival of the traditional parish system in industrialising Britain could preserve the social fabric and permanently improve the
condition of the labouring orders. He was convinced that the creation of
closely-knit parish communities among the urban proletariat would encourage a communal benevolence, in which the labouring orders would strive
for personal self-sufficiency through thrift and delayed marriage, and would
care for the disadvantaged in their midst. By the early 1830s, he was widely
regarded as Britain's leading apologist for the idea of an established church.

In 1830, two years after Chalmers's move to Edinburgh, John Gladstone
purchased the estate of Fasque in Kincardineshire, fulfilling a long-term
dream of being a Scottish landowner; in the early 1830s, he also acquired
a town house in Edinburgh. As the Gladstones settled again in Scotland,
William grew close to Chalmers. In Edinburgh during the winter of
1833–34, he breakfasted with Chalmers on at least two occasions, and
attended one of his college lectures. They developed a mutual regard, despite
the nearly thirty-year difference in their ages. Gladstone was struck by
Chalmers's 'extreme' modesty, and by the 'very eloquent, earnest and
impressive' manner in which he spoke of his Christian social ideal. 'He does
indeed', Gladstone had noted in his diary on 8 January 1834, 'seem to be
an *admirable* man'.[15] Chalmers, in turn, was attracted to this talented son of

his old friend, who had achieved a double-first at Oxford and was now a rising Tory MP, committed to using his political gifts for the advancement of church interests.

Gladstone's political abilities and connections would have been particularly attractive to Chalmers at this time. In 1833, Chalmers was the leader of the Popular, or Evangelical, party in the Church of Scotland. He was committed to reviving the influence and authority of the established Church of Scotland and for this he would need political support in parliament. A moderate Scottish Whig for most of his life, Chalmers had broken with the Whigs in the early 1830s over the Reform Bill and what he perceived as Whig indifference to the needs of the established churches. By 1833, he was looking for a connection with the Tories, as the party most favourable to established Christianity. 'Originally I think a Liberal', Gladstone later recalled, '[Chalmers had] drifted with the religious movement to the side of the Conservatives.'[16] The young Gladstone offered Chalmers a contact with the parliamentary Tory party.

In May 1834, the Evangelical party under Chalmers's leadership gained control over the General Assembly, or supreme court, of the Church of Scotland. The Evangelical-dominated Assembly took immediate action to strengthen the established church as a force in national life. To begin with, the Assembly reformed the system of patronage, by which patrons, most of them landowners, had the power to present candidates to church livings. Patronage was part of the civil law, and there was some uncertainty about whether or not the church alone had the authority to reform the practice. None the less, the General Assembly passed the Veto Act, giving male heads of families in congregations the power to veto unacceptable patronage appointments to parish livings. The aim was to make the established church a more popular body. The Assembly of 1834 also launched a church extension campaign, under Chalmers's direction, which aimed at building hundreds of new churches. Chalmers's church extension plan was two-fold. First, the church would raise private funds in order to erect the church buildings – mobilising popular giving, including 'penny-a-week' subscriptions from the poor. Second, it would approach parliament for a grant to provide a modest endowment for each new church, sufficient to pay a portion of the minister's stipend. The endowment grant would ensure that the new churches were not overly dependent on attracting prosperous members who could contribute financially to the payment of the minister and upkeep of the buildings. Rather, with endowments, the churches would be able to conduct an aggressive home mission among the poor. Further, the grant would demonstrate parliament's commitment to the Scottish religious establishment.

Chalmers had suffered a stroke in January 1834, and his health remained precarious. By the late summer, however, he had recovered sufficiently to begin organising the church extension campaign, and his committee began forming scores of local church-building societies across Scotland. On 24

September 1834, Chalmers wrote to William Gladstone, asking his advice on how best to approach parliament for the grant, and suggesting that Gladstone might speak with his 'influential friends'.[17] On 29 September, Gladstone responded from Fasque with a lengthy letter, full of practical advice and political information. He opened with a bleak picture of the prospects for a parliamentary grant while the Whigs remained in power. The Whig government of Viscount Melbourne, he explained, was dependent on the support of English Dissenting MPs – who were increasingly committed to bringing down the established churches throughout the United Kingdom and who would thus strenuously oppose any grant of public money to the established Church of Scotland. That said, Gladstone maintained that the Church of Scotland should press its case for the grant, as the Dissenters' demands for disestablishment would be 'most effectually met by retaliated aggression'. The Church of Scotland's struggle, he insisted, was one for the principle of established Christianity throughout the United Kingdom.[18] For Chalmers, the advice was most welcome. 'I have received and read with the greatest interest your son's most important letter to me,' he enthused to John Gladstone on 4 October. 'It is indeed a masterly document; and I feel that I shall derive much advantage from it both in the way of guidance and information.'[19] Acting on Gladstone's advice, Chalmers's committee organised the collection of local petitions and prepared to send a deputation to meet leading politicians in London.

Then in December 1834 came the unexpected news that the King had dismissed the Whig government and called on the Tory leader, Sir Robert Peel, to form an administration. Gladstone, now known among Scottish church extensionists as Chalmers's 'enlightened correspondent', entered the government as a Junior Lord of the Treasury.[20] The prospects for the parliamentary grant suddenly brightened, and Gladstone advised Chalmers to press forward vigorously with the Scottish petitioning campaign. Peel's government, Gladstone confided, was unlikely to survive for long, but there might just be a possibility of getting the Scottish endowment grant through parliament before the government fell.[21] Knowing that Chalmers was diffident about approaching Peel directly, Gladstone offered to serve as intermediary between Chalmers and the Prime Minister – assuring Chalmers that he was 'very confident Sir Robert Peel will never regard me as an intruder when I go to him on your business'.[22] John Gladstone further reassured Chalmers that he understood Peel was 'very *warmly*' disposed to Scottish church extension.[23] During the early months of 1835, there was a constant exchange of letters, with Gladstone carrying communications to Peel and advising Chalmers on practical parliamentary politics – including how best to present the church's grant request and how to lobby individual MPs.[24] Chalmers followed Gladstone's advice closely and described in detail his approaches to individual MPs.[25] In the event, Peel's government fell before it could introduce the Scottish church extension grant. 'May God be with our country,' Gladstone wrote to Chalmers on 2 April 1835, in intimating that the ministers would soon resign office.[26] None the less, although short-lived, Peel's government had raised hopes in the Church of Scotland that parliament would provide the endowment grant. This, in turn, greatly stimulated private giving for Scottish church-building. Chalmers was able to report to the General Assembly of the Church of Scotland in May 1835 that the campaign was off to an excellent start, with subscriptions of £65,626 and 64 new churches completed or being built.[27]

Early in July 1835, Chalmers travelled to London with a Church of Scotland deputation to discuss the endowment grant with members of the Whig government. They met, however, a chilly reception and their hopes for an imminent grant faded. Melbourne's government was now even more dependent on the support of Dissenters than before, and less disposed to support new grants to the established churches. Gladstone was sympathetic when he met the disheartened Chalmers on 6 July, but could only confide to his diary that he felt 'ashamed of my uselessness' to him.[28] Chalmers was now beginning to experience serious difficulties as leader of the Church of Scotland. In Scotland, Dissenters had organised a petitioning campaign against the proposed endowment grant, and the country became a religious battleground, with church extensionists and Dissenters holding demonstrations and counter-demonstrations, issuing tens of thousands of tracts, and abusing one another with less than Christian charity. Confronted by the intense religious strife and conflicting claims in Scotland, the Melbourne government decided in late July to appoint a Royal Commission to investigate the extent of church accommodation in Scotland. Chalmers suspected, probably correctly, that the Commission was a stalling device, intended to dampen enthusiasm for church extension, and that the Whigs had no intention of providing the endowment grant.[29]

Gladstone spent most of the latter half of 1835 in Fasque. His mother died there after a long illness on 23 September 1835, and on 1 October he wrote to Chalmers, evidently a favourite with his mother, to inform him of the manner of her death.[30] For the last weeks of 1835 and the first weeks of 1836 Gladstone was at the family home in Edinburgh. He and Chalmers were especially close during this period. They took a number of long walks together. Chalmers had recently begun a model church extension operation in a working-class district in the Dean village, on the outskirts of Edinburgh, and on at least one occasion, he took Gladstone with him for a day of house-to-house visiting among the cottages. William was evidently favourably impressed, for his father soon after made a large financial contribution to Chalmers's Dean village operation.[31] Chalmers was in serious personal financial difficulties at this time. The Edinburgh town council had refused for two years to pay him his professorial salary, owing to a legal dispute over who was responsible for its payment.[32] The matter, Gladstone later recalled, 'was a very grave one, and I think it materially affected the prospects, and even the status of himself and his family'. None the less, Gladstone was impressed to find that Chalmers regarded his own financial crisis as of little importance when compared with his 'favourite and engrossing' subject – 'that of evangelising the country by means of manageable districts, each with its church and minister'. Chalmers at this time was, Gladstone later recalled, 'one of nature's nobles', with 'his rich and glowing eloquence, his warrior grandeur, his unbounded philanthropy, his strength of purpose, his mental integrity, his absorbed and absorbing earnestness', and above all 'his singular simplicity and detachment from the world'.[33] Many years later Gladstone would often refer to his long walks with Chalmers. 'We rarely drove between Edinburgh and Dalmeny', Lord Rosebery recalled in 1915, 'without Mr Gladstone pointing out with affectionate interest the spot where, when they were walking together on the Queensferry Road, Dr Chalmers's hat had been blown off across a dyke, and the future statesman had to run a considerable distance to catch it.'[34] Chalmers, for his part, had reason to be grateful to Gladstone for using his political influence to get Chalmers's professorial salary paid, which included bringing the matter to Peel's attention.[35]

III

Despite their personal friendship, however, the two men soon moved apart. At issue was the nature of the church they were seeking to revive. Their co-operation in 1834–35, like that which began between Chalmers and Gladstone's father in 1817–18, had been based largely on their shared Evangelical commitment to restoring the parish system of the established churches among the rapidly growing industrial populations of England and Scotland through a programme of church extension. Differences between the Anglican and Presbyterian establishments had seemed to them relatively insignificant when compared with the aim of realising the ideal parish system. Although one recent biographer has suggested that Gladstone had embraced a high view of episcopal church government by 1832,[36] this had not stopped him from working closely with Chalmers in 1834–35 on behalf of Presbyterian church extension in Scotland or commending in 1835 the 'comparative purity' of the Scottish establishment to his constituents at Newark.[37] However, Gladstone's attitudes soon changed, as he moved away from the Evangelicalism of his father and Chalmers, and came increasingly under the influence of the Oxford-based Tractarian movement that had emerged in 1833. The Tractarians embraced a high doctrine of the visible church, with emphasis on the ancient and apostolic character of the Church of England. For them, Anglican liturgy and discipline were rooted in the first centuries of Christianity and preserved through the apostolic succession of bishops – a mystical and unbroken chain, stretching back to Christ laying his hands on the apostles. From 1835, Gladstone was drawn to the Tractarian conception of the church, and to new High Church friendships. In

April 1835, he began a regular correspondence with the High Church rector
of Lavington, Henry Manning.[38] In the spring of 1836, he began his friendship with the High Church Scottish Episcopalian lawyer, James R. Hope.[39]
Both Manning and Hope encouraged Gladstone in viewing apostolic succession as a necessary mark of the true church.

This, in turn, transformed Gladstone's perception of the Scottish establishment. For the Tractarians, the Presbyterian Church of Scotland was not
a true church because it had rejected episcopacy. In the first two tracts,
published in 1833, John Henry Newman had maintained that without the
commission conveyed through the apostolic succession of bishops, no individual could claim authority to preach or administer the sacraments.[40] The
Presbyterian clergy of the established Church of Scotland were by implication 'uncommissioned' – without the essentials of ecclesiastical government
and discipline. Presbyterianism was a schismatic movement, a Protestant
sect. Such ideas spread among High Church Anglicans. In April 1835, for
example, Gladstone's friend, the High Church Anglican cleric Samuel Wilberforce, had become convinced that Presbyterianism was unscriptural and
'that the Episcopal form of Government is the appointment of God through
his inspired apostles'.[41] In October 1835, the High Church *British Critic* published a sympathetic account of Chalmers's Scottish church extension campaign, but expressed doubts about the spiritual integrity of a Scottish
establishment that lacked episcopal government.[42] As they questioned the
claims of the Scottish Presbyterian establishment, High Church Anglicans
looked more favourably upon the tiny Episcopal Church of Scotland. This
church, they observed, had preserved its episcopate and thus the apostolic
succession despite enduring persecution and dire poverty through most of the
eighteenth century. It was a martyr church, deserving the sympathetic support of Anglicans. It, and not the Presbyterian establishment, was the true
church in Scotland.[43] Gladstone was attracted to the Scottish Episcopal
Church, and when in Scotland preferred worship in an Episcopal chapel to
that in a Presbyterian church.[44] He was thus susceptible when his High
Church friends argued that his support for Presbyterian church extension
was damaging the true church in Scotland. Though Gladstone defended the
principle of state support for Scottish Presbyterianism to Manning in April
1837, his confidence in what he now termed the Church of Scotland's 'una-
postolic ministry' was wavering.[45] By August 1837, the High Churchman
E. B. Pusey was reporting to James Hope that Gladstone had come around to
their position that the establishment of Presbyterianism in Scotland had been
'very injurious' to the interests of the apostolic church.[46]

By this date, criticisms from High Anglicans were only one of Chalmers's
problems as leader of the Presbyterian Church of Scotland. The Scottish
establishment continued to encounter violent attacks from Scottish Dissenters and cold hostility from the Whig government, while the Commission
appointed to investigate church accommodation in Scotland proceeded

slowly in its work. There were growing criticisms of church extension, even within the Church of Scotland. For its opponents, the real aim of the church extension movement was not to evangelise among the urban labouring orders, but rather to impose a Presbyterian theocracy in Scotland. Chalmers and his supporters were derided as Presbyterian zealots, eager to revive the seventeenth-century 'Solemn League and Covenant'.[47] There was also growing opposition in Scotland to the church's Veto Act, which had given male heads of families in congregations the right to veto patrons' candidates for church livings. For critics of the Veto Act, it was an illegal infringement of the civil rights of patrons, and would lead to ministers being selected more for their ability to pander to democratic sentiment in congregations than for their education and Christian life.

In March 1838, Chalmers's church extension campaign was dealt a devastating blow when Melbourne's government finally announced in parliament that it would not support any new grant of public money to endow the churches being built in Scotland. This threatened the end of church extension. The church extensionists had raised private funds for church-building in the expectation that the churches would be endowed, and thus be enabled to pursue an aggressive home mission among the labouring poor. They had virtually promised the private contributors to church-building that state endowments would be forthcoming. By now, the church extensionists had built or were completing nearly 200 new churches in Scotland.[48] Without the expected support from the state, subscribers would feel betrayed and private giving would cease. In April 1838, Chalmers travelled to London to present a series of lectures on the establishment and endowment of national churches. His aim was to appeal for Scottish church extension beyond the Whig government to the English governing classes as a whole. Setting aside the differences between episcopal and Presbyterian government, he focused instead on the similar functions of the English and Scottish establishments. The essential feature of an established church, he argued, was its parochial organisation, through which it provided religious instruction and pastoral care to the entire population by way of territorial churches. In order to create a coherent parochial system, the state was bound to choose one denomination to be the established church. The precise organisation and doctrine of the chosen denomination was, Chalmers insisted, a matter of relative indifference, provided the denomination was both Protestant and Evangelical.[49] In short, supporters of the Church of England could, and should, make common cause with the Presbyterian Church of Scotland.

Gladstone attended the lectures regularly, and Chalmers no doubt expected support from his friend, a fellow advocate of the establishment principle who had done so much for Scottish church extension in 1834–35.[50] He was in serious difficulties, and needed Gladstone's help. However, Gladstone distanced himself. When a Scottish church extension deputation visited him on 26 April, in the midst of the lecture series, to ask his support, they received a cool reception. He could not, he explained, on 'conscientious grounds' support Scottish church extension, because the Church of Scotland lacked apostolic succession.[51] Though he had 'a great reverence for Dr. Chalmers', Gladstone later recalled, he 'could not stand' Chalmers's 'crude and raw' theory of church and state.[52] In his *State in its Relations with the Church*, published later in 1838, Gladstone maintained that Chalmers was wrong to claim that it was a matter of relative indifference which denomination a state chose to establish. The state, Gladstone maintained, was morally bound to acknowledge 'revealed' religious truth and to enter into a connection only with a branch of the true church. Chalmers, he suggested, had 'surrendered the condition without which all others fail, in omitting from his calculation the divine constitution of the visible church'.[53] 'The Scottish establishment', Gladstone insisted, 'has deprived herself of the episcopal succession, and therein, we cannot but believe, of her strongest argument as an establishment against the competing claims of any other religious body.'[54] For Chalmers, with his life's work for church extension being shattered by the Whig government's refusal to support the Church of Scotland against the 'competing claims' of Scottish Dissenters, Gladstone's book was a cruel blow. Gladstone effectively sought to 'unchurch' the Scottish establishment at a time when Chalmers was desperately seeking Tory-Anglican support. Chalmers's lectures, meanwhile, failed to reverse the government's decision against the endowment grant, and the Scottish church extension campaign soon came to an end.

IV

The Church of Scotland soon faced a more serious challenge. In May 1838, the Court of Session, the supreme civil court in Scotland, declared the church's Veto Act to be an illegal encroachment on the civil rights of patrons, and instructed the church to ordain patrons' candidates as parish ministers regardless of the wishes of the parishioners. The church appealed against the decision to the House of Lords, but in the spring of 1839, the Lords decided in favour of unrestricted patronage. The civil courts, supported by a substantial minority in the church, now insisted that the Veto Act be withdrawn. The Evangelical party, however, refused to accept the Lords' decision, arguing that the church could not allow the civil courts to impose unrestricted patronage and flout the desires of parishioners without sacrificing its spiritual independence. By mid-1839, it began to appear that the Church of Scotland would break up over the patronage question.

Chalmers's friendship with John Gladstone was brought under strain by the patronage controversy. In 1838, John Gladstone had agreed to build and endow in his native Leith a church in connection with the Church of Scotland. By now, the anti-patronage Evangelical majority in the church was insisting that newly erected churches should not have patrons, but rather that the male heads of family in the congregation should be permitted to elect the minister. Gladstone, however, a staunch supporter of patronage, insisted that his proposed Leith church must have full rights of patronage, with the nomination of the minister to be vested in himself and, after his death, his son William. When the General Assembly of the Church of Scotland considered the constitution of the Leith church in May 1839, it was challenged by leading Evangelicals, who insisted either that Gladstone withdraw his demand for the patronage, or that the Assembly decline his offer to build the church. Chalmers was torn between the anti-patronage principles of his Evangelical party and his long-standing friendship with the Gladstones. In the event, he spoke in support of Gladstone's pro-patronage constitution, using his personal authority to get Assembly approval for the unpopular measure.[55] This, however, damaged his leadership in the church. The *Presbyterian Review*, the leading organ of the Evangelical party, announced its 'unfeigned sorrow and bitter regret' over Chalmers's behaviour and called the decision in favour of Gladstone's patronage 'deplorable'.[56]

If Chalmers hoped that his support for John Gladstone's patronage might revive his prior connection with William, he was soon disappointed. Chalmers's last chance to preserve the Church of Scotland from disruption was to secure parliamentary legislation that would legalise the church's Veto Act. In January 1840, he appealed to William Gladstone for help. Gladstone was not entirely unsympathetic to the anti-patronage position.[57] He sent Chalmers a gracious reply on 7 February, expressing the hope that his efforts to find a legislative solution would prove successful but offering no assistance. He referred to their break, writing that he could not allow the opportunity to pass 'without assuring and endeavouring to convince you of the deep pain with which I have found myself at variance upon some ecclesiastical questions from one so distinguished for the highest qualities as yourself'.[58] Chalmers responded with equal good grace on 17 February 1840, assuring Gladstone that 'no difference of opinion has at all shaken the feelings of esteem and friendship wherewith I have ever regarded you'. The closing of his letter was poignant. 'Let me implore', he wrote, 'your best services on behalf of our Religious Establishment in Scotland, if not as a True Church, at least as an efficient practical organ for the distribution of Christian truth and principle among the families of our land.'[59] Gladstone did not respond, and Chalmers's hopes for a legislative solution soon faded.

There was, in truth, little chance of Chalmers gaining Gladstone's 'best services'. After 1839, Gladstone's attention was focused, not on rescuing the Presbyterian Church of Scotland, but on his work, in conjunction with his High Church friend, James Hope, for the revival of the Scottish Episcopal Church. There is evidence that Gladstone perceived the impending break-up of the Church of Scotland as opening the way for an Episcopalian revival in Scotland. In October 1839, Gladstone wrote to Hope that the prospects were good for the revival of the Scottish Episcopal Church, as the coming months

were likely to prove 'critical to the Kirk, both as an Establishment, I fear –
and as Presbyterianism'.[60] By 1840, Gladstone and Hope had conceived the
plan of establishing a college at Glenalmond, in Perthshire, aimed at educat-
ing both ordinands for the Episcopal Church of Scotland and Episcopalian lay
leaders, and they were busy raising subscriptions. One recent biographer has
maintained that Gladstone and Hope 'wanted nothing less than to turn the
country back from Presbyterianism to the Episcopalianism it had intermit-
tently professed in the seventeenth century'.[61] Gladstone admitted to Hope on
25 August that 'perhaps it is perverseness', but with the 'Vetoists' in the
church being driven to extremes and the future of the Church of Scotland
uncertain, this seemed the time to press forward with their college plans.[62]

The Tories returned to power in the summer of 1841, and Gladstone
entered the government. He was, however, immersed in his plans for
Glenalmond College, and kept his distance from Chalmers. Then in June
1842, John Gladstone broke with Chalmers over the patronage question.
Chalmers had by now committed himself to a decided anti-patronage line,
and for the elder Gladstone this represented an attack on the rights of property, on the social hierarchy and on due order within the church. Chalmers
sought to avoid the break. 'Verily', he wrote to John on 27 June, 'we are
both of us too old for controversy. Let me, therefore, fondly hope ... that
henceforth we may live in mutual goodwill and die in charity and peace.'[63]
He received no response. On 3 December 1842, Chalmers wrote once more
to William Gladstone on the Scottish church question, sending him a copy
of the church's Claim of Right, a document that represented the church's
final appeal to parliament. 'I feel encouraged', he wrote, 'by our old acquain-
tanceship to send a copy to you.' Gladstone sent a cordial but cool response,
assuring Chalmers of his wish that 'an honourable and a satisfactory' solution could be found.[64] None the less, he apparently made no effort within the
government to avert the break-up of the Church of Scotland. When the
Commons debated on whether or not to receive the church's Claim of Right
on 7–8 March 1843, Gladstone did not speak, and he voted with Peel
against the House receiving the document.[65] Chalmers now lost all trust in
Peel, and claimed that the Tory government intended to impose an Erastian
state control over the Scottish church. Some two months later, the Church
of Scotland was broken up at the Disruption, with over a third of the clergy
and nearly half the lay membership following Chalmers out of the establishment to form the Free Church.

Four months after the Disruption, on 29 September 1843, an anonymous
letter appeared in the *Montrose Standard* bitterly attacking Chalmers for his
role in the Disruption. Chalmers's enquiries revealed what he had probably
suspected: the letter had come from John Gladstone of Fasque, now a notorious opponent of the newly formed Free Church. In conversation, according to Chalmers's informant, Gladstone spoke of Chalmers 'very much as if
he were sunk and gone for ever'.[66] The two men published a caustic

THE PROCESSION ON THE 18TH OF MAY.

2 Procession at the Disruption of the Church of Scotland, 1843

exchange of letters in November 1843, with Gladstone blaming the Disruption on Chalmers's lust for power and popularity.[67] After reading the exchange in the *Montrose Standard*, William decided that his father was right.[68] Several months later, William Gladstone published his own views on the Disruption in the *Foreign and Colonial Quarterly Review*. He expressed, on the one hand, admiration for the 'great effort and magnificent sacrifice' of those who had left the established church.[69] The amount of money the new Free Church had raised for building new churches was astounding, and put the far wealthier Church of England to shame.[70] None the less, he insisted, the outgoing ministers were wrong to claim that the Disruption vindicated the spiritual independence of the church and that their Free Church represented the true church in Scotland. Because all Presbyterians had rejected the apostolic succession – the only true basis of ecclesiastical authority – none of them was capable of resisting the Erastian doctrine that authority over the church's spiritual functions lay ultimately with the civil magistrate. Without the divine commission conveyed through an episcopacy with apostolic succession, a Presbyterian church could have no independent spiritual authority. 'We repeat it,' he asserted, 'those who deny the succession, those who strip the sacraments of their power, have no solid ground on which to resist the doctrine of Erastus.'[71] He closed the article by appealing for the revival of the Episcopal Church of Scotland, as representing 'the beauty and the glory of the Lord's own house'.[72]

Chalmers eventually responded to such High Church criticisms in early 1846, in a pamphlet advocating the aims of the 'Evangelical Alliance', an organisation of Protestant denominations formed in late 1845. For Chalmers, the objects of the Evangelical Alliance should be two-fold – first, to oppose the revival of 'Popery' and second to support home mission work.[73] In his pamphlet, he unleashed his anger at 'the bigots of a lordly and exclusive High Churchism', those 'who monopolise for themselves, as being the only true Church upon earth, whatever of real piety or saving faith is to be met with in Christendom'.[74] The 'old priest-craft of the Middle Ages', he insisted, was 'lifting its head again'. The 'Antichrist' now appeared, not only in Roman Catholicism, but also in 'the no less dangerous ... form of Puseyism'.[75] 'Puseyism and High Churchism' were the 'great feeders of Popery in our own island'.[76] If for Gladstone, then, the Free Church was essentially Erastian, for Chalmers, High Church Anglicanism was one step away from 'Popery'. Their break was complete.

V

There was apparently no further communication between Gladstone and Chalmers after the Disruption. Chalmers died in late May 1847, and Gladstone made no mention of the event in his diary. When Chalmers's son-in-law, William Hanna, published the exhaustive four-volume *Life of Dr Chalmers* between 1849 and 1852, he avoided discussing Chalmers's connection with the Gladstones. A veil was drawn over the former friendship. In the mid-1830s, the relationship between Chalmers and William Gladstone had been full of promise for the established churches. The two had shared an Evangelical Protestantism and a commitment to the co-ordinated defence and extension of the established churches in both England and Scotland. For them the differences between the episcopal and Presbyterian establishments had seemed minor when compared with their similar parochial systems. But amid the religious controversies of the 1830s, as both men had taken an increasingly serious view of the church as a divine institution, they had drawn apart. Gladstone embraced the High Anglican view of episcopacy as a divine institution, and became unable to regard the Scottish Presbyterian establishment as a true Christian church. In his correspondence with James Hope after 1837 he seemed almost to view the crisis in the established Church of Scotland as providential and to look for a Scottish Episcopalian revival on the ruins of the Presbyterian establishment. Chalmers, for his part, came to view Peel's Tory government, of which Gladstone was a prominent member, as essentially Erastian, while he eventually denounced Tractarianism, or 'Puseyism', with its insistence on apostolic succession, as the work of the Antichrist. The break between Gladstone and Chalmers was probably unavoidable in the heated religious atmosphere of the late 1830s and early 1840s. Gladstone and Chalmers had, in the early 1830s, existed on the cultural borders of Anglican England and Presbyterian Scotland, and both had sought to serve as bridges between the two national establishments. The religious crisis had forced them to define their respective doctrines of the church, at the expense of their co-operation for the principle of religious establishment, and bridges had been burnt.

Gladstone would later change his views on the Disruption. Indeed, by the 1870s, he would emerge as the great champion of the Scottish Free Church that had arisen from the Disruption. When parliament proposed in 1874 to abolish patronage in the established Church of Scotland, Gladstone insisted that it must first consult the interests of the Free Church, which he portrayed as the aggrieved party in 1843.[77] Anglican politicians, he argued, must put aside their prejudices when considering Scottish religious matters. The Disruption, he asserted in the Commons on 6 July 1874, had been an event which 'drew a universal burst of applause and congratulation from all Christendom irrespective of religious persuasion'.[78] Parliament, he asserted, had been wrong in its treatment of Chalmers and the seceders of 1843, and it now owed a 'confession of penitence' to the people 'whom you drove out of the Established Church'.[79] After 1874, he sympathised with the Free Church campaign for the disestablishment of the Church of Scotland. When in 1880 the Free Church planned to commemorate the centenary of the birth of Chalmers, Gladstone was the first to be invited, and although unable to attend the event, he sent a letter, reminiscing on his friendship with Chalmers.[80] His close support of the Free Church in his later years may have been a gesture of penitence over his break with Chalmers, a man whom he later described as having 'the energy of a giant and the simplicity of a child'.[81]

Notes

1   J. Morley, *The Life of William Ewart Gladstone*, 3 vols, London, Macmillan, 1903, vol. 1, pp. 169–75.

2   J. Brooke and M. Sorensen (eds), *The Prime Ministers' Papers: W. E. Gladstone*, 4 vols, London, HMSO, 1971–81, vol. 1, *Autobiographica*, p. 252.

3   There has been only one study of the relationship between Gladstone and Chalmers. W. Forbes Gray, 'Chalmers and Gladstone: An Unrecorded Episode', *Records of the Scottish Church History Society*, Vol. 10, 1948, pp. 9–17.

4   For an account of the tour, see W. Hanna, *Memoirs of Dr Chalmers*, Edinburgh, Thomas Constable, 1849–52, vol. 2, pp. 92–107.

5   S. G. Checkland, *The Gladstones: A Family Biography, 1764–1851*, Cambridge, Cambridge UP, 1971, p. 87.

6   Hanna (1849–52), vol. 2, p. 106.

7   T. Chalmers to J. Gladstone, 6 August 1817, Glynne–Gladstone MSS, Flintshire Record Office, Harwarden, G.G. 98; J. Gladstone to T. Chalmers, 12 August 1817, Thomas Chalmers Papers, New College Library, Edinburgh [hereafter TCP], CHA 4.6.16.

8   T. Chalmers to J. Gladstone, 13 February, 17 June 1818, Glynne–Gladstone MSS, G.G. 98; J. Gladstone to T. Chalmers, 17, 26 February, 23 March, 14 April 1818, TCP, CHA 4.8.1–4.

9   T. Chalmers, *Collected Works of Thomas Chalmers*, Glasgow, Collins, 1835–42, vol. 14, p. 227.

10   Checkland (1971), p. 127.

11   J. Gladstone to T. Chalmers, 5, 21 September 1825, TCP, CHA 4.44.12–14; T. Chalmers to J. Gladstone, 17 September 1825, Glynne–Gladstone MSS, G.G.98.

12   T. Chalmers to J. Gladstone, 3 April 1821, Glynne–Gladstone MSS, G.G.98.

13   GD, 25 December 1826, 26 May 1828.

14   Gladstone, *Autobiographica* (1971), p. 217; Gray (1948), p. 9.

15   GD, 13, 16, 17, 18, 24 December 1833; 8 January 1834; Morley (1903), vol. 1, pp. 109–10.

16   Gladstone, *Autobiographica* (1971), p. 42.

17   T. Chalmers to W. E. Gladstone, 24 September 1834, GP 44354, ff. 58–59.

18   W. E. Gladstone to T. Chalmers, 29 September 1834, TCP, CHA 4.223.33.

19   T. Chalmers to J. Gladstone, 4 October 1834, Glynne–Gladstone MSS, G.G. 98.

20   C. Fergusson to T. Chalmers, n.d. [December 1834], TCP, CHA 4.222.35; J. Gladstone to T. Chalmers, 27 December [1834], TCP, CHA 4.205.50.

21   W. E. Gladstone to T. Chalmers, 30 December 1834, TCP, CHA 4.223.37.

22   W. E. Gladstone to T. Chalmers, 2 February 1835, TCP, CHA 4.236.62.

23   J. Gladstone to T. Chalmers, n.d. [probably early 1835], TCP, CHA 4.223.29.

24   W. E. Gladstone to T. Chalmers, 30 December 1834, 9, 16, 26 January, 2, 13, 15, 18 February, 12, 28 March 1835, TCP, CHA 4.223.31, CHA 4.223.37, CHA 4.236.60–70, CHA 4.336.4–6.

25   T. Chalmers to W. E. Gladstone, 13, 27 December 1834, 28 January, 10, 14, 16, 21 February, 7, 19 March 1835, GP 44354, ff. 108, 134, 153, 172, 174, 176, 177, 182, 186.

26   W. E. Gladstone to T. Chalmers, TCP, CHA 4.236.74.

27   T. Chalmers, *First Report of the Committee of the General Assembly on Church Extension*, Edinburgh, John Waugh, 1835, pp. 1–16.

28   GD, 6 July 1835.

29   S. J. Brown, 'Religion and the Rise of Liberalism: The First Disestablishment Campaign in Scotland, 1829–1843', *Journal of Ecclesiastical History*, Vol. 48, 1997, pp. 694–96; S. J. Brown, *Thomas Chalmers and the Godly Commonwealth in Scotland*, Oxford, Oxford UP, 1982, pp. 245–56.

30   W. E. Gladstone to T. Chalmers, 1 October 1835, TCP, CHA 4.236.78.

31   T. Chalmers to J. Gladstone, 14 March 1836, Glynne–Gladstone MSS, G.G. 98.

32   T. Chalmers to W. E. Gladstone, 12 December 1835, GP 44354, f. 233; W. E. Gladstone to T. Chalmers, 14 December 1835, TCP, 4.236.80.

33   GD, 22, 24 December 1835; W. E. Gladstone to H. Wellwood Moncreiff, March 1880, in *The Chalmers Centenary: Speeches delivered in the Free Assembly Hall, Edinburgh, on 3 March 1880*, Edinburgh, John Maclaren, 1880, pp. 15–16; Morley (1903), vol. 1, p. 110.

34 Lord Rosebery, *Miscellanies, Literary and Historical*, London, Hodder & Stoughton, 1921, vol. 1, pp. 249–50.
35 T. Chalmers to J. Gladstone, 14 March 1836, Glynne–Gladstone MSS, G.G. 98; T. Chalmers to W. E. Gladstone, 9 March, 17 August 1836, GP 44355, ff. 29–30, 105–06; W. E. Gladstone to T. Chalmers, 15 August 1836, TCP, CHA 4.336.14.
36 P. J. Jagger, *Gladstone: The Making of a Christian Politician*, Allison Park, Pennsylvania, Pickwick, 1991, pp. 154–55.
37 H. C. G. Matthew, *Gladstone 1809–1874*, Oxford, Clarendon Press, 1986, p. 44.
38 P. Butler, *Gladstone: Church, State and Tractarianism: A Study of his Religious Ideas and Attitudes, 1809–1859*, Oxford, Clarendon Press, 1982, pp. 70–71.
39 Ibid., pp. 72–73.
40 [J. H. Newman], *Thoughts on the Ministerial Commission*, London, Rivingtons, 1833; [J. H. Newman], *The Catholic Church*, London, Rivingtons, 1833.
41 D. Newsome, *The Parting of Friends: The Wilberforces and Henry Manning*, London, John Murray, 1966, p. 173.
42 'Dr Chalmers and the Scotch Church', *British Critic*, Vol. 18, 1835, p. 453.
43 P. Nockles, '"Our Brethren in the North": The Scottish Episcopal Church and the Oxford Movement', *Journal of Ecclesiastical History*, Vol. 47, 1996, pp. 655–82.
44 Butler (1982), p. 164.
45 W. E. Gladstone to H. E. Manning, 23 April 1837, in *Correspondence on Church and Religion of William Ewart Gladstone*, ed. D. C. Lathbury, 2 vols, London, John Murray, 1910, vol. 1, pp. 33–39.
46 E. B. Pusey to J. R. Hope, *Very Private*, 4 August 1837, National Library of Scotland [hereafter NLS], Hope-Scott Papers, MS 3675, ff. 192–93.
47 For example, D. Aitken to Lord Minto, Chairman of the Royal Commission on Religious Instruction, 30 January 1836, NLS, Minto Papers, MS 11802, f. 26.
48 T. Chalmers, *Fourth Report of the General Assembly Committee on Church Extension*, Edinburgh, William Whyte, 1838, p. 12.
49 T. Chalmers, *Lectures on the Establishment and Extension of National Churches*, in Chalmers (1835–42), vol. 17, pp. 185–355.
50 GD, 27 April, 1, 3, 8, 10, 12 May 1838.
51 J. F. Leishman, *Matthew Leishman of Govan and the Middle Party of 1843*, Paisley, Alexander Gardner, 1921, pp. 93–96.
52 Gladstone, *Autobiographica* (1971), p. 43.
53 W. E. Gladstone, *The State in its Relations with the Church*, London, John Murray, 1838, p. 21.
54 Ibid., p. 105.
55 J. Gladstone to T. Chalmers, 10 October 1838, TCP, CHA 7.2.1; G. Bell to T. Chalmers, 25 November, 29 December 1838, TCP, CHA 4.270.75–77; J. Gladstone to T. Chalmers, 11 January 1839, TCP, CHA 4.282.50; *Presbyterian Review*, Vol. 12, 1839, pp. 184–86; Checkland (1971), pp. 291–92.
56 *Presbyterian Review*, Vol. 12, 1839, pp. 185–86.
57 C. S. Parker, *Life and Letters of Sir James Graham*, London, John Murray, 1907, vol. 1, pp. 374–75.
58 W. E. Gladstone to T. Chalmers, 7 February 1840, TCP, CHA 4.291.30.
59 T. Chalmers to W. E. Gladstone, 17 February 1840, GP 44357, ff. 72–74.
60 W. E. Gladstone to J. R. Hope, 24 October 1839, NLS, Hope-Scott Papers, MS 3672, ff. 44–45.

61 D. W. Bebbington, *William Ewart Gladstone: Faith and Politics in Victorian Britain*, Grand Rapids, Michigan, Eerdmans, 1993, p. 66.

62 W. E. Gladstone to J. R. Hope, 25 August 1840, NLS, Hope-Scott Papers, MS 3672, f. 73.

63 John Gladstone published their correspondence of June 1842 in the *Montrose Standard*, 24 November 1843; Checkland (1971), pp. 337–38.

64 T. Chalmers to W. E. Gladstone, 3 December 1842, GP 44359, f. 235; W. E. Gladstone to T. Chalmers, 8 December 1842, TCP, CHA 4.336.18.

65 *Hansard's Parliamentary Debates*, 3rd series, vol. 67, col. 511; the question, he confided to his diary, was 'a most painful and menacing one'. *GD*, 8 March 1843.

66 W. Nixon to T. Chalmers, 5 October 1843, TCP, CHA 4.310.69; see also W. Nixon to T. Chalmers, 6, 9 October 1843, TCP, CHA 4.310.73–75.

67 *Montrose Standard*, 17, 24 November 1843.

68 Checkland (1971), p. 338.

69 W. E. Gladstone, 'The Theses of Erastus and the Scottish Church Establishment' (1844), in *Gleanings of Past Years*, 7 vols, London, John Murray, 1879, vol. 3, p. 3.

70 Ibid., pp. 37–38.

71 Ibid., p. 34.

72 Ibid., p. 40.

73 Brown (1982), pp. 350–65; Hanna (1849–52), vol. 4, pp. 384–90.

74 T. Chalmers, *On the Evangelical Alliance*, Edinburgh, Oliver & Boyd, 1846, pp. 44, 21.

75 Ibid., pp. 28–29.

76 Ibid., pp. 33–34.

77 P. Carnegie Simpson, *The Life of Principal Rainy*, London, Hodder & Stoughton, 1909, vol. 1, pp. 256–73; N. L. Walker, *Robert Buchanan*, London, Nelson, 1877, pp. 479–81.

78 *Hansard*, 3rd series, vol. 220, col. 1123.

79 Ibid., col. 1127.

80 *The Chalmers Centenary* (1880), pp. 14–16.

81 Gladstone, *Autobiographica* (1971), p. 42.

'The Strict Line of Political Succession'? Gladstone's Relationship with Peel: An Apt Pupil?

Eric Evans

3 Sir Robert Peel, 2nd Bt, by John Linnell, 1838

The author of this volume is a young man of unblemished character, and of distinguished parliamentary talents, the rising hope of those stern and unbending Tories, who follow, reluctantly and mutinously, a leader, whose experience and eloquence are indispensable to them, but whose cautious temper and moderate opinions they abhor.[1]

His [Peel's] enormous energies were in truth so lavishly spent upon the gigantic work of government which he conducted after a fashion quite different – I mean as to the work done in the workshop of his own brain – from preceding and succeeding prime ministers, that their root was enfeebled, though in its feebleness it had more strength probably remaining than fell to the lot of any other public man.[2]

THESE two contemporary quotations form an appropriate backdrop to an investigation of William Gladstone's relationship with Sir Robert Peel. The first is the opening sentence of the Whig historian T. B. Macaulay's famous *Edinburgh Review* polemic of April 1839 which attacked Gladstone's long and tendentious defence of the political importance of High Anglicanism, *The State in its Relations with the Church*. The first part of Macaulay's sentence is as well known as it is misquoted; the second presents an implicit judgement about Gladstone's political relationship with Peel. Macaulay's assessment might be dismissed as mere political mischief-making. He was better known in 1839 as a Whig party politician – something of a 'rising hope' himself – and not yet as a historian. Within six months he would enter Melbourne's cabinet as Secretary for War. On the other hand, as we shall see, the reaction of the Tory leader to the book's appearance was certainly cool.

The words of the second quotation are less well known. As aficionados will instantly recognise from their tortured syntax, they are Gladstone's. They were written about his old chief in 1851, after the immediate shock of Peel's premature death had worn off. They speak of respect for immense political achievement rather than indicating love for a man he would judge in 1853 'my great teacher and master in public affairs'.[3] The emphasis on the public rather than the private sphere is probably significant. Recent studies of Gladstone have noted his less than effusive references. Richard Shannon has identified the Earl of Aberdeen, rather than Peel, as 'a kind of father-figure substitute' on account of the former's much more obvious Christian piety.[4] Edgar Feuchtwanger implies that a lack of close personal accord derived from differences over Peel's political leadership after the Conservative split of 1846. He argues that Gladstone had 'found [Peel's] refusal to lead and organize increasingly irksome and frustrating'.[5] Gladstone's own words seem to support the verdict. His assessment quoted above begins with the judgement, 'Great as he was to the last, I must consider the closing years of his life as beneath those that had preceded them.'

Roy Jenkins refers, somewhat prissily, to 'some delicate curtain' which came between the two and to Gladstone's 'surprisingly cool' reaction to Peel's death.[6] This judgement may reflect a misreading of the evidence. As is frequently noted, Gladstone made only a brief speech in seconding a motion for the adjournment of the Commons the day after Peel's death. It ended with rehashed verses from Sir Walter Scott first used when the younger Pitt died more than forty years earlier. The occasion, however, was one more for an immediate mark of respect than for prepared eulogies. Gladstone noted in his diary that the whole house had been taken by surprise when Joseph Hume moved an amendment to adjourn out of respect for Peel and that he was left to 'make the best of it'. Moreover, Gladstone was clearly embarrassed by the absence, in a thin house just beyond noon, of more senior colleagues who had known Peel for longer than he. Gladstone did not want to court charges of presumption. His brevity has been cited – almost certainly wrongly – as evidence of 'coolness' towards Peel. His words may have been formal but they were intended to mark what his chief would most have valued: his service to the country. Peel's premature death deprived members of the fond hope that 'in whatever position he was placed, by the weight of his character, by the splendour of his talents, by the purity of his virtues, he would still have been spared to render to his country the most essential services'. Gladstone's diary recorded the private view of the 'great calamity which the nation has suffered in the death of its greatest statesman' and his fretting about getting his tribute in the *Morning Chronicle* right after necessarily brief remarks in the Commons. These reactions do not suggest any coolness in Gladstone's response.[7]

This piece will argue that Gladstone's relationship with Peel was in no way 'cool'. Gladstone, especially in the early part of his political career, was cool about nothing and Peel was among the first to recognise his immense, if wayward, talent. Gladstone's response to Peel was grounded in more than the natural respect and gratitude accorded to a mentor and, in effect, political sponsor. In 1838, Gladstone published *The State in its Relations with the Church*; in 1850 and 1851 he had to accommodate himself to the premature death of Peel and the conversion of his leading High Anglican friends – Manning and James Hope – to the Roman Catholic Church. During the years 1838–51, Gladstone undertook an immense ethical pilgrimage. It encompassed crises in relationships with men he believed would be lifelong friends and helpmeets on his effortful journey to spiritual fulfilment. It was to Manning in 1838 that he confided his view that he would never be 'seduced by ambition' into a conventional political career.[8] Gladstone's pilgrimage was the more painful since he had to acknowledge that his earlier vision of the spiritual governing the temporal was an impractical one in an industrial age.

The whole experience was traumatic and it brought him closer to Peel. This was not just because of their growing political relationship. Gladstone recognised that his mentor had had to undergo similar anguish over a religious question with profound political consequences – in Peel's case, of course, Catholic emancipation. Peel told the House of Commons that emancipation was 'the severest blow which it has ever been my lot to experience'. In commenting on the appearance of Peel's *Memoirs*, Gladstone interpreted what he called Peel's 'agony' as the decisive moment which transformed him. It 'seems to have [at] once forced into expansion and ripeness Sir R. Peel's political character'.[9] Peel survived the devastating accusations in 1829 of 'ratting' and apostasy from High Tories who had previously been among his staunchest supporters[10] and went on to lead the Conservative party with distinction in the 1830s and 1840s. In so doing, he had wrestled with a major dilemma and had had the courage to change his mind. Gladstone drew from this not only a political lesson but a form of ethical guidance.

Peel was, of course, the dominant influence on Gladstone's early political career. Gladstone served in five government posts under him, two of them in cabinet. He obtained his first ministerial post in December 1834, just before his twenty-fifth birthday, when Peel appointed him Junior Lord of the Treasury in his minority government. He had time to graduate to Under-Secretary for War and the Colonies in 1835 before the government fell in the spring. He was one of the first men Peel contacted about joining his new government after the Conservative general election victory of 1841. In the famous government of 1841–46 Gladstone was Vice-President of the Board of Trade, becoming a cabinet minister as President in May 1843 when he was thirty-three. He resigned office over Maynooth in January 1845 but returned to the cabinet as Secretary for the Colonies in December. Thereafter, he gave Peel staunch support during the Corn Law crisis which ended with the fall of the government in June 1846.

Peel's resignation also had a decisive impact on Gladstone. Trained for office, and with some reason to expect almost as long a lease as the young Sir Robert had enjoyed (during the twenty years from 1810 to 1830 Peel was out of government for only four), Gladstone found himself out of office for all but two years and two months of the next thirteen years. When in June 1859, with that characteristically fissile Gladstonian combination of reluctance, ambition and distaste, he joined Palmerston's government, it was as a Liberal and not as the Conservative he assumed he would always remain. A study of Gladstone's relationship with Peel may cast significant light on that elusive admixture of the personal and the political which is so vital to understanding how his priorities changed in the 1830s and 1840s and why Gladstone never fulfilled Macaulay's expectations of him as a 'stern, unbending' Tory.

4 Sir John Gladstone, calotype by David Octavius Hill, c. 1844

II

Gladstone was first elected to the House of Commons in December 1832 as one of the two members for the borough of Newark. He appeared thanks to the patronage of the Duke of Newcastle who had been impressed by the young Gladstone's defence of the unreformed constitution at the Oxford Union. His maiden speech was delivered on 3 June 1833. It was a response to an attack by Lord Howick, the son of the Prime Minister, Earl Grey, which had alleged cruelty towards, and even murder of, West Indian slaves on the estate in Demerara owned by Gladstone's father. The speech played on impugned family honour as a springboard to refute Howick. Its peroration balanced humanitarian sympathies against the rights of the propertied Englishman: 'he deprecated slavery; it was abhorrent to the nature of Englishmen; but, conceding all these things, were not Englishmen to retain a right to their own honestly and legally acquired property?'. The speech impressed both Stanley and Althorp, and Gladstone noted that Peel 'came up to me most kindly & praised the affair [speech] of Monday night'.[11]

It seems to have been Gladstone's maiden speech which persuaded Peel to invite him to a dinner for political friends and acquaintances three weeks later. Conversation between the two was slight but Gladstone excitedly wrote to his father the following day that 'he paid me the compliment of drinking wine with me'.[12] Thereafter, though they did not become intimate political colleagues immediately, contact was regular. Gladstone met Peel at a dinner given by the High Tory MP for Oxford, Sir Robert Inglis, in March 1834 and found the conversation 'delightful listening'. When he dined at the Peels in July, he noted that his host had been 'very kind'. He also wrote to his mother that 'Sir Robert Peel caused me much gratification by the way in which he spoke to me of my speech, and particularly the great warmth of his manner'.[13] By 1836, he knew Peel well enough to comment on his home life. He wrote to his father that 'in addition to everything else Sir R. And Lady P[eel] are so domestic and kind in their own family, that it is a pleasure to see them in that character alone ... when in his family Sir Robert is, of the two, rather taciturn than garrulous ... I do not mean that he is a silent man, but that only he is not so continuous a talker as the world expects great men to be for its amusement.'[14]

Peel clearly saw Gladstone as a valuable recruit to a party seriously reduced in numbers by the heavy election defeat of December 1832. He was able to provide his talented young colleague with an early taste of ministerial office because of William IV's quixotic, and entirely unexpected, decision to dismiss Melbourne's ministry in November 1834.[15] Peel, in Italy at the time, rushed back to England to accept office as Prime Minister on 9 December. Four days later he wrote to Gladstone asking for an interview. It took Gladstone, who was spending the autumn at his father's estate in Scotland, a week to receive the summons and then journey to London. He accepted office after a brief discussion during which, he told his father, Peel had been '*extremely* kind'. Inglis, no lover of modern ways, paid Gladstone the backhanded compliment of noting: 'You are about the youngest lord who was ever placed at the treasury on his own account, and not because he was his father's son.'[16]

His second promotion occurred serendipitously. Peel's original selection to lead on the colonies in the Commons, John Stuart-Wortley, lost his seat at the general election. On this occasion, Peel was more confiding. He informed the young minister before most colleagues that he intended asking the King for a dissolution of parliament to improve the Tory position in the Commons. He also left Gladstone in no doubt how highly his abilities were appreciated: 'I give you my word that I do not know six offices which are at this moment of greater importance than that to which is attached the representation of the colonial department in the House of Commons, at a period when so many questions are in agitation.' Gladstone noted in his diary that he accepted 'this great responsibility' and took the trouble to note, also, the cordiality of Peel's wishes at his departure: 'May God bless you wherever you are.'[17] The tone of Gladstone's effusive letter to his father might perhaps be explained by a Prime Minister's ability to turn the head of an ambitious young politician. It did, however, draw attention to the contrast between Peel's public image and his private persona in a pre-echo of many such tributes from cabinet ministers during, and after, the protection crises of 1844–46 which tore the Conservative party apart. Peel appeared an arrogant, driven and glacially remote figure to many on his own backbenches. His ministerial subordinates tended to be much more charitable. 'I can only say', Gladstone assured his father, 'that if I had always heard of him that he was the warmest and freest person of all living in the expression of his feelings, such description would have been fully borne out by his demeanour to me.'[18] Since the government fell in April there was no time for Gladstone to carry any legislation. He did, however, develop plans for negro education in the West Indies and impressed his civil servants. Henry Taylor noted that 'Gladstone was far the most considerable of the rising generation, having besides his abilities an excellent disposition and great strength of character.'[19] Gladstone also began to forge a political relationship with the Earl of Aberdeen which would become second in influence only to that of Peel and which would last a decade longer.

III

James Stephen, another shrewd senior official at the Colonial Office, commented on Gladstone's easy mastery of detail and voracious capacity for work as ideal in a minister committed to legislative achievement. He doubted, however, whether he had sufficient appetite for the rough and tumble of political life. No one could at any moment in his career consider Gladstone as effete. His opinions were strongly held, always supported by voluminous evidence and, when thwarted or crossed, he could unleash a fearful temper. Stephen's perception concerned Gladstone's commitment to political life and he thus touched upon the key issue which initially divided Gladstone from Peel. For the Gladstone of the 1830s, theology took precedence over politics. The outward trappings of an Evangelical upbringing having been shaken off at Oxford, Gladstone emerged from Christ Church as a High Church anti-reformer. A visit to Rome in 1832, where he marvelled at the 'magnificent temple' which was St Peter's, also removed some of his anti-Catholic prejudices and strengthened his awareness of what he called 'the pain and shame which separates us from Rome',[20] though it did nothing to remove his revulsion at the temporal power exercised by the Pope. This High Anglican, as Boyd Hilton has shown, still 'clung fervently to the central tenets of moderate evangelicals: providence, sin, conversion, conscience, Atonement, salvation, and Judgment'.[21] Mixed by someone with Gladstone's ferocious determination, his theological views coalesced into a dangerous brew which disconcerted a far wider spectrum of political opinion than that represented by the notoriously sceptical Viscount Melbourne who resumed office as Prime Minister when Peel's minority government fell.

Peel's own religious views have been fairly assessed by his biographer as 'a simple, rational, pious Protestantism'.[22] He was by no means indifferent to the state church. Much the most precise declarations of intent in his Tamworth Manifesto of December 1834 concerned the Church of England and the most important outcome of the minority government was the establishment of the Ecclesiastical Commission which proposed a series of reforms enacted by the Melbourne government from 1836 to 1840.[23] He did not see the church as the focal point for political action; Gladstone at this time did.

Discussion of reforms in the 1830s has concentrated upon parliamentary representation in 1832 and, to a lesser extent, the Poor Law Amendment Act of 1834. These priorities reflect the concerns of a later, and predominantly secular, age. Contemporaries generally saw things differently. There is a very strong case for considering the 1830s 'the decade of church reform' – the more so if that decade is permitted to extend back to 1828. The Dissenters aimed to profit from the climate of reform. If disestablishment was, like democracy for the Chartists, a step too far, then the pursuit of sturdy self-determination, by refusing to pay church rates and denying the Church of England monopoly over popular education, was not. Even the Duke of Wellington, for whom vigorous theological dispute was certainly not an activity of choice, argued in 1838 that 'The real question that now divides the country and which truly divides the House of Commons, is church or no church.'[24]

Temperament and political circumstance alike impelled Gladstone to strong partisanship on these questions. He spelled out his priorities at the end of 1835:

> My birthday. Here closes an important year. Its first section brought to my life an enhancement of public interest: and its second has been not lightly charged with domestic cares. But the question for these anniversaries – special to them, but fit for every day – is, has the soul gained any growth into the Father's image? Is the mind which was in Christ more seen and known and transferred? I can only answer thus much: the heart condemns, but God is greater than the heart, and the evidences of His love in warnings and monitions and Providential combinations, remain abundant to sustain the soul. Onward then upon another year.[25]

In discharge of this self-appointed task, Gladstone's priorities out of office from 1835 did not so much emphasise the theological over the political; rather he attempted to meld the two into a kind of theocratic view of state polity. The result was two treatises: *The State in its Relations with the Church* (1838) and the less well-known *Church Principles Considered in their Results* (1840). The theological bases of these two works, in which Gladstone invested so much and whose reception cast him down, have received exten-sive recent scholarly attention.[26] Here it is necessary only to consider their effects on Gladstone's development as a politician and, particularly, on his relationship with Peel.

Gladstone was aware that his own religious priorities could alienate Peel. To friends of like religious mind, he indicated that Peel's literally mundane politics militated against the kind of action they wished to encourage. In a letter to the Bishop of Exeter, Henry Phillpotts, in 1840, he noted that 'There is a manifest and peculiar adaptation in Peel's mind to the age in which he lives and to its exigencies and to the position he holds as a public man.'[27] We should not infer that Gladstone's politics at this stage were other-worldly. His concerns were highly political. The Whigs, in his view, had failed the nation because their libertarian and Erastian assumptions saw church and state inhabiting separate spheres. For Gladstone, the two were inseparable. He summed up the views he held in the 1830s and 1840s in an uncharacteris-tically laconic observation made a year before he died: 'My doctrine was that the State was a person with a conscience.' By contrast, 'Sir R. Peel who was a religious man was wholly anti-church and unclerical.'[28]

The Tory revival, well underway when Gladstone launched his theocratic observations on to an unsuspecting political world, would shortly see the party back in office. As Colin Matthew has observed, his 'general defence of Anglican hegemonic nationalism' was intended 'as a guide to Conservatives as they prepared for office'.[29] Gladstone wanted the legislation of an incom-ing Tory government to reflect the beliefs and moral precepts of the estab-lished church along lines adumbrated in Gladstone's two striking theological publications. Peel, equally clearly, did not.

At this time the church, for Gladstone, subsumed 'individual morality'. Citizens should be seen 'only as constituents of the active power of ... the life of the state'.[30] In the battle which had raged since the early sixteenth cen-tury between freedom of conscience and the authority of the state, Gladstone presented himself as an out-and-out authoritarian. He deprecated the pre-vailing trend towards unrestricted liberty of conscience. Freedom for the individual impoverished a church which embraced the highest moral ideals. The state, asserted Gladstone, had a 'true and a moral personality'. Its long association with the church gave it a higher and more profound authority than individual conscience could ever claim. The business of government was to put the highest ideals of its church into practice. Thus purified, it could speak for the nation.

The State in its Relations with the Church was Gladstone's first major pub-lication and he was 29 when it appeared. His agitation is understandable. He was cognisant of his reputation as a 'coming man'. He also knew how far his ideas challenged conventional political as well as theological wisdom. Along with that intellectual self-confidence which bordered on arrogance went considerable personal vulnerability and insecurity. Despite the strong early impression he had made on Peel and other Conservative leaders, he remained an inexperienced politician who had launched a controversial pub-lication before his political position was secure. In early 1839, he awaited reactions to his book with considerable anxiety. His diary noted a dinner with Peel where he obviously felt that the subject had been studiously avoided: 'Not a word from him, S[tanley] or G[raham] yet even to acknowl-edge the receipt of my poor book'. He later alleged that Peel 'was repelled and dismayed when my book on Church and State appeared. I remember that when I came back from the Continent in January 1839, he (not rudely) shirked me in the street and I went after him and spoke to him.'[31] At the end of his life, he called the work 'crude' and recorded that it 'entailed upon me great embarrassments over and above the dissatisfaction of Sir Robert Peel, my political leader and guide, whose confidence I think I never again quite fully acquired'.[32] He also confessed to his sense of isolation. There was little place in a party led by Peel for his backward-looking Anglicanism: 'Scarcely had my work issued from the press when I became aware that there was no party, no section of a party, no individual person probably, in the House of Commons, who was prepared to act on it. I found myself the last man on a sinking ship.'[33]

Gladstone's fears about long-term damage to his relationship with Peel seem misplaced. There is little to suggest that Peel considered the appear-ance of Gladstone's anguished outpourings as specially significant. Rather too much has been made by historians of the dismissive comment recorded by Gladstone's exact contemporary, the Conservative MP and poet Richard Monckton Milnes. Milnes was a guest of Peel at his Staffordshire residence of Drayton Manor at the time Peel was reading the book. Peel was alleged to have thrown it on the floor, exclaiming as he did so: 'That young man will ruin his fine political career if he persists in writing trash like this.'[34] Peel was doubtless irritated that Gladstone should have exposed a raw ecclesias-tical nerve while he was busy rebuilding the Conservative party around a very different conception of church–state relations. However, this outburst – if accurately reported anyway – was an isolated one. Peel knew that Glad-stone, for all his promise, was too junior for his heterodox views to threaten party unity. The period of coolness was brief; Gladstone was quickly back in Peel's favour. He was dining again at Peel's by February 1840 when he took part in detailed 'rumination on the probable course of politics & party'.[35] During the protracted final months of Melbourne's government, his views were frequently sought and, it seems, increasingly respected.

Gladstone's parliamentary role was also undiminished. In April 1839 Peel asked him to follow up his own attack on the Whig proposal to suspend the constitution of the colony of Jamaica following the breakdown of relations between governor and Assembly there over the implementation of liberalis-ing legislation in respect of recently emancipated slaves. Gladstone responded with a highly competent, well-argued speech. He thus contributed to the destabilisation of the government which led to Melbourne's temporary resignation on 7 May and the so-called Bedchamber Crisis.[36] In April 1840, he delivered a characteristically 'Christian' attack on the government for going to war against China in support of the opium trade. Justice, he argued, was with the Chinese and 'whilst they, the Pagans, and semi-civilised barbarians, have it, we, the enlightened and civilised Christians, are pursuing objects at variance both with justice, and with religion'. Palmerston, the Foreign Secretary, to whom Gladstone had already taken a personal dislike, was lambasted for 'indolence and apathy'.[37] His speech of 10 May 1841 on the Whig government's proposal to reduce sugar duties was judged by Greville to be one of the two best which came from the opposition during the debates that finally administered the quietus to Melbourne's beleaguered and increasingly demoralised government.[38]

Just before his speech on the sugar duties, however, Gladstone had written a long and reflective piece in his diary. It revealed that 'the principle of National Religion' was his 'bond to Parliamentary life'. If that principle were 'to be upheld, or saved from utter overthrow, it must be by the united action of the Conservative party ... of the party as a whole & moving under its leaders'. Concerning his relationship with Peel:

> If I have differences from my leader they are as I am convinced not political but religious. I think both his cast of sentiments and of abilities such as to be a great Providential gift to this country, wonderfully suited to her need: thus I have ever thought since knowing him. I have the most implicit confidence in his integrity and honour. If I believe in the Catholic Church historical & visible, & consequently in claims generically different from those of sects, and if he does not, this will naturally lead me to aver some things which he must, & on his own principles I think reasonably and consistently, shrink from upholding: but even if I be right in my belief as far as it may differ from his, I set down that difference to the periods & circumstances of education.[39]

Though he never read this statement, Peel would shortly accustom himself to many similar examples of that ponderous prolixity with which Gladstone unburdened himself when actuated by conscience. And conscience was Gladstone's invariable guide.

However, he was to recant at least on the practicalities, if not the theory, of his church and state thesis. In two diary entries from Easter 1842 and on his birthday in 1843 – both occasions on which he was liable to develop ideas more extensively than was normal in the diaries – he belatedly recognised the impracticability of his earlier views. He acknowledged that 'we have passed the point' at which it was possible to harmonise the actions of the state to the laws of the church, though he still looked for further 'adjustment' in relations between the two. By December 1843, he was more explicit: 'Of public life I certainly must say every year shows me more & more that the idea of Christian politics can not be realised in the State according to its present conditions of existence. For purpose sufficient ... I am more than content to be where I am.'[40] He wrote a paper in July 1894 entitled 'Some of my Errors'.[41] It listed eight, all related to his political career between 1838 and 1892. The first was the publication of *The State in its Relations with the Church*:

> Undoubtedly that work was written in total disregard or rather ignorance of the conditions under which alone political action was possible in matters of religion ... In the sanguine fervour of youth, having now learned something about the nature of the Church and its office, and noting the many symptoms of revival and reform within her borders, I dreamed that she was capable of recovering lost ground and of bringing back the nation to unity in her communion ... the effort seems contemptible.

Nevertheless, he was anxious to explain that his position had justification at the time:

> The land was overspread with a thick curtain of prejudice. The foundations of the historic Church of England except in the minds of a few divines were obscured. The Evangelical movement with all its virtues and merits had the vice of individualising religion in a degree perhaps unexampled and of rendering the language of Holy Scripture about Mount Zion and the Kingdom of Heaven little better than jargon.[42]

IV

Gladstone returned to office with Peel in August 1841. After the elections in his Newark constituency were over, he returned to London and found himself, as on several previous occasions in the last few years, involved in discussions about the formal ending of Melbourne's ministry. Between 21 and 31 August, he attended four meetings of senior Conservatives, including Graham, Lyndhurst, Stanley, Goulburn and Hardinge. His perception of his recovery from the publication of *The State in its Relations with the Church* was such that he harboured genuine expectations of an immediate cabinet post. Characteristically, though, he found himself wrestling with his conscience before Peel even offered him a post. He confided to his diary concerns about 'a stumbling block at present in my way' if Peel intended to continue the previous government's policy of pressing the Chinese for compensation for losses concerning the opium trade: 'May God grant me in this juncture a cool head and earnest resolute heart that I may neither be bewildered by imagination on one side, nor by interest or vanity or even a *general* desire to serve the country on the other.'[43]

Peel's offer came on 31 August, the day after he kissed hands as Prime Minister, and it did not contain either the promotion or the specific post that

Gladstone wanted. He had wished to walk in Peel's footsteps as Chief Secretary: 'the idea of Ireland had nestled imperceptibly in my mind'.[44] Unlike Peel, however, he also hoped to enter the cabinet in this post. The Whigs had often included the Chief Secretary within the cabinet,[45] although the Tories had not. Peel had to wait until 1822 to enter the cabinet as Home Secretary. Gladstone considered that his good start in government six years earlier and what he called the 'forward position in the party'[46] he had retained since then made this a natural progression. When the dispositions had been made, he reconfirmed his hope to have been offered 'Ireland with the Cabinet' in view of 'the degree of confidence which Sir Robert Peel had for years, habitually I may say, reposed in me ... I am sorry now to think that I may have been guilty of an altogether absurd presumption.'[47]

Peel had neither Ireland nor the cabinet in mind for Gladstone. Like all Prime Ministers, he had internal balances to strike, longer-term loyalties than Gladstone's to reward and political debts to repay.[48] He saw the immediate need to promote older, if substantially less gifted, men. Peel was also sensible, as almost any leading Conservative other than Gladstone must have been, that the triumphalist utterances of *The State in its Relations with the Church* rendered its author utterly unsuitable to exercise administrative control over a country 80 per cent of whose population was Roman Catholic, which saw the Church of Ireland (the name of the Anglican communion in Ireland) as perhaps the most irritating single symbol of alien authority and which had, in Daniel O'Connell, an impressive rallying point for nationalist disaffection. Accordingly, the Chief Secretaryship went to the far less controversial but, as events were to prove, equally impulsive Lord Eliot.

Peel's offer of the Vice-Presidency of the Board of Trade was intended to be a fit match for Gladstone's abilities. He explained that 'In this great struggle in which we have been & are to be engaged, the chief importance will attach to questions of finance'.[49] Gladstone's reaction has been widely documented.[50] He objected to Peel that he had 'no general knowledge of trade whatever' – an unlikely assertion from a man with a substantial knowledge of early nineteenth-century Liverpool, with which city's fortunes his family's wealth was intimately intertwined. He also confided to his diary: 'It has always been my hope, that I might be able to avoid this class of public employments: on this account I have not endeavoured to train myself for them.' However, Peel told him that the Vice-Presidency was 'an office of the highest importance'. Gladstone, although nominally Lord Ripon's deputy, would lead on trade in the Commons, a responsibility which Peel had 'unbounded confidence' he would be able to discharge effectively. Moreover, Gladstone would find Ripon 'a perfect master on the subject' who would quickly initiate him into the details of the work. This proved a hopeless exaggeration. Ripon, the erstwhile F. J. Robinson and Lord Goderich, was now a burnt-out case. Gladstone sardonically noted later that on the subject of Ripon's mastery 'I was early undeceived.'[51]

Though grateful for the friendliness and warmth of Peel's 'whole language & demeanour' during the interview, Gladstone accepted the post, and the membership of the Privy Council which went with it, with less than good grace. He noted in his diary: 'I must forthwith go to work, in sum, as a reluctant schoolboy meaning well.' He later acknowledged the churlishness of his reaction. The Vice-Presidency 'was really at the time a much more important appointment than the other [the Chief Secretaryship] ... I did not appreciate duly the fact that for years Protection was to form the hinge of British politics.'[52]

Whatever the relevant experience of trade on Gladstone's *curriculum vitae* to that point, Peel knew well that his transferable skills were ideal for the post. Peel's assessment of the 'chief importance' in his new ministry was not intended merely as an inducement for Gladstone to take up an uncongenial portfolio. Matters were dominated by finance. Peel already knew about Gladstone's ambition, his predilection for hard work and his obsessive attention to detail as the necessary precondition of effective policy formation. He calculated that all of these would be sunk in his new labours and that he would emerge from them a more mature and formidable operator. Graham famously asserted that 'Gladstone could do in four hours what it took any other man sixteen to do, and he worked sixteen hours a day.'[53] Even better, Peel doubtless calculated, devilling among myriad trade regulations was just the ticket for pushing to the back of that capacious cranium implausible and atavistic certainties about church–state relations.

What came increasingly to the front of it, of course, was trade liberalisation. Gladstone had been what might be termed an ill-informed protectionist. He had spoken for protection in support of his brother's candidacy for the Walsall by-election in 1840, when calling the Anti-Corn Law League 'no better than a big borough-mongering association' – and got roasted by Richard Cobden. This he later called 'my first capital offence in the matter of Protection: released from public condemnation only by obscurity'.[54]

He had considered trade issues beneath the high concerns of the aspiring statesman: 'In a spirit of ignorant mortification I said to myself at the moment: the science of politics deals with the government of men, but I am set to govern packages.'[55] Immersion in these minutiae, however, did not deflect Gladstone from the pursuit of higher moral purposes. His recollection in 1895 was that it had taken him 'two or three years' of 'transition' before he was prepared to champion free trade as a 'cause'. Before 1845, although he generally considered his actions at the Board of Trade to have been 'on the right side', he acknowledged that he committed 'political sins against the principles of Free Trade'. By 1845, however, free trade was at the core of his political being and, as such, the revelation of divine providence. As Boyd Hilton puts it: 'For him, as for Peelites generally, Free Trade and sound (non-interventionist) finance were less matters of *enrichissez-vous* and social progress ... than of leaving providence to its own devices, the better to display God's handiwork, his wise and moral economy of the world.'[56]

The moral dimension was also prominent in the article, 'The Course of Commercial Policy at Home and Abroad', which Gladstone published anonymously in 1843 in the *Foreign and Colonial Quarterly* magazine. This celebrated the substantial reductions in more than six hundred tariffs which had been effected in 1842 as a means of stimulating trade, and thus providing employment. Most of the detailed preparatory work had been undertaken by Gladstone. He expressed his satisfaction over the policy in terms which would never have occurred to Peel. He argued that the tariff reductions represented the 'natural and proper consequence of [Britain's] possessing, in a superior degree, the elements of industrial greatness'. More, they derived from the belief that 'religion and Christian virtue, like the faculty of taste and the perception of beauty, have their place, aye and that the first place, in political economy, as the means of creating and preserving wealth'.[57]

Gladstone's mastery of the technicalities of Board of Trade business was achieved in months, rather than years. By early 1842, he was offering advice on the direction of government economic policy. This brought him into a disagreement with Peel which, for a time – and entirely characteristically – Gladstone thought could be resolved only by resignation. The diary entries for the first half of November 1841 make frequent reference to work on 'corn'; he presented Peel with a long paper on the subject in the same month. When Peel discussed his own proposals the following January, he had suggested 56 shillings as the level 'at which a considerable quantity of foreign corn can be imported ... the point I also had assumed as the general result of my inquiries'.[58] In later discussions, however, the qualifying domestic price was pushed up. Gladstone noted that Peel 'would not be averse to abatement – but wishes to feel the pulse of the agricultural folks'.[59] The erstwhile protectionist Gladstone had become convinced, within months of joining the Board of Trade, that 'The present law ... appears to me to have been a very stringent and severe one'.[60]

In early February, when it was clear that the cabinet (which had already lost the protectionist Duke of Buckingham on the issue) would only agree on levels of protection higher than Gladstone thought necessary, he sought a personal interview with the Prime Minister:

[I] represented to him that I had such serious doubts on the subject of the scale as proposed that I thought it right to mention them – and to him rather than to any other person. I feared it might still be found to operate as virtual prohibition up to 70/- – that I should like to think somewhat more upon the point – and I hinted at retirement as being perfectly ready to adopt it if that could be done without perplexing the Government.[61]

Peel, if not perplexed, was certainly vexed. A junior minister's views – however well founded on commercial grounds and however much the Prime Minister might privately sympathise with them – could hardly be expected to prevail against cabinet. There was no more sensitive issue in contemporary politics. As Peel well knew, the offer of resignation would damage Gladstone's career without changing government policy: a pretty fair definition of a pointless sacrifice. In the circumstances, he handled Gladstone gently, telling him the facts of political life – 'that it was impossible for everyone to have precisely that which he thought best' – while admitting that Gladstone's behaviour had left him 'thunderstruck'. Gladstone's remorse was as sudden as his concern for political survival was real:

> I fear Peel was much annoyed & displeased for he would not give me a word of help or of favourable supposition as to my own motives & belief. And indeed I am a poor creature, vain enough I suppose and yet not enabled even by vanity to know what is expected of a person in my office. I wish I could have seen that he was at all soothed: he used nothing like an angry or unkind word, but the negative character of the conversation had a chilling effect on my feeble mind. I came home sick at heart in the evening.[62]

Gladstone's palpable mishandling of the situation still pained him when he recalled it more than fifty years later. He acknowledged that Peel's compromise was 'as much as the Cabinet or the party would adopt ... Undoubtedly in this proceeding I was absolutely without comprehension of the political situation, and acted like a schoolboy which indeed I still was to no small extent.' He remembered going home 'well intimidated, and in very low dumps indeed'.[63]

Peel's irritation was short-lived. Having talked some sense into Gladstone, he continued to rely on his formidable energies in administration and on his effective speeches on commerce in the House of Commons. Gladstone describes a journey of discovery which ended with his wholehearted commitment to free trade. Peel's journey had been undertaken earlier and he had reached the same destination, however much (at least in 1842–43) he still felt the need for compromises and accommodations[64] in the interests of party unity. There seem to have been few, if any, significant disagreements between them on commercial matters throughout the ministry. In June 1842, Peel wrote in the warmest terms to Gladstone's father:

> I cannot resist the temptation, if it be only for the satisfaction of my own feelings, of congratulating you most warmly and sincerely, on the distinction which your son has acquired, by the manner in which he has conducted himself throughout these discussions and all others since his appointment to office. At no time in the annals of parliament has there been exhibited a more admirable combination of ability, extensive knowledge, temper and discretion.[65]

The reference to 'discretion' was perhaps more kindly than accurate, especially concerning church matters where Gladstone continued to be headstrong and intemperate. His determination to parade his conscience when offered preferment must also have been extremely irritating. In May 1843 Peel promoted him to the cabinet as President of the Board of Trade. The promotion was entirely on merit; Westminster gossip had long installed Gladstone in that office in reality, since Ripon was only a cipher. Nevertheless, Peel waited until the death of Vesey Fitzgerald, President of the Board of Control, before shuffling Ripon there. Gladstone recorded his interview with Peel in some detail in his diary. Peel could by now probably anticipate Gladstone's reaction. Peel expressed warm appreciation of his service and told him that promotion within the Board of Trade was 'obviously the right arrangement' given Gladstone's obvious command of the brief.

Gladstone responded that it was his 'duty to examine my mind and consider whether I had any sentiments upon points of public policy which I deemed it possible he might think exceptionable'. Barely pausing for breath, it seems, he unveiled his shopping list. He remained concerned about the opium trade and was glad to learn that Peel remained sound on the need to do more about the Corn Laws. He was also anxious to steel his chief to resist any proposals which reduced the influence of the Church of England in educational matters. He bent Peel's ear at greatest length over the ongoing proposal to merge the bishoprics of Bangor and St Asaph in order to create a new bishopric for Manchester. Naturally, Gladstone was opposed to a measure which he interpreted as weakening the historic Anglican communion. He threatened to make it into a sticking point: 'I have to consider with God's help by Monday whether to enter the Cabinet, or to retire altogether: at least such is probably the second alternative.'[66] It was left to Gladstone's High Anglican friends Manning and Hope to warn him against risking his political career on such a point of ecclesiastical detail and he attended his first cabinet two days later.

Gladstone's later career in Peel's cabinet was not trouble-free but it can be discussed in less detail since the nature of the political relationship between the two men was clear by the middle of 1843. Gladstone and Peel were at one on the broad objective of policy, which was to rebuild the nation's finances. Gladstone, as was natural in the much younger and less experienced politician, wished to move the faster, but this caused few difficulties once Peel became accustomed to Gladstone's mode of operation. Gladstone was at one with Peel on the controversial proposal to reduce the sugar duties in 1844. He acted as the unlikely broker of an attempted compromise with the leading Conservative opponents of the measure in June to prevent the government's resignation after a Commons defeat. He was, however, sure that Peel's speech which made his resentment of backbench Tories all too clear was ill judged – 'hard, reserved, and introspective', he called it. 'I heard his speech with great pain ... At the end of the speech we all felt ourselves out. The House seem resolved into its primordial elements ... Conversations with members of Parliament subsequently convinced me that a deep wound had been inflicted upon the spirit & harmony of the party: that a great man had committed a great error.'[67]

For his part, Peel continued to admire Gladstone's work at the Board of Trade, not least the pioneering Railways Bill. Gladstone, however great his satisfaction at piloting the bill through parliament in 1844, felt cast down when he was unable to prevent an amendment to ensure that his cheap 'parliamentary trains' ran on Sundays as well as weekdays. He wrote to Peel: 'I do not know how to reconcile it to myself to be responsible for the enactment or the execution of a law concerning a provision so dangerous in its immediate and ultimate results to public morality.'[68]

Church affairs, however, continued to be a point of mutual incompatibility, if not incomprehension. The cabinet had been discussing, on and off, the funding of the Roman Catholic seminary at Maynooth, just outside Dublin, since November 1842.[69] Gladstone's unease was certainly obvious to Peel by 1844, though he was by now familiar with Gladstone's conscience and, in particular, the contortions into which it put him when church principles clashed with state policy. To get himself off an unwelcome hook, he went so far as to suggest to Peel in July that he might appoint him envoy to the Vatican. Not surprisingly Peel refused to take the suggestion seriously. Gladstone later recalled it as the second of his eight 'recorded errors' (though he had the chronology wrong): 'a blunder which was the silliest action probably that I ever committed: due to religious fanaticism, for fanaticism may be very strong in a character which for purposes of religion is very weak'.[70]

Gladstone prepared for what he called his 'catastrophe' during a cabinet meeting on 9 January 1845 which finally decided to increase the Maynooth grant. He reasserted his decision to resign if the matter was pursued since 'I viewed the matter as one of personal pledge: that it was wholly unconnected with any thing like alienation of feeling.'[71] What Gladstone actually meant was uncertain and it took most of the rest of the month for costive discussions to work their way through. Gladstone resigned on 28 January, Peel implausibly expressing himself 'staggered ... I had resigned because of Maynooth'. He had an audience with the Queen on 3 February.[72] Graham and Peel exchanged bewildered notes. Peel wondered why Gladstone had marked a private letter secret when it 'came in the post to me this morning open. It may have been read in every post office through which it has passed.' Graham acknowledged that Gladstone's loss 'is serious and on every account to be regretted; but I do not think that we should be justified in averting it by abandonment of a most important part of our Irish policy'. Peel had said: 'I really have great difficulty sometimes in comprehending what Gladstone means.' Graham agreed, though more sardonically: 'It is always difficult through the haze of words to catch a distant glimpse of Gladstone's meaning.'[73] So Gladstone went, though he nevertheless supported

Peel's motion to increase the grant when it came before the Commons in April. This thoroughly confused even most of those who had supported him to that point. Gladstone could justify it to his conscience, but he never succeeded in explaining it to his colleagues. Colin Matthew's explanation is neat: 'Principle rejected the Maynooth grant: good government demanded it. Thus Gladstone both resigned from the cabinet and voted for the grant: the man of theory and the man of government.'[74] To this it might only be added that the Conservative party was rarely a natural home for 'men of theory'.

Gladstone was not away long. He returned to office as Colonial Secretary on 22 December 1845 after Russell's failure to form a Whig administration to carry Corn Law repeal. Peel wanted him as perhaps the staunchest supporter of the cause for which it was now clear he was ready to sacrifice his party. In this judgement he was to be proved absolutely correct. Gladstone had told Lord Lincoln (the son of his political patron the Duke of Newcastle), during 'a talk over matters of trade' at dinner as recently as 6 December, the old Corn Law 'was a delusion'. This view he had held since 1841, but had not pressed it out of deference to Newcastle and his Newark constituents. However, 'I now held myself at liberty to vote for its abolition.'[75]

Gladstone nevertheless took office with the usual expressions of self-abasement: 'Never did I feel a poorer creature', '... accepted office – in opposition, as I have the consolation of feeling, to my leanings & desires: & with the most precarious prospects'.[76] He was, however, reassured to find Peel 'most kind, nay fatherly – we *held* hands instinctively & I could not but reciprocate with emphasis his "God bless you"'. The decision, though it gave Peel reliable support in cabinet, deprived him of it where it now mattered more. Gladstone felt obliged to resign his seat at Newark and did not return to the Commons until 1847 when, with Robert Inglis, he represented Oxford University. It thus happened that perhaps the most forceful debater in the Commons was not on hand to combat the stratagems of certainly the wiliest, most poisonously ambitious and probably the wittiest performer there: Benjamin Disraeli, self-appointed and incongruous spokesman for the protectionist interest.

V

Gladstone came closest to open criticism of Peel during the four-year period between the former Prime Minister's resignation and his death. It is not difficult to see why. Peel had been forced from office by the split within his party over free trade but he retained enormous authority as the leading statesman of the age. The tides of political change generally, and rapidly, engulf outgoing Prime Ministers. Many leaders harbour delusions that they will be able to swim against that tide only to find themselves paddling furiously downwards to the vasty deeps of political oblivion. Baroness Thatcher represents only the most recent, if much the most strident and repining, example. Peel was different. He had indeed been forced from office, but he left with both honour and policies intact. He had won the most important political argument of the day. The mid-Victorian period would witness the apotheosis of free trade and Peel had made that unequivocally into his cause. Frequently during the later 1840s the Whig government of Lord John Russell seemed to be swimming weakly in his slipstream. Not infrequently, it looked to Sir Robert for direction and fresh impetus. For this reason, it is difficult to agree with Roy Jenkins's judgement that 'Peel had ... no possibility of return to Downing Street after 1846'.[77]

Certainly, Gladstone would have disagreed. When Peel resigned, Gladstone was 35 years of age and had been a cabinet minister for just over two years, having briefly, but successfully, controlled two major ministries: trade and the Colonial Office. Though sometimes a difficult and frustrating colleague, he had proved his value. He saw no reason why his ministerial career should not rapidly resume if only his revered chief could be persuaded to exert his still enormous authority to unseat unworthy Whig successors. To his immense frustration, however, Peel showed no signs of wishing to do so. Gladstone had a long conversation with Peel a fortnight after they left office. Peel informed Gladstone that 'he had been twice Prime Minister and nothing should induce him again to take part in the formation of a government: the labour and anxiety were too great'. Gladstone demurred:

> You have had extraordinary physical strength to sustain you: and you have performed an extraordinary task. Your government has not been carried on by a Cabinet but by the heads of departments each in communication with you ... The question is not whether you are entitled to retire but whether after all you have done and in the position you occupy before the country you can remain in the House of Commons as an isolated person and hold yourself aloof from the great movements of political forces which sway to and fro there.[78]

But Peel was determined to remain 'aloof'. Gladstone became the more vexed as time passed and the Whig government ran into trouble, not least over its handling of the Irish famine. At the end of 1847, Peel agreed with Sir John Young, the Peelites' Chief Whip, that 'there should be some attempt at organising the scattered individuals who had either belonged to the late government or had adhered to their policy to the last'. In consequence, Gladstone held a dinner attended by Young and Lord Lincoln. The conclusion from this table talk was predictable:

> we all felt the great and special difficulty of the case to arise from the relation in which we should stand to Sir R. Peel combined with his determination to hold himself aloof from party and not to contemplate the resumption of office... It was easy to feel the great difficulties attending any organisation among us in which he was not to be included. We could not be in communication with him and yet

not commit him virtually as the leader of a party to the position he had abjured: we could not act together out of communication with him, without being in the constant hazard of thwarting his views or of being thwarted by him.[79]

What Gladstone saw as Peel's abrogation of responsibility increasingly festered during 1848. He spoke against the Whigs over the issue of sugar duties, arguing that their proposals afforded insufficient relief to the West Indian planters, and resented the overriding priority which Peel gave to keeping the Whigs in office rather than risk returning to protection. Gladstone, almost certainly correctly, judged the risk to be minimal. He wrote a bitter private note demonstrating his resentment of the fact that Peel 'continues to tolerate every kind of financial error and mischief' perpetrated by the government. By refusing to take office 'he may cause an accumulation of evil too great to be got rid of except by social convulsion entailing perhaps other and heavier calamities'.[80] The note reflected a wider political concern. Gladstone was intellectually and temperamentally averse to Liberal radicalism, which had increased its support at the general election in 1847, and he could not accept Cobden's assumption that the adoption of free trade would somehow cure original sin as well as bringing commercial benefit.[81] The Gladstone of the late 1840s was still a Conservative.

The Peelites maintained no evident unity during 1849. Gladstone spoke in favour of reciprocal arrangements for free trade with other countries rather than the unconditional repeal of the Navigation Laws, which the Whigs proposed and Peel supported. Gladstone returned to the theme of Peel's leadership in a discussion with Aberdeen:

> Yesterday morning we had been on Peel's political position which I described as false and in the abstract almost immoral – as he, and still more Graham, sit on the opposition side of the House professing thereby to be independent members of Parliament but in every critical vote are governed by the intention to keep the ministers in office & sacrifice every thing to that intention.[82]

In 1850, a yet more obvious split emerged when Gladstone supported a motion to relieve agricultural distress by adjusting arrangements for local taxation. Peel opposed it. The Peelites split almost equally on the issue. Young informed Peel: 'They will stand by Free Trade ... But they have no sympathies with and no confidence in the present government.'[83] By the time of Peel's death, it was difficult to maintain that the Peelites were acting as a party at all.

VI

After Peel's death, Gladstone crystallised the harsh judgements he had reached about his chief's career after 1846. He deprecated his decision to remain in the Commons when, as he often asserted, he had no intention of resuming office: 'The question may be fairly raised whether he would not have set as a greater luminary if he had been taken from us in 1846'. 'Prime Ministers unattached are dangerous: as great rafts would be dangerous floating unmoored in a harbour ... the position of Sir Robert Peel for the last four years of his life was a thoroughly false position.'[84] Gladstone's attack is explained partly by personal ambition. He yearned for further office and he saw in Peel the means to achieve it. But a deeper explanation may be offered. The two men took divergent views about political parties and their role in the modern state. Gladstone talked about Peel's 'reconstruction of that great Party which he has reared'. Peel considered this as a relatively light achievement, if achievement at all. He saw party as the subordinate means to achieve the great end of proper governance. In Angus Hawkins's words, Peel viewed 1846 'as the triumphant reassertion of his freedom from the shackles of party'.[85] Gladstone at this stage of his career had a view of party which was paradoxically much closer to that of Disraeli when he so viciously attacked Peel as an apostate during the Corn Law debates in the spring of 1846. By 1856, Gladstone was calling for a strengthened and more disciplined party system as the only means of shoring up executive government.[86] Arguably in no area of public life, even the church, did Gladstone differ so profoundly from Peel as on the role of political parties.

Was it the case, then, that Gladstone was Peel's 'apt pupil'? John Morley's view is worth quoting in some detail:

> It was during these years of labour under Peel that he first acquired principles of administrative and parliamentary practice that afterward stood him in good stead: on no account to try to deal with a question before it is ripe; never to go the length of submitting a difference between two departments to the prime minister before the case is exhausted and complete; never to press a proposal forward beyond the particular stage at which it has arrived ... We cannot forget that Peel and Mr Gladstone were in the strict line of political succession. They were alike in social origin and academic antecedents. They started from the same point of view as to the great organs of national life, the monarchy, the territorial peerage and the commons, the church, the universities. They showed the same clear knowledge that it was not by its decorative parts, or what Burke styled 'solemn plausibilities', that the community derived its strength; but that it rested for its real foundations on its manufactures, its commerce, and its credit. Even in the lesser things, in reading Sir Robert Peel's letters, those who in later years served under Mr Gladstone can recognise the school to which he went for his methods, the habits of mind, the practices of business, and even the phrases which he employed when his own time came to assume the direction of public affairs.[87]

That assessment was written in 1903. Like so much else in what is one of the great biographies written in the twentieth century, it has stood the test of time. No scholar can provide a rounded assessment of Gladstone without acknowledging his enormous debt to Peel. This paper has attempted to show that it was a relationship of mutual warmth as well as of respect. Even when they disagreed openly in the Commons over agricultural relief in 1850, Peel went out of his way to pay tribute to Gladstone's abilities and achievements. Peel's personal regard for, and many kindnesses to, colleagues whom he respected rarely manifested themselves at the level of contemporary public awareness, where his alleged arrogance and lack of regard for those with fewer gifts were cited as contributory reasons for his downfall.[88] Morley's 'manufactures, commerce and credit' are at the heart of the relationship between Peel and Gladstone. Both men knew relatively little about economic policy until they took up new responsibilities: Peel with the bullion committee in 1819 and Gladstone at the Board of Trade from 1841. Both used their formidable powers of concentration to assimilate large amounts of arcane material. Mastery of such detail also set them apart from most contemporary politicians. Peel's perception that Gladstone's ferocious energies would be more effectively channelled into economic policy than into theocratic speculation probably saved Gladstone's political career.

Without the example of Peel, Gladstone could not have developed into the formidable politician he later became. Indeed, he might well have left politics altogether at any time between 1839 and 1843 to pursue what he later acknowledged to be his wilder ecclesiastical passions. However, in one sense Peel had something to learn from Gladstone. Once Gladstone had resolved his personal dilemma and had become convinced that politics could be used to pursue a great end – the moralising and liberalising force of free trade – he became a believer in party to achieve that end. His was to become an authoritarian view of party; it was there to be led. He was, however, clear that without party the political function could no longer be discharged.

Gladstone was born in 1809, almost four years after the death of the younger Pitt. Peel took his seat in the House of Commons in the same year. Peel had grown up under Pitt's patriotic coalition of order from the 1790s and his view of party was much closer to Pitt's than Gladstone's could ever be.[89] Pitt called himself a 'liberal Whig', connoting by this attachment a cautiously reformist value system under the direction of the nation's property owners. He resisted any assertion that his governments – even after 1794 – were Tory by arguing that the adoption of this label implied faction and an inappropriately narrow view of national interests and priorities. Peel's view was much the same, but he tried to uphold it almost half a century later. Revolutionary social and political developments in the meantime compelled a reappraisal. However great Gladstone's debt to Peel – and it was massive – their views on party were fundamentally different. Despite his reputation for modernity, Peel's view of party as a subordinate vehicle for progress placed him in the eighteenth-century tradition. Gladstone belonged firmly in the nineteenth.

Notes

1   T. B. Macaulay, 'Gladstone on Church and State' in *Critical and Historical Essays*, 3 vols, London, Longman, 1843, vol. 2, p. 430.

2   J. Morley, *The Life of William Ewart Gladstone*, 3 vols, London, Macmillan, 1903, vol. 1, p. 275.

3   In a letter written on 20 April 1853 and preserved in the Peel MSS, British Library. Quoted in N. Gash, *Sir Robert Peel: The Life of Sir Robert Peel after 1830*, London, Longman, 1986 edn, p. 708.

4   R. Shannon, *Gladstone, 1809–1865*, London, Hamish Hamilton, 1982, p. 224.

5   E. J. Feuchtwanger, *Gladstone*, London, Allen Lane, 1975, p. 68.

6   R. Jenkins, *Gladstone*, London, Macmillan, 1995, p. 63.

7   *Hansard's Parliamentary Debates*, 3rd series, vol. 112, col. 857, 3 July 1850. *GD*, 2, 3 and 4 July 1850.

8   Shannon (1982), p. 67. See also P. Butler, *Gladstone: Church, State and Tractarianism: A Study of his Religious Ideas and Attitudes, 1809–1859*, Oxford, Clarendon Press, 1982, pp. 66–73.

9   J. Brooke and M. Sorensen (eds), *The Prime Ministers' Papers: W. E. Gladstone*, 4 vols, London, HMSO, 1971–81, vol. 3, p. 77. This extract is quoted in B. Hilton, 'The Ripening of Robert Peel', in M. Bentley (ed.), *Public and Private Doctrine: Essays presented to Maurice Cowling*, Cambridge, Cambridge UP, 1993, pp. 63–84, at 63–64.

10 G. I. T. Machin, *The Catholic Question in English Politics, 1820–30*, Oxford, Clarendon Press, 1964; G. I. T. Machin, 'The Catholic Question and the Monarchy, 1827–29', *Parliamentary History*, Vol. 16, 1997, pp. 213–20. On Catholic emancipation as part of a broader blitz on Irish legislation in 1828–30, see P. J. Jupp, *British Politics on the Eve of Reform: The Duke of Wellington's Administration, 1828–30*, London, Macmillan, 1998, pp. 157–64.

11 *GD*, 5 June 1833. See also Morley (1903), vol. 1, p. 77. The speech is reported in *Hansard*, 3rd series, vol. 18, cols 330–37. See also H. G. C. Matthew, *Gladstone, 1809–1874*, Oxford, Clarendon Press, 1986, p. 31, and Shannon (1982), p. 46.

12 A. Tilney Bassett (ed.), *Gladstone to his Wife*, London, Methuen, 1936, p. 28.

13 *GD*, 31 March and 29 July 1834; Morley (1903), vol. 1, p. 84.

14 Bassett (1936), pp. 31–32

15 This was the last occasion on which a monarch dismissed a ministry. For recent, and rather conflicting, interpretations of the reasons which lay behind William's decision, see L. G. Mitchell, *Lord Melbourne*, Oxford, Oxford UP, 1997, pp. 146–50, and I. Newbould, *Whiggery and Reform, 1830–41: The Politics of Government*, London, Macmillan, 1990, pp. 152–54.

16 *GD*, 17–20 December 1834; Morley (1903), vol. 1, p. 89.

17 Morley (1903), vol. 1, p. 91; *GD*, 26 January 1835.

18 Morley (1903), vol. 1, p. 91. A useful assemblage of evidence about Peel's private kindness to government subordinates is found in Gash (1986), pp. 662–69.

19 Feuchtwanger (1975), p. 26; Morley (1903), vol. 1, p. 94.

20 Matthew (1986), p. 37.

21 B. Hilton, *The Age of Atonement: The Influence of Evangelicalism on Social and Economic Thought, 1795–1865*, Oxford, Clarendon Press, 1988, p. 340. See also D.

Schreuder, 'Gladstone and the Conscience of the State', in *The Conscience of the Victorian State*, ed. P. T. Marsh, New York, 1979, pp. 73–143.

22 Gash (1986), p. 185.

23 The literature on church reform in this period is substantial. G. I. T. Machin, *Politics and the Churches in Great Britain, 1832–68*, Oxford, Clarendon Press, 1977, O. Chadwick, *The Victorian Church*, London, A. & C. Black, 1966, vol. 1, and E. J. Evans, *The Contentious Tithe*, London, Routledge, 1976, offer a representative introduction.

24 Morley (1903), vol. 1, p. 114.

25 *GD*, 29 December 1835.

26 See, for example, P. Butler (1982), Hilton (1988) and B. Hilton, 'Gladstone's Theological Politics' in *High and Low Politics in Modern Britain*, ed. M. Bentley and J. Stevenson, Oxford, Clarendon Press, 1983, pp. 28–57.

27 GP, 44819, f. 50. Quoted in Shannon (1982), p. 55.

28 Brooke and Sorensen (1971–81), vol. 1, *Autobiographica*, 1971, p. 57.

29 Matthew (1986), p. 41.

30 W. E. Gladstone, *The State in its Relations with the Church*, 4th edn, London, John Murray, 1841, quoted in Hilton (1988), p. 341.

31 *GD*, 9 February 1839; *Autobiographica* (1971), p. 44.

32 *Autobiographica* (1971), p. 125.

33 Quoted in Morley (1903), vol. 1, p. 133.

34 T. W. Reid, *The Life, Letters and Friendships of Richard Monckton Milnes, First Lord Houghton*, London, Cassell & Co., 1890, vol. 1, p. 316. Milnes, who supported Peel over free trade in 1846, joined the Liberals in 1848 rather than become a Peelite. He was ennobled by Palmerston in 1863. The famous quotation is recorded, among many other places, in Shannon (1982), p. 81.

35 *GD*, 1 February 1840.

36 *Hansard*, 3rd series, vol. 68, cols 921–33, 6 May 1839. Gladstone recorded that the speech was 'dry' and delivered 'to a somewhat reluctant House'. *GD*, 6 May 1839. See also Morley (1903), vol. 1, pp. 164–65. For the Bedchamber Crisis, see Gash (1986), pp. 220–27; R. Brent, *Liberal Anglican Politics*, Oxford, Clarendon Press, 1987, chap. 7; P. Ziegler, *Melbourne*, London, Collins, 1976, chap. 21; Mitchell (1997), pp. 241–43.

37 *Hansard*, 3rd series, vol. 53, cols 819–20, 8 April 1840. The whole speech is reported in cols 800–20. See also *GD*, 8 April 1840, where Gladstone mentions having been 'authorised' by the party leadership to speak out.

38 H. Reeve (ed.), *The Greville Memoirs*, 8 vols, London, Longmans, 1888, vol. 5, p. 7. For Gladstone's speech, see *Hansard*, 3rd series, vol. 58, cols 160–80, 10 May 1841. Its peroration includes an attack on T. B. Macaulay, perhaps a belated repayment for his stinging review of *The State in its Relations with the Church*. On the end of the Melbourne government see Newbould (1990), pp. 305–13; Mitchell (1997); Ziegler (1982); P. Mandler, *Aristocratic Government in the Age of Reform: Whigs and Liberals, 1830–1852*, Oxford, Clarendon Press, 1990, pp. 197–99.

39 *GD*, vol. 3, p. 106, 9 May 1841.

40 *GD*, 27 March 1842 and 29 December 1843.

41 This retrospective appears in two versions in GP, 44790, ff. 131–41 and 44791, ff. 29–44. Both versions are published in *Autobiographica* (1971), pp. 246–50 and 125–34 respectively.

42 *Autobiographica* (1971), p. 246.

43 GD, vol. 3, p. 133, 25 August 1841.

44 GD, 2 September 1841.

45 Stanley had been Chief Secretary for Ireland in the cabinet from 1831 to 1833 as Morpeth was in the last two years of Melbourne's government. Henry Labouchere acted similarly from 1846 to 1847 in Russell's government. No Tory or Conservative government made the Chief Secretaryship a cabinet post until the third Derby administration of 1866–68.

46 *Autobiographica* (1971), p. 44.

47 GD, vol. 3, p. 140, 16 September 1841.

48 On Peel's government-forming priorities, see Gash (1986), pp. 273–88.

49 GD, vol. 3, p. 135, 31 August 1841.

50 The interview between Peel and Gladstone is recorded, for example, in Morley (1903), vol. 1, pp. 178–81, and discussed in Shannon (1982), pp. 108–11, Feuchtwanger (1975), p. 41 and Jenkins (1995), pp. 66–67. Gladstone's later reflections, from which, with GD, 31 August 1841, this discussion derives, are in *Autobiographica* (1971), pp. 44–46.

51 He confirmed this impression at least once: 'In a very short time I came to form a low estimate of the knowledge and information of Lord Ripon.' Morley (1903), vol. 1, p. 185.

52 GD, vol. 3, p. 135, 31 August 1841; *Autobiographica* (1971), p. 44.

53 Shannon (1982), pp. 115–16.

54 Morley (1903), vol. 1, p. 181; *Autobiographica* (1971), p. 60.

55 *Autobiographica* (1971), p. 58. Morley (1903), vol. 1, p. 181.

56 Hilton (1988), p. 351.

57 *Foreign and Colonial Quarterly*, 1 January 1843, pp. 222–73, quoted in Shannon (1982), pp. 120–24.

58 GD, vol. 3, p. 173, 20 January 1842. See also Morley (1903), vol. 1, p. 187 for Gladstone's account of developments concerning the sliding scale for corn during January and February 1842

59 GD, vol. 3, p. 173, 21 January 1842.

60 GD, vol. 3, p. 174, 21 January 1842.

61 GD, vol. 3, p. 178, 5 February 1842.

62 *Ibid.*

63 *Autobiographica* (1971), p. 45. For Peel's view of the incident, see Gash (1986), pp. 313–14.

64 The view that Peel had become since the 1820s rather a rigid, even doctrinaire, free-trader has not been effectively challenged since it was put forward in B. Hilton, 'Peel: A Reappraisal', *Historical Journal*, Vol. 22, 1979, pp. 585–614.

65 Quoted in Morley (1903), vol. 1, p. 189.

66 GD, vol. 3, p. 280, 13 May 1843, and GP 44819, ff. 92–93. See also Morley (1903), vol. 1, p. 192, and Shannon (1982), p. 139.

67 GD, vol. 3, p. 383, 17 June 1844. For a discussion of the government's reverse on the sugar duties, see Gash (1986), pp. 445–53, and Shannon (1982), pp. 150–52. See also *Autobiographica* (1971), pp. 61–62.

68 GD, 22 July 1844, Gladstone to Peel, 26 July 1844, quoted in Shannon (1982), p. 146. On government railway policy see H. Parris, *Government and the Railways in Nineteenth-Century Britain*, London, Routledge, 1965; F. E. Hyde, *Mr*

Gladstone at the Board of Trade, London, Cobden-Sanderson, 1934; J. Simmons and G. Biddle, *The Oxford Companion to British Railway History*, Oxford, Oxford UP, 1997, pp. 176–77.

69 Gash (1986), pp. 400–01, 414–17.

70 *Autobiographica* (1971), p. 127. Gladstone's letter to Peel of 12 July 1844 offering to serve in communications 'with the Court of Rome' is published in C. S. Parker (ed.), *Sir Robert Peel: From his Private Papers*, 3 vols, London, John Murray, 1899, vol. 3, pp. 160–61. He evidently preferred this solution to Peel's of appointing a Roman Catholic to the post. Peel did not reply. See also Morley (1903), vol. 1, pp. 200–02.

71 *GD*, vol. 3, p. 425, 9 January 1845.

72 *GD*, vol. 3, pp. 429, 431, 28 January and 4 February 1845.

73 C. S. Parker (ed.), *The Life and Letters of Sir James Graham, 1792–1861*, 2 vols, London, John Murray, 1907, vol. 2, pp. 2–3. See also Parker (1899), vol. 3, pp. 163–69.

74 Matthew (1986), p. 69.

75 *GD*, vol. 3, p. 500, 6 December 1845. See also further conversations with Lincoln on 19 and 20 December, in Brooke and Sorensen (1971–81), *Autobiographical Memoranda, 1845–1866* (1978), pp. 13–15.

76 *GD*, 21 and 22 December 1845.

77 Jenkins (1995), p. 61.

78 Meeting on 13 July 1846, in *Autobiographical Memoranda, 1845–1866* (1978), p. 29.

79 Meeting on 7 December 1847, in ibid., pp. 33–34.

80 12 December 1848, in ibid., p. 38.

81 *GD*, vol. 4, p. 82, 6 December 1842. See also the discussion in Shannon (1982), pp. 207–13, and Feuchtwanger (1975), pp. 65–66.

82 *GD*, vol. 4, p. 161, 19 October 1849.

83 Young to Peel, 22 February 1850, Peel MSS 40603, ff. 92–97, British Library. Quoted in J. B. Conacher, *The Peelites and the Party System, 1846–52*, Newton Abbot, David & Charles, 1972, p. 58.

84 GP, 44745, f. 190. See also the discussion in Conacher (1972), pp. 18–20, 62–65.

85 A. Hawkins, '"Parliamentary Government" and Victorian Political Parties, *c.* 1830–1880', *English Historical Review*, Vol. 104, 1989, p. 655.

86 W. E. Gladstone, 'The Declining Efficiency of Parliament', *Quarterly Review*, Vol. 99, 1856, pp. 521–70. During the 1850s, it was increasingly assumed that party was the necessary vehicle not only for debate but for the efficient discharge of executive business. See Hawkins (1989), pp. 638–69, and his *British Party Politics, 1852–1886*, London, Macmillan, 1998, pp. 9–58.

87 Morley (1903), vol. 1, p. 199.

88 Much the best biography of Peel, if overly sympathetic to its subject, remains that in two volumes by Norman Gash, *Mr Secretary Peel: The Life of Robert Peel to 1830*, London, Longman, 1961, and *Sir Robert Peel: The Life of Sir Robert Peel after 1830*, London, Longman, 1972. Peel's reputation is surveyed in D. Read, *Peel and the Victorians*, Oxford, Blackwell, 1987. Important studies which appraise his achievements somewhat more coolly include R. Stewart, *The Foundation of the Conservative Party, 1830–67*, London, Longman, 1978; P. Harling,

The Waning of 'Old Corruption': The Politics of Economical Reform, 1779–1846, Oxford, Clarendon Press, 1996; B. Hilton, 'Peel: A Reappraisal', *Historical Journal*, vol. 22, 1979, pp. 585–614; and I. Newbould, 'Sir Robert Peel and the Conservative Party, 1832–1841: A Study in Failure', *English Historical Review*, Vol. 98, 1983, pp. 529–57. Studies which engage with more recent reappraisals include T. A. Jenkins, *Sir Robert Peel*, London, Macmillan, 1999, and E. J. Evans, *Sir Robert Peel: Statesmanship, Power and Party*, London, Routledge, 1991.

89 For Pitt, see the classic three-volume biography, J. Ehrman, *William Pitt: The Years of Acclaim* (1969), *The Reluctant Transition* (1969) and *The Consuming Struggle* (1996), all London, Constable. On politics in the 1790s, see F. O'Gorman, 'Pitt and the "Tory" reaction to the French Revolution, 1789–1815' in *Britain and the French Revolution, 1789–1815*, ed. H. Dickinson, London, Macmillan, 1989; J. Mori, *William Pitt and the French Revolution, 1785–95*, Keele, Keele UP, 1997; J. Mori, 'The Political Theory of William Pitt the Younger', *History*, Vol. 83, 1998, pp. 234–48; and E. J. Evans, *William Pitt the Younger*, London, Routledge, 1999.

Gladstone and Homer

David Bebbington

5 Bust of Homer, Hawarden Castle

GLADSTONE'S Homeric studies have not fared well with commentators, either past or present. Contemporaries were particularly dismissive of the statesman's apparent obsession with Homer's account of the divinities of Olympus. Sir George Cornewall Lewis, Gladstone's successor as Chancellor of the Exchequer in 1855 and a considerable classical scholar, told a correspondent that Gladstone's estimate of Homer as an exponent of religion was 'fundamentally wrong'.[1] Lord Tennyson thought Gladstone's opinions on the subject 'hobby-horsical'.[2] Lord Acton reported to his wife from Hawarden that he had spent 'a dreadful hour' listening to Gladstone's theories about Homer.[3] Even the loyal John Morley was forced to admit that his hero's ideas in this area were 'commonly judged fantastic'.[4] Historians have tended to echo these judgements and to have assumed that Gladstone's treatment of the poet was an idiosyncratic foible.[5] Sir Philip Magnus is an exception, for he rightly locates Gladstone's preoccupation with Olympian religion within the framework of Christian apologetic.[6] Another exception is the classicist Sir Hugh Lloyd-Jones, who, in a sparkling sketch, brings out the high quality of the statesman's feeling for the heroic society that Homer depicts and the sensitivity of Gladstone's appreciation of the poetry as literature.[7] J. L. Myres, Agatha Ramm and Colin Matthew have each offered sympathetic assessments of Gladstone's Homeric scholarship, and Frank Turner has given the fullest and most perceptive exposition of his views on the religion and politics of Homer's poems, at the same time stressing Gladstone's desire to vindicate the classical curriculum of the University of Oxford.[8] What has been neglected, however, is the extent of change in Gladstone's theories. Far from remaining constant, his attitude to Homer, and especially to the poet's Olympian pantheon, altered considerably over time. Neither Lloyd-Jones nor Turner registers the modification; Agatha Ramm has noticed it, but does not pursue it. The account that follows, after exploring the reasons for Gladstone's Homeric project and examining its salient features, attempts to bring out the significance of the substantial shift in his views.

Why, then, did Gladstone study the earliest of Greek poets with such enthusiasm? One answer is that the task provided a diversion from politics, a way of spending spare time profitably. Gladstone first turned to the careful examination of the poet in the autumn of 1846 when out of parliament and freshly retired from the Colonial Office. Likewise his second campaign of work was during the later 1850s, following the fall of the Aberdeen coalition, when he was chafing at exclusion from government. The beginning of his voyage of Homeric discovery in the 1840s was without any particular destination in view. At Fasque, the family home in Kincardineshire, Gladstone, in pursuing his normal vigorous programme of reading, passed from Virgil's *Aeneid* to Homer's *Iliad* and was surprised by the pleasure it gave him. The description of the shield of Achilles in book 18, for example, thrilled him: 'how beautiful!', he burst out in his diary.[9] He made copious notes of stray thoughts suggested by the text relating to literary equivalents, biblical parallels, Adam Smith, Coleridge and much else.[10] One line, he told his brother-in-law, Lord Lyttelton, gave him a hint that the origin of customs duties might be found in the book of Genesis. 'I find', he justly remarked to Lyttelton, 'Homer full of interesting matter collateral to the practical purpose.'[11] He moved on to the *Odyssey*, started writing papers on Homeric geography, sacrifice and other themes, and then, in the new year, began exploring the secondary literature. The whole exercise bore fruit in an article for *The Quarterly Review* defending the unity of authorship of the Homeric oeuvre against the latest German critical effort, by Carl Lachmann, to split the poetry into separate units by different hands – no fewer than 18, according to Lachmann.[12] Gladstone's interest in Homer was already of the ablative variety – concerned with anything by, with or from the poet. It gave rise, in 1858, to substantial sections of his three-volume *Studies on Homer and the Homeric Age* about geography, beauty, number and colour in the poet. Later, in the 1860s and 1870s, he was to project, and substantially compose, a thesaurus embracing all the contents of Homer together with much else besides. A published sample on the poet's use of the word for 'speckled' allowed Gladstone to record the results of his enquiries about piebald horses, noting the 'predominance of the chestnut in Shropshire'.[13] There can be little doubt that much of Gladstone's preoccupation with Homer was a species of eclectic antiquarianism, originally begun, as he once put it, 'without theory or prepossession of any kind'.[14] It was a typically intense form of Gladstonian relaxation.

Inevitably, however, the statesman's ideological standpoint impinged on his Homeric researches. A second explanation of his dedication to Homer, in fact, is that he was eager to attack the opinions of George Grote, the leading authority of the day on ancient Greece. Grote was a quintessential philosophic radical, notorious as the champion of the secret ballot, a Benthamite republican who despised the landed aristocracy, the Church of England and all Gladstone stood for in his early career. In the spring of 1846 Grote published the first two volumes of a monumental *History of Greece* that was completed in ten more over the following decade. Although Gladstone did not record taking up the *History* until March 1847, six months into his Homeric studies, he was provoked by what he read there. The world of Homer, according to the Benthamite rationalist, must remain totally unknown to us because archaic Greece is forever shrouded in legend.[15] The rebuttal of this point of view was the mainspring of much of Gladstone's classical work. He insisted on the basic reliability of the poet as a witness to a vanished world, for Homer was painstakingly accurate. Even the epithets of movement in his poetry, Gladstone once declared, are 'scientific', differing in their specification of the relative amount of momentum derived either from quantity of matter or from velocity.[16] Gladstone's eagerness to assert the historicity of Homer's record betrayed him in 1878 into premature endorsement of the theories about Troy published by the fanatically egoistic German archaeologist

Heinrich Schliemann.[17] In *Homer and the Homeric Age* there is a long section taking issue with Grote's case that the *Iliad* should be divided into two poems, and much of the account of Homer's political institutions is designed to show, against Grote, that the poet depicted an assembly that was essentially free.[18] Agamemnon, on Gladstone's showing, was almost as constitutional a monarch as Queen Victoria. The smiting of Grote, hip and thigh, was one of Gladstone's overriding aims.

A third reason for the Homeric enterprise, added in the 1850s and looming very large thereafter, was distinctly religious. During that decade Gladstone was becoming troubled by the growth of the assumption that little or nothing about religion was supernatural. This conviction was to be expected of freethinkers, but now it was making ground even among clergymen in the University of Oxford, which Gladstone represented in parliament. In 1855 Benjamin Jowett, who became Regius Professor of Greek in the same year and later contributed to *Essays and Reviews*, published an essay on 'Natural Religion' in his commentaries on the epistles of Paul. He rejected the traditional contrast between religion as natural, a form of spontaneous spirituality, and religion as revealed, what was disclosed by the Almighty. The difference, Jowett claimed, was a matter 'rather of words than ideas' because the two ran into each other.[19] Gladstone looked at Jowett's book while on a visit to Oxford in June 1855, and must have been alarmed. E. B. Pusey, the Tractarian leader whom he visited two days later, would almost certainly have stressed the evil consequences of such doctrines making headway in Oxford. Belief in divine revelation was being imperilled. A fortnight later Gladstone lamented in a memorandum that society's hold on the essence of Christianity was growing weaker and weaker. Within another week he had conceived the idea of recommencing his studies on Homer with a more specific object.[20] The resolve led to *Homer and the Homeric Age*. In the book Gladstone mounted an assault on the notion that religion is merely an expression of human instincts, deploying Homer's depiction of the pagan gods and goddesses for his purpose. Jowett, when asked for his opinion of Gladstone's work, produced a terse reply: 'It's mere nonsense.'[21]

How could Homer's pantheon be deployed in the struggle between the liberal theology of Jowett and the dogmatic faith that Gladstone shared with Pusey? The conservatives faced a rising scholarly claim, buttressed by romantic sensibilities, that awe in the presence of the powers of nature had given birth to the spirit of worship. In an age of enduring classical interests, the generalisation was applied first and foremost to ancient Greece – in Germany by the disciples of B. G. Niebuhr such as Carl Otfried Müller, and in England by their imitators such as Connop Thirlwall, the liberal-minded bishop who was to be buried in Westminster Abbey in the same grave as Grote. The Greeks, seeing life in every part of nature, supposed Thirlwall, must have associated divinities with each one.[22] Gladstone had Thirlwall read the proofs

6 "My Old Friend Homer", *Punch* 14 December 1872

of his book while it was in the press with the request that the bishop should point out extravagant conclusions so that they could be toned down. It was a typical Gladstonian ploy to spike the guns of a potential opponent in advance. Thirlwall did express reservations about Gladstone's case, though too late for any modifications to be made in the text.[23] What worried Thirlwall was Gladstone's alternative explanation of Greek religion, the theory of primitive revelation. At the dawn of history, according to Gladstone, the Almighty had revealed a body of truth to Adam and then to Noah, whose posterity had carried authentic religion with them as they dispersed over the globe. Over time, however, the purity of the tradition became sullied as valid memories faded and false conjectures took their place. Among the migrating peoples were the Greeks, whose religion was a mingling of the original revelation with its subsequent debasement. Homer therefore portrayed 'not strictly a false theology, but a true theology falsified'.[24] Here was an alternative explanation of ancient religion that, by insisting on a place for divine revelation, provided a buttress for the supernatural.

This understanding of Homeric religion has often been seen as a Gladstonian oddity. It seems to bear all too strong a resemblance to the arcane and fruitless efforts of Casaubon, in George Eliot's *Middlemarch*, to discover the key to all mythologies. When *Homer and the Homeric Age* came out, Cornewall Lewis, in a private letter, ridiculed Gladstone for his 'three thick volumes'.

> There is a volume on the mythology, in which he traces a large part of the Greek mythology to traditions from the patriarchs, to whom he moreover assumes that Christianity was in some way revealed by anticipation. Hence he finds the doctrine of the Trinity in Homer, and holds that Latona is compounded of Eve and the Virgin Mary.[25]

But Lewis, apart from being pleased to poke fun at a political rival, was also an ideological opponent. He had translated Carl Otfried Müller's main work into English and, like Connop Thirlwall, maintained the naturalistic interpretation of Greek religion. Gladstone's views were not, as Cornewall Lewis or Jowett liked to suggest, a personal idiosyncrasy. They rested on a long tradition of scholarship stretching back to Grotius and Pufendorf in the seventeenth century. Bishop Samuel Horsley, the most powerful mind in the High Church party at the turn of the nineteenth century, upheld the idea that the worship of Jehovah had originally been universal, that this faith had gradually degenerated into superstition but that relics of the early tradition had survived among the Gentiles.[26] Others who maintained a similar position in the years around 1850 included William Mure, the author of the standard history of ancient Greek language and literature, and J. B. Friedreich, one of the leading German authorities on Homer, whom Gladstone was delighted to cite in his own support.[27] Those with a conservative axe to grind in scholarship and religion often took the general line adopted by Gladstone. He was by no means alone in wanting to defend the idea of a primitive revelation against its detractors.

There was also, however, a fourth reason why Gladstone took up Homeric studies, and it, too, was religious. After Gladstone had painfully shed his early ideal of state–church confessionalism during the Maynooth affair of 1844–45, he had seen the hope for the nation in the rise of a vibrant Tractarianism within the Church of England. The departure of leading Tractarians to the Roman Catholic Church was deeply painful because it threatened the progress of 'Catholic principles' in their former communion. John Henry Newman's *Essay on the Development of Christian Doctrine*, the chief intellectual apologia for secession, attracted Gladstone's attention as soon as it appeared in 1845. Unlike Bossuet and traditional defenders of the Roman position, Newman did not argue that the church professed the same beliefs as those held in the days of the apostles. Instead the future cardinal contended that over the centuries the church had gradually unfolded the implications of the original deposit of faith. This case seemed to do much greater justice to the evidence; it also had superior appeal for a generation brought up under romantic influences to appreciate metaphors of growth.[28] Such a theory, remarked Gladstone in a memorandum of July 1845, is 'fatal to us if proved'.[29] Repeatedly during 1846 and 1847, at the very time he was beginning his Homeric studies, Gladstone penned objections to the *Essay on Development*. Among the many points he jotted down was the suggestion that, while it was true that a great public institution such as the Roman Catholic Church was unlikely to have remained unaltered over time, the process of change would probably not be development of the kind Newman envisaged, leading to a firmer grasp of truth. On the contrary, it would be a 'deteriorating process'.[30] Was that not what had happened, as Homer was reminding him, in the early history of humanity, when the original revealed doctrines gradually fell into decay? The seed of a potential critique of Newman had been sown.

The harvest was not reaped until the second burst of Homeric exploration from 1855. Meanwhile, in the years around 1850, as Colin Matthew has shown, Gladstone had undergone an anguished crisis compounded of political impotence, sexual temptation, family bereavement and the loss to Rome of his closest comrades in the Anglo-Catholic revival, James Hope and Henry Manning.[31] Gladstone's pent-up feelings found issue in fierce diatribes against the Pope such as his translation of Luigi Carlo Farini's denunciation of the recent exercise of the temporal power in Italy.[32] On the other hand, Gladstone had warmed to the irenical Catholic stance of the Munich theologian Ignaz von Döllinger and to his German liberal Catholic mentor Johann Adam Möhler; he had also been introduced to the champion of liberal Catholicism in France, the Comte Montalembert.[33] Perhaps the liberal Catholic tendency would supply the tools for resisting the rising tide of ultramontanism. In early 1853 Gladstone turned to read the *Essai sur l'indifférence* (1817–23) by Montalembert's master, the Abbé de Lamennais, whom he was later to call 'the greatest genius of the French clergy of his day'.[34] In it he found much that was congenial: the claim that private judgement had caused social disintegration; the idea that faith needed to be based on communal convictions; and, supremely, the argument, developed at length in the third volume, that the universality of certain beliefs in the ancient world demonstrated the existence of 'une révélation primitive'. Homer, according to the Frenchman, contained, amidst all his fictions, a wealth of true doctrines derived from this source.[35] Lamennais, like Newman, believed in a sacred tradition but, unlike Newman, he held that it decayed over time. That was the liberal Catholic message Gladstone wanted to hear. By following Lamennais's understanding of Homer as a quarry of revealed truths, he could vindicate a dogmatic, supernatural religion against those who were undermining it. But he could do so in a way that implicitly revealed the redundancy of Newman's idea of development. The material on

Greek religion in *Homer and the Homeric Age* should be read as anti-Roman Catholic polemic inspired by a Roman Catholic apologist. It was a typically convoluted Gladstonian ploy.

The view of Homer's 'theo-mythology' that emerged for these four reasons can easily be misunderstood. In 1864 Max Müller, the Taylorian Professor of Modern European Languages at Oxford, associated Gladstone in a public lecture with the schools of interpretation that saw in Greek mythology either shadows of Bible characters or else memories of past heroes. A nettled Gladstone despatched to the professor a detailed letter of repudiation. So vast was it that Max Müller's servant, having been instructed to forward only letters, failed to send on what seemed to him a parcel.[36] The misunderstanding that afflicted the Oxford professor had to be dispelled. Gladstone took pains in the following year, when delivering an address as rector of the University of Edinburgh, to distinguish his own position sharply from that of those who, like Milton, derived pagan gods from Jewish sources. He was prepared to reject the patristic case, as expounded by Clement of Alexandria, that the Greeks were responsible for the theft of Hebrew ideas. What was true in Homer sprang from universal revelation, not from the particular revelation to the Jews. Equally he repudiated what Max Müller called 'eheumerism', a theory popular in the French Enlightenment to the effect that exploits of ancestors had been magnified into tales of the gods.[37] In England this interpretation had been elaborated during the 1770s in a series of disorderly dissertations by the immensely erudite Jacob Bryant. Cornewall Lewis privately scorned Gladstone's mythological researches as 'a *réchauffé* of old Jacob Bryant',[38] but Lewis was entirely mistaken. Gladstone's enterprise was of a different order from Bryant's, an attempt to discover traces of eternal verities rather than of contingent events on Homer's Olympus. Myth, in Gladstone's view, contained echoes of the wisdom of the Almighty as he had revealed it to the patriarchs.

In one significant respect Gladstone went beyond many of the advocates of the theory of primitive revelation that he espoused. Unlike Lamennais, though like others such as Friedreich, he postulated that the revelation contained distinctly Christian elements. It was this notion that made the easiest target for Cornewall Lewis's quips and that Max Müller found most difficult to take seriously.[39] Minerva and Apollo, on Gladstone's account, both displayed many of the qualities of Jesus Christ himself. Minerva, as the goddess of wisdom, represented the tradition of the *logos*, identified with Christ by John the Evangelist. Her persistent care of Ulysses, as described in the *Odyssey*, is treated as nothing less than the exercise of a providential role. Apollo, in a similar way, is presented as a redeemer figure. He is unique, explains Gladstone, as 'an exhibition of entire harmony with the will of Jupiter', so reflecting the Son of God who was always at one with his Father.[40] Minerva and Apollo, as substantially pure embodiments of the messianic traditions inherited from the beginnings of human history, stood apart from all the other divinities in whom invented elements predominated. Shortly before publication of *Homer and the Homeric Age*, in December 1857, when the text was already being set up in print, Gladstone was assailed with doubts about whether he had gone too far in magnifying the messianic element in Homer. He paid a flying visit to Oxford, en route from London to Hawarden, in order to consult Pusey, the natural intellectual resource for his whole project. Pusey was able to lend him a work by Christian Schöttgen, an early eighteenth-century German scholar who had assembled an array of testimonies from Hebrew sources in order to demonstrate to the Jews that their own literature bore witness to Jesus as the Messiah.[41] Schöttgen's case suggested that expectations of a promised deliverer were to be found outside the Old Testament, that they rested on ancient tradition, and therefore, by implication, that Homer might also contain them. The German's analysis, which is substantially reproduced in *Homer and the Homeric Age*, bolstered Gladstone's confidence. It seemed legitimate, on Pusey's authority, to discern uniquely Christian teaching in the pages of Homer.

Gladstone's whole approach was also undergirded by many of the assumptions of contemporary social anthropology. Until the 1850s the dominant school, calling itself 'ethnology', was associated with James Cowles Prichard, a Bristol physician who fitted his researches into a biblical framework based on the dispersion of the descendants of Noah. Culture, on this view, had advanced more by diffusion than by development. Comparative philology enabled the scholar to trace the interplay of races during their migrations.[42] The bulk of the first volume of Gladstone's *Homer and the Homeric Age*, headed 'Ethnology of the Greek Races', was an exemplary instance of this technique. Gladstone carefully sifts Homer's vocabulary in order to establish the characteristics of the constituent elements of the Greek nation, the earlier Pelasgians and the later Hellenes. Most of his discussion raised few eyebrows. Its culmination, however, was more fanciful. Ignoring the leading British authority on the Pelasgians, Bishop Herbert Marsh, who had maintained that this migrant people could be traced back only to their settlement in Thrace,[43] Gladstone held that they descended from Low Iranian tribes, or Medes, while the Hellenes originated among the High Iranians, or Persians. He was eager to establish links with Persia because, it was generally agreed, the earliest known Persian religion embraced belief in a single supreme God and the worship of the host of heaven. Such a pattern, Gladstone asserts, reflected the monotheism of the earliest human faith together with the beginnings of a deviation.[44] The Persian connection seemed to provide the route by which the traditions of a primitive revelation reached Greece. At the same time that he was in touch with Pusey, Gladstone anxiously enquired of George Rawlinson, shortly to become Camden Professor of Ancient History at Oxford, whether the Persian theory was tenable. Rawlinson warned him off part of it, but not the whole.[45] Gladstone recognised the weakness of his Persian proposal before it was published, but clung to it because it reinforced his fundamental hypothesis about the transmission of a universal revelation.

The basic premise was the feature of his *Homer and the Homeric Age* which attracted the sharpest criticism in the reviews. Two among them stand out for their ability. An anonymous reviewer in *The Times*, whom Gladstone admitted to be 'extremely clever',[46] censured him for the debating style that made ridiculous theories seem respectable. On Persia, according to the reviewer, Gladstone made far too much out of a small matter. His theological extravaganza would find favour only with the clergy. If Apollo contained intimations of the Messiah, why was the resemblance not total? The whole hypothesis about primitive traditions made very little allowance for the natural workings of the human mind, and it was unreasonable to doubt whether true thoughts about God are possible without divine revelation. Gladstone had failed to carry conviction. It was regrettable, concluded the reviewer, that 'so much fertility should be the fertility of words'.[47] *Blackwood's* published a similar line of argument by W. H. Smith, not the newsagent and politician but a leisured man of letters. Smith complained that Gladstone neglected Homer the artist for the sake of studying him as theologian. One fact was sufficient to disprove Gladstone's 'fanciful and visionary' theory. The idea of creation was entirely absent from early Greek mythology. Could so prominent a doctrine be lost in transmission? The messianic dimension was particularly weak. Why, if Apollo was supposed to represent Christ, should he be just as indifferent as the other Olympian deities to the future destinies of men? Gladstone's analogies between Homer and the Jewish Talmud, Smith remarked, were expressions of 'perverted ingenuity'. The enterprise was mistaken because scholarship had shown that the pagan gods were based on the phenomena of nature. Smith appeals explicitly to the authority of Carl Otfried Müller.[48] Like the contributor to *The Times*, Smith had grasped Gladstone's case, but had rejected it. The naturalistic interpretation of Greek religion had become too widely accepted to be dislodged.

Accordingly, when Gladstone revised his Homeric theories, he capitulated. In the autumn of 1867 he set to work on what was originally intended as a recasting of *Homer and the Homeric Age* but emerged in 1869 as *Juventus Mundi: The Gods and Men of the Heroic Age*. Because the single volume was a popularisation, many supposed that it was simply an abridgement of the three-volume work. In reality, however, the argument was substantially modified. It is not that the belief in an original divine revelation or in its subsequent degeneration was abandoned. The theory remained, though stated more guardedly. What changed, first and foremost, was the notion that Greek religion could not have sprung from awe before the elemental forces of nature. A passage in *Homer and the Homeric Age* had declared that the poet did not authorise the belief that nature worship ever preceded the Olympian system. Gladstone marked this passage in his own copy, now in St Deiniol's Library, Hawarden, with a cross, the sign of disagreement.[49] Consequently in *Juventus Mundi* he was willing to treat the religion of the Pelasgians as essentially the worship of nature. He abandoned the term 'inventive', which had been used in *Homer and the Homeric Age* to describe features of the Olympian pantheon not derived from the pure tradition. Gladstone's decision to accept the naturalistic understanding may well have been swayed by the reinforcement of that position by Max Müller, who had gained much support for his view that all mythology sprang from solar phenomena. Gladstone certainly assured the professor in a letter of 1864 that he was willing to admit that Greek myth grew from nature worship.[50] Perhaps the crucial influence was the latest German treatise on the Hellenic divinities, published by F. G. Welcker between 1857 and 1863, which Gladstone read thoroughly as his summer holiday task at Penmaenmawr in 1863.[51] In any case, he accepted in the 1860s that he could no longer hope to convince the world that Greek religion did not arise from the veneration of the forces of nature.

   Another change in Gladstone's views related to foreign influence on the Greek theo-mythology. In his own copy of *Homer and the Homeric Age*, Gladstone also put a cross against his earlier remark that Persia was probably the cradle of Achilles's family.[52] In *Juventus Mundi* the Persian hypothesis virtually disappears. Although at one point Gladstone comments that the Persian race may have contributed an element to the formation of the Greek nation, there is no further discussion of the link and at another point he admits that it is impossible to trace the route by which the legacy of original revelation reached the Greeks.[53] Nevertheless Gladstone retains the diffusionist model of cultural change. Now the chief agents of the spread of ideas to Greece are the Phoenicians. Already in *Homer and the Homeric Age* he had postulated that this people, the great seafarers of the Mediterranean world, had transmitted many of the tales of the *Odyssey*,[54] but during the preparation of *Juventus Mundi* he convinced himself, partly from the pages of Ernest Renan's *Mission de Phénicie* (1864–67), that they were the schoolmasters of Greece.[55] The exaggeration may be excused when it is appreciated that Gladstone mistakenly associated the Phoenicians with the Minoan civilisation of Crete, which the twentieth century has shown to be a taproot of Greek culture. But the large place for the Phoenicians posed a problem for Gladstone's theory of the origin of Homeric mythology. This people seemed to be linked with the worship of Aphrodite, a character 'odious on the side of lawless indulgence', Dionysus, a god praised by drunken women, and the Oxen of the Sun, mere brute beasts.[56] Hence the Phoenicians were responsible for blatantly immoral features of the cult together with the veneration of animals, which Gladstone scorned as debased. It was implausible to see the Phoenicians as those who transmitted to Greece the substance of primitive revelation. The form of diffusion theory that alone seemed acceptable in the 1860s tended to undermine belief in the spread of revealed truth.

   Gladstone was faced by twin difficulties. On the one hand, he had been compelled to concede that the forces of nature were worshipped in archaic

Greece, and on the other, he had decided that the Phoenicians taught the Greeks to kneel before animals. Ancient Greek religion contained elements of rampant idolatry. How could he nevertheless argue that the pages of Homer bore witness to revealed truth? The answer was to exalt the poet himself as the creator of a synthesis that kept the veneration of the natural and animal worlds in its place. He argued, for instance, that Pelasgian river worship was incorporated within Hellenic religiosity, but in a strictly subordinate role. Homer's 'plastic powers as a poet' had forged a new theo-mythology.[57] It is true that Gladstone, in a manner typical of those who had absorbed German romantic thinking, treats the poet's individual part as secondary to the corporate spirit of 'the people' in generating their thought-world. But the statesman claims that Homer exerted a greater personal influence over the nation than 'any other Greek, whether legislator, poet, or philosopher' – which includes even Aristotle.[58] That was because Homer was the architect of a belief-system that bound together the Pelasgian and Hellenic tribes as a new people. As the 'great bard of the nation', he was responsible for welding the various sections of the Greek population into a unity.[59] In order to avoid compromising their sense of nationality, according to Gladstone, the poet scrupulously avoids all reference to the foreign origin of his themes. Homer may have used material from overseas, but he did not say so. The status of the poet, now seen as the father of his people, is much higher in *Juventus Mundi* than in *Homer and the Homeric Age*.

The great achievement of Homer was the creation of what Gladstone calls 'the Olympian system'. Its keynote was the anthropomorphic principle, the ascription of human characteristics to the gods. It might be expected that the lies, jealousies and sexual irregularities of Olympus would be seen, like the worship of rivers or oxen, as a debasing feature of Homeric religion. In *Homer and the Homeric Age*, in fact, that is Gladstone's prevailing view. He coins the word 'anthropophuism' (there is no previous recorded instance of its use) to convey his belief that human nature had 'obtruded' into the sphere of deity, implying that the human was an alien force in the realm of divinity.[60] By the time of *Juventus Mundi*, however, his attitude had been transformed. The human is regarded no longer as a contaminant of deity. Gladstone's very term for the depiction of the gods in human form changes. He drops 'anthropophuism', replacing it with 'anthropomorphism', which was intended to have no unfavourable connotations. His treatment of Homer's Zeus well illustrates the alteration. In *Homer and the Homeric Age* Zeus is presented as a repulsive personality because of his carnal behaviour, but in *Juventus Mundi* he possesses grandeur as the moral governor of the universe. Gladstone now alludes to the carnality in a masterpiece of understatement: 'the individual character of Zeus', he remarks, 'is of a far lower order than his public capacity would lead us to expect'.[61] Zeus earns Gladstone's approval since Homer has successfully transposed the qualities of earthly life into a heavenly key. The god is a brilliant invention because of the 'humanising or anthropomorphic element'.[62] The category of the human now enjoys Gladstone's benediction.

The alterations evident in *Juventus Mundi* remain in Gladstone's later Homeric work. He never again toyed with the idea that Greece was free of nature worship. His belief in the foreign origin of motifs in the theo-mythology actually expanded in scope. He delved behind the Phoenicians to examine the putative debt of the Greeks to the Assyrians and Babylonians, drawing in particular on the writings of A. H. Sayce, Professor of Assyriology at Oxford from 1891. Gladstone was impressed by Sayce's 1888 study of Babylonian religion, which he annotated favourably and copiously, and on which he drew for a lecture on *Archaic Greece and the East* delivered before the Oriental Congress at Oxford in 1892.[63] Such overseas influences could be accommodated because Gladstone continued to stress Homer's role as the synthesiser of Greek religion. In his last book on the poet, *Landmarks of Homeric Study* (1890), there is a laudatory chapter on Homer as a maker of religion. *The Times* reviewer found the speculations 'rather ingenious than convincing' and the claim that Homer fostered the national idea was 'strange' and 'unexpected'.[64] Most strikingly, Gladstone regularly insisted on the importance of the human element in Homer. The humanism was not confined to the representation of individual divinities but extended to the pantheon as a whole: 'the government of the world by the Olympian gods', he wrote in 1892, '... is essentially modelled upon the basis of human action'. By that date he no longer used the word 'anthropomorphism', with its implication that the gods were misunderstood when they were presented in human form. He preferred 'theanthropy', a word suggesting merely that human qualities were incorporated in divinity. This, he argued, was the most remarkable characteristic of Homer's pantheon.[65] It was to have been a chief theme of the unfinished treatise on 'Olympian Religion' on which he was still working within five months of his death.[66]

What, then, was the significance of Gladstone's half-century of engagement with Homer? Although conducted partly for relaxation, it was an exercise profoundly charged by ideology. The initial impetus of countering Grote, though never entirely abandoned, faded in importance; so did the underlying desire to do battle with Newman. But the aim of vindicating divine revelation against less definite theological positions was never dropped. It is restated in a set of articles of 1892 targeting an American audience; and it reappears in the manuscript preface for the intended book on 'Olympian Religion', where it is said to be the content of the work's concluding portion. In the preface Gladstone explains that the error in his early *Homer and the Homeric Age* was not to attribute some of the Olympian deities to authentic tradition, but rather to fail to attribute all of them to that source. In each of the Homeric divinities, he had come to believe, there were traces of a universal revelation and so elements shared with other old religious traditions and especially with the Holy Scriptures.[67] Demonstrating the parallels would increase the plausibility of an original divine disclosure. Moreover if religion

in ancient Greece, like the mechanical arts, had made progress over time, as
many claimed, then it could be explained, like those arts, by the human
capacity for invention. If, however, religion had become steadily more corrupt, as Gladstone wished to show, then there were grounds for seeing its
origin as superhuman, since how could human beings create what they
could not conserve?[68] It might have been expected that when, during the
1860s, Gladstone admitted that Greek religion had natural origins, his grand
theory would have collapsed. If the pagan divinities sprang from nature, the
idea of a primitive revelation should appear redundant. But he never conceded that the whole of classical theo-mythology derived from nature worship. In Homer, the earliest known stage in its evolution, Gladstone believed
he could discern glimmers of truth. It continued to be worthwhile drawing
attention to them because, as he was well aware, theism was on the decline.
The theological liberalism of the 1850s had been followed among the intelligentsia by more open and more widespread avowals of disbelief. Gladstone
might try to rebut T. H. Huxley on minor battle-grounds such as the swine
miracle of the gospels in order to resist the inroads of agnosticism,[69] but the
attempt to vindicate revelation by means of Homer was his most sustained
response to the Victorian crisis of belief.

   Furthermore Gladstone's Homeric studies provide an index to the nature
of the religious views he was trying to defend. The transition evident in his
attitude to the human element in the pantheon reflects a distinct development in his theological position. Between *Homer and the Homeric Age* in 1858
and *Juventus Mundi* in 1869, as we have seen, Gladstone ceased to think of
the Greek gods as debased by their human attributes and began to glory in
the anthropomorphic principle. Behind the anthropomorphism lies the doctrine of the incarnation. In *Juventus Mundi* the depiction of the gods in
human form is confidently presented, as it had not been in *Homer and the
Homeric Age*, as a memory of the divine promise of a coming God-man.[70] The
incarnation was now at the centre of Gladstone's Christian view of the
world, structuring his intellectual activities. The union of the human with
the divine, he had explained before the University of Edinburgh in 1865,
means that the Almighty places a high value on everything human – on
respect for life, on art and philosophy, on all the components of civilisation.
Ancient Greece was appointed by God to provide a model in these respects,
a way of preventing the ascetic temper in religion from cramping the human
spirit.[71] Gladstone was making a very similar point to Matthew Arnold's rec-
ommendation of a balance between Hebraism and Hellenism. There must be
no one-sided religious fanaticism. The statesman, in fact, was coming close
to the Broad Church position that Arnold occupied. Although Gladstone still
retained an Anglo-Catholic's grasp on dogma, he was willing to commend
J. R. Seeley's humanistic picture of Christ in *Ecce Homo* in a way that made
Pusey despair.[72] Gladstone's celebration of the human dimension in Homer's
pantheon was in fact a counterpart of Seeley's dwelling on the human side

of Christ. It would be quite mistaken to number Gladstone among the Broad Churchmen without qualification, but the incarnationalism reflected in his later Homeric writings carried him far in their direction.

The same shift towards a higher estimate of things human also had implications for Gladstone's politics. When preparing *Homer and the Homeric Age* in the 1850s he was still a Conservative, albeit a progressive and footloose Peelite. Original sin, so often a crucial component of a Conservative worldview, did much to shape his representation of the Olympian pantheon. Human sin had corrupted the true revelation by its invention of falsehood and its attribution of vice to divinity. Gladstone's attitude to the Homeric gods meshed easily with the political assumption that the state existed primarily to keep its unruly charges in order. By 1869, in *Juventus Mundi*, however, the Liberal Prime Minister gave the concept of humanity altogether more favourable treatment. In that book the human factor actually enhances the dignity of the gods. The rhetoric of humanity studded Gladstone's later speeches, whether in regard to Bulgarians suffering under the Turkish yoke or Irish people oppressed by English coercion. Perhaps it reached its apogee in the peroration of the second Midlothian speech about concern for 'the sanctity of life in the hill villages of Afghanistan' being the duty of fellow human beings 'in the same flesh and blood'.[73] The humanity that transfigured Olympus and the humanity required of British foreign policy were one and the same, a core value of Gladstonian Liberalism. Although Jonathan Parry has properly stressed the persistence of Gladstone's High Church Peelite inheritance into his years as Liberal leader,[74] the Homeric writings give a hint that there was significant ideological development between the phases of his career. That is not to propose that the study of Homer was a cause of Gladstone's blossoming into a humanitarian Liberal: political experience had far more to do with the change and such intellectual roots as there were have to be sought in other aspects of his pilgrimage. Nevertheless the labour on the Greek poet should not be seen merely as an arcane hobby, totally divorced from the public sphere. Rather Gladstone's Homeric project was shot through with the same values as his politics, for the two were the products of a single evolving mind.

Notes

1   Sir G. C. Lewis to H. Reeves, 16 September 1858, in *Letters of the Rt Hon. Sir George Cornewall Lewis, Bart*, ed. Rev. Sir G. F. Lewis, Bart., London, Longmans, Green, 1870, p. 345.

2   L. A. Tollemache, *Talks with Mr Gladstone*, 3rd edn, London, Edward Arnold, 1903, p. 16.

3   Lord Acton to Lady Acton, 'Wednesday', Cambridge University Library, Add. MSS Acton, Box 18, quoted by O. Chadwick, *Acton and Gladstone*, London, Athlone Press, 1976, p. 18.

4   J. Morley, *The Life of William Ewart Gladstone*, 3 vols, London, Macmillan, 1903, vol. 3, p. 545.

5   E.g. R. Jenkins, *Gladstone*, London, Macmillan, 1995, pp. 14–15, 181–83, 392.

6   P. Magnus, *Gladstone: A Biography*, London, John Murray, 1954, pp. 122–25.

7   H. Lloyd-Jones, 'Gladstone on Homer', *The Times Literary Supplement*, 3 January 1975, pp. 15–17, reprinted in his *Blood for the Ghosts*, London, Duckworth, 1982.

8   J. L. Myres, 'Gladstone's View of Homer', in *Homer and his Critics*, London, Routledge & Kegan Paul, 1958, pp. 94–122; A. Ramm, 'Gladstone as Man of Letters', *Nineteenth Century Prose*, vol. 17, 1989–90, pp. 12–17; H. C. G. Matthew, *Gladstone, 1809–1898*, Oxford, Clarendon Press, 1997, pp. 152–57; F. M. Turner, *The Greek Heritage in Victorian Britain*, New Haven, Connecticut, Yale UP, 1981, pp. 159–70, 236–44.

9   *GD*, 21 November 1846.

10   'Iliad. Notes. 1846', GP 44736, ff. 42–76.

11   Gladstone to Lord Lyttelton, 15 December 1846, Glynne–Gladstone MSS, Flintshire County Record Office, Hawarden, 35, f. 107v.

12   W. E. Gladstone, 'Lachmann's *Essays on Homer*', *The Quarterly Review*, Vol. 81, 1847, pp. 381–417.

13   W. E. Gladstone, 'Homerology. V. Ailos', *The Contemporary Review*, Vol. 28, 1876, p.307.

14   W. E. Gladstone, 'The Olympian Religion. I. Its Sources and Authorship', *The North American Review*, Vol. 154, 1892, p. 232.

15   See D. W. Bebbington, 'Gladstone and Grote', in P. J. Jagger (ed.), *Gladstone*, London, Hambledon Press, 1998, pp. 157–76.

16   W. E. Gladstone, 'On Epithets of Movement in Homer', *The Nineteenth Century*, Vol. 5, 1879, pp. 463–66.

17   W. E Gladstone, 'Preface', in H. Schliemann, *Mycenae: A Narrative of Researches and Discoveries at Mycenae and Tiryns*, London, John Murray, 1878.

18   W. E. Gladstone, *Studies on Homer and the Homeric Age*, 3 vols, Oxford, Oxford UP, 1858, vol. 3, pp. 366–69, 1–144.

19   B. Jowett, 'Natural Religion', in *The Epistles of St Paul to the Thessalonians, Galations, Romans*, 2nd edn, 2 vols, London, John Murray, vol. 2, p. 456.

20   *GD*, 17, 19 June, 1, 7 July 1855.

21   Tollemache (1903), p. 12.

22   C. O. Müller, *The History and Antiquities of the Doric Race*, trans. H. Tufnell and G. C. Lewis, 2 vols, Oxford, John Murray, 1830, vol. 1, p. 16; C. Thirlwall, *A History of Greece*, 8 vols, London, Longman, Rees, Orme, Brown, Green & Longman, 1835, vol. 1, pp. 183–90.

23   C. Thirlwall to W. E. Gladstone, 24 October, 10, 14 November 1857, 19 February 1858, GP 44388, ff. 212, 246, 252; 44389, f. 68v.

24   Gladstone, *Homer and the Homeric Age*, vol. 2, p. 9.

25   Sir G. C. Lewis to Sir E. W. Head, 3 May 1858, in Lewis (1870), p. 333.

26   S. Horsley, 'A Dissertation on the Prophecies of the Messiah dispersed among the Heathen', *Nine Sermons on the Nature of the Evidence by which the Fact of our Lord's Resurrection is Established*, London, Longman, Hurst, Rees, Orme and Brown, 1815. Gladstone's annotations of the copy in St Deiniol's Library, Hawarden, show a debt to Horsley.

27   [W. Mure], 'Archdeacon Williams's Homerus', *The Edinburgh Review*, vol. 77, 1843, p. 58; J. B. Friedreich, *Die Realien in der Iliade und Odyssee*, 2nd edn,

Erlangen, Verlag von Ferdinand Enke, 1856, pp. 635n, 689; Gladstone *Homer and the Homeric Age*, vol. 2, pp. 138–39.

28   O. Chadwick, *From Bossuet to Newman*, 2nd edn, Cambridge, Cambridge UP, 1987.

29   GP 44735, f. 51. Nevertheless Gladstone had his own understanding of the development of doctrine. See D. Nicholls, 'Gladstone and the Anglican Critics of Newman', in *Newman and Gladstone Centennial Essays*, ed. J. D. Bastable, Dublin, Veritas Publications, 1978, pp. 121–24.

30   GP 44736, f. 299v; *GD*, 20 September, 11 November 1846, 10, 24 January, 8 August 1847.

31   Matthew (1997), chap. IV.

32   L. C. Farini, *The Roman State from 1815 to 1850*, trans. W. E. Gladstone, 4 vols, London, John Murray, 1851–54.

33   P. C. Erb, 'Gladstone and German Liberal Catholicism', *Recusant History*, vol. 23 1997, pp. 450–69; L. Allen, 'Gladstone et Montalembert: correspondence inÈdite', *Revue de Littérature Comparée*, Vol. 30, 1956, pp. 28–52.

34   W. E. Gladstone, 'The Sixteenth Century Arraigned before the Nineteenth' (1878), in *Gleanings of Past Years, 1844–79*, 7 vols, London, John Murray, 1879, vol. 3, p. 255; *GD*, 23, 30 January, 13 February, 20 March 1853.

35   F. de la Mennais, *Essai sur l'indifférence en matière de religion*, 4 vols, Paris, Tournachou-Molin et H. Seguin, 1817–23, vol. 3, pp. 23, 268–70.

36   F. Max Müller to W. E. Gladstone, 19 October [1864], GP 44251, f. 275.

37   W. E. Gladstone, 'Place of Ancient Greece in the Providential Order' (1865), *Gleanings*, vol. 7, pp. 35–44.

38   Lewis (1870), p. 333.

39   F. Max Müller, *Lectures in the Science of Language*, 6th edn, 2 vols, London, Longman, Green, 1871, vol. 2, p. 466.

40   Gladstone, *Homer and the Homeric Age*, vol. 2, p. 71.

41   *GD*, 12, 13 December 1857. Gladstone to E. B. Pusey, 24 December 1857, 13 March 1858, LBV 86, ff. 48, 53, Pusey House Library, Oxford. The book is mistakenly, though tentatively, identified in the *Diaries* as Schöttgen's *Jesus, der wahre Messias*, but seven days later Gladstone describes it as 'Hor. Talm.' (*GD*, 20 December 1857). It was therefore Christian Shöttgen, *Horae Hebraicae et Talmudicae*, Dresdae et Lipsiae, Fredericum Hekel, 1742.

42   G. W. Stocking, Jr, *Victorian Anthropology*, New York, Free Press, 1987, chaps 1, 2.

43   H. Marsh, *Horae Pelasgicae, Part the First*, Cambridge, J. Smith for J. Murray, 1815, p. 19.

44   Gladstone, *Homer and the Homeric Age*, vol. 1, pp. 561–62.

45   G. Rawlinson to Gladstone, 22 December 1857, 11 March 1858, GP 44282, ff. 330–31, 335.

46   Gladstone to Lord Lyttelton, 19 August 1858, Glynne–Gladstone MSS, 35, f. 192v.

47   *The Times*, 12 August 1858, p. 7; 13 August 1858, p. 5.

48   [W. H. Smith], 'Gladstone's Homer', *Blackwood's Edinburgh Magazine*, vol. 84, 1858, quoted at pp. 128, 143.

49   Gladstone, *Homer and the Homeric Age*, vol. 2, p. 410.

50   Gladstone to F. Max Müller, 28 September 1864, GP 44251, f. 269 (printed in Max Müller (1871), vol. 2, p. 441).

51 F. G. Welcker, *Griechische Götterlehre*, 3 vols, Göttingen, Berlag der Dieterischen Buchhandlung, 1857–63; *GD*, 3–29 September 1863.

52 Gladstone, *Homer and the Homeric Age*, vol. 2, p. 452, St Deiniol's Library, Hawarden.

53 W. E. Gladstone, *Juventus Mundi: The Gods and Men of the Heroic Age*, 2nd edn, London, Macmillan, 1870, pp. 310, 200.

54 Gladstone, *Homer and the Homeric Age*, vol. 3, p. 251.

55 W. E. Gladstone, 'Phoenicia and Greece', *The Quarterly Review*, Vol. 124, 1868.

56 Gladstone, *Juventus Mundi*, pp. 314–15, 319, 322–23.

57 Ibid., pp. 192–93.

58 Ibid., pp. 175–76.

59 Ibid., p. 181.

60 Gladstone, *Homer and the Homeric Age*, vol. 2, p. 174.

61 Gladstone, *Juventus Mundi*, p. 233. In this book, by contrast with *Homer and the Homeric Age*, the names of divinities are given in their Greek rather than their Latin form.

62 Ibid., p. 234.

63 A. H. Sayce, *Lectures on the Origin and Growth of Religion as illustrated by the Religion of the Ancient Babylonians*, 2nd edn, London, Williams & Norgate, 1888, St Deiniol's Library, Hawarden.

64 *The Times*, 16 October 1890, p. 6.

65 W. E. Gladstone, 'The Olympian Religion. II. Outline of its Particulars (Concluded)', *The North American Review*, Vol. 154, 1892, pp. 623–24.

66 GP 44713, f. 80 (20 December 1897).

67 GP 44713, f. 126.

68 W. E. Gladstone, 'The Olympian Religion. Its Sources and Authorship (Continued)', *The North American Review*, Vol. 154, 1892, pp. 371–72.

69 W. E. Gladstone, 'Professor Huxley and the Swine–Miracle' (1891), in *Later Gleanings*, London, John Murray, 1897, pp. 246–79.

70 Gladstone, *Juventus Mundi*, p. 288.

71 Gladstone, 'Place of Ancient Greece', pp. 59–87.

72 E. B. Pusey to Gladstone, 3 January [1868], GP 44281, ff. 339–39v.

73 W. E. Gladstone, *Midlothian Speeches 1879*, ed. M. R. D. Fort, Leicester, Leicester UP, 1971, p. 94.

74 J. P. Parry, *Democracy and Religion: Gladstone and the Liberal Party, 1867–1875*, Cambridge, Cambridge UP, 1986, chap. 3.

Gladstone and Parliamentary Reform

Roland Quinault

TINCT: REFORM: COMP:

7 Gladstone and Disraeli, *Punch*, 26 May 1866

GLADSTONE'S connection with parliamentary reform is best remembered with regard to his role in the genesis of the 1867 Reform Act and the passage of the 1884 Reform Act. Yet Gladstone's involvement with parliamentary reform extended over a much wider field and time span than the second and third Reform Acts. As an Oxford undergraduate, he was a vociferous opponent of the 1832 Reform Act and as a middle-aged cabinet minister, he supported reform bills in the 1850s and early 1860s. As a Liberal Prime Minister he was responsible for the 1872 Ballot Act and the 1883 Corrupt and Illegal Practices Act. Gladstone also sponsored various reforms of parliamentary procedure including the closure of debates and the amendment of members' oaths to accommodate atheists. After 1885, he dedicated his last years to another form of parliamentary reform: home rule for Ireland. Thus Gladstone was concerned with one or other aspect of parliamentary reform throughout his long career.

Since Gladstone was a voluminous writer and speaker, there is plenty of evidence about his views on reform at almost every stage of his career. He made many speeches on reform – both in parliament and on the platform – and wrote extensively on the subject in published articles and in private correspondence and memoranda. Gladstone's diaries also provide much information about his reading on reform – evidence which is now easily accessible in the superb edition initiated by M. R. D. Foot and completed by H. C. G. Matthew. Unfortunately, the sheer bulk of all this evidence, together with the prolixity and ambiguity of Gladstone's prose, makes interpretation and analysis difficult.

At first sight, however, it appears that Gladstone's stance on parliamentary reform can be divided into two distinct phases of roughly equal length: in the first phase, he was a Tory anti-reformer; and in the second phase, he was a Liberal reformer. Gladstone certainly began his parliamentary career as a Tory opponent of the 1832 Reform Act, but he became a convert to moderate reform while he was still a Peelite Tory. When he introduced the 1866 Reform Bill, he still described himself as a 'Liberal Conservative'. Subsequently, as the leader of the Liberal party and Prime Minister, he remained a cautious and pragmatic reformer. Thus Gladstone's attitude to reform did not advance in a simple linear progression from a stance of Tory opposition to one of Liberal support.

Gladstone's Liverpool upbringing gave him early experience of a large electorate and popular politics. In the early nineteenth century, Liverpool's freeman constituency increased rapidly to over 4,400 electors in 1830. Gladstone's father had been chairman of the Liverpool election committee which had secured Canning's return without recourse to bribery.[1] But the candidates at the 1830 Liverpool by-election spent more than £100,000 bribing the electors, which Gladstone was told by his father was an 'Insanity' which called 'loudly for Reform'.[2]

Gladstone, in later life, described Canning as 'the dominant influence' on his early political ideas.[3] Canning was strongly opposed to parliamentary reform based on the abstract principles of 'the rights of man' associated with the French Revolution.[4] His influence was evident in Gladstone's private comments on reform in 1827. He wanted to 'Extend the blessings of the constitution to all who can enjoy them without endangering it', but added, 'While I have the period of the French Revolution stamped deeply on my memory, I cannot but feel distrust of the principles of Whiggism, and of its tendency.'[5]

Gladstone's reservations about reform increased while he was an undergraduate at Oxford, where he played a prominent part in the Debating Society which became the Oxford Union. Most members of the society were strongly opposed to reform and, early in 1830, they debated a motion that 'the purity and independence of Parliament was now better secured than it would be under any system of reform'. Gladstone thought that this motion 'seemed very strong as entirely denying the possibility of improvement', but he voted for an anti-reform resolution which was carried almost unanimously.[6] Later that year, Gladstone supported Acland's motion – 'That the Declaration of Rights made by the National Assembly of France in 1789, was founded on false principles' – which was carried without a division.[7]

Gladstone recalled, in old age, that 'the general tendencies of my mind were not in the time of my youth illiberal'. He claimed that it was 'the accident of the Reform Bill of 1831' which made him an anti-Liberal Tory.[8] This was reinforced by his early religious views which led him to believe that there was 'a certain element of AntiChrist in the Reform Act'.[9] Yet Gladstone was not, initially, a strong opponent of the Reform Bill. In March 1831 he wrote in his diary: 'Heard with mixed feelings of the passing of the Ref[orm] Bill.'[10] It was not until the first bill had been defeated and a general election called that Gladstone became alarmed by the tide of popular sentiment which demanded reform. After attending a Warwick county meeting on reform, he observed that the multitude were 'now eagerly rushing or heedlessly sauntering along the pathway of revolution'.[11]

Gladstone's fear that reform would lead to revolution was prompted mainly by events outside, rather than inside, the United Kingdom. The French Revolution of July 1830 led Gladstone to predict that 'the present vast struggle on the Continent ... will be as Canning foretold, a war of principles'.[12] At the 1831 general election, he had printed, at his own cost, placards on which he declared that new constitutions had brought chaos to South America, France and Belgium and he called on the electors 'TO RESIST REVOLUTION TO THE DEATH'.[13] While canvassing at the Oxfordshire election, he harangued a working man on the text that reform was revolution: 'To corroborate my doctrine I said, "Why, look at the revolutions in foreign countries", meaning of course France and Belgium. The man looked hard at me and said these very words, "Damn all foreign countries, what has old England to do with foreign countries?"'[14] Gladstone later concluded that he had received an important lesson from a humble source, but he was not so easily reassured at the time. For the 1830 revolution in France convinced many Tories, including the party's leader, the Duke of Wellington, that large-scale reform would lead to revolution.[15]

Gladstone's fears about reform were shared by many of his Oxford debating friends, such as Robert Lowe.[16] During a debate in May 1831, Gladstone moved a rider which alleged that the Reform Bill would break up the whole frame of society.[17] He had prepared for the debate by reading the anti-reform speeches of Canning, whose son, Charles, was his friend and contemporary at Christ Church.[18] Gladstone also read Burke's *Reflections on the French Revolution* and later admitted that he was 'completely under his mastery with regard to the French Revolution'.[19] In 1832 he told his father that 'the abstract rights of man to political power, so fatal to organised communities', were now 'unblushingly advanced and ... universally and readily applied'.[20]

Ironically, however, Gladstone's pronounced opposition to reform enabled him to enter the first reformed parliament. At Oxford, his Christ Church contemporary Lord Lincoln joined him in his anti-reform speeches and activities.[21] They co-organised a university petition to the House of Commons against the Reform Bill. The petition claimed that the bill was a rash surrender to popular clamour which would increase Roman Catholic influence in parliament and undermine the influence of the 'Aristocratical Order' in the House of Commons.[22] These arguments strongly appealed to Lord Lincoln's Tory father, the Duke of Newcastle, who was a strong opponent of Catholic emancipation and a prominent borough-monger with a strong stake in the unreformed electoral system.[23] The duke's antipathy to reform was reinforced by his fear of revolution, which may have stemmed from his internment on the continent during the Napoleonic Wars. The duke was one of the small minority of peers who voted against the Reform Bill in June 1832 and soon afterwards, he invited his son's friend, Gladstone, to stand for Newark, where he had much territorial influence.

Gladstone was returned for Newark at the general election in 1832 and represented the borough until 1846. Thus he partly owed his early ministerial career (in Peel's two governments) to his strong opposition to reform. Yet Newark provided Gladstone with direct experience of working-class electors which encouraged his subsequent support for working-class enfranchisement. Many of the Newark electors were working men, who had qualified under the old scot-and-lot qualification, and Gladstone wooed them by personal canvass and specific election promises. In 1865 he stated that his experience at Newark had convinced him that working men would not vote together as a class and he lamented the abolition of scot-and-lot constituencies.[24] He regretted that the Great Reform Act had extinguished 'the truly popular franchises' of Newark and other boroughs.[25]

In the later 1830s and earlier 1840s, Gladstone combined a *de facto* acceptance of the Great Reform Act with a continuing fear of revolutionary change. Around 1835, he set out the principles of concession or resistance to radical or revolutionary demands by citing the historical examples of Charles I and Louis XVI.[26] His retrospective mentality was typical of contemporary Tories, for whom, as Kitson Clark noted, 'the French Revolution was still the fecund mother of potent ... nightmares'.[27] Gladstone later recalled that he had continued to view parliamentary reform with 'some lingering feeling of prejudice as late as about 1848', but he added that at no time had he spoken a word against it.[28] In 1848, however, another French Revolution encouraged a revival of Chartism in Britain which prompted many leading politicians to conclude that reform was preferable to revolution.

Two weeks after the 1848 revolution in Paris, an outbreak of rioting in London's West End led Gladstone to enrol as a special constable. He spent two hours on duty on 10 April – the day of the Chartist demonstration at Kennington Common – and wrote in his diary: 'May our hearts feel profoundly the mercies of this very remarkable day.'[29] Gladstone's service as a special constable reflected his opposition to violence and revolution, but did not imply that he was opposed to peaceful reform.[30] When parliament debated Hume's reform resolutions, in June 1848, Gladstone dealt with a number of suffrage petitions and spent more than five hours listening to the closing speeches.[31] He heard his Peelite colleague Sydney Herbert (an old associate from Oxford Union days) endorse Russell's support for further parliamentary reform in the not-too-distant future.[32]

In the early 1850s, Gladstone supported, without fuss and without public declaration, the case for further reform. As Chancellor of the Exchequer, in Aberdeen's coalition, he was 'Thoroughly with Lord John Russell in his [reform] proposal and should not I think have disliked a larger measure.'[33] Although he regarded the outbreak of the Crimean War as a good reason for abandoning the 1854 Reform Bill, he later criticised Palmerston's first ministry for not redeeming the reform pledges which had been 'given to the people from the mouth of the Sovereign on the throne'.[34]

Gladstone's first major speech on parliamentary reform was made in 1859 on the second reading of Derby and Disraeli's Tory Reform Bill. He welcomed the extent of consensus, within the House of Commons, on what he termed 'this great and transcendent subject'. He declared that his 'paramount and overbearing motive' was to ensure 'the early and satisfactory settlement of this question'.[35] He thought that the nation would suffer if reform was further delayed:

It is bad for the nation that this House, which has so much business to transact, on the part of this country and our vast empire, should be perpetually engaged in constitutional and organic questions ... We cannot afford – as a mere matter of time – ... to fritter away the principal part of each Session in debating the question of Parliamentary Reform.[36]

Gladstone feared that the prolonged debates on reform would diminish 'the stability of our institutions' and prevent the nation from performing its great world duties. He voted for the Tory bill, not for party reasons, but because he wanted to settle the issue.[37]

Gladstone's strong support for reform in 1859 has been underplayed by historians, partly because he endorsed a Tory bill and partly because of his conservative views on the redistribution of seats. His opposition to the disfranchisement of small boroughs has been described, by Roy Jenkins, as 'not an obvious way in which either to mark his transition to Liberalism or to support a measure which disfranchised seventy of them'.[38] But Gladstone still regarded himself as a 'Liberal Conservative' and he feared that the disfranchisement of small boroughs would be 'injurious to the efficiency of the House of Commons' – which he hoped that reform would promote.[39]

The defeat of the 1859 Tory Reform Bill led to a general election which left the Liberals in a strong position. Gladstone's decision to join Palmerston's government was partly prompted by his belief that the Liberals now had a better chance than the Tories of settling the reform question.[40] In 1860 the Liberal government introduced its own measure and Gladstone 'spoke at much length on Reform Bill to an adverse and difficult House'.[41] He began by again stressing the need to settle the issue, claiming that the failure to deal with reform had baffled and bewildered the public and raised 'doubts as to what is the real value of the pledges of public men'.[42] He believed that the public would become disillusioned if parliament continued to dally with the reform question.[43]

Gladstone also called, in his 1860 speech, for the enfranchisement of a substantial proportion of the working classes:

> I do not admit that the working man, regarded as an individual, is less worthy of the suffrage than any other class. I do not admit the charges of corruption ... I do not believe that the working men of this country are possessed of a disposition to tax their neighbours and exempt themselves; nor do I acknowledge for a moment that schemes of socialism, of communism, of republicanism, or any other ideas at variance with the law and constitution of this country are prevalent and popular amongst them.[44]

Gladstone endorsed Disraeli's observation – made a decade earlier – that parliament would have to deal with the admission of the working classes and he argued that a large measure of that kind would increase working-class support for the constitution. He admitted that the proposed £6 borough franchise would not make the working classes a majority of the total borough electorate, but he claimed that 'even with a very extended suffrage you would probably still continue to see the monarchy and aristocracy flourish as they do now'.[45]

Gladstone described Palmerston's cabinet as divided, on the reform issue, into two camps: on one side the ultra-Conservatives, and on the other those with no fear of the working classes who believed 'that something *real* though limited should be done towards their enfranchisement'. He listed the ministers who favoured enfranchisement as Russell, Somerset, Newcastle, Argyll, Gibson and himself; and those who were 'fearful or opposed' as Palmerston, Villiers and Herbert. But he noted that all the ministers who favoured suffrage extension also opposed a large redistribution of seats – with the sole exception of the Duke of Newcastle, who was his old anti-reform friend from Oxford and the son of his patron at Newark.[46] The fact that Newcastle wanted a bolder reform measure than Gladstone illustrates how far the Peelites had advanced their thinking on reform. In cabinet, Gladstone opposed the withdrawal of the 1860 Reform Bill, but he was overruled.

In 1864 Gladstone made a speech on Edward Baines's Borough Franchise Bill which attracted much attention and which has been regarded by many historians as a political watershed. Justin McCarthy even claimed that Gladstone's 1864 speech effectively established the principle of popular representation.[47] Gladstone himself noted, at the time, that his speech had caused 'some sensation', but he thought that this was caused less by what he had said, than by the change in the public mood since 1859.[48] Certainly Gladstone said very little in 1864 which he had not already said in 1860, or 1859. He attempted to lay the ghost of the French Revolution, by pointing out that, whereas most MPs had been brought up, during the period of reaction to the excesses of the first French Revolution, to believe that the masses were hostile to the constitution, this was clearly no longer the case. He then declared, in what became a notorious phrase, 'that every man who is not presumably incapacitated by some consideration of personal unfitness or of political danger is morally entitled to come within the pale of the Constitution'.[49] This principle sounded novel and radical, but Gladstone, as he pointed out to Palmerston, had not committed the government, or himself, to any particular form of franchise.[50] His principle echoed the statement he had made in 1827, when he had wished to 'extend the blessings of the constitution to all who can enjoy them without endangering it'. On that occasion, he had expressed his fear that reform might lead to revolution and in 1864 he also stressed his opposition to 'sudden, or violent, or excessive, or intoxicating change'.[51]

Nevertheless Gladstone's 1864 speech was widely interpreted as an endorsement of the democratic principle. Palmerston wrote to him: 'You lay down broadly the Doctrine of Universal Suffrage which I can never accept.'[52] *The Times* accused Gladstone of using 'the language of sweeping and levelling Democracy', which preached 'the divine right of multitudes ... equality against Liberty, Theory against Practice, abstract dogmatism against experience'.[53] In *Punch*, Tenniel depicted Gladstone as a jockey unable to control his steed – 'Democracy' – to the anger of the course steward, Palmerston.[54]

The press response to Gladstone's speech led the Radicals to believe that he now supported the principle of manhood suffrage. This embarrassed Gladstone, who told Palmerston: 'The applause which I do not deserve vexes me at least as much as the criticism.'[55] He later admitted that his franchise principle, although 'apparently of wide scope', had been reduced 'by large and scarcely definable exceptions within rather narrow limits'. He acknowledged that he had not attempted to solve 'problems of real intricacy, which belong wholly to the future, and which are little likely to become practical except for another generation'. He regretted that his declaration had produced expectations which were likely to be disappointed.[56] He privately stated that he wanted a reform measure which 'promises by reasonably widening the basis of our institutions to strengthen the structure above'.[57]

Gladstone's intentions may have been conservative, but his critics sternly denounced his apparent espousal of the egalitarian principle. Robert Lowe claimed that Gladstone's argument amounted 'to that assumption of the *a priori* rights of man which formed the terror and ridicule of that grotesque tragedy, the French Revolution'.[58] Gladstone responded by defining Liberal principles as 'Trust of the people only qualified by prudence' and Tory principles as 'mistrust of the people only qualified by fear'.[59] The shadow of the French Revolution was also evident when the Commons debated the 1866 Liberal Reform Bill. Disraeli reminded Gladstone of his 1831 Oxford Union motion, which had predicted that the Reform Bill would destroy social order.[60] Gladstone replied:

> What he has stated is true. I deeply regret it; but I was bred under the shadow of the great name of Canning: every influence connected with that name governed the politics of my childhood and my youth. With Canning ... and under the shadow of that yet more venerable name of Burke, I grant, my youthful mind and imagination were impressed with the same idle and futile fears which still bewilder and distract the mature mind of the right honourable gentleman.[61]

Gladstone later concluded that Burke was wrong about the French Revolution and 'under the influence of a thoroughly one-sided view of French history'.[62]

Gladstone's attitude to reform was also influenced by political developments in the United States. In 1860 he declared that it would be 'a miserable day for England when she thinks fit to adopt America as her example ... England ... has much to teach to America and little to learn from her.'[63] The subsequent outbreak of the Civil War initially increased Gladstone's doubts about America, but in 1864 he acknowledged that the war had unleashed 'a kind of volcanic force not yet suspected to exist' in the American people.[64] After the end of the war, he observed that the heroic resistance of the Confederacy and the courage and perseverance of the Federals which finally overcame it, represented energies which 'surpassed our scale and measure'.[65]

The American Civil War influenced Gladstone's thinking on parliamentary reform in 1866. He read many works on the USA and the Civil War while he was involved with the Liberal government's Reform Bill.[66] In a speech at Liverpool, he declared that American institutions could no longer be held up as a bugbear to prevent franchise extension: 'Recent events which have taken place on the other side of the Atlantic have demonstrated to us how, by enlarging the franchise, augmented power can be marshalled on behalf of the government and increased energy given to the action of a nation.'[67] Gladstone claimed that England stood between the feudal, class-based society of Europe and the principles of equality which formed the basis of society in America. His analysis was inspired by Tocqueville's *Democracy in America* which he had read in 1840.[68] Gladstone regarded Tocqueville as 'the Burke of our age'.[69] But his comments on democracy, at Liverpool, balanced the views of Tocqueville with those of Burke:

> The word 'democracy' has very different senses, if by democracy be meant liberty ... the extension to each man in his own sphere of every privilege and of every franchise that he can exercise with advantage to himself and with safety to the State – then I must confess I don't see much to alarm us in the word democracy. But if by democracy be meant the enthroning of ignorance against knowledge, the setting up of vice in opposition to virtue, the disregard of rank, the forgetfulness of what our fathers have done for us ... then ... I ... am an enemy of democracy.[70]

When Gladstone introduced the 1866 Reform Bill, he declared that since reform had already been proposed by five governments, it would be superfluous to debate the general question.[71] He justified the principle of franchise extension on the grounds that 'Liberty is a thing which is good not merely in its fruits, but in itself.'[72] He also argued that reform would improve the work of the House of Commons.[73] But he denied that the government wanted to 'import American principles' and claimed that the reduction of the borough franchise was a return to old English principles. This was a reference to the scot-and-lot and freemen borough franchises which had been abolished in 1832. But his final assertion that 'You cannot fight against the future. Time is on our side' – suggested that he had a Tocquevillian belief in the inevitable rise of democracy.[74]

Gladstone's stance on reform mirrored respectable opinion in the country at large. He defended the moderate nature of the 1866 Reform Bill by reference to the conservative state of public opinion.[75] When a deputation from Lancashire asked him to speak there on reform, he thought the request 'without precedent ...dangerous ... unfavourable in its effect on the temper of the House'.[76] Soon afterwards, however, he spoke 'at length and wholly on the Bill' to an enthusiastic audience of 4,000 at Liverpool – which prompted *The Times* to restate his own reservations about such a performance.[77]

Nevertheless Gladstone did nothing further directly to stimulate 'pressure from without' for reform. He cited the quiescence of the Lancashire operatives during the cotton famine, not their pro-reform militancy, as evidence of their fitness for the franchise.[78] In 1866, he declined to attend a meeting of the London Working Men's Association who wished to thank him for his efforts on their behalf.[79]

The defeat of the 1866 Reform Bill led to the resignation of the Liberal government, although Gladstone would have preferred to hold a general election. He told the Queen that the repeated failure to enact reform discredited not just ministries and parties, but parliamentary government itself.[80] Consequently he promised to support Derby and Disraeli's new Tory ministry if it dealt with reform 'in an effectual manner'.[81] In February 1867, he again pledged Liberal support for a speedy and effectual settlement.[82] When the Tory Reform Bill was debated in the Commons, Gladstone's attendance was second to none.[83] As the leader of the largest party in the Commons, he played a crucial role in the successful passage of the bill and he was largely responsible for several of its provisions such as the removal of the dual vote, voting papers and fancy franchises. His retrospective verdict on the 1867 Reform Act was both positive and self-effacing: 'it was for the purpose of the hour, and as the work of a government in a decided minority, an extraordinary piece of parliamentary success'.[84]

When Gladstone returned to office, as the Liberal Prime Minister, in December 1868, his priority was the reform of the Irish church, but he did not forget what he called 'the great question of parliamentary reform'. In his first speech as Prime Minister, at Greenwich, he observed that although 'We have attained to a great stage of advancement with regard to popular suffrage that forms an epoch in the history of the country', further action was required to protect the franchise rights of compound householders and to ensure free voting for all electors.[85] He had previously opposed the introduction of the ballot, but after the passage of the 1867 Reform Act he concluded that secret voting was necessary to protect the new working-class voters from intimidation.[86] He announced his conversion to the Commons in 1870, when he pointed out that the 1867 Reform Act had 'practically adopted in principle an extension that is unlimited'. He declared that it was now 'a simple question of time and convenience' when 'every man who is not disabled' would possess the vote. He rejected any long-term suffrage discrimination between either householders and lodgers or boroughs and counties.[87] A Ballot Bill was introduced in 1871 and enacted in 1872.

Gladstone also gave a lead to the Commons on other aspects of parliamentary reform. In 1872 he declared that 'the present condition of the county franchise cannot very long continue', but he refused to make a pledge of immediate action because there was no party unanimity on an issue which would take up much parliamentary time.[88] Commenting on a private member's Female Suffrage Bill, in 1871, he referred to 'a presumptive case for *some* change in the law', but he strongly opposed any reform which would enable women to participate directly in the 'masculine turmoil of elections'.[89] On this issue, his views did not advance, for three premierships and twenty years later, he expressed similar reservations about another private member's Female Suffrage Bill.[90]

After Gladstone's resignation from the premiership and the Liberal leadership, he returned to the question of parliamentary reform, in a published debate with Lowe, in 1877–78. He again called for the enfranchisement of all adult males 'not specially disabled and duly identified by public authority as to place and particulars'. He thought that enfranchisement should be based on qualifications – such as paying taxes and heading a family – rather than on 'rights' – a word which he admitted had 'a maddening effect' on some people (such as Lowe). He rejected the concept of equality as a 'bastard political theorem' and asserted that the English people loved the aristocratic principle. He hoped to prevent the emergence of a plutocracy by effecting a great reduction in the cost of elections.[91]

Gladstone also stressed the need for constitutional reform in his writings and Midlothian campaign speeches in 1879. He believed that the House of Commons was not capable of efficiently discharging its functions and he predicted that the question of local government might 'transcend all others for the time in the urgency of its pressure and in the promise of advantage from its adjustment'.[92] In his second Midlothian speech, he noted the need for electoral reform in Scotland and then declared:

> In the matter of local government, there may lie a solution of some national and even Imperial difficulties ... I desire, I may almost say I intensely desire, to see Parliament relieved of some portion of its duties ... The Parliament is almost overwhelmed. If we can take off its shoulders that superfluous weight by the constitution of secondary and subordinate authorities, I am not going to be frightened out of wise measures of that kind by being told that in that I am condescending to the prejudices of Home Rulers.[93]

Gladstone insisted that nothing should be done to undermine the supremacy of the imperial parliament in the United Kingdom, but he was clearly flagging his support for some form of devolution.

When Gladstone returned to power, in 1880, the critical state of Ireland and the economic depression ensured that reform was not a top priority. Nevertheless, in 1882, Gladstone reiterated his support for household suffrage in the counties, arguing that it would strengthen labour representation in the Commons. But he again refused to make a pledge which he could not immediately redeem.[94] He supported the 1883 Corrupt and Illegal Practices Bill, which he had inspired, but he left the details to his Attorney-General, Henry James. Gladstone was far more interested in the Affirmation Bill (prompted by the Bradlaugh case) on which he made one of his most notable

speeches.[95] In 1884, moreover, he took personal responsibility for the introduction and passage through the Commons of a new Reform Bill.

When Gladstone introduced the bill he stressed that it enjoyed wide public
support:

> It commonly happens with regard to these large and constitutional questions –
> and it is well that it should so happen – that, before they are proposed [by the]
> Government, they have attained to an advanced stage of progress in the public
> mind through discussion out-of-doors; and, in consequence, it is not necessary
> very long to detain this House with general arguments.[96]

Gladstone also argued that 'the enfranchisement of capable citizens ... gives
an additional strength to the State'. He believed that this had been demonstrated in the USA during the Civil War – a point he had originally made in
1866. He claimed that the Union had been able to defeat the Confederacy
because it was 'a nation where every capable citizen was enfranchised, and
had a direct and an energetic interest in the well-being and the unity of the
State'.[97] Gladstone made a clear distinction between enfranchisement, which
he regarded as a national and imperial question, and redistribution which
he considered merely a local issue.[98]

Historians have recently stressed the conservative character of the 1884
Reform Bill, which fell far short of universal male suffrage and avoided radical proposals such as female suffrage or proportional representation.[99] But
Gladstone did not want to give the Tory majority in the House of Lords an
easy excuse for rejecting the bill. In the event, the Lords refused to pass the
bill without a measure of redistribution and Gladstone hammered out, with
Salisbury and Northcote, a bipartisan compromise. This included the division of large constituencies into single-member districts – a measure which
favoured the Tories. Gladstone's main concern, however, was to extend the
franchise, rather than to gain party advantage. He later noted that the 1884
Reform Act had enfranchised far more men than all the previous reform
acts, but he added, significantly, that the main benefit of the measure 'was
not mainly numerical but moral'.[100]

The initial refusal of the House of Lords to accept the Franchise Bill led
Gladstone to complain to the Queen that the House of Lords 'has for a long
period been the habitual and vigilant enemy of every Liberal Government'.
He was reluctant, however, to raise the question of Lords reform, even
though it was in the interests of the Liberal party to do so. But he warned
the Queen that a conflict between the two Houses could end only in the victory of the Commons and would threaten the hereditary nature of the Lords
and isolate the crown.[101]

Gladstone's attitude to the House of Lords, in 1884, was consistent with
his past record. Despite his close personal and political ties with many peers,
he had frequently criticised the legislative record of the upper House. When

RAISING THE " FIERY CROSS."
MIDLOTHIAN, AUGUST, 1884.

8 Gladstone raising the fiery cross of reform, *Punch*, 30 August 1884

the peers rejected Gladstone's proposal to repeal the paper duty in 1860, he resisted 'to the uttermost of my power the encroachment of the House of Lords'. He asserted the principle that 'the Lords are not to tax the people without their consent'.[102] When the Lords amended the 1869 Irish Church Disestablishment and Disendowment Bill, Gladstone declared that the peers were wholly out of touch with public opinion, but he welcomed the subsequent bipartisan compromise as 'an escape from a formidable constitutional conflict'.[103] In 1871, when the Lords rejected the Army Bill which proposed the abolition of the purchase of commissions, Gladstone used a royal warrant to end the practice. In the same year, he described the summary rejection of the Ballot Bill by the Lords as 'a great and grievous error'.[104] The bill was reintroduced in 1872 and passed by the Lords. In 1877 Gladstone claimed that the people revered the peers, not for their legislative record in the House of Lords, but for their role in local government and society.[105] In 1881, Gladstone refused to accept the Lords' amendments to the Irish Land Bill, even though his old friend, the Duke of Argyll, resigned from the cabinet. Gladstone's support for Irish home rule in 1886 was even more unpopular with the peers and left the Liberals in a tiny minority in the Lords. In 1893 the

House of Lords rejected the second Home Rule Bill by an overwhelming majority and in 1894 it savaged the Employers' Liability Bill and the Parish Councils Bill. Gladstone reluctantly accepted these decisions, but in his farewell speech to the Commons, he expressed his dissatisfaction with the conduct of the Lords over the previous half-century. He accused the Lords of seeking 'to annihilate the whole work of the House of Commons' and declared that the conflict between the two Houses must be resolved by the nation.[106] Asquith regarded Gladstone's comment as 'The legacy which he left his party', and when Asquith became Prime Minister, in 1908, he treated the veto of the House of Lords as 'the dominating issue in politics'.[107] Thus the 1911 Parliament Act, which abolished the permanent veto of the House of Lords, fulfilled Gladstone's last objective in the field of parliamentary reform.

Viewed in perspective, Gladstone's record on parliamentary reform was not one of steady progress from Tory reaction to ever greater measures of Liberal reform. As a very young man, he was not averse to some extension of the franchise, but his fear of French-style revolution made him a strong anti-reformer in 1831–32. Ironically, it was another French Revolution, in 1848, which convinced Gladstone – following in the wake of his Peelite colleagues – that reform was the best antidote to revolution. From the mid-1860s, he virtually advocated the principle, if not the practice, of universal manhood suffrage, although he continued to oppose revolutionary methods and egalitarian theories.

Gladstone injected into the reform debate all his formidable powers of eloquence, energy and execution, but his exact influence on reform policy is not always easy to assess. He did not have a major influence on either the reform debate or reform legislation until the mid-1860s and thereafter he often let other sections of the Liberal alliance take the initiative on reform. Gladstone acted both as a catalyst of reform and as a brake upon it – often at the same time. His speeches on reform balanced commitment with caution and he qualified his bold statements of principle with conditions which were carefully vague. This was classically the case in 1864, but it was also evident in 1870, 1877 and 1884.

Gladstone added his own characteristic stamp to the reform debate in other ways as well. He consistently refused to exploit the reform issue for party or electoral advantage and he always sought bipartisan support for reform legislation. In both 1859 and 1867, he supported a Tory Reform Bill, because he thought that the interests of the nation required a speedy settlement. The same motive prompted his reform compromise with the Tories in 1884. Gladstone attached great importance to ministerial pledges on reform. He attacked the Tories, not for defending or deserting their principles, but for cynically playing with the reform issue – which he regarded as a dangerous game. He believed that 'the consistency of parties and Parliaments' was essential if the public was to retain its confidence in the British constitutional system.[108] He feared that the government of Britain and the empire would suffer if the reform question was allowed to drag on to the exclusion of other issues. His attitude to reform was deeply influenced by his own long experience as a government minister. His alarm at the growing volume of parliamentary business – evident in 1859, 1879 and 1886 – partly explains his change of heart on parliamentary reform and Irish home rule.

There were other striking continuities in Gladstone's approach to reform. He was consistently conservative in his attitude to the redistribution of parliamentary seats – as in 1859, 1866 and 1884. His bad experience in 1866 convinced him that redistribution was an obstacle to further enfranchisement, but he also feared that redistribution would undermine the 'legitimate' political influence of landowners and local communities. Yet Gladstone consistently opposed special electoral arrangements, such as proportional representation, which would have ensured the separate representation of political minorities. From the 1850s, Gladstone's attitude to franchise extension was distinctly Liberal and implicitly Radical. He favoured the maximum enfranchisement consistent with consensual parliamentary sanction and political stability. Although his main measure of parliamentary reform – the 1884 Reform Act – fell well short of universal male suffrage, it had, as Colin Matthew has pointed out, distinctly democratic consequences.[109]

Gladstone's desire to extend the suffrage to most men was not matched by a similar commitment to female suffrage. On that question, he was disposed 'to take no step in advance until I am convinced of its safety' – an attitude which corresponded closely to his attitude to male enfranchisement. But Gladstone did not believe that the female suffrage campaign was analogous to its male counterpart, because it was not generally supported by the public or by women themselves.[110] Thus Gladstone applied a crude sort of 'democratic test' to assess the relative validity of male and female claims for enfranchisement.

Gladstone's policy on parliamentary reform generally followed, rather than led, public opinion. His support for reform, from the 1850s, was largely a response to the growing liberal mood of the age. He himself noted that the orator had to be 'what his age will have him, what it requires in order to be moved by him, or else not to be at all'. Walter Bagehot concluded that since Gladstone could not impose his creed *on* his time, he had to learn his creed *of* his time.[111] Gladstone openly acknowledged that his major initiatives on reform were responses to well-established popular sentiment.

Gladstone's reform legislation greatly expanded the political nation and popularised parliamentary government. His reform rhetoric powerfully supported the *de facto* (though not the *de jure*) arguments for political equality and popular sovereignty. Yet Gladstone has recently been given little credit for his reforming achievements and has been described as 'not a democrat'.[112] Yet Gladstone *did* favour democracy, providing individual liberty was consistent with stable government. Moreover he believed that the extension of the franchise strengthened both the state and the individual and was one of the best methods of moral improvement. For Gladstone, parliamentary reform – like free trade or home rule – was not just a political question, it was also a moral question.

Notes

1 *Hansard's Parliamentary Debates*, 3rd series, vol. 22, col. 474.
2 J. to W. E. Gladstone, 18 March 1831, quoted in Michael Brock, *The Great Reform Act*, London, Hutchinson, 1973, p. 149.
3 W. E. Gladstone, 'My Earlier Political Opinions (I) The Descent', in *The Prime Ministers' Papers: W. E. Gladstone I: Autobiographica*, ed. J. Brooke and M. Sorensen, 4 vols, London, HMSO, 1971–81, vol. 1, p. 33.
4 P. Dixon, *Canning: Politician and Statesman*, London, Weidenfeld & Nicholson, 1976, p. 287.
5 W. E. Gladstone to W. W. Farr, 14 September 1827, in *Autobiographica* (1971), p. 197.
6 W. E. Gladstone to W. W. Farr, 4 February 1830, in *Autobiographica* (1971), p. 213.
7 *GD*, 2 December 1830.
8 W. E. Gladstone, 'Autobiographical Retrospect', in *Autobiographica* (1971), p. 38.
9 W. E. Gladstone, 'My Earlier Political Opinions (II) The Extrication', in *Autobiographica* (1971), p. 40.
10 *GD*, 22 March 1831.
11 *Standard*, 7 April 1831.
12 W. E. Gladstone to W. W. Farr, 13 September 1830, in *Autobiographica* (1971), p. 218.
13 Gladstone's draft handbill, 23 April 1831, in *Autobiographica* (1971), p. 231.
14 W. E. Gladstone, 'My Earlier Political Opinions (I) The Descent', in *Autobiographica* (1971), p. 37.
15 R. Quinault, 'The French Revolution of 1830 and Parliamentary Reform', *History*, vol. 79, 1994, pp. 383–84.
16 R. Lowe. 'A Chapter of Autobiography', in A. P. Martin, *Life and Letters of the Right Honourable, Robert Lowe, Viscount Sherbrooke*, 2 vols, London, Longmans, Green, 1893, vol. 1, p. 16.
17 W. E. Gladstone to his brother, 20 May 1831, in J. Morley, *The Life of William Ewart Gladstone*, 3 vols, London, Macmillan, 1903, vol. 1, p. 73.
18 *GD*, 19 April, 18 May 1831.
19 *GD*, 1 June 1831; W. E. Gladstone: 'My Earlier Political Opinions (I) The Descent', in *Autobiographica* (1971), p. 36
20 W. E. Gladstone to J. Gladstone, 7 January 1832, in *Autobiographica* (1971), pp. 225–26.
21 *GD*, 23, 27 April, 16, 17 May 1831.
22 See the text of the university petition against the Reform Bill in A. F. Robbins, 'Mr Gladstone's Ancestry and Early Years', in *The Life of William Ewart Gladstone*, ed. W. T. Reid, London, Cassell, 1899, pp. 107–08.
23 J. Golby, 'A Great Electioneer and his Motives: The Fourth Duke of Newcastle', *Historical Journal*, Vol. 8, 1965, pp. 201–18.

24 Gladstone's speech at Chester, *The Times*, 1 June 1865.
25 W. E. Gladstone, 'The County Franchise and Mr Lowe Thereon', in his *Gleanings of Past Years* [hereafter Gladstone, *Gleanings*], London, John Murray, 1879, vol. 1, p. 148.
26 Gladstone's undated memorandum, in R. Shannon, *Gladstone, 1809–1865*, London, Hamish Hamilton, 1982, p. 53.
27 G. K. Clark, *Peel and the Conservative Party: A Study in Party Politics 1832–41*, London, Frank Cass, 1964, pp. 320–21.
28 W. E. Gladstone, 'My Earlier Political Opinions (II) The Extrication', in *Autobiographica* (1971), p. 52.
29 *GD*, 10 April 1848.
30 R. Quinault, '1848 and Parliamentary Reform', *Historical Journal*, Vol. 31, 1988, pp. 836–37.
31 *GD*, 26 May, 20 June 1848.
32 *Hansard*, 3rd series, vol. 99, col. 213.
33 W. E. Gladstone, 'My Earlier Political Opinions (II) The Extrication', in *Autobiographica* (1971), p. 52.
34 *Hansard*, 3rd series, vol. 153, col. 1051.
35 Ibid., cols 1046, 1050.
36 Ibid., cols 1065–66.
37 Ibid., col. 1067.
38 R. Jenkins, *Gladstone*, London, Macmillan, 1995, pp. 201–02.
39 *Hansard*, 3rd series, vol. 153, col. 1054.
40 Gladstone to Sir William Heathcote, 16 June 1859, in Morley (1903), vol. 1, p. 468.
41 *GD*, 3 May 1860.
42 *Hansard*, 3rd series, vol. 158, col. 628.
43 Ibid., col. 649.
44 Ibid., col. 632.
45 Ibid., cols 645, 633, 643, 644.
46 W. E. Gladstone, 'Memorandum on the Political Attitudes of Cabinet Ministers', in *The Prime Ministers' Papers: W. E. Gladstone*, ed. Brooke and Sorensen, vol. 3, *Autobiographical Memoranda, 1845–1866*, pp. 234–34.
47 J. McCarthy, *The Story of Gladstone's Life*, London, A. & C. Black, 1898, pp. 228–29.
48 *GD*, 11 May 1864.
49 *Hansard*, 3rd series, vol. 175, col. 324.
50 Gladstone to Palmerston, 11 May 1864, in *Gladstone and Palmerston: Being the Correspondence of Lord Palmerston with Mr Gladstone, 1851–65*, ed. P. Guedalla, London, Victor Gollancz, 1928, p. 280.
51 *Hansard*, 3rd series, vol. 175, col. 324.
52 Palmerston to Gladstone, 12 May 1864, in Guedalla (1928), p. 281.
53 *The Times*, 12 May 1864.
54 'The False Start', *Punch*, 28 May 1864; 'Out of the Race', *Punch*, 11 June 1864.
55 Gladstone to Palmerston, 21 May 1864, in Guedalla (1928), p. 286.
56 W. E. Gladstone, *Speeches on Parliamentary Reform in 1866*, London, John Murray, 1866, pp. 313–14.
57 W. E. Gladstone to Lord Lyttelton, 9 April 1865, in Morley (1903), vol. 2, p. 238.

58 *Hansard*, 3rd series, vol. 178, col. 1424.
59 *The Times*, 1 June 1865.
60 *Hansard*, 3rd series, vol. 183, col. 95.
61 Ibid., col. 129.
62 *GD*, 8 July 1881; W. E. Gladstone, 'My Earlier Political Opinions (I) The Descent', in *Autobiographica*, (1971), p. 36.
63 *Hansard*, 3rd series, vol. 158, col. 642.
64 Lord Stanley's journal entry for 23 June 1864, in *Disraeli, Derby and the Conservative Party: Journals and Memoirs of Edward Henry, Lord Stanley, 1849–69*, ed. J. Vincent, Hassocks, Harvester Press, 1978, pp. 219–20.
65 W. E. Gladstone to C. Sumner, 25 August 1865, in Shannon (1982), p. 553.
66 *GD*, 13, 19 January, 8 February, 17 April 1866, etc.
67 *The Times*, 7 April 1866.
68 *GD*, 23 April, 18 June 1840.
69 W. E. Gladstone, 'Kin Beyond the Sea', in *Gleanings*, vol. 1, p. 203.
70 *The Times*, 7 April 1866.
71 *Hansard*, 3rd series, vol. 182, col. 20.
72 Ibid., col. 58.
73 *Hansard*, 3rd series, vol. 183, cols 144–45.
74 Ibid., col. 152.
75 *Hansard*, 3rd series, vol. 182, col. 58.
76 *GD*, 20 March 1866.
77 *GD*, 6 April 1866; *The Times*, 7 April 1866.
78 *Hansard*, 3rd series, vol. 183, cols 144–45.
79 Gladstone to the London Working Men's Association, 2 July 1866, in Gladstone, *Reform Speeches* (1866), p. 308.
80 Gladstone's memorandum, 26 June 1866, in Morley (1903), pp. 209–10.
81 *Hansard*, 3rd series, vol. 184, col. 1144.
82 *Hansard*, 3rd series, vol. 185, cols 243, 486.
83 W. E. Gladstone to Duchess of Sutherland, 9 July 1867, in Morley (1903), vol. 2, p. 234.
84 Gladstone's memorandum on 'The Resignation of 1866 and Household Suffrage in Towns', in *Autobiographica* (1971), p. 93.
85 *The Times*, 22 December 1868.
86 *Hansard*, 3rd series, vol. 203, cols 1030, 1033.
87 Ibid., cols 1030–31.
88 *Hansard*, 3rd series, vol. 210, cols 1908–11.
89 *Hansard*, 3rd series, vol. 206, col. 91.
90 *Female Suffrage: A Letter from The Rt Hon. W. E. Gladstone MP to Samuel Smith MP* (London, 1892).
91 W. E. Gladstone, 'The County Franchise, and Mr Lowe Thereon', *Gleanings* (1879), vol. 1, pp. 143, 148, 164–65.
92 W. E. Gladstone, 'The Country and the Government', *The Nineteenth Century*, Vol. 6, 1879, p. 225.
93 W. E. Gladstone, *Political Speeches in Scotland, November and December 1879*, Edinburgh, Andrew Elliot, 1880, pp. 86–87.
94 *Hansard*, 3rd series, vol. 267, cols 1469–75.
95 Lord Askwith, *Lord James of Hereford*, London, Ernest Benn, 1930, pp. 119, 126.

 96 *Hansard*, 3rd series, vol. 285, col. 106.
 97 Ibid., cols 107–08.
 98 Ibid., col. 126.
 99 Jenkins (1995), p. 492.
100 W. E. Gladstone, '1884–5 Household Suffrage in Counties', in *Autobiographica* (1971), p. 107.
101 Gladstone's memorandum to the Queen, 19 August 1884, in *GD*, vol. 11, pp. 191–94.
102 Gladstone's memorandum of 1 July 1860, in *GD*, vol. 5, p 501.
103 W. E. Gladstone to Queen Victoria, 22 July 1869, in Morley (1903), vol. 2, p. 278.
104 Gladstone's speech at Greenwich, in *The Times*, 30 October 1871.
105 Gladstone, *Gleanings* (1879), vol. 1, p. 148.
106 *Hansard*, 4th series, vol. 21, cols 1149–52.
107 *Hansard*, 4th series, vol. 169, col. 597; vol. 176, cols 1507–12; *The Times*, 12 December 1908.
108 Gladstone, *Reform Speeches* (1866), pp. 313–14.
109 H. C. G. Matthew, *Gladstone, 1875–98*, Oxford, Clarendon Press, 1995, p. 177.
110 W. E. Gladstone, *Female Suffrage: A Letter to Samuel Smith, MP* (London, 1892).
111 Walter Bagehot, 'Mr Gladstone', in *Biographical Studies*, ed. R. H. Hutton, London, Longmans, Green, 1881, pp. 94, 112.
112 I. Machin, 'Gladstone', *The Historian*, Winter 1995, p. 19.

Gladstone, Liberalism and the Government of 1868–1874

Jonathan Parry

THE END OF THE SEASON.

Butler. "BEFORE TAKING LEAVE FOR MY HOLIDAY, MY LADY, MAY I VENTURE TO HOPE THAT MY
CONDUCT, AND THAT OF THE OTHER SERVANTS, HAS GIVEN YOU EVERY SATISFACTION."
Britannia. "TAKE YOUR HOLIDAY, EWART. THE LESS SAID ABOUT THE REST THE BETTER!"

9 'The End of the Season', *Punch*, 26 August 1871

THE extent and diversity of the activity of the first Gladstone government were its most distinguishing characteristics, and present as great a challenge to the historian as to the weary MPs who had to respond to it. Why was the legislation so varied and controversial? What was the particular role of Gladstone, a new Liberal leader? How far did he alter the direction of the party? The Liberals were traditionally a vibrant but undisciplined coalition, held together very loosely under Palmerston. The 1867 Reform Act galvanised them further, unleashing many expectations and fears. This chapter suggests a way of classifying the most significant projects pursued by Liberals between 1868 and 1874. It then explores the tensions between these different Liberal ideals, and their contribution to the difficulties that the government faced from 1871. It also suggests that these tensions were exacerbated by the continental crisis of 1870–71, which exposed the weakness of the Palmerstonian myth that Britain had an unusually blessed influence on the international scene.

The government's activity may profitably be divided into four main classes. The first was legislation for social and moral improvement, involving an unprecedented degree of state interference in local affairs, with the particular object of elevating the condition and morals of the working classes. The two most familiar and controversial examples of this were the 1870 Education Act and the 1872 Licensing Act, but also relevant were such measures as the 1869 Habitual Criminals Act, the 1870 Factories and Workshops Act and the 1872 Mines Regulation Act. This interventionist legislation did not, on the whole, engage Gladstone's enthusiasm; he was instinctively suspicious of curbs on free trade in beer, or on the independence of church schools.[1] Rather, the measures were inspired by five main influences. There was Lord John Russell, the departing leader of the Liberal party, an advocate of great improving causes to rally the party, and a particular supporter of increased state involvement in elementary education. He hoped that this would rescue children from vice and sensuality, raise the religious and moral character of the people, and assist the electorate's sober and sound judgement on political affairs.[2] There was a trio of Christian socialist cabinet ministers, and longstanding friends, H. A. Bruce, Earl de Grey and Ripon, and W. E. Forster. Having entered politics in the 1850s primarily out of anxiety about the condition of the people, in Gladstone's first government they found themselves in charge of education policy (de Grey and Forster) and the Home Office (Bruce).[3] There was pressure from social scientific opinion – among local doctors, professional men and philanthropists – which was represented by backbench MPs, often sitting for large cities, who wanted to see parliament devote more energies to promoting a constructive legislative programme; A. J. Mundella was typical of these.[4] There was cross-party support from Conservatives since, in the uncertainties of the post-1867 climate, many MPs on both sides of the house were extremely anxious to preserve social order and to improve moral and educational standards in the new electorate.[5] And there was Robert Lowe, Chancellor of the Exchequer, who admired talented civil servants such as John Simon at the Medical Department of the Privy Council, and believed in giving them the resources to execute beneficial strategies such as Simon's expansion of the vaccination and general health inspectorates.[6] Though in many ways a strident advocate of laissez-faire, Lowe was a supporter of state interference for 'rational' ends, such as in reforming the statutes of ancient endowed schools so that they might offer a more modern educational syllabus training middle-class pupils in scientific habits of mind. He was one of several influences on the 1869 Endowed Schools Act.[7]

A second strand of legislation was concerned with the development of the democratic principle. One obvious example here was the secret ballot, introduced in 1872. In 1869, the municipal franchise was extended, and single women ratepayers were allowed to vote in all local government elections. School boards, established in 1870, were to be directly elected by ratepayers. These measures symbolised the fervour for participatory politics in some quarters of the party. Also relevant were measures such as the Married Women's Property Act of 1870, and the trade union legislation of 1871 (soon found to be imperfect), which demonstrated an anxiety to broaden the scope of the political nation to previously marginalised social groups. The Assessed Rates Act of 1869 extended eligibility for the parliamentary franchise to tenants whose landlords paid their rate bill themselves, collecting the money out of rent. This was a Liberal response to the Conservatives' insistence on personal payment of rates as a qualification for the borough franchise in 1867. It was one of the few measures widely foreshadowed by party leaders in the election campaign.[8] In most other cases, however, 'democratic' pressure came not from the established leadership but from individual MPs, such as Jacob Bright, Grosvenor Hodgkinson and G. O. Trevelyan. Gladstone was a famously late convert to the principle of the ballot, under pressure from John Bright among others; he had spoken against it in his 1868 campaign.[9] This is not to say that he was an anti-democrat. On franchise issues he tended to reflect the consensus rather than lead opinion. And at this stage the Liberal party as a whole was not agreed on a major extension of democratic ideas, such as the principle of household suffrage in the counties, or ratepayer control of licensing.

Gladstone, then, was not a prime mover in either of these categories of legislation. His major concerns in his first government were with the other two main strands of its activity. One was the Irish issue, which both Russell and Gladstone wished to highlight after Palmerston's neglect. Gladstone's objective was to bind Ireland to Britain in 'harmony and concord', by removing symbols of injustice and division and increasing respect for law and institutions. In his 1868 speeches, he concentrated overwhelmingly on Irish church disestablishment as a way to do that. He argued that the policy of associating the state with one minority creed had been 'the plague and the scourge of the country', dividing 'man from man' and 'class from class'. Disestablishment would strip the state of its disabling religious personality.[10]

This policy had a series of advantages. It allowed him to paint the Conservatives as instinctive advocates of the endowment of all Irish sects, including the Catholics, a charge that he made in virtually every speech of his campaign. It excited Dissenters in Britain; in their eyes, no previous Liberal leader had talked as sympathetically as Gladstone now did about the damage done to civil society and religious zeal by state favouritism in religion. And it rallied the whole party by reminding the older Whigs of the appropriation pledge of 1835, without having to promise Irish MPs that Ireland would see radical secular changes. It was no wonder that the Liberal parliamentary party kept together so well during the 1869 and 1870 sessions, which were dominated by the Irish Church and Land Bills. But the latter, which had been kept in the background in 1868, proved more divisive in the party's higher echelons, even though Gladstone at this period was pursuing a conservative strategy, attempting to restore the historic rights of landlords and tenants.[11] Gladstone's real problems over Ireland emerged after 1870. Disorder did not abate, and the third leg of his programme, the Irish university question, proved intractable: there was little Irish support for Gladstone's policy of not endowing sectarian teaching colleges, while British Liberal anticlericalism and anti-Catholicism became increasingly vocal.[12]

The other plank of Gladstone's election campaign was the drive for economy and efficiency in government. Like Ireland, this was a traditional Liberal theme to which Gladstone brought an altered perspective and a new intensity. Gladstone disliked complacent and careless misgovernment, was anxious to extend principles of accountability and was aware of the popularity of tax cuts. In his 1868 campaign, he made retrenchment his guiding policy, alleged that the Conservatives were too lenient in dealing with demands from local lobbies and vested interests, and urged the public to remain vigilant against 'this Continental system of feeding the desires of classes and portions of the community at the expense of the whole'.[13] By making significant cuts in colonial defence in 1869, the government was able to reduce military and naval spending by about 15 per cent. Another major step in purifying the state's administrative image came in 1870, with the imposition on most civil service departments of entry by competitive examination, which allowed Gladstone to claim that he had voluntarily reduced the scope for the government to exercise 'special patronage'.[14] The abolition of the purchase system for army commissions, in 1871, was similarly presented as an attempt to improve standards in the public service.

Despite concentrating on these last two concerns, Gladstone believed in the principle of action by a public-spirited and vigorous executive. For this reason, and because of the need to unite a broadly based and energetic party of which he had only recently become leader, he allowed departmental colleagues and to some degree backbenchers considerable scope for their interventionist and democratising enthusiasms. This stimulated great activity in government. It also engendered tensions within the party. There is no room here to discuss the difficulties that emerged over Irish policy, significant though they were. This chapter, instead, seeks to explore some of the tensions between the other three themes outlined above: central government initiative, democracy and economy. It argues that the interaction of these three principles contributed to the party's loss of direction and defeat in the 1874 election. The chapter is divided into two sections. The first looks at the controversies caused by both government intervention and democratic principles, and the ways in which they collided to frustrate the socially improving instincts of the government. The second examines the clash between economy and the tradition of gentlemanly expertise in government.

There is no doubt that the Education and Licensing Acts, the two most significant measures of social and moral improvement, were also among the most controversial pieces of legislation passed between 1868 and 1874. The conflicts over the 1870 Education Act were particularly crippling. Many Dissenters had only with great reluctance been converted to the need for state intervention in education in the late 1860s; their whole historical tradition encouraged them to think of the state as likely to favour the interests of the established church. Therefore it was hardly surprising that they were so susceptible to claims that that was what the 1870 act did. Section 25 became a symbol of the act's tenderness to existing and prospective church schools. In 1872, only 67 backbench Liberals voted against a motion to abolish it, and many MPs looked to ministers to adopt an anti-clerical policy of this type.[15] This Russellite strategy would have been a natural way of rallying Whigs and Radicals. John Bright must have hoped for something along these lines when he returned to the cabinet in August 1873.

On the other hand, the Dissenters' reaction to the 1870 act, and Liberal backbench sympathy for them, drove some moralistic Anglicans, such as Thomas Hughes, into the church defence camp, fearing that Dissenting pressure from without would lead the Liberals into a campaign for secular education or church disestablishment. Anxiety about this was exacerbated by proposals of the Endowed Schools Commissioners to remove some of the safeguards for denominational teaching in Anglican foundations, for example by giving the Birmingham town council and school board power to appoint a majority of the governors of the King Edward VI Grammar School, Birmingham. The House of Lords defeated that and similar schemes for other schools such as the Emmanuel Hospital in London.[16]

Thus the education difficulty showed how the state, by muscling into an area previously dominated by vested interests, alienated powerful elements in both church and Dissent, and made further short-term major reform of the elementary education system almost impossible. The same pattern, of interventionist legislation offending opinion on both sides, can be discerned in the case of licensing: free traders in beer and the United Kingdom Alliance were both left dissatisfied by the bills of 1871 and 1872.[17]

Moreover, the education issue was not just about religion; it was also about taxes and rates. The imposition of a rate for board schools caused considerable local irritation, especially in suburban areas among those social classes just too respectable to deign to send their children to these institutions. These were often the same classes who could be persuaded to become aggrieved by the Endowed Schools Commission plans to end free education for local children at ancient grammar schools in favour of entry by scholarship examination. For these reasons, the education issue became caught up in the controversy over the burden of local taxation. This was a major issue in the early 1870s because of the perception that central government was taking more powers from localities but imposing extra costs on ratepayers which other categories of wealth were escaping. Advocates of relief for local ratepayers from central funds repeatedly invoked the spectre of central government domination. As the Conservative MP Clare Read put it in 1871, 'we [are] gradually drifting into the centralization of France, where ... they could not repair a parish pump without a correspondence with the Minister at Paris'.[18] Some ministers indeed lamented English localism: Childers regretted that Gladstone was not as keen as he was on the notion of a French-style 'administration'.[19] In 1872 there was a major rebellion of Liberal MPs when the government refused to accept the Conservative motion that it should pay for some charges – the police, lunatics, care of prisoners and so on – out of national rather than local taxes. This was largely a move by Liberal county MPs, but also had a major suburban London component – only 4 of the 17 Liberal backbench MPs for London voted with government, and the Conservative motion was carried by 100.[20] The local taxation grievance undoubtedly helps to explain the loss of 8 of the 20 Liberal seats in London, and 20 of their 47 English county seats, in 1874.[21]

Ratepayer anxieties were part of a broader defensive reaction among propertied voters after 1867, who feared that pressure from newly enfranchised electors would produce legislation favouring the working classes. In the spring of 1871, this alarm prompted a revolt of county Liberal MPs against two government schemes, to establish county financial boards and to increase succession duties, both of which had to be dropped.[22] The prospect that the government might capitulate to democratic ideas alarmed Edward Cardwell, Secretary of State for War, who offered to resign in 1872 after he opposed the government's adoption of a backbench amendment to the Ballot Bill which made it an imprisonable offence for a voter to show his ballot paper after he had voted. He told Gladstone that this was a proposal of 'democratic tyrants' and that if the trend towards over-regulation by legislation did not stop, there would be a reaction against the Liberals like that of the Restoration against the Puritans.[23] (The amendment was defeated by an insurrection of Liberal backbenchers, led by William Harcourt.) Ironically it was Cardwell himself who had been responsible for another so-called tyrannical act of government, the decision to carry the abolition of purchase in 1871 by royal warrant after the Lords had defeated the Army Regulation Bill.

The fact that some Radicals also criticised the decision to proceed by royal warrant reminds us that government activity could kindle fears of executive autocracy as well as of democratic supremacy.[24] In 1872–73, Harcourt launched a campaign against 'grand-maternal government', which he hoped would unite Whig and Radical MPs.[25] There were several apparently autocratic acts of government that libertarian MPs could exploit. The 1871 Licensing Bill proposed a special police inspectorate for public houses, to be appointed by the Home Office, a proposal which led the old Chartist J. R. Stephens to claim that this was a French-style government spy system designed to restrict the liberties of Englishmen. Even the milder version of the bill which became law in 1872, and which put the police inspectorate under local not central control, still restricted opening hours, which inspired protests at which 'Rule Britannia' was sung.[26] Lowe's attempt to sell most of the remaining crown land in Epping Forest, which was a very popular spot for working-class East Enders' recreation, also created an outcry and was defeated by a Liberal backbench revolt in 1871.[27] In 1872, Harcourt protested, at length and eventually successfully, against new regulations for public access to the royal parks in London, traditionally a sensitive issue for Radicals.[28] Another increasingly vigorous libertarian agitation was that against the Contagious Diseases Acts of 1864 and 1866, under which prostitutes suspected of infection could be incarcerated in special hospitals on the orders of a salaried permanent official staff.[29]

One reason why government activity could provoke fear of autocracy as well as democracy was the continental crisis of 1870–71. The Franco-Prussian War and its aftermath had the effect of significantly increasing awareness of Britain's distinctness from the continent, and the importance of maintaining that distinctness. In 1870–71 the continent presented two images; neither was at all appealing to British Liberalism. One was the might of the Prussian army, supplied with modern technology and mass popular backing, and directed by an all-powerful central autocracy. But if the idea of an omnipotent illiberal government manipulating technical know-how and the masses was scarcely alluring, the French alternative was no more so: an effete, corrupt and luxurious imperial regime, undermined by its own materialist excesses and giving way to a bloody anarchy in the 1871 Commune. Here were examples of the failings of autocracy – in both countries – and of unbridled democratic licence in France.[30] The effect was to stimulate agitation in Britain against the importation of overly 'continental' governing practices. For example, this assisted the campaign against the Contagious Diseases Acts. Josephine Butler's argument was that the continental system of official regulation of prostitution betrayed the proper responsibility of a Christian people to safeguard public morals themselves. By enfeebling the Protestant conscience in this way, the Prussian state was being left free to pursue inhumane militarist policies, endangering European peace.[31] The argument that French government behaviour had weakened the nation's public morality was even easier to make.[32] Such views were grist to the mill of, say, Dissenters who argued for the disestablishment of the Church of England.

This chapter has argued that the interplay of central initiative and democracy was very awkward for the Liberal party after 1867. On the whole, this strengthened opponents of state action, because those who feared democracy often suspected centralisation as its ally, while many Radicals saw centralisation as an autocratic threat to local control. These tensions made it difficult for the Liberals to make further progress on issues such as education and licensing. But it is important to qualify the negativism of this conclusion. Some Liberals – again from both Whig and Radical wings – concluded after 1874 that these difficulties made it all the *more* important to work on sober measures of state improvement. They believed that these were more socially advantageous than the enthusiasms of the sectional pressure groups in the party, while Britain had lessons to learn from the success of Prussian organisation in 1870. One Liberal MP, Sir John Trelawny, in continuing to defend the Contagious Diseases Acts, argued that for the state to try to prevent diseases – in a manner similar to that practised in much of Europe – was preferable to indulging in 'childish' measures such as the secret ballot.[33] The pursuit of constructive, dull, practical social legislation as an antidote to negative sectionalism in the party was Forster's policy, and his good showing in the leadership election of 1875 indicates that it had supporters.[34] The legislation of 1874–76 shows how much support there was for it in the Conservative party too, and how bipartisan were attitudes to the role of the state in social affairs at this time.[35]

As befits someone who was not a major instigator of the centralising or the democratising initiatives of the government, Gladstone has hitherto played a small role in this discussion. Of course, as Prime Minister, he was bound to incur blame from opponents of these initiatives, though it is striking how comparatively unscathed he was by the educational controversy. Perhaps this was because his private willingness to consider the idea that school boards should limit themselves to funding secular education was fairly well known, as were other remarks of his which showed his suspicion of excessive government intervention.[36] None the less, Gladstone was all too conscious of the damage done to the party by these quarrels. This made it important to find a unifying alternative. From 1871 he knew that the best, indeed only, way of restoring vigour to the Liberal cause lay in economy. County franchise reform would divide the party (though he toyed with the idea in 1873). He was not an advocate of a social reform programme. But neither could he attempt the other obvious strategy which might keep the bulk of the party enthusiastic, an anti-clerical policy. If applied to England, this would damage the church schools, and Gladstone was not prepared to do that. He was equally opposed to the sort of anti-clerical policy on the Irish university question that Fawcett was advocating.[37] (This became more and more attractive to Protestant Liberals owing to another continental crisis – the Vatican Council – and the increased publicity given to priestly interference in Irish elections.) So Gladstone had no alternative to economy, especially since between 1871 and 1873 a major concern of his was to win John Bright back to the cabinet in order to pacify the Dissenters. He also felt personally pledged to the economy issue as a result of his 1868 campaign.

But here too Europe cast a long shadow. The conduct of the Franco-Prussian War suggested that Britain did not matter very much in Western European politics. Meanwhile, the war gave Russia the opportunity, in November 1870, to abrogate the Treaty of Paris signed at the end of the Crimean War and to announce that its ships would once again enter the Black Sea. And the European crisis made it important for Britain to settle its quarrels with the United States; the cabinet decided to agree to negotiate a treaty with the USA, conceding that the *Alabama* dispute should be settled by international arbitration. The Black Sea and *Alabama* issues were controversial within the party, damaged the government's standing with the metropolitan press and probably weakened it in the country. But of more concern here is that these events also weakened the cause of economy. In the short term, this was because the anxiety created by the Franco-Prussian War forced the government to ask for a £2 million vote of credit and an extra 20,000 troops in August 1870, in order to give substance to its treaty obligations to defend Belgium from attack by either of the participants. It also led to the expensive decision to abolish purchase in the army and to buy out the officers; the Commons would have been reluctant to sanction such an expense at a more peaceful time. In the medium term, anxieties about threats to Britain's world supremacy, and increased consciousness of continental autocracy, created a climate receptive to invasion stories and other manifestations of insecurity about home defence.[38] The 1868 election had given the advocates of retrenchment the appearance of popular support, but the fears of 1870–71 dissipated it. Thereafter, Gladstone never quite succeeded in regaining the initiative. Defence expenditure grew from £21.5 million in 1869–70 to £23.6 million in 1873–74. The enormous surpluses of the later years of the government were the result of buoyant economic conditions rather than fierce retrenchment.

It is in this context that we should consider the second set of tensions within Liberalism to be discussed in this chapter, that between the movement for economy and the professionalism of central government. In a number of spheres of policy, a style of Liberalism represented by proud expert government servants came to feel threatened by the new principles associated with retrenchment fever, Treasury control and competitive examination. Two examples of this tension are particularly instructive, touching on defence and domestic expenditure respectively. One involved the technical advisers at the Admiralty; the other concerned some of the most respected men in the London artistic and scientific communities. Liberal government under Palmerston and Russell had given these men considerable scope to put their experience at the service of the nation. Russell believed that honour and expertise were the best guarantees of good government. Politicians of character and integrity should be given the freedom to take initiatives around which their followers could rally, and the freedom to appoint to posts in the public service those well suited by temperament and achievement rather than by an abstract, amoral definition of merit. Therefore Russell staunchly opposed entry by competitive examination.[39] The quarrels of 1868–74 were partly about that. But some advocates of competitive examination, such as Lowe, also took the side of the government experts; in opposing franchise extension in 1866, he had warned of the damage that would be done to efficient government by giving too much political weight to ignorance. Indeed Lowe's behaviour was one of the reasons why Gladstone's economy drive after 1871 was only half successful, and why Lowe's stewardship of the Treasury lost Gladstone's confidence by 1873.[40] Instead, Gladstone's ministerial allies in these two cases were, respectively, Hugh Childers (First Lord of the Admiralty) and Acton Ayrton (First Commissioner of Works).

Childers presented himself as the man who would bring rationality and accountability to the Admiralty, in the spirit of Gladstone's election campaign. In a memorandum of January 1869 he announced that 'business methods' would now be applied there. He reformed the decision-making structure in the Admiralty in order to appease the Radicals in parliament who complained that the existing structure of a five-man Admiralty Board made it impossible to assign responsibility for official blunders. The Childers reforms ignored the Board and concentrated power with three people. The First Sea Lord was to take responsibility for all personnel issues and the Controller of the Navy for ships and equipment; both were answerable personally to Childers himself. There were very few meetings; business was conducted by memorandum, and Childers could play his two senior naval advisers off against each other.[41]

The first major test of this system arose out of the continental crisis of 1870. It was necessary to save national face by mounting a great demonstration of British naval strength in home waters. On 4 September 1870, the pride of the British fleet set sail for Gibraltar. No ship received more attention than HMS *Captain*, which was on its maiden voyage and, to quote a subsequent court-martial report, had been 'built in deference to public opinion'.[42] The *Captain* was the result of a seven-year battle between the professionals in the Admiralty on the one hand, and newspaper and economical opinion on the other. It combined heavy turret guns with masts, resulting in an exceptionally low freeboard. *The Times*, Cobden and Childers were among those who had welcomed the new prototype design as economical because of the concentration of heavy firepower which could be rotated flexibly to meet the source of danger. The two leading technical experts on ship design in the Admiralty believed that the *Captain* was too low in the water to be safe. These were the Controller, Sir Spencer Robinson, and the Chief Constructor, Edward Reed, who had designed two higher-sided turret-ships, the *Monarch* and *Devastation*, with which the future was in fact to lie. Robinson and Reed were both Liberals[43] who were highly respected as scientifically minded modernisers within the Admiralty, men who favoured 'applying the superior power of mind and forethought' to the Navy rather than 'mere money and brute force'.[44] But they were forced to consent to the public clamour for the *Captain*. Unfortunately, the doubters were proved right. The ship overturned in a moderate gale in the Bay of Biscay; only 18 of the 499 people on board survived. Among the dead were the ship's designer, and a son of Childers.

Childers was anxious, on Gladstonian principles, to allocate responsibility for the disaster. But, hardly surprisingly in view of his son's death, he could not allocate it to himself, and he rejected the views of the court martial. His reforms had made it easy to direct the blame, so he wrote and published a minute in which Robinson, his Controller, was censured for not advising him strongly enough of the instability of the *Captain*. Robinson was outraged by this and wished to defend himself, and an unedifying squabble followed, for Robinson was not an easy colleague. When his term of office ran out in February 1871, Gladstone refused to renew it, effectively dismissing him. (Childers had by now gone abroad after suffering a nervous breakdown and later resigned his post.) In doing this, Gladstone took the high executive line that Robinson and Reed, who had resigned earlier in 1870, were political appointees and that the government must be allowed total control over their appointments.[45]

The bad news for the Admiralty did not end there. Two more ships ran aground in the summer of 1871, the *Agincourt* and the *Megaera*, the latter during a nine-month voyage to Australia. In each case the court martial blamed the Admiralty rather than the ship's captain. The *Megaera*'s hull was badly corroded and she was so obviously unseaworthy even at the beginning of her journey that a question was asked in the House of Commons about her state when she docked in Ireland, though it was dismissed loftily by the government junior minister. The *Megaera* incident left the public with the impression that the Admiralty was parsimonious and inefficient, incapable of spotting necessary ship repairs.[46] This was blamed partly on the regime of economy and partly on the collapse of the old policy-making board of expert naval men. Earlier in the year, Whigs and Conservatives had joined forces in the Lords and the Commons to make both points, especially the need to professionalise naval administration.[47] As it was, at the height of the panic about the shortcomings of home defence, there was little evidence of grip at the Admiralty, in the absence of the First Lord and of Robinson.

"ALL IN THE DOWNS."

Mr. Bull. "THAT MY *ARMY* SHOULD BREAK DOWN WAS, NO DOUBT, TO BE EXPECTED; BUT—*FOR MY NAVY!!!*—'ZOUNDS! (*plaintively*) I *DID* FONDLY THINK I WAS ALL RIGHT WITH MY *NAVY!*"

10 'All in the Downs', *Punch*, 19 August 1871

When George Goschen was appointed to succeed Childers, the Liberal MP Edward Bouverie pointed out that, like Childers, 'probably he is not able to do much more than distinguish between the stem and the stern of a ship'.[48] It was essential for Goschen to repair the Admiralty's reputation by meeting some of the criticisms about the lack of professional influence; he instituted daily meetings of the senior naval lords in order to improve communication. He also resisted much of the pressure for further naval cuts, pleading an increase of prices, the demands of protecting commerce and anti-slave trade missions, and the state of the public mind.[49] None the less, relations between ministers and their professional servants had been severely tarnished, and the retrenchment policy had lost credit as a result.

The second example of tension concerns a branch of domestic policy, involving a clash between an exuberant populist advocate of Treasury-controlled expenditure reduction, and much of the artistic and scientific establishment of London. Acton Ayrton, Radical MP for Tower Hamlets, was a tireless advocate of economy and of local self-government. He was appointed a junior Treasury minister in 1868, and immediately entered on the Gladstonian project of economy with great gusto. A particular responsibility of his was the superintendence of the unusually large number of public building schemes in London which had been sanctioned over the previous few years. This involved close co-operation with the First Commissioner of Works, and this created a clash of cultures. The First Commissioner was Henry Layard, also a Liberal MP professedly keen on value for money, but of an earlier generation, who wished to build an alliance between government and art in order to improve the minds of the British people.[50] Layard was a quintessential Russellite who believed in the importance of men of vision and honour offering inspiring political leadership in order to raise the cultural standards of the people, and to defeat vulgar and insular philistinism and materialism.[51] British public life would benefit from the state undertaking the increased role played by the states of the continent in elevating the intellect and taste of the people. Layard was excited at the prospect of becoming First Commissioner of Works because it gave him the chance to save London 'from the reproach of being the ugliest capital in the civilized world'.[52] His particular enthusiasm was for a major development of the land cleared by the Thames Embankment project, on which he wanted to place the new Law Courts and the projected Natural History Museum, surrounded by pleasant gardens which would attract working men and lead them naturally to be educated by the exhibits inside. This was widely admired by the architectural establishment, and would certainly have cost a great deal of money. But both schemes fell foul of Ayrton and the Treasury, as well as of the solicitors who preferred the Carey Street site for the Law Courts. Ayrton stirred up parliamentary and public opposition to the aesthetes' lavish architectural plans, leaving Layard with so little room for manoeuvre that he asked to surrender domestic office for a diplomatic post in autumn 1869. Exiled to Madrid, he fulminated about the control of the Treasury and the narrow-minded Radical MPs who ganged up against his plans; the First Commissioner had become little more than 'a clerk in the Treasury'.[53] 'We shall probably ere long come to the same condition as the United States – no man of honourable feeling or of any refinement will go into public life.' Public affairs would be left to men like Ayrton who reflected popular taste.[54] To Layard's annoyance, Gladstone appointed Ayrton to be the new First Commissioner. Ayrton presided over the move of the Natural History Museum to South Kensington, saving over half the £373,000 originally projected, and engaged in a prolonged battle to reduce costs on the cramped Law Courts site, behaving so roughly to the architect, G. E. Street, in forcing him to keep to his original estimate, that Street complained to Lowe, who supported him. Lowe also caused difficulties for Ayrton in his determination to make the Metropolitan Board of Works rather than the government pay for the new area of Thames Embankment south of the Palace of Westminster, and by 1873 the two were not on speaking terms. Ayrton was by now a figure of hatred among aesthetic types, on account of a series of disputes with artists in which he usually had the upper hand. He dismissed Edward Barry as consulting architect to the Houses of Parliament, a job that Barry seems to have believed was in his family's gift but that Ayrton, reasonably enough, treated as a terminable Treasury contract.[55] Layard predicted the triumph of 'monotonous vulgar Office of Works architecture'.[56]

Ayrton entered into a very similar struggle in another realm of his operations as First Commissioner, this time with the gentlemen of science, the leaders of the scientific lobby. The bone of contention was Kew Gardens. Ayrton expected to have oversight of the expenditure of the gardens. He believed that the director of Kew, Joseph Hooker, was an extravagant man who, having inherited the directorship from his father, regarded Kew as a family fiefdom. Ayrton thought that some of Kew's research functions could be transferred to the new Natural History Museum. But the causes of dispute between them were pettier than that: the Treasury objected to the cost of new heated plant houses, and also interfered with the appointment of an office clerk, insisting that the post should be filled by competitive examination. An under-gardener got the job, despite admitting that he was not suitable for the duties in question, and Hooker refused to train him. Angry at these challenges to his authority, Hooker rallied his scientific friends in the Commons, and complained also to Russell, who was a long-standing friend of Kew (he had been instrumental in getting the state to take over management of it in 1841 and the leading influence in appointing both Hooker's father and Hooker as directors). Lowe, a friend of science, also gave Hooker tacit support. Hooker demanded not only an apology from Ayrton for his behaviour but also security – 'I want to have the position of Director of Kew recognised as one of authority, trust, and responsibility: given a status, in short that cannot be attacked by an Ayrton.'[57] One of Hooker's parliamentary supporters said that he had been treated like an under-gardener, not like a gentleman.[58] The Whiggish intelligentsia found petty-bourgeois assertiveness difficult to bear. The metropolitan press gave a great deal of coverage and support to Hooker, but Ayrton was protected by Gladstone and was never asked to apologise.[59]

The press coverage of these incidents indicated the continuing political influence of a vocal group of literary people in the London clubs and salons. This group played a significant part in the general criticism of the government that developed during the early 1870s. Indeed, on the whole, the metropolitan press never recovered its enthusiasm for Gladstonian Liberalism thereafter, as Gladstone himself was well aware.[60] By 1873, the government could be assailed on a number of grounds, and one small episode, slight in itself, shows how metropolitan critics could make fun of it. On 3 March 1873, there opened at the Royal Court Theatre a burlesque written by the *Punch* writer Gilbert A'Beckett and a respected young playwright hiding behind the exotic pseudonym of F. Latour Tomline: W. S. Gilbert. The burlesque was called *The Happy Land*. On 6 March it was visited by the Lord

Chamberlain. On 7 March he prohibited further performances.[61] What was so shocking about this play? It was set in fairyland, and the fairies were in need of guidance about how to run their land. So, hearing that England was uniquely blessed by a system of popular government, they decided to ask for three representatives of that system to visit them. There appeared Mr G, Mr L and Mr A. The fairies were slowly but terribly disabused of their enthusiasm for popular principles. Mr A told them to paint all their public buildings slate-colour because it did not show the dirt, and that if they wanted to be trained in the right mode of government it must be by competitive examination. Mr L told them that their principles of foreign policy were to save halfpence here and halfpence there and, 'when we get hit, we don't hit back again'. Mr G told them that, when their country had to 'submit to an unparalleled series of humiliations in the eyes of surrounding nations', the best response was to appoint a First Lord of the Admiralty who knew nothing about ships. The fairies, carrying out the advice of the three men, found that their whole fleet had run aground, despite putting a retired solicitor in command.[62] The fairies concluded that popular government was a sham, and that popular ministers did no good to anyone, clung desperately on to place, sent everybody to bed at seven o'clock by act of parliament and betrayed the principles of patriotism. Having despatched Mr G, Mr L and Mr A back whence they came, the fairies end by singing, 'Poor Britannia, Although she rules the waves, Britons ever, ever, ever shall be slaves'.[63]

The cry of economy, apparently so powerful in 1868, waned in force in the early 1870s. Overall expenditure rose from £67.1 million in 1869–70 to £74.6 million in 1873–74. Cabinet support for retrenchment was lukewarm, especially with Childers and Bright marginalised.[64] Chancellor Lowe was relatively friendly to public health and education expenditure, and was an advocate of a strong navy and of the retention of the income tax as a great engine of finance. (His rebarbative and flippant public image, however, ensured that he received no credit for this.) The War and Colonial Offices also did their best to resist the Prime Minister; Gladstone complained that he could not interfere in the decision to send a military expedition to the Gold Coast in 1873 because the War Office would not let him know the facts.[65] In November 1872 Gladstone admitted to Goschen that for the past two years he had 'given in considerably to the wish of the Cabinet' about expenditure.[66] Though he forced Cardwell to make army cuts in 1872–73, in the following winter he could not get the defence departments to give him the £1 million extra that he needed for his proposed initiative of abolishing the income tax. This drove him to dissolve parliament in January 1874 and to make a doomed appeal to the electorate over the heads of the spending departments for abolition.[67] Relatively good economic conditions made it more difficult to excite voters about abolition. The local taxation quarrel, the difficulties over art and science, and activity by other pressure groups illustrate the large number of lobbies that were now asking for extra expenditure. Indeed, it was for that reason that Gladstone was so anxious to abolish the income tax, the source of temptation for popularity-seeking governments.[68]

The upshot was that the government ran out of steam on the policy on which Gladstone most hoped that the party could be united – after it had lost its enthusiasm for his other crusade, on Ireland, and had revealed deep divisions on the other Liberal ideals of interventionist legislation and the extension of democracy. It is noteworthy that one factor in the failure of all these ideas was the international tension of 1870–71, from which different groups of Liberals could draw very different conclusions and, according to taste, advocate more defence or domestic spending, less government activity, or a celebration of British Protestant national identity. For a series of reasons, of which this was merely one, the travails that beset the government came upon it in a rush in the spring of 1871. There were embarrassments over the 1871 budget, which stemmed from the need to find money for military spending, and which damaged the Liberals' reputation for financial competence stretching back to the 1840s.[69] There was disquiet at harassing licensing, local government and army legislation. There were grass-roots agitations against 'autocratic' measures concerning education, open spaces and contagious diseases. There were fears expressed by propertied Liberals that such agitations set the tone for the new democratic politics. There were suggestions that the government itself was willing to pander to popular economising pressure rather than to pursue rational administration, for example in defence. There was regret at the apparent unwillingness of the Catholic Irish to accept the boons of 1869–70. And there was anger at Gladstone's perceived inability to maintain British interests vis-à-vis Russia and the United States in the shape that Palmerston had left them. Hardly any of these problems went away thereafter, and discipline in the Commons became very difficult; two parliamentary diarists both believed that Gladstone had lost his hold on the Commons by the end of the 1871 session.[70] The government held on for two and a half years from that point, but with less and less authority. It lost an unprecedented 20 by-elections between 1871 and 1874. The situation was like the 1830s, when the power-base of Melbourne's government also collapsed, yet it retained so much residual advantage over the opposition, as a result of the Reform Act, that it was to almost no one's advantage to unseat it.

But it would be unfair to end on this note. The Gladstone government had an almost impossible task in reconciling a great diversity of expectations. That diversity ensured that Gladstone was merely one among many influences on policy. It is arguable that he learned from this, and that by the time of his return to power in 1880 he had, through his mastery of the media, found a way of achieving greater control over party, parliament and sectional legislative enthusiasms. By subordinating demands for legislation to a strategy of personalising politics around his projected values, he did much to discipline Liberal exuberance. It is worth reflecting that this was a reversion to a previous Liberal leader's approach, adapted to different circumstances and exploiting different values. Palmerston would have been highly amused.

Notes

1 B. Harrison, *Drink and the Victorians: The Temperance Question in England 1815–1872*, London, Faber & Faber, 1971, p. 263; J. P. Parry, *Democracy and Religion: Gladstone and the Liberal Party, 1867–1875*, Cambridge, Cambridge UP, 1986, pp. 166–67.

2 J. Parry, 'Past and Future in the Later Career of Lord John Russell', in *History and Biography: Essays in Honour of Derek Beales*, ed. T. C. W. Blanning and D. Cannadine, Cambridge, Cambridge UP, 1996, p. 150.

3 For their support for sanitary measures, see R. Lambert, *Sir John Simon, 1816–1904, and English Social Administration*, London, Macgibbon & Kee, 1963, pp. 412–13.

4 J. Parry, *The Rise and Fall of Liberal Government in Victorian Britain*, New Haven, Connecticut, Yale UP, 1993, pp. 229–30.

5 See Harrison (1971), pp. 281–84.

6 Lambert (1963), pp. 325–28, 413–14, 450–52.

7 See D. W. Sylvester, *Robert Lowe and Education*, Cambridge, Cambridge UP, 1974, pp. 154–61.

8 See Gladstone, e.g. at Liverpool, *The Times*, 15 October 1868, p. 7.

9 Ibid, and at Garston, *The Times*, 16 November 1868, p. 5. For Bright's influence on Gladstone, see B. Kinzer, *The Ballot Question in Nineteenth-Century English Politics*, New York, Garland, 1982, p. 101.

10 Gladstone at Southport, *The Times*, 22 October 1868, p. 6, and at Wavertree, *The Times*, 16 November 1868, p. 5.

11 E. D. Steele, *Irish Land and British Politics: Tenant Right and Nationality, 1865–1870*, Cambridge, Cambridge UP, 1974.

12 Parry, *Democracy and Religion* (1986), pp. 343–68.

13 At Leigh, *The Times*, 21 October 1868, p. 8.

14 In his Blackheath speech of 1871: *Gladstone's Speeches: Descriptive Index and Bibliography*, ed. A. T. Bassett, London, Methuen, 1916, p. 408.

15 Parry, *Democracy and Religion* (1986), p. 337.

16 Ibid, pp. 310, 380; *Hansard's Parliamentary Debates*, 3rd series, vol. 216, col. 74, 19 May 1873.

17 Harrison (1971), pp. 262–96.

18 *Hansard*, vol. 204, col. 1076, 28 February 1871.

19 To Gavan Duffy, 19 April 1872, in S. Childers, *The Life and Correspondence of the Right Hon. Hugh C. E. Childers, 1827–1896*, London, John Murray, 1901, vol. 1, p. 209.

20 *Hansard*, vol. 210, col. 1404, 16 April 1872.

21 See e.g. Arthur Hobhouse's view: Parry, *Democracy and Religion* (1986), p. 311.

22 See ibid., p. 321.

23 Cardwell to Gladstone, 12 April, 19 April 1872, GP 44120, ff. 21, 23. See Kinzer (1982), pp. 207–10.

24 *Hansard*, vol. 208, col. 1387, 1417, 1658, 10 August, 15 August 1871 (Torrens, Harcourt, Fawcett).

25 A. G. Gardiner, *The Life of Sir William Harcourt*, London, Constable, 1923, vol. 1, p. 240.

26 Harrison (1971), pp. 267, 276.

27 Parry (1993), p. 235.

28 Gardiner (1923), vol. 1, pp. 236–39.

29 J. L. and B. Hammond, *James Stansfeld: A Victorian Champion of Sex Equality*, London, Longmans, 1932, pp. 118–81.

30 I hope to write at greater length on this subject. See the many articles appearing in the periodical press between autumn 1871 and summer 1872 about the lessons of continental events.

31 G. Petrie, *A Singular Iniquity: The Campaigns of Josephine Butler*, London, Macmillan, 1971, pp. 127–28.

32 See e.g. W.M. Torrens, 'Localism and Centralism', *Contemporary Review*, Vol. 17, June 1871, pp. 399–413.

33 T. A. Jenkins (ed.), 'The Parliamentary Diaries of Sir John Trelawny, 1868–73', *Camden Miscellany*, vol. 32, 1994, p. 456, 8 April 1872.

34 Parry, *Democracy and Religion* (1986), pp. 112–16; P. Jackson, *Education Act Forster: a Political Biography of W. E. Forster (1818–1886)*, Madison, New Jersey, Fairleigh Dickinson UP, 1997, chap. 10.

35 P. Smith, *Disraelian Conservatism and Social Reform*, London, Routledge, 1967.

36 See e.g. his remarks at Blackheath in October 1871, in Bassett (1916), p. 423; his letters to Bright about education, 25 November 1871 and 27 January 1874, in *GD*, vol. 8, pp. 67–69, 449–50; and his talk with Josephine Butler in December 1872, in Hammond (1932), p. 180.

37 Parry, *Democracy and Religion* (1986), pp. 343–51.

38 I. F. Clarke, *Voices Prophesying War, 1763–1984*, London, Oxford UP, 1966, pp. 30–44.

39 In 1870 Bruce arranged for the Home Office to be exempt from the competitive examinations on the ground that 'great trustworthiness' was needed in senior civil servants there: M. Wright, *Treasury Control of the Civil Service, 1854–1874*, Oxford, Clarendon Press, 1969, p. 83.

40 Parry (1993), p. 269.

41 N. A. M. Rodger, 'The Dark Ages of the Admiralty, 1869–85: Part I, "Business methods", 1869–74', *Mariner's Mirror*, Vol. 61, 1975, pp. 334–38.

42 S. Sandler, '"In Deference to Public Opinion": the Loss of HMS *Captain*', *Mariner's Mirror*, Vol. 59, 1973, p. 64. Sandler and Rodger (1975) provide the necessary background to this and the next paragraph.

43 They both stood in by-elections as Liberal candidates after their resignations.

44 E. J. Reed, *Our Naval Coast Defences*, London, John Murray, 1871, p. 23.

45 *Hansard*, vol. 205, col. 1320, 18 April 1871.

46 N. McCord, 'A Naval Scandal of 1871: The Loss of HMS *Megaera*', *Mariner's Mirror*, Vol. 57, 1971, pp. 115–34.

47 *Hansard*, vol. 204, col. 295, 16 February 1871, and vol. 205, col. 1280, 18 April 1871.

48 Ibid., col. 1319.

49 See Rodger (1975), pp. 340–42, and A. R. D. Elliot, *The Life of George Joachim*

Goschen, First Viscount Goschen, 1831–1907, London, Longmans, 1911, vol. 1, pp. 115–18.

50 See his lecture on Pompeii, *The Times*, 10 November 1869, p. 8.

51 Parry, (1996).

52 *The Times*, 10 November 1869, p. 8.

53 M. H. Port, 'A Contrast in Styles at the Office of Works; Layard and Ayrton; Aesthete and Economist', *Historical Journal*, Vol. 27, 1984, p. 161.

54 Layard to Gregory, 29 July 1870, 21 February 1871, Layard Papers, British Library, Add MSS 38949, ff. 59, 83.

55 Ayrton was even supported by *The Times*, 28 June 1871, p. 9.

56 Layard to Gregory, 6 April 1870, Layard Papers, 38949, f. 31. For this whole paragraph, see Port (1984).

57 R. M. Macleod, 'The Ayrton Incident: A Commentary on the Relations of Science and Government in England, 1870–1873', in *Science and Values: Patterns of Tradition and Change*, ed. A. Thackray and E. Mendelsohn, New York, Humanities Press, 1974, p. 60.

58 Cowper-Temple in *Hansard*, vol. 213, col. 757, 8 August 1872.

59 For this whole paragraph, see Macleod (1974); *Hansard*, vol. 213, col. 709, 8 August 1872.

60 One of Gladstone's first public criticisms of the bias of the London press came in his speech at Whitby in September 1871, just after a famous by-election defeat in East Surrey. See Parry, *Democracy and Religion* (1986), pp. 322–23.

61 The problem was that the text was much more politically pointed than that which the Lord Chamberlain had approved; the more pointed version would presumably not have been approved in the first place.

62 Devotees of *HMS Pinafore* (1878) will recognise here the prototype of Sir Joseph Porter, KCB, who rose to be First Lord by sticking to his desk and never going to sea. It is arguable that Porter was modelled on Childers much more than on the First Lord of 1878, W. H. Smith.

63 F. Tomline and G. A'Beckett, *The Happy Land: A Burlesque Version of 'The Wicked World'*, London, J. W. Last, 1873.

64 Childers left the cabinet in March 1871 and returned from August 1872 to September 1873, to be replaced by Bright, who had resigned with effect from January 1871.

65 H. C. G. Matthew, *Gladstone 1809–1874*, Oxford, Clarendon Press, 1986, p. 190.

66 [9 November 1872,] *GD*, vol. 8, p. 234.

67 W. H. Maehl, 'Gladstone, the Liberals and the Election of 1874', *Bulletin of the Institute of Historical Research*, Vol. 36, 1963, pp. 53–69.

68 Matthew (1986), p. 222.

69 After great protests, the government had to withdraw its proposals for a match tax and increased succession duties, and to raise the income tax by 2d instead.

70 Jenkins, 'The Parliamentary Diaries of Sir John Trelawny' (1994), p. 435; *A Selection from the Diaries of Edward Henry Stanley, 15th Earl of Derby (1826–93) between September 1869 and March 1878*, ed. J. Vincent, London, Royal Historical Society, 1994, p. 88.

Gladstone and Cobden

Anthony Howe

11 Richard Cobden, c. 1865

IN his dotage, Gladstone writing to James Bryce described himself as 'a dead man, one fundamentally a Peel–Cobden man'.[1] In doing so he was not simply lamenting the passing of the mid-century order of free trade, peace and stability but paying tribute to two very different statesmen who had exerted a decisive influence on the shaping of his political outlook and his major legislative achievements, especially with regard to finance and free trade. Sir Robert Peel's influence was undoubtedly the more immediate and personal, and he remained late into Gladstone's life a favourite topic of conversation. Peel was, for Mr G, a 'perfect God', his former private secretary Sir Edward Hamilton recorded, to whom Gladstone 'always refers with the greatest possible admiration and respect'.[2] In recent years there have been many insights into this 'Peelite' element in Gladstone's makeup, as Professor Evans's chapter in this volume well shows.[3] The 'Cobdenite' element has been less extensively analysed. On the one hand, John Vincent has stoutly denied that Cobden exerted any influence on Gladstone, concluding that 'Gladstone dismantled what Cobden had built'; on the other, following in the wake of W. E. Williams's older study, Edsall, Matthew and Searle have offered more positive assessments.[4] This chapter sets out to rectify this overall imbalance by outlining in some detail the 'Cobdenite' component in Gladstone's self-proclaimed ideological 'corpse', suggesting that in many ways his later career revealed the lasting and decisive impact made by Cobden's precepts and example.

That Gladstone would have described himself as in any sense a Cobdenite would probably have come as a surprise to Cobden himself. For even shortly after the time when they had closely co-operated over the Anglo-French commercial treaty in 1860, Cobden wrote to Gladstone in January 1862, 'We stand on such different grounds, & our careers of action in public life must ever be so separate, that I sometimes think it hardly fair to try to take a common view with you into the future'.[5] By contrast, Gladstone recorded in retrospect that at the time of the Anglo-French treaty 'my union of sentiment with him [Cobden] on this and I think most other subjects was complete'.[6] Certainly over the next 30 years that unity of sentiment was abundantly displayed, such that there can be little doubt as to the suitability of Gladstone's description of himself as 'a Peel–Cobden man'. There is also much truth in Gladstone's assessment that by the mid-1890s 'Peel–Cobden' men were defunct, the dinosaurs of a lost generation. In so regarding the Cobdenite world-view as steeply in decline, Gladstone reflected a common contemporary opinion. Thus, when the jubilee of the repeal of the Corn Laws was celebrated in 1896, formerly loyal members of the Manchester School, such as Goldwin Smith, lamented its seemingly irreversible decline while critics, from right as well as left, enthusiastically pronounced the 'death of Cobdenism'.[7] Gladstone himself on receiving a copy of the printed proceedings of the jubilee commended their seemingly quixotic publisher, Thomas Fisher Unwin, the husband of Cobden's daughter Jane, for what Gladstone hailed as 'an act of great gallantry, for the Cobdenian faith is in all points at a heavy discount – Peace, Retrenchment, Free Trade and all the rest of it, to my great grief I must confess'.[8] Gladstone's grief and sense of isolation as one of the 'Cobdenian faith' had itself been painfully exposed on his resignation from office only two years earlier. For in January 1894, in preparing to resign in protest over 'swollen expenditure' on armaments, Gladstone had affirmed his consistency since the 1840s as a 'Peel–Cobden man' in what Colin Matthew has described as 'a memorandum remarkable in the annals of British radical writing'. He would not, he wrote, 'break to pieces the continuous action of my political life, nor trample on the tradition received from every colleague who has ever been my teacher'.[9] Gladstone classed Peel among the critics of excessive military establishments but far more decisively, as we shall see, Gladstone's growing 'union of sentiment' with Cobden had been based on their common opposition to military expenditure during the Palmerston government of 1859–65.[10] This link between economy and hostility to militarism had been at the heart of the morality of free trade which, in varying degrees, Peel, Gladstone and Cobden had consistently espoused. For, as Morley noted, the Conservative party in the 1840s had been 'the economic party' with 'Peel its leader being a Cobdenite'.[11] Above all, for Gladstone, the 'Peel–Cobden man', this intertwining of economy and opposition to armaments provided the crucial lifelong secular belief which lent unity to his career in domestic politics as well as to his European stature, as 'a symbol of the policy of peace, moderation, and non-aggression'.[12]

But if Gladstone ended his career as a 'Cobden man', at the start of that career he had been, far more than Peel himself, a bitter critic of Cobden. This was in part through accident of family circumstance, for on the occasion of his brother's becoming the first parliamentary candidate opposed by the Anti-Corn Law League at Walsall in a by-election in 1841 the young Gladstone found himself inveighing, in the sort of language Disraeli would use in 1846, against the unconstitutional proceedings of the League.[13] He later recounted, if not quite recanted, 'an impertinent letter to him who was afterwards my master'.[14] However, such recognition of Cobden's overarching contribution to free trade was extremely gradual, despite some evidence that Gladstone soon more generously appreciated Cobden's political abilities. But for the most part, by virtue of office at the Board of Trade, Gladstone found himself put up in the house to oppose Cobden, and to defend the Corn Laws as he did sometimes rather unconvincingly.[15] More fundamentally, Gladstone strongly dissented from Peel's famous praise of Cobden for his part in the repeal of the Corn Laws. For while he admitted Cobden's 'power of discussion great and his end good', he found his tone 'harsh and his imputation of bad and vile motives to honourable men incessant'.[16] Gladstone's own ideas and policies on free trade in this period owed little to Cobden directly, however much they coincided in practice. For example, Hirst in 1931

reported the view of Sir Thomas Farrer, himself one of the most economically orthodox of civil servants, that 'Even when the Corn Laws were about
to be repealed, he [Gladstone] did not, I think, take the broad views of
Cobden and the Free Traders.'[17] Rather than recognising Cobden as his
master, Gladstone was still very much in the 1840s the pupil of Peel, with
the leading principles of his budgetary strategy derived from Peelite practice.[18] It should also be remembered that Gladstone entered office at the
Board of Trade with a relative innocence of political economy. It was only
in 1841 that he read *The Wealth of Nations* and he seems never to have read
other fundamental works such as Ricardo's *Political Economy*.[19] As a result,
Gladstone approached the issue of free trade largely from the technical angle
seen in his Board of Trade memoranda.[20] But perhaps more importantly,
as Hilton has shown, Gladstone's ideological approach to economic policy
in these years owed far more to his religious worldview derived from Bishop
Butler than to the precepts of political economy itself. In the 1840s, Gladstone was in fact far more reluctant than Peel to move beyond the politics
of atonement in order to embrace Cobden's more secular, optimistic and cosmopolitan model of free trade.[21] If we leave aside Morley's incidental and
perhaps exaggerated claim that Peel himself was already a 'Cobdenite', it
seems clear that well into the 1850s Gladstone's approach to free trade was
primarily governed by his Peelite budgetary principles.

At this stage, too, there was no direct rapprochement between Gladstone
and the Manchester School. For however much his policy may have been
informed by his links with his brother Robertson's involvement with the Liverpool Financial Reform Association, Gladstone remained critical of Cobden's
fiscal policy as outlined in his famous 'National Budget'.[22] It is also indicative
of their mutual distance that when Gladstone, like most eminent Victorians,
did pay his ritual obeisance to the power of industrial Manchester, visiting it
in 1853 to unveil a statue of Peel, the members of the 'Manchester School'
were conspicuous by their absence from what was far more of a 'civic' (this
was Manchester's first public statue) than a 'free trade' celebration.[23] But
Gladstone's speech on this occasion foreshadowed his later approach to free
trade in three important ways. First, in perhaps an *amende honorable* for his
'impertinent letter' of 1840, he now acknowledged the 'advanced intelligence' which Manchester represented, 'and the prominent part which that
intelligence has enabled Manchester to bear in influencing in particular
during recent years, the fortunes and the destinies of this country'. Second,
Gladstone commended the tendency to settle questions by international
negotiation, 'towards the substitution of arbitration for war', a significant
nod towards the cause to which Cobden himself had been primarily devoted
since repeal, and which on the very day Gladstone spoke in Manchester,
Cobden was supporting at the Peace Conference in Edinburgh.[24] Third, Gladstone affirmed that the principles of Britain's financial and commercial legislation, on which 'argument and statement alike are needless', had proved not

only beneficial to Britain but provided advantages for the world as a whole. The overriding moral benefit of free trade was proclaimed by Gladstone to lie in 'rendering the relative attitudes of nations more peaceful from the opening up of channels of commerce, bringing about a more constant intercourse, and thus tending to abate the rivalries that have divided and estranged the countries of Christendom from one another'. This speech announced in a sense Gladstone's progression from the budgetary principles of Peel towards the international vision of free trade, peace and arbitration that Cobden had promoted since 1846.[25]

As the Crimean War unfolded, Gladstone's linkage between commerce and peace proved unfortunate in its timing, but the creed he outlined here provided over the next four years the basis for his decisive realignment with the Manchester School. For although Gladstone initially at least supported the justice of Britain's cause in the Crimea, that war also sharpened his sense that the potential benefits of free trade in terms of the social and moral union of nations had been jeopardised. Gladstone's own increasing dislike for British policy towards the Crimean War now pulled him towards Cobden as the most articulate and principled opponent of that war. They were therefore increasingly aligned in debate in the House of Commons (the members of the Manchester School even ceded their usual seats in the Commons to Gladstone and his allies in 1855), although not all Cobden's suspicions of Gladstone as 'a reasoning machine for the moment, with his moral sense put in abeyance' had yet been removed.[26] At this stage too, neither Gladstone nor Cobden discerned any clear instruments by which free trade and peace were to be linked. As a peacetime Chancellor, Gladstone was ready to operate on the causes of war-fever through fiscal means, but he was not yet a recruit to a belief in commercial treaties as the appropriate 'peace bonds' between nations. This in turn reflected the earlier vital change in Gladstone's economic beliefs when at the Board of Trade in the 1840s. For Gladstone had then abandoned the liberal Tory belief in reciprocity treaties, seen as fruitless and unnecessary entanglements in the exigencies of foreign states, in favour of the brand of unilateral free trade favoured by Peel and Cobden but which Gladstone himself now supported only at the cost of a painful rift with his Huskissonite father.[27] After 1846, like Peel, Cobden, and the Whigs, Gladstone put his faith simply in the power of the British example of free trade to draw other nations in its wake. Thus his 1853 budget had included certain items designed specifically to appeal to Prussia, although Gladstone at this stage felt no need to go beyond 'non-diplomatic free trade'.[28] But in the late 1850s what drew Cobden and Gladstone closely together for the first time was not so much the promotion of free trade as their joint opposition to Palmerston over the *Arrow* incident in China in 1857. In condemning this episode of 'gunboat diplomacy', they shared a powerful distaste for high-handed executive actions against weaker nations in pursuit of morally questionable goals. It was during these famous foreign policy debates that

Cobden and Gladstone became regular correspondents and lasting allies.[29] Hence it was when Gladstone re-entered office in 1859 (Cobden refused Palmerston's offer, which Gladstone had encouraged, of the Board of Trade) that Cobden's influence (or 'mastery') over Gladstonian policy was to be first felt. But it was felt less in terms of financial policy than in terms of international relations. For on Gladstone's return to office, the scope for Cobden's impact was enlarged by Gladstone's own sense of change since the 1840s. Comparing 1859 with the days of Peel, Gladstone was now keenly impressed by the scale of Britain's international responsibilities, 'the increasing complexity of the relations & obligations we multiply abroad'.[30] But it was the particular form those responsibilities took with regard to the peace of Europe that opened the way for what in some ways was the chief piece of constructive legislation of Gladstone's career, the Anglo-French commercial treaty of 1860. For this treaty not only marked the culmination of Peelite–Gladstonian budgetary policy since 1842 but now tied its operation into a European diplomatic structure designed to consolidate the Anglo-French entente cordiale as the essential basis of peace in Europe.[31] In the ripening of this international vision, the impact of Cobden was now strong, for it was during their garden stroll in the grounds of Hawarden in September 1859 that Gladstone became an enthusiastic convert to the idea of an Anglo-French commercial treaty.[32] Moreover, given the indifference of some and hostility of other members of the cabinet to the idea of a commercial treaty with France, it was largely through Gladstone's pertinacious support that the Cobden–Chevalier treaty was signed and completed through a tortuous process in 1860.[33]

In view of Gladstone's earlier distaste for treaties this bouleversement requires some explanation. This Gladstone himself provided in terms of the danger of war between England and France in the context of the Italian question and invasion scare of 1859–60.[34] But it was combined with the huge possibilities which opened up in his fertile mind through the combination of a treaty with France and a new budgetary instalment of free trade. Yet, as he explained to Acton, the budget of 1860 grew out of the treaty, rather than the treaty out of the budget.[35] But it seems above all to have been the prospect of war with France in the wake of the annexation of Nice and Savoy which encouraged Gladstone now to abandon his previously adamant hostility to commercial treaties whose negotiation in the 1840s he had found 'profitless' and 'false in principle'. Gladstone's reasoning here is not fully convincing, for the panic over Nice and Savoy grew in intensity only in the period February–March 1860, well after the treaty was under way. Even so, the treaty undoubtedly grew in attractiveness in the minds of both Cobden and Gladstone as 'the only sedation' for panic. It was, Gladstone wrote, a 'counter-irritant; and it aroused the sense of commercial interest to counteract the war passion. It was, and is my opinion that the choice lay between the Cobden treaty and, not the certainty but the high probability, of a war with France.'[36]

The details of the treaty are well known and need not detain us, but two important consequences stemmed from the treaty beyond the budgetary sphere.[37] First, Gladstone embraced the wider Cobdenite (and Napoleonic) project whereby a series of interlocking commercial treaties between the European states could become the bastion of a new international order in which military power would be constrained by budgetary stringency. Commercial treaties themselves promised a reinvigoration by new means of the public law between nations but at the same time implied the reordering of states domestically in a way that encouraged peace. This was perhaps best seen in Gladstone's approach to the new Italy, where he strongly urged that only a liberal tariff would promote domestic harmony, wealth and power, while gaining the friendship of foreign nations.[38] Gladstone retained strong doubts as to how far Britain should intervene domestically in the affairs of other states, but as late as 1866 he was prepared to offer fiscal inducements to Austria as a means of accelerating her inclusion in a common European economic whole.[39] Britain's pursuit of commercial treaties between 1860 and 1866 was not perhaps quite, as Metzler has argued, the creation of an 'entente commerciale' by which Britain would economically dominate Europe, but it was a rare interlude in which trade did briefly dominate the practice even of aristocratic diplomacy.[40] Interestingly, Gladstone himself, sometimes suspicious of the diplomatic profession as morally dangerous, found many redeeming features in Cobdenite diplomacy.[41]

Second, Gladstone's co-operation with Cobden over the 1860 treaty led to an intense, if short, political alliance, which helped shape in fundamental ways Gladstone's subsequent Liberal politics. Ideologically, Gladstone shared Cobden's deep antagonism to many aspects of Palmerstonian diplomacy, but crucially he grew in sympathy with Cobden's analysis of war scares and the inflated public demands for military expenditure. In what Morley and Hirst characterised as Gladstone's 'battle for economy', Cobden's mark was writ deep, with Gladstone gradually conceding Cobden's case that in terms of military expenditure, 'we are the leaders, and the French the followers'.[42] Not only did he seek (in vain) Cobden's official assistance as chairman of the Board of Audit, but more influentially he read 'with feelings of painful interest, the humiliating narrative which you have given to the world in your *Three Panics*'.[43] This was the influential pamphlet of 1862 in which Cobden had indicted the irrationality of military expenditure dictated by public 'scares' rather than controlled by wise and economical administration, itself grounded in mutual trust and negotiation. Gladstone's apparent public support for Cobden's views led to a brief spat with Palmerston, but Gladstone by no means accepted all of Cobden's conclusions.[44] He was, far more than Cobden, prepared to accept the popular origins of the demand for war expenditure, and after his own successful paring of the British estimates, believed by 1863 that the onus for reduction had passed to France.[45] Even so, at home, Gladstone now identified as the problem for the future how to restrain 'the spirit of expenditure', a spirit he believed was unleashed by income tax, 'the bottom-less purse into which everyone may dip and take out what he pleases'.[46] But Gladstone also derived from his Cobdenite tutoring in the early 1860s a grow-ing suspicion of the court and services as the originators of demands for expenditure, and a growing appreciation of the forces which would vastly increase the spectre of European militarism in the coming generation.

Politically, Gladstone's 'union of sentiment' with Cobden represented a delayed fulfilment of Cobden's own vision, following the repeal of the Corn Laws in 1846, of a Liberal–Peelite convergence based on broad middle-class support; as Morley put it, '[I]n substance it [Cobden's scheme] was destined to be partially realized one day, not by Peel, but by the most powerful and brilliant of his lieutenants.'[47] More widely defined, this ideological alliance also now informed Gladstone's ambition that the Liberal party should become the instrument by which to revive the old Peelite spirit of economy and retrenchment, the spirit in which Gladstone, as Colin Matthew has demonstrated, approached the question of parliamentary reform, and which, as Biagini has shown, in many ways dominated the ministry of 1868–74, with its culmination in the attempt to abolish income tax.[48] At the same time, Gladstone's role in the treaty negotiations removed most of Cobden and Bright's suspicions of Gladstone. Cobden now recognised 'the democracy of the Chancellor of the Exchequer – for the latter is at heart a democrat of the purest type! I mean in his desire to serve the interests of the millions & not of a class.'[49]

The political friendship between Cobden and Gladstone proved short-lived with Cobden's death occurring in April 1865. Yet not only had its sincerity and impact helped lastingly to define Gladstone's subsequent career but also it had left to the Liberal party a considerable political legacy. Gladstone him-self of course had already done much to cement his alliance with the bour-geoisie, partly through his advocacy of free trade. In his provincial speeches, as at Newcastle and Leith in the early 1860s, free trade and Cobden's contribution had formed a staple element.[50] But following Cobden's death, Gladstone in many ways proved to have the keenest appreciation of Cobden's political message. He thus confided to his diary on the day of Cobden's funeral – Gladstone had been a pall-bearer – 'Cobden's name is great and will be greater' and famously to his brother 'ever since I really came to know him I have held him in high esteem ... till he died I did not know how high it was'.[51] After Cobden's death, Gladstone was a ready con-fidant for Mrs Cobden, who believed 'no other public man in England misses my husband from his side so much as yourself'. Gladstone also acted (with Chevalier) as Mrs Cobden's literary executor, approving in 1878 the appointment of John Morley as Cobden's biographer.[52]

Significantly too Gladstone readily identified himself in 1866 with the Cobden Club set up by the somewhat vainglorious but 'true-hearted' Thomas Bayley Potter, Cobden's successor as MP for Rochdale.[53] After 1865,

Potter set himself the task of keeping Cobden's ideas alive through the Cobden Club, the public face of the Manchester School embodied in political dinners, speeches and a vast propaganda machine. This was a work of commemoration in which Gladstone readily played his part, speaking not only at the inaugural dinner in 1866 but also in 1870 – at the time of the Franco-Prussian War – when he affirmed England's free trade vocation as a 'special design of Providence'.[54] Gladstone also took an interest in the club's publications, especially on land reform, and the club in turn published several of his ephemeral speeches in the form of leaflets designed to appeal to agricultural labourers. Gladstone's addresses on cottage gardening to the residents of Hawarden became a particular favourite, one of which Potter thought Cobden himself would have warmly approved.[55] Gladstone's readiness to associate himself with the club reflected his esteem for the permanence of Cobden's political message and the club's value as a 'fountainhead of pure doctrine'. But it also paid a handsome political dividend in terms of binding an important group of MPs to Gladstone's leadership of the Liberal party. In addition, it brought to the party the valuable electoral work of the Cobden Club in the election of 1880 and especially among the new rural electorate in 1885. Gladstone himself, increasingly distrustful of the selfish propensities of the urban electorate, saw in the agricultural labourers a useful bastion against a return to protection.[56] However simplistic the club's message of 'free trade, peace, and goodwill', it was one which Gladstone permanently embraced. For as he wrote to Potter, the main ideas of Cobden 'attach themselves directly to the common interests of mankind. They are entitled to universal acceptance.'[57]

But to what extent can such Cobdenite watchwords, 'entitled to universal acceptance', be held to have influenced practically Gladstone's own later career? Here the record is more complex and must now be traced in the three fields in which Cobden's impact on Gladstone had been greatest, those of commercial diplomacy, the defence of free trade, and the control of military expenditure. The practice of Cobdenite diplomacy – the period of 'Gladstone–Cobdenism' to use the critical term of Lord Overstone – had been defined by the making of commercial treaties in the early 1860s. But such treaty-making came under strong internal and external pressures after the Austro-Prussian War of 1866.[58] This war not only seemed to augur the supersession of 'cotton goods internationalism' by the age of 'blood and iron' but immediately undercut the progress of the Anglo-Austrian commercial treaty. When this was belatedly completed in 1870, it proved more a footnote to the 1860 treaty than the completion of the European free trade edifice.[59] More seriously, as the renegotiation of the Anglo-French treaty approached, itself vastly complicated by the Franco-Prussian War, Gladstone found himself faced by growing domestic opposition to a renewal of the treaty, with France also wishing in substantial ways to reverse course. Detailed negotiations not only gave an opportunity for the treaty's critics to mobilise at home but also undermined Gladstone's own faith in treaties by threatening a return to the 'higgling' of the 1840s, thus exposing the state once more to the pressure of vested interests from which unilateralism in 1846, and in a qualified sense in 1860, had proved an escape. The early 1870s were therefore to see an effective impasse in commercial diplomacy in which, as Chevalier had warned Gladstone, Britain's moral ascendancy of the 1860s would be undermined to Bismarck's benefit.[60] In this context, as continental states came under renewed pressures to return to tariffs (primarily for fiscal reasons), Britain lost her ability to reshape the European order.

When Gladstone returned to office in 1880, the situation had in many ways deteriorated still further. Not only had the Eastern Question erupted, drawing Disraeli and the Tory party for the first time, Gladstone believed, towards war rather than peace, but Germany had swiftly returned to a protectionist tariff in 1879 and in Britain the fair trade movement seriously challenged Britain's free trade orthodoxy.[61] Gladstone's own former private secretary, Sir Stafford Northcote, now at the Exchequer under Disraeli, had been unable to avoid plunging into the mire of military-induced expenditure which Gladstone, in the subtext of his Midlothian speeches, assailed with the abhorrence Cobden had reserved for Palmerstonian extravagance.[62] But more widely, the Liberal indictment of Beaconsfieldism led, as Colin Matthew has shown, to Gladstone's formulating a new liberal understanding of the 'Concert of Europe' in which Britain's mission to hold out an example of free trade to the world would be buttressed by the Concert taking political steps towards the avoidance of war.[63] Gladstone here reaffirmed his belief in a European community whose moral goals would be best achieved by low armaments and low taxes, the world, it had seemed, free trade had made possible in the 1860s. For this reason, despite his renewed doubts as to the desirability in principle of commercial treaties, Gladstone's ministry of 1880–85 was to show considerable interest in the possibility of further commercial negotiations. Gladstone himself was back at the Exchequer and his budget of 1880 provided scope for commercial bargaining by setting aside £250,000 from the wine duties in the event of a successful renegotiation of the Cobden treaty. Gladstone expressed 'little hope' in the success of such negotiations, and despite the best efforts of Charles Dilke, the intricacies of French domestic politics left little scope for success. Gladstone regretted this failure on political grounds but consoled himself with the belief that no great economic damage would ensue.[64]

Despite failure in Paris, the Foreign Office still pursued a range of commercial negotiations, securing a renewal of the Anglo-Italian commercial treaty in 1883, and a convention with Portugal which had been begun whilst Gladstone had been at the Board of Trade in the 1840s. Even Gladstone's 'home rule' ministry achieved one unsung success, the negotiation of a commercial treaty with Spain that had consistently eluded all British diplomats since the 1830s. Gladstone's ministry also kept a watchful eye on the spread of German, Austrian and Russian protectionism and with this in mind negotiated commercial treaties with Montenegro, Greece and Turkey, all attempts to keep south-eastern Europe and the Levant open freely to British goods.[65] Despite therefore the unfavourable climate for free trade diplomacy created by Treasury fiscal orthodoxy (which now held that Britain had no more tariffs left which could be safely reduced), by the swing to protection in Germany, and by the growing stridency of the fair trade movement, and despite Gladstone's own scepticism, the attempt to buttress Britain's free trade mission by political and diplomatic instruments was by no means abandoned. As Colin Matthew has argued, these efforts failed to amount to a sustained attempt by the world's leading industrial power to preserve an open world market and by comparison with the efforts of the German industrial state, Gladstonian fear of the state was pronounced.[66] Even so, it seems difficult to imagine that retaliation of the type briefly mooted by Chamberlain in 1882 would have remedied this situation. Not only was retaliation of doubtful efficacy, but it was an expedient Gladstone had, like most Liberals, curtly and finally dismissed.[67] However, with ministers such as Dilke, Chamberlain and later Bryce fully alive to the needs of trade, some progress had been made, and even the muted Anglo-French treaty of 1882 preserved for a few more years the shadow of the old Cobdenite project.

Despite the relative failure of Britain's commercial diplomacy after 1870 Gladstone remained wholly committed to a belief in the benefits of free trade for Britain, Europe and the empire, repudiating vigorously ideas of retaliation and preference and the variety of heterodox economic nostrums which British politics spawned from the early 1880s. In parliament and in public, he continued to voice the 'platitudes' of the 1840s, affirming that only free trade was congruent with prosperity, publishing in 1880 an encomium of the material results of free trade, and leading the attack on fair trade in his Leeds speeches of 1881.[68] The almost covert rise of colonial protectionism in the 1870s also found in Gladstone a stern critic of this abandonment of the principle of the community of values as well as of interests upon which empire should be based.[69] Moreover, as evidence of depression in British agriculture and industry mounted, Gladstone firmly opposed the idea of a Royal Commission of inquiry and orchestrated Liberal abstention from the Commission set up by Salisbury's minority government of 1885. When in part the evidence of that Commission was used to encourage support for protection within the Tory party, Gladstone was also ready to lead the attack, as in his speech at Dover in December 1887.[70]

Most interestingly, in 1890 Gladstone confronted the increasingly perplexing issue as to how Britain should respond to the inveterate protectionism of the United States. For, like Cobden, Gladstone had long identified the United States as Britain's potential successor as the world's leading economic power. Consistent with his creed since 1846, the belief that 'human greed

"RULE, BRITANNIA!" (?)

12 Gladstone and the shade of Cobden, *Punch* 18 November 1893

and selfishness are interwoven with every thread of the Protective system', Gladstone proclaimed in the face of the McKinley tariff that protection would damage most the long-term interests of the United States while prophetically he outlined the responsibility of the world's greatest economic power to adopt free trade.[71] Gladstone also returned to the theme of free trade in several speeches in the early 1890s. For example, at Dundee in 1890 he reiterated the benefits of free trade for Britain and the damage of protection for the United States while hailing somewhat prematurely the emergence of a 'powerful body' of free traders in the United States.[72] Gladstone continued to see for Britain the duty to uphold free trade, identifying his case still with that of Cobden, in the belief that 'if we have courage and persistence in the right ... we shall convert the world'. Gladstone continued to the end to wrestle with free trade as the peculiar 'care of Britain'.[73] Perhaps one of the last such occasions was, intriguingly, during a visit, too late to be recorded in the diary, by George Peel, the grandson of Sir Robert, to Hawarden in the summer of 1896 before setting out for the United States. Peel later recalled, 'Gladstone administered to me, for some three or four hours altogether what I could only regard as a prophylactic against my contemplated contact with American realities. This took the form of an account ... of those principles of economic policy which had animated and guided Sir Robert Peel ... and himself.'[74]

But however tenaciously Gladstone held to Peelite principles, we may finally suggest that in his later years, governed by the rise of European militarism and protectionism, Gladstone found a surer guide in the precepts which had guided Cobden and himself in the early 1860s when pursuing Britain's 'Providential' mission to support free trade and peace. This, as Gladstone recognised, had become a task on a wholly different scale with the rise in military expenditure in Europe following the Franco-Prussian War. In this context, Gladstone painfully recognised his own growing ineffectiveness as a critic of militarism and expenditure. For example, he was forced in 1884 to accept larger estimates than he wished. Out of office, while he still upheld Britain's mission 'to help peace', he was reduced to the role of bystander in the face of rising estimates after 1887, and in the wake of the Naval Defence Act of 1889, which now became a new benchmark in military spending to set beside the scale of Palmerstonian estimates in 1859–60.[75] In opposition after 1886, he remained naturally a stern critic of Conservative extravagance, lamenting in 1887, 'So few come up to Cobden's doctrine that public economy is a part of public virtue.'[76] Gladstone also strongly reasserted the importance of an Anglo-French entente for Europe's peace and prosperity. In particular, in 1887 he recounted and defended the making of the Cobden–Chevalier treaty of 1860, for the benefit of the readers of the fledgling *English Historical Review*. But, afforced by lengthy memoranda from Hamilton at the Treasury, he was now more confidently able to regard the treaty as justified by results, despite the recent revival of continental protectionism.[77] At Paris, too, in 1889, when enjoying the spectacle of the World Exhibition, he reiterated the importance of the entente cordiale for the peace of Europe.[78] On similar lines, in 1892 Gladstone acknowledged an unusual fellow spirit in the Italian economist Pareto, affirming for an Italian audience the need to oppose as a threat to liberty the alliance of protection and militarism, while also identifying Crispi's Italy as a leading contributor to Europe's 'accursed militarism'.[79]

Ironically, however, outside Crispian Italy, it was within the Liberal cabinet of 1892–94 that Gladstone now found the leading danger to peace in Europe. A readiness to succumb to military alarmism unprecedented since 1859–60 now seemed to Gladstone to grip the cabinet and eventually prompted his own resignation in February–March 1894.[80] During this protracted resignation, Gladstone's thinking was to a remarkable degree still dominated by the memory of his partnership with Cobden in the early 1860s. In particular, he became obsessively concerned with justifying his own actions over expenditure in 1859–60, above all holding the peace-reinforcing treaty of 1860 to exculpate his partial bowing to the Palmerstonian panic in that year. But he also found in that earlier crisis over military expenditure a benchmark against which to define the illegitimacy of Liberal expenditure upon armaments in the 1890s, as tending not to avoid but to encourage war. In this way, the permanent mark left by Cobden's arguments and example in the early 1860s was still deeply imprinted on Gladstone's consciousness.[81] As he found himself, during his resignation, 'encouraged by voices from the dead', we may well surmise that Cobden's was loud among those dead voices. For even in resigning, Gladstone did so avowedly, as he wrote to Harcourt, 'on the ground laid down by Cobden (which has a real solidity of its own)'.[82] Moreover, having resigned on 'Cobdenic' grounds, among the topics Gladstone revisited in his autobiographical memoranda was that of the history of protection. Significantly, we find there primary tribute not to Peel, as we might expect, but to Cobden, with whom, he wrote, 'it is futile to compare any other man ... as the father of our system of Free Trade'.[83] While of course this implies no deliberate underestimation of Peel, it affords clear testimony to Gladstone's evaluation of Cobdenite principles as a guide to public conduct.

If those principles now served to isolate Gladstone within the Liberal cabinet in 1894, they nevertheless proved ripe for preservation after his death in 1898. For in the choice of Morley as biographer the Gladstone family appointed not simply the biographer whom Gladstone himself had approved for Cobden but the Liberal politician on whose mind, Lord David Cecil wrote, 'The study of Cobden's unselfish character and international statesmanship left impressions ... which were never effaced. Most of the principles which guided him thenceforth as critic or director of public policy were essentially those of Cobden.'[84] Significantly too, Morley's devil in his biography of Gladstone was Francis Hirst, later the husband of a great-niece of Cobden, as well as custodian of Cobden's Sussex home, Dunford House. Conventionally, Hirst has been regarded as the 'last of the Cobdenites' but he was equally the last of the Gladstonians, for whom the principles of Gladstonian finance represented the sum of governmental wisdom whether in the context of the Boer War, the First World War, or indeed the Second World War.[85] During the Boer War and the Edwardian arms race, Hirst readily associated Gladstone with Cobden as a leading opponent of the 'scaremongering' *mentalité*, for example, in the Cobden Club's volume *The Burden of Armaments* and in his tract, *The Six Panics*.[86] Interestingly, this Cobden–Morley–Hirst nexus proved long-lived and enjoyed a late flowering in the crisis of Liberalism, as well as of Labour and finance, in 1931. For in that year Hirst produced his study of Gladstone as financier, instigated by his son, Henry Neville Gladstone, who was also to unveil in Heyshott parish church a memorial to Cobden, making, in the words of his biographer, 'a strong appeal for a return to those principles of free trade and economy advocated by Cobden and pursued by Mr Gladstone'.[87] While Henry Neville displayed no doubts as to his father's likely course of action in the crisis of 1931, others close to Gladstone were by no means so certain. Interestingly, his former private secretary, J. A. Godley, now Lord Kilbracken, speculated that Gladstone himself in the circumstances of 1931 would have abandoned his Cobdenite loyalties and might have proved 'unfaithful to free trade'.[88] We need not enter this speculation. Suffice it to say that during his own lifetime Gladstone had acquired and consistently displayed a deep and lasting faith in Cobden as the epitome of free trade and of morality in foreign policy. This 'Cobdenite' strand had in turn been crucial to Gladstone's contribution to the definition and history of 'Liberal England', pursuing its Providential mission of free trade and peace.

Notes

1 Letter dated 15 January 1896, cited in H. C. G. Matthew, *The Liberal Imperialists*, Oxford, Oxford UP, 1973, p. vii; see also H. C. G. Matthew, *Gladstone, 1809–1898*, Oxford, Clarendon Press, 1997, p. 639.

2 D. W. R. Bahlman (ed.), *The Diary of Sir Edward Walter Hamilton, 1887–1906*, Hull, University of Hull Press, 1993, p. 57 (18 March 1887) and p. 240 (19 February 1894).

3 See especially H. C. G. Matthew, 'Disraeli, Gladstone and the Politics of Mid-Victorian Budgets', *Historical Journal*, Vol. 22, 1979, pp. 615–43; B. Hilton, *The Age of Atonement: The Influence of Evangelicalism on Social and Economic Thought, 1785–1865*, Oxford, Clarendon Press, 1988; F. W. Hirst, *Gladstone as Financier and Economist*, London, Ernest Benn, 1931; F. E. Hyde, *Mr Gladstone at the Board of Trade*, London, Cobden-Sanderson, 1934.

4 J. Vincent, *The Formation of the British Liberal Party, 1857–68*, Harmondsworth, Penguin Books, 1972, pp. 71–72; W. E. Williams, *The Rise of Gladstone to the Leadership of the Liberal Party, 1859 to 1868*, Cambridge, Cambridge UP, 1934, esp. pp. 19–33, 60–69; Matthew (1997), pp. 75–6, 133, 137; N. C. Edsall, *Richard Cobden, Independent Radical*, Cambridge, Massachusetts, Harvard UP, 1986, esp. chaps 21, 22; G. R. Searle, *Entrepreneurial Politics in Mid-Victorian Britain*, Oxford, Oxford UP, 1993, pp. 147–49, 151–52.

5 15 January 1862, GP 44136, f. 160.

6 J. Brooke and M. Sorensen (eds), *The Prime Ministers' Papers: W. E. Gladstone*, 4 vols, London, HMSO, 1971–81, vol. 1, *Autobiographica*, p. 84 (dated 31 August and 1 September 1897).

7 A. Howe, *Free Trade and Liberal England, 1846–1946*, Oxford, Clarendon Press, 1997, pp. 191–92.

8 23 June 1896, Cobden Papers 981, West Sussex Record Office.

9 *GD*, vol. 12, p. lxx; vol. 13, p. 364, 20 January 1894.

10 *Autobiographica* (1971), vol. 1, p. 124, where Gladstone recalls, 'Peel in 1842 had expressed his belief '"That European states had then, and for many years before, military establishments unnecessarily large".'

11 J. Morley, *The Life of William Ewart Gladstone*, 3 vols, London, Macmillan, 1903, vol. 3, p. 507.

12 Ibid.; see also Gladstone to A. J. Mundella, 6 February 1894, *GD*, vol. 13, pp. 372–73.

13 Gladstone to Cobden, 23 January 1841, GP 44135, f. 3; Morley (1903), vol. 1,

   p. 232; Matthew (1997), p. 56; N. McCord, *The Anti-Corn Law League,
       1838–1846*, London, George Allen & Unwin, 1958, pp. 83–87.
14 *Autobiographica* (1971), vol. 1, p. 48.
15 In 1857 Cobden still recalled Gladstone's protectionist speeches as a barrier to
       political trust between them. Cobden to Henry Richard, 27 January 1857,
       Cobden Papers, British Library, Add. MS 43658, f. 252. As late as 1892, the
       aged Earl Grey also critically recalled Gladstone's protectionist speeches of 1843.
       The Times, 8 July 1892, p. 10.
16 Morley (1903), vol. 1, p. 291; *GD*, 30 June 1846, vol. 3, pp. 552–55, and 10
       July 1846, esp. pp. 555–56.
17 Hirst (1931), p. 98.
18 Above, note 3; 'The latter [Gladstone] has not I think originated any great prin-
       ciple. He has merely ably carried on Peel's policy,' noted the Board of Trade offi-
       cial Sir Louis Mallet to M. E. Grant Duff, 4 November 1868, Grant Duff Papers,
       MS Eur. F 234/37, India Office Library.
19 *GD*, vol. 14, Index, for Gladstone's reading, e.g. *Wealth of Nations*, 12 March
       1841 *et seq.*; Gladstone soon became well read in the pamphlet literature con-
       cerning free trade and the Corn Laws.
20 For a recent analysis, see J. Maloney, 'Gladstone, Peel and the Corn Laws', in
       Free Trade and its Reception, 1815–1960, ed. A. Marrison, London, Routledge,
       1998, pp. 28–47.
21 Hilton (1988), esp. chap. 9 and pp. 64–70.
22 Matthew (1979); Searle (1993), pp. 64–65; W. E. Gladstone to Robertson Glad-
       stone, 27 December 1848, Glynne–Gladstone MSS, 569, Flintshire Record Office,
       Hawarden.
23 *GD*, 12 October 1853; *The Times*, 13 October 1853, p. 7; see also *The Papers
       of William Ewart Gladstone, Printed Speeches and Newspaper Cuttings from St
       Deiniol's Library, Hawarden*, Microfilm edn, Primary Source Media, Reel 1,
       ff. 423–51.
24 Edsall (1986), pp. 270–72; J. A. Hobson, *Richard Cobden: The International Man*,
       London, Fisher Unwin, 1918, p. 105; D. Nicholls, 'Richard Cobden and the
       International Peace Congress Movement, 1848–1853', *Journal of British Studies*,
       Vol. 30, 1991, pp. 351–76; M. Ceadel, *The Origins of War Prevention: The British
       Peace Movement and International Relations, 1730–1854*, Oxford, Clarendon
       Press, 1996, pp. 504–11.
25 Aberdeen thought Gladstone's speech at Manchester on 12 October had 'much
       promoted the cause of peace'. Aberdeen to Gladstone, 17 October 1853, GP
       44088, f. 201. For further insights into Gladstone's dilemmas in the 1850s, see
       A. B. Hawkins, 'A Forgotten Crisis: Gladstone and the Politics of Finance during
       the 1850s', *Victorian Studies*, Vol. 26, 1983, pp. 287–320.
26 Morley (1903), vol. 1, p. 509; Cobden to Richard, 27 January 1857, Cobden
       Papers, Add. MS 44658, f. 252; Edsall (1986), pp. 361–62; Hobson (1918), pp.
       200–02. See also M. Taylor, *The Decline of British Radicalism, 1847–60*, Oxford,
       Clarendon Press, 1995, p. 269.
27 Maloney (1998), pp. 42–44; Howe (1997), pp. 22–23.
28 Howe (1997), p. 88 and n. 101; J. Davis, *Britain and the German Zollverein,
       1848–66*, London, Macmillan, 1997, pp. 105–06. For a good statement of Glad-
       stone's faith in the 'mighty force' of British example, see his speech at Inverness,

27 September 1853, in *Speeches and Newspaper Cuttings from St Deiniol's Library*, Microfilm edn, Reel 1, ff. 418–21.

29 Morley (1903), vol. 1, p. 509; 'I know not when I have given a vote that I am so thankful to have given,' wrote Gladstone to Cobden following Palmerston's defeat, 20 June 1857, GP 44135, ff. 13–14; Taylor (1995), pp. 269–75.

30 Gladstone to Cobden, 12 October 1859, GP 44135, ff. 29–30.

31 Morley (1903), vol. 2, chap. 2; J. Morley, *The Life of Richard Cobden*, 2 vols, London, Chapman, Hall, 1881, esp. vol. 2, pp. 236–69, 335–45; Howe (1997), pp. 92–99.

32 Matthew (1997), pp. 113–14; Gladstone to Catherine Gladstone, 12 September 1859, in A. T. Bassett (ed.), *Gladstone to his Wife*, London, Methuen, 1936, p. 125; Gladstone to Sir J. Acton, 6 January 1864, GP 44093, f. 37.

33 The most comprehensive discussion is still that of A. L. Dunham, *The Anglo-French Treaty of Commerce of 1860*, Ann Arbor, University of Michigan Press, 1930.

34 *Autobiographica* (1971), p. 85; W. E. Gladstone, 'The History of 1852–1860, and Greville's Latest Journals', *English Historical Review*, Vol. 2, 1887, pp. 281ff.; for a modern account, A. Iliasu, 'The Cobden–Chevalier Treaty of 1860', *Historical Journal*, Vol. 14, 1971, pp. 65–98.

35 Gladstone to Acton, 6 January 1864, GP 44023, f. 40; Morley (1903), vol. 2, p. 1.

36 *Autobiographica* (1971), pp. 84–85; R. Shannon, *Gladstone, 1809–1865*, London, Hamish Hamilton, 1982, vol. 1, p. 412.

37 Dunham (1930); most recently, Howe (1997), pp. 92–99.

38 W. E. Gladstone to J. Lacaita, 1 December 1860, GP 44233, ff. 155–62; P. Bolchini, 'Anglo-Italian Economic Relations (1861–1883)', unpublished PhD thesis, University of London (1967), pp. 23ff.

39 K. F. Helleiner, *Free Trade and Frustration: Anglo-Austrian Negotiations, 1860–70*, Toronto, University of Toronto Press, 1973; Howe (1997), pp. 102–03.

40 G. Metzler, *Grossbritannien-Weltmacht in Europa: Handelspolitik im Wandel des europaischen Staatssystems 1856 bis 1871*, Berlin, Akademie Verlag, 1997, pp. 139–57; J. W. Gaston, 'Trade and the Late Victorian Foreign Office', *International History Review*, Vol. 4, 1982, pp. 317–38.

41 Morley (1903), vol. 2, p. 641.

42 Morley (1903), vol. 2, chap. 3; Hirst (1931), pp. 241–52; Gladstone to Cobden, 8 October 1861, GP 44136, f. 118.

43 Gladstone to Cobden, 25 April 1862, GP 44136, f. 180. For the genesis of this pamphlet, see Cobden to H. Richard, 17 August 1861 *et seq.*, Cobden Papers, Add. MS 43569, f. 86.

44 Shannon (1982), pp. 457–58; P. Guedalla, *Gladstone and Palmerston*, London, Victor Gollancz, 1928, pp. 205–16. Cobden himself remained critical of the degree to which Gladstone funded Palmerstonian 'excesses'; Cobden to Richard, 3 March 1861, Cobden Papers, Add. MS 43569, f. 88; Matthew (1997), p. 111.

45 Gladstone to A. Fould, 4 April and 29 December 1863, GP 44400, ff. 156, 287; see also Fould to Gladstone, 24 December 1865, GP 44408, f. 240.

46 Gladstone to Cobden, 5 January 1864, GP 44136, f. 217; Matthew (1997), pp. 120–28.

47 Morley (1881), vol. 1, p. 408.

48 Matthew (1997), pp. 120–28; E. F. Biagini, 'Popular Liberals, Gladstonian Finance and the Debate on Taxation, 1860–1874', in *Currents of Radicalism*, ed. E. F. Biagini and A. J. Reid, Cambridge, Cambridge UP, 1991, pp. 134–62.

49 Cobden to Bright, 25 August 1860, Cobden Papers, Add. MS 43651, f. 174; see also Morley (1881), vol. 2, p. 308.

50 *The Times*, 13 January 1862, p. 6 (Leith); 25 April 1862, p. 7 (Manchester); 9 October 1862, p. 7 (Newcastle); 14 October 1864, p. 7 (Liverpool); 19 December 1867, p. 7 (Oldham); Matthew (1997), pp. 134–35.

51 *GD*, 7 April 1865; W. E. Gladstone to Robertson Gladstone, 5 April 1865, Glynne–Gladstone MSS, 573, quoted Morley (1903), vol. 2, p. 143.

52 Mrs C. A. Cobden to Gladstone, 26 April 1866, GP 44410, ff. 104–7; and 8 January 1866, GP 44409, ff. 47–50; Sir L. Mallet to Gladstone, 28 January, 8 March 1878; memorandum by Sir H. Thring, GP 44486, ff. 71–72, 128–31, 132.

53 C. J. L. Brock and G. Jackson, *A History of the Cobden Club*, London, Cobden-Sanderson,1939; for a recent account of the Club, Howe (1997), pp. 116–41; for Gladstone on Potter, *GD*, 22 August 1884.

54 Morley (1903), vol. 2, p. 213; Cobden Club, *Report of Annual Dinner*, London, Cassell, 1870, p. 24.

55 *W. E. Gladstone on Cottage Gardens and Fruit Culture*, Cobden Club, 1889; T. B. Potter to W. E. Gladstone, 23 August 1889, GP 44282, f. 201.

56 Gladstone to T. B. Potter, 29 August 1881, *GD*, vol. 10, p. 116; Howe (1997), pp. 129–31.

57 W. E. Gladstone to T. B. Potter, 18 July 1866, in Cobden Papers, Add. MS 43678, f. 52.

58 A. Howe, 'Free Trade and the Victorians', in Marrison (ed.), *Free Trade*, pp. 172–74; Howe (1997), pp. 156–65.

59 Howe (1997), p. 158; Helleiner (1973), pp. 112–33.

60 Chevalier to Gladstone, 11 October 1872, GP 44127, f. 105; Gladstone to Chevalier, 24 January 1872, *GD*, vol. 8, pp. 98–99.

61 Bahlman (1993), p. 82; Howe (1997), chap. 5; S. Zebel, 'Fair Trade: An English Reaction to the Breakdown of the Cobden Treaty System', *Journal of Modern History*, Vol. 12, 1940, pp. 161–85.

62 W. E. Gladstone, *Political Speeches in Scotland*, 1st and 2nd ser., Edinburgh, Andrew Elliot, 1879 and 1880; A. J. P Taylor, *The Trouble Makers: Dissent over Foreign Policy, 1792–1939*, Harmondsworth, Penguin, 1985, p. 85.

63 *GD*, vol. 9, pp. xxxviii–xli.

64 Howe (1997), pp. 177–80; J. W. Gaston, 'Policy-Making and Free Trade Diplomacy: Britain's Commercial Relations with Western Europe, 1869–1886', unpublished PhD thesis, University of Saskatchewan, 1975.

65 Howe (1997), pp. 181–85.

66 *GD*, vol. 10, pp. xxx ff.

67 D. W. R. Bahlman (ed.), *The Diary of Sir Edward Hamilton, 1880–85*, 2 vols, Oxford, Oxford UP, 1972, vol. 1, p. 310 (21 July 1882); Gladstone to Chevalier, 26 October 1872, GP 44127, f. 109.

68 W. E. Gladstone, 'Free Trade, Railways, and the Growth of Commerce', *Nineteenth Century*, Vol. 7, 1880, pp. 367–88; Gladstone, *Speeches, delivered at Leeds, 7 and 8 October 1881*, London, National Press Agency, 1881.

69   *GD*, vol. 8, p. 87; Howe (1997), p. 189.

70   B. H. Brown, *The Tariff Reform Movement in Great Britain, 1881–1895*, New York, Oxford UP, 1943, p. 65; *The Times*, 28 December 1887, p. 4.

71   W. E. Gladstone, 'Protectionism, 1840–1860' (12 July 1894), in *Autobiographica* (1971), p. 74; Gladstone, 'Free Trade', *North American Review*, Vol. 150, 1890, pp. 1–27; *GD*, vol. 12, pp. xlii–xliii.

72   *The Times*, 30 October 1890, p. 4 (Newcastle); also 8 July 1889, p. 7 (Cardiff); 5 October 1891, p. 12 (Newcastle); 8 July 1892, p. 5 (West Calder).

73   *Autobiographica* (1971), p. 75.

74   G. Peel, *The Economic Impact of America*, London, Macmillan, 1928, pp. vi–vii.

75   *Hansard's Parliamentary Debates*, 3rd ser., vol. 334, 4 April 1889, esp. col. 1631, 'The case of 1860 is no precedent.' Gladstone clearly differentiated 1859–60 from 1889, but criticised the bill largely on grounds of the Peelite 'doctrine of annual provision for the wants of the year out of the means of the year' (col. 1625).

76   For Gladstone on Lord Randolph Churchill as a 'champion of economy', Morley (1903), vol. 2, p. 365; on Cobden, Gladstone to Sir R. E. Welby, 26 October 1887, Murray Papers, Blair Castle; the comment was repeated in Gladstone's speech at Edinburgh, 27 October 1890, *The Speeches of W. E. Gladstone, 1888–1891*, ed. A. W. Hutton and H. J. Cohen, London, Methuen, 1902, p. 264.

77   Above, n. 34; Sir Edward Hamilton Diary, 16 February 1887, Hamilton Papers, Add MS. 48645; Hamilton to Gladstone, 14 and 15 February 1887, GP 44191, ff. 114–15, 117–18.

78   *Journale des Economistes*, vol. 45–46, pt 2, 1889, pp. 449–51; Gladstone's host was the free trader Leon Say. Gladstone was also a keen supporter of the Channel Tunnel, a Cobdenite–Chevalier cause *par excellence*.

79   For Gladstone to Pareto, 30 April 1892, in *GD*, vol. 13, p. 23 n. 5. For Crispi's Italy, *Autobiographica* (1971), p. 121.

80   For Gladstone's thinking on naval expenditure, 1893–94, see especially *Autobiographica* (1971), pp. 121–25; *GD*, vol. 13, pp. 348–51, 354–61, 364, 372–73, 376–78; Matthew (1997), pp. 600–06; Bahlman (1993), esp. pp. 215–42; Morley (1903), vol. 3, pp. 507–08, 563.

81   See especially Gladstone to A. J. Mundella, 6 February 1894, in *GD*, vol. 13, pp. 372–73.

82   Matthew (1997), p. 602; Gladstone to Harcourt, 25 February 1894, *GD*, vol. 13, p. 384.

83   *Autobiographica* (1971), p. 73.

84   For the choice of Morley, see *GD*, vol. 1, pp. xxv–xxvii; M. R. D. Foot, 'Morley's Gladstone: A Reappraisal', *Bulletin of the John Rylands Library*, Vol. 51, 1968–69, pp. 368–87; Cecil, 'John Morley', DNB.

85   *F. W. Hirst by his Friends*, London, Oxford UP, 1958; F. W. Hirst, *Richard Cobden and John Morley*, Heyshott, Cobden Club, 1941. M. R. D. Foot has also suggested Gilbert Murray as the 'last of the Gladstonians'.

86   F. W. Hirst, *The Burden of Armaments*, London, Fisher Unwin, 1905; F. W. Hirst, *The Six Panics*, London, Methuen, 1913.

87   Howe (1997), p. 282; *The Times*, 5 October 1931; H. N. Gladstone, introduction, Hirst (1931), pp. ix–xx; cf. *The Times*, 8 December 1931, p. 8; I. Thomas,

Gladstone of Hawarden: A Memoir of Henry Neville, Lord Gladstone of Hawarden, London, John Murray, 1936, pp. 227–28; H. N. Gladstone also became one of the governors of the Dunford House (Cobden Memorial) Association.

88   Kilbracken to G. H. Murray, 8 April 1931, Murray Papers, 1676, Blair Castle.

Networking through Sound Establishments: How Gladstone Could Make Dissenting Sense

Clyde Binfield

13 Gladstone and his family at Hawarden Castle, c. 1875

$\mathcal{S}$IDNEY Checkland's invaluable collective biography, *The Gladstones*, prompted comparisons between the Gladstones and the Kennedys.[2] In each case a patriarch, more domineering than dominating, single-mindedly accumulated the property, influence, connections and children from which a dynasty could grow. The public and business lives of each patriarch, Sir John for the Gladstones and Joseph for the Kennedys, were as questionable as the public and business lives of any successful newcomers were bound to be in cities like Liverpool or Boston. What neither could determine was the myth engendered by the political empires which each had launched. For the Kennedys it was not just the glamour of Camelot and the allure of a culture which dragged Polish princes and English dukes and grave statesmen in its train, it was also the glow of great (and therefore Liberal) causes. For the Gladstones it was not just the battlements of Hawarden and decades at the political heart of the world's greatest empire and first industrial nation, it was also the thrill of disinterested moral adulation. For Kennedys and Gladstones alike there was the support of men and women whose views would have given Joseph and Sir John the shivers. And for students of both Kennedys and Gladstones there is the vexed question of how far any of them ever identified with those supporters.

The parallels between Gladstones and Kennedys should be enjoyed rather than taken seriously. Certainly the name 'Gladstone' has become synonymous with a myth which would have disturbed Sir John as much as it has perplexed posterity. The constituent parts of that myth, however, would have thrilled Sir John, for they were the houses in the country, the seats at Westminster, the offices of state, the marriage alliances, consolidated by the steady application of superior intellectual ability, which confirmed the prime position in the traditional political nation on which one hardy Liverpool merchant had set his sights. This chapter first considers the extent to which the Gladstones became part of that traditional, though already changing, nation and then it suggests how they yet could be seen to represent a steadily enlarging, and therefore still changing, political nation.

This nation was intelligent, urban and, to a significant extent, Dissenting. It was conservative because it was propertied, but it was sceptical about endowments, primogeniture and most other appurtenances of a hierarchical society. Its own hierarchies were based on common sense. It preferred respect to flunkeyism. Its society was a nice balance of self-reliance and mutuality. It distrusted established ways, at least until it had proved their practical application to the circumstances of up-to-date living. It found moral judgements exciting. All this made for movement. It turned naturally conservative people into Radicals, or at least Liberals.

These people travelled on railway trains, frequently to support good causes or to pack annual assemblies. They read newspapers, often in reading rooms furnished by an institute, or a YMCA, or even a club. They read periodicals too, often religious ones, and often in the train. They knew all about leadership because they exercised it in chapels or Sunday schools or a host of societies, each one with a committee and an annual general meeting. Many of them exercised it in business, and all of them experienced it. They also knew about leadership because they read about it in their Bibles; they debated about it; they recognised it in their pulpits where, having called it into being, they sat under it. Increasing numbers of them had municipal and parliamentary votes and were able to use those votes. They too were now in the political nation. What they did not have was a leader whose image they could fashion to their satisfaction.

And then, almost overnight, for all that he had been in the public eye for 30 years, they had Mr Gladstone: first, from the 1860s, as the People's William and then, from the 1870s, as the Grand Old Man. It was marvellously convenient for all concerned. Urban, Dissenting Britain convinced itself that it had found a leader who yet belonged socially, intellectually and confessionally to the Establishment and it played him for all he was worth. He played them too. On both sides there was genuine fascination, great admiration, some common ground, more sympathy, and infinite scope for mutual incomprehension. Dissenters liked it that way. They had Dickens in literature, Livingstone in foreign mission, Ruskin in culture and now, with similar enthusiasm and quite as much justification, they had Gladstone in politics.

II

It is surprisingly difficult to place the Gladstones socially. If Liverpool had been Hamburg or Amsterdam one might speak of a 'patriciate' or *haute bourgeoisie* with overtones not conveyed by the English term, 'upper middle class'. The origin of their fortune was mercantile rather than industrial or professional, with a consequent effect on mentality, networks and escape routes. The Gladstones became landed gentry in Scotland when they purchased Fasque in 1830 and in Wales when they became associated with Hawarden, although Hawarden Castle was Gladstone property only from 1874 and was only W. E. Gladstone's property for a few months in 1874.[3] In England W. E. Gladstone's naval brother had a seat in Wiltshire from the 1840s: Tory Bowden, set in the lee of Whig Bowood, had all the makings of a well-connected country property. And between 1903 and 1921 Gladstone's third son had a house on the Wirral, Burton Manor. But the Wirral was the haunt of Ismays, Levers and Roydens, and Burton, meticulously planned and gardened, recalled 'contemporary houses on the East coast of America' rather than landed gentry.[4] The Welsh and Scottish estates, unlike Bowden and Burton, have been strategically conserved by successive generations and the dynasty launched so powerfully by Sir John in the first decade of the nineteenth century has survived beyond the last of the twentieth. Its social integration can be charted in several ways.

For example, an established family should make a creditable showing in the older professions. One of the patriarch's sons became a naval officer, a grandson was in the Coldstream Guards, one great-grandson was killed in action, a second was taken prisoner, and a third mentioned in despatches, all in the Great War.[5] One grandson became a clergyman and three grand daughters married clergymen, two of whom became deans.[6] A son, two grandsons and a great-grandson had Oxford careers of enviable distinction and the son and great-grandson were presidents of the Oxford Union.[7] That son, moreover, was Lord Rector of two Scottish universities while one grandson became President of a Welsh university college and another taught in an Oxford college.[8] A granddaughter was Vice-Principal of a women's college in Cambridge and others in the family circle were promoters of a women's college in Oxford. A great-granddaughter, indeed, became the first woman to gain first class honours in Oriental Languages at Cambridge.[9] Male descendants included two masters at Eton, one of them subsequently headmaster of Lancing, and a grandson-in-law was Master of Wellington.[10]

Theirs was a family circle which encountered and entertained established scholars, writers and artists as a matter of course rather than of duty, finding enjoyment in Lord Acton and charm in John Ruskin, who was determined not to be charmed. Hawarden was not Camelot but it was on serious terms with high culture.

Theirs was also a family circle which took care to balance the social and political facts of dynastic life with commercial necessity. The Liverpool connection switched its focus from the West Indies to the East, usefully sustained by cadet branches as well as by the second son of the patriarch, grandsons and two great-grandsons. Those business interests made that second son mayor of Liverpool in 1842. They took one grandson to India for several years, brought a directorship of the Bank of England to a great-grandson, and found their fittest civic expression in a great-nephew turned grandson-in-law: he chaired Liverpool's Docks and Harbour Board for 11 years, sat on Liverpool's bench for 32, was treasurer of its University College for 22, and promoted the building of its cathedral 'for which he was mainly instrumental in adopting the site'.[11] They were all Eton but he was Eton and Edinburgh, Liverpool underneath, completing the circle of a statesman's credibility at the point where masses as well as classes were finding their way within the pale of the constitution.

Even so, that statesman's credibility remained grounded in land. The Gladstone commercial fortune sustained two solid estates which by 1883 ran to 45,062 Scottish acres belonging to the patriarch's eldest son, who was the largest landowner in his county, and 6,908 Welsh acres belonging to a grandson.[12] The Scottish estates sustained the baronetcy which came to the patriarch in 1846. A viscountcy came to one of his grandsons in 1910 – with no land to uphold its dignity – and a barony came to another grandson in 1932.[13] As it happened, that grandson was living in the family's Welsh castle, whose estates in the previous century had been thought inadequate to uphold the earldom which could have been his father's at any point between 1874 and 1898.

The family's marriages reflected this hereditary respectability. Two of the first baronet's sons married baronets' daughters, both of them what might be called parliamentary baronetcies, one of them anciently as well as nobly connected, the other the prelude to a peerage, the former largely Welsh and the latter largely Ulster.[14] Of the first baronet's grandsons, two married baronets' daughters and two married the daughters of peers, one of them again anciently and nobly connected, this time Scottish. Of his grand-daughters, one married a baronet, and her sister married an Irish earl.[15] And there were town houses to match: Albany, Upper Brook Street, and Berkeley Square, Buckingham Gate, Carlton House Terrace, and Harley Street, all of them political houses.[16]

For there were Gladstones in one or other house of parliament from 1818 to 1935 with one break between 1827 and 1832. Although the Gladstone peerages lasted only a quarter of a century, there were four generations of Gladstone MPs between 1818 and 1915, with two intermissions at peaks of constitutional crisis (1827–1832, January 1910–September 1911). Those four generations saw seven Gladstones in the Commons, who between them represented 19 constituencies: Berwick, Kilmarnock, Kincardine and Midlothian in Scotland; Portarlington in Ireland; Chester, Leeds, South Lancashire and Whitby in the north of England; East Worcestershire, Leicester, Newark and Walsall in the Midlands; Greenwich, Oxford University, Queenborough and Woodstock in the south; with Ipswich and Devizes as outliers to east and west.[17]

No doubt one should not read too much into this generous coverage; or at least one should make due allowance for the vagaries of small electorates, residual patronage and frequently changing party labels. None the less, it remains impressive, the more so if Greenwich is seen as reaching into London, or Midlothian into Edinburgh, or south Lancashire into the cottonopolis of Manchester and Salford. The coverage, moreover, is further extended if family connections are brought into it: Lord Frederick Cavendish, for example, sitting for North West Yorkshire between 1865 and 1882, reminding the Commons of the grand Whiggery's indefinable lustre, while his wife's Lyttelton kinsmen enlarged on it in the Lords.[18] The patriarch's eldest grandson certainly benefited from that sort of link. When he stood for Chester in 1865, it was with Earl Grosvenor as his Whig running mate in a nice balance of traditional territorial neighbourliness; and when he stood for East Worcestershire in 1880 it was in succession to a Whig Lyttelton uncle whose properties lay conveniently to hand. It was in such a way that Wales came into the picture. The 6,000 acres in Flint were naturally reflected locally in a High Shrievalty or a Lord Lieutenancy, or a seat on the county council after 1888. In the 1830s and 1840s they were reflected in parliament by a Gladstone brother-in-law.[19] In the changed circumstances of 1890 this Welsh connection was pleasantly enhanced when a Gladstone married the daughter of the MP for Montgomery, who was also president of

the North Wales Liberal Federation and chairman of the Welsh parliamentary Liberals.[20]

What did this amount to in local honour and national office? Lord Lieu-
tenancies in Flint and Kincardine; junior posts in the Treasury (held by three
Gladstones), the War, Home and Colonial Offices, and the Board of Trade;
the Offices of Lord Privy Seal, President of the Board of Trade, Home Secretary, Colonial Secretary, Chancellor of the Exchequer, and Prime Minister,
as well as Chief Whip and Leader of the Commons; and two Privy Council-
lorships, one High Commissionership, and one Governor-Generalship. There
was even a Gladstone briefly attached, by way of apprenticeship, to the
British embassy in Washington.[21]

This panoply of public service worked through each of the nation's main
political parties. Of the seven Gladstone MPs, three sat as Tories (two of them
unseated on petition), three as Liberals and the seventh was both. It may be
doubted whether their shared assumptions varied greatly.[22] Their service
also drew on their country's intelligentsia (through Oxford University) and
its industrial, commercial and professional acumen (through Leeds, Lancashire and Midlothian). More remarkably it drew on the religious nerve of
three nations. It was astoundingly well earthed. When he was MP for Oxford
University, W. E. Gladstone represented the mind of the English National
Church in and to the House of Commons. Thereafter, though his devotion
to that church remained part of his innermost being and he and his family
went beyond the call of lay duty in conserving its catholic communion in
Wales and Scotland, Gladstone also represented other religious minds and
so, by association, did his MP sons and grandson. At Midlothian the chairman of his election committee (and of the local Liberal Association) was
a leading Free Church of Scotland man. When the last Gladstone to sit in
the Commons was returned for Kilmarnock Burghs in 1911 he succeeded a
son of that formidable Free Church wire-puller and ally of the Grand Old
Man, Principal Rainy.[23] The Free Church of Scotland was crucial to Lowland
Liberalism. The English Free Churches also required careful cultivation.
Gladstone must have found them disconcertingly like the Queen: to be
painstakingly respected, and ignored only after the courtesies had been
scrupulously observed. If the Queen retained many of the characteristics of
an old-fashioned Whig country gentlewoman, and all the prejudices, the
Nonconformists exhibited an obstinately conservative radicalism. And they
remained integral to organised Liberalism for at least as long as there were
Gladstones in the House of Commons. The electoral careers of Gladstone's
two parliamentary sons bear this out.

III

William Henry Gladstone (1840–91) liked outdoor pursuits and lived in
Berkeley Square. He also had a respectable degree in classics and an envi-

able knowledge of music as well as a gift for it. His was the proverbial silver spoon. In two of his three constituencies he depended greatly on the traditionary influences of family, property, connection and obligation. Hawarden and Eaton Hall counted for something in Chester and Hagley counted in East Worcestershire. However, he also depended on other interests. At Chester he had a Grosvenor running mate but he was in fact stepping into the shoes of a Welsh Congregationalist, Enoch Gibbon Salisbury, who had briefly held the seat in the 1850s and would stand again when Gladstone moved on.[24] At Whitby, where there were no traditionary influences to help him, he needed to rely all the more on local Dissenters who were only too ready to bask in this youthful outworking of family glamour. Michael Bentley has explored their non-meeting of minds.[25] The unhappy experiment lasted for 12 years and then Whitby turned to the local clout, wealth and birthright Quakerism (and, alas, as it turned out, Liberal Unionism) of Arthur Pease,[26] while William Henry Gladstone's career, which had begun so promisingly with a Lordship of the Treasury, ended on Flint County Council.

Herbert John Gladstone (1854–1930) was more hopeful in every way. He too began in his twenties as a Lord of the Treasury but, though he too did duty on Flint County Council, he ended in the House of Lords, having sat in the cabinet and served as a Governor General. And his electoral alliance with Leeds endured for 30 years.

The enthusiasm with which that alliance began shines from the diaries of Katharine Roubiliac Conder, a thoroughly normal girl from the professional classes.[27] Her diaries, which survive for the years 1874–76 and 1880, suggest three things about such Gladstonians. First, the conservatively prosperous, responsible, civic tenor of their lives. Here is conscience with a stake in society. It has a history and a culture in counterpoint but not in opposition to established ways. The books read, the lessons learned, the places visited by the young Conders of Newton Grove, Leeds, could in most respects have been those read, learned or visited by the young Robert Gladstones of Woolton Vale, Liverpool. These are the voting classes of 1832, thickened by 1867, who live in villas, take holidays, sometimes run to a carriage and have friends who might number newly created baronets among their acquaintance or even as marriage connections, the Robert Gladstones, perhaps, or even the Robertson Gladstones. Secondly, there is the mutually useful glow of recognition released, warmed and disciplined by the fine-honed arts of electioneering. Thirdly there is the concomitant release, warmth and discipline of intelligent Evangelical religion, chapel-style, fine-honed in the pulpit. Here is the earthing of Mr Gladstone, a realm ready for a Gladstonian dynasty.

Katharine Conder had been educated at home by governesses and her stepmother, a youngish woman in her later thirties, then at Cheltenham Ladies' College, and finally at Leeds High School. Hers was a life of examinations and competitions, college boys to be flirted with at the Philharmonic Concerts and horizons to be widened by a sister, Ethel Mary, at Girton,[28] and a family circle in which her parents' broad cousinhoods had been hugely extended by those of her stepmother. These determined a busy round of quietly prosperous doings, punctuated by domestic excitements such as scarlet fever, or visiting lecturers, or trips into the West Riding or across to the coast. There are readings of great authors and there is the fixed point of church, which means chapel, either by tramcar or a friend's carriage to the town centre (no Low Church nonsense here about walking to worship), or closer to hand in Newton Park, in a dual-purpose building served by students. Very occasionally church was Church, Leeds Parish Church: 'Had the pleasure of hearing the curate, Mr Knaggs, a fearful specimen ...'

The following entries set the scene for the prosperous normalcy and instinctive networking of that apparently seamless provincial force, chapel Gladstonianism. Names and enthusiasms jostle artlessly. None is there by chance.

1874: March 1 Sunday: This morning being very gloomy and wet, we went to Newton Chapel, and heard Mr Bolton ... Papa preached at Newton Chapel this evening ... I enjoyed it very, very much.

Papa had to go to London, and started at half-past nine this evening: it seems so strange to think of him travelling all Sunday night ...[29]

March 8 Sunday: This morning we all went to E.P.C. [East Parade Chapel]. I rode down and walked up. This afternoon I played with Baby, read, learnt a hymn, and read Helena's household ... this evening ... Laurie and I went to the 'little chapel' and heard a student ... at the very beginning of the service, Laurie 'exploded' and nearly made me laugh by saying, 'The student's a little drunk!' which he certainly was not, though he did roll about a little as he walked ...[30]

March 23 Monday: Min asked us to go with her to a lecture by Mr Flitch and as Mamma said we might, we went this evening. The lecture was announced 'The record of a noble life' and who should it be about but Hampden. It was most interesting, and a very great deal being taken from Macaulay, but that made it all the nicer because we knew it so well. Mr Flitch is very handsome, and reads beautifully ...[31]

March 24 Tuesday: This morning we heard that Dr Livingston's [sic] body had arrived in England, so now no hope is left that he may still be alive ...[32]

April 1 Wednesday: The dear, dear, dear Jubilee singers are coming to Leeds! ... Oh! joy! joy!! joy!!!

April 14 Tuesday: dinner at St Ann's where Aunt Jainie is staying with Grandpapa B ....[33]

July 21 Tuesday: ['dear Filey again, and it looks just the same as ever!'] ... After tea, Mamma read some of 'Diary of Mrs Kitty Trevylyan' aloud while we went on with our sea-weeds; I have read the book twice before, but I don't like it any the worse for that; it is a most charming book![34]

By 1880 Katharine's hair is up and the purposeful round of cousinhood has intensified:

1880: January 5 Monday: Went down with Miss Jowitt ... Aunt Janie Crossley came to dinner. Ethel and I went to call on the Barrans ... Edie and Maggie Baines drove me home.[35]

January 7 Wednesday: Read Kingsley ... Went to dinner at the Scattergoods', and then with Lilly to the Little Owl at Dr. Heaton's Capital meeting ...[36]

January 12 Monday: Comfortable journey to Halifax. Aunt Janie's carriage met us ... drove in it to Dean Clough for Uncle Edward ... Then on to Moorside [and thence to Bermerside, where Aunt Janie and Uncle Edward lived] ... Mr Clarke, from Italy was staying ...[37]

January 13 Tuesday: To Mrs Marchetti at Broomfield ... dined at Nathan Whitley's ... and we played clumps and logarithms.[38]

January 14 Wednesday: ... a humorous lecture at the Dean Clough Institute on 'Public Speaking'...

January 15 Thursday: ... the Grammar School theatricals. Uncle Edward and Auntie Janie went to a tea-meeting ... into the Observatory. Had a splendid two hours there. Saw Mars, Saturn, the nebula near Orion's Belt and Castor...[39]

February 5 Thursday: Up to Chapel Allerton Hall to practise some hymns for the work-house ... went over the conservatories ... then on to East Parade Chapel, where we had a very interesting missionary lecture on Madagascar.[40]

February 12 Thursday: ... I went to Papa's Butler class at the YMCA, which was very interesting.[41]

February 13 Friday: [To see Grandpapa Baines, now almost stone deaf; then with Louise Barran, to the workhouse]. Had a very nice, in a sad way, time there, singing and talking to the people. Mr Barran's carriage came for us....Read 'Yeast'.[42]

This was a world of civic rights and duties whose prime movers were a young woman's friends and relations. Thus were foundations laid for the transforming of charity into social strategy, of knowledge into understanding, of mission into responsibility. The implications were intellectual, administrative, political. All of them had to do with how establishments were perceived and worked, and by whom. This young woman's friends and family were no doubt new to national establishments, but they were not novices. They were also loyal. Katharine's vicarious pleasure at the new Duchess of Edinburgh's entry to London marked a general admiration for the whole royal family:

> *1874: March 10, Tuesday:* We had a jolly reading class with Papa; reading the accounts of the reception at Windsor of Prince Alfred and his bride. How I sh[ou]ld like to have been there! We had a Scripture class with Mamma ... after which we went out ... and we snow-balled each other and the windows ...[43]

> *March 14, Saturday:* We had a very nice walk up to the coal mines ... This evening at tea, Mamma read us the account of the grand procession of the Prince and Duchess into London. Auntie Katie has gone to London to see it all.[44] How I should like to have seen it above most things!
>
> At the station, the platform was covered with crimson cloth, and so thickly strewn with beautiful hot-house flowers that it looked as if a splendid hot-house had suddenly been transplanted there. The whole route was gloriously decorated, and exquisite flowers must have had a very prominent part. Our favourite Prince Arthur was there, in his officer's uniform, giving orders to the soldiers. The last of the six carriages in the processions, held the Queen, Princess Beatrice, Prince Alfred and his bride. How I should like to have seen her! She was dressed in a blue silk with a white fur mantle, and her sweet face, and innocent almost childlike expression and winning smile have one [sic] the hearts and the affections of the people.[45]
>
> When they reached the palace, the Queen presented herself on the balcony bowing graciously, and then returning, led forth by the hand of the Princess Alexandrovna. Then came the Prince of Wales with him his two eldest sons. Then, the Queen, seeming to miss someone, went back and brought out the beautiful Princess of Wales! They were all received with loud and prolonged cheers and stood there for several minutes. What a beautiful thing it must have been and how I should love to have seen it and them all!

That loyalty, predictably enmythed, was naturally projected back. Macaulay met Kingsley and Elisabeth Rundle Charles; Trollope bowed to Mrs Oliphant. A summer with relations in Cheltenham numbered among its high spots dinner at Sudeley Castle with its antique oak memories of Henry VIII's Protestant Queen. 'Mrs S [Swinburne] had given us the idea of the Castle being very grand but very uncomfortable but we were most agreeably disappointed.' There follows a perfect evocation of the genesis of Whig history:

pouring rain in August and a room 'All oak with a thick Turkey carpet in the middle', and a portrait of Henry VIII, his six wives and three children. Their hostess, Sudeley's chatelaine, Mrs Dent, was 'most distinguished looking, tall, with very good features, pretty hands, and a very sweet expression, and beautiful silver white hair done most becomingly. She looked fit for Catherine Parr herself'.[46]

There, of course, is the key. Catherine Parr is Katharine Conder's heroine. So through the Chinese bedroom, and Amy Robsart's room (her bed, her washstand, her wardrobe), and the French room to Queen Catherine's room, 'a most queer little room' with her hair ('found perfect, when she was dug up'), her letters; and then there were Charles I's wooden spoon, Wellington's order and a lock of his hair and the hair of his horse Copenhagen, Prince Rupert's room, Cromwell's armour, and their hostess's pendant jewellery from abroad. And then dinner, eight of them in the dark library. 'Mrs Dent does talk *so* well! ... Mrs Swinburne told us that they generally had very poor dinners at the Castle, but we did not.'

That was in 1875. Election fever hit Leeds and the Conders in March 1880. Their candidates were a dream ticket of the national and the local: W. E. Gladstone, past Prime Minister with nearly 50 years of parliament behind him, and John Barran, future baronet, present Baptist and father of Katharine Conder's great friend Louie, with almost four years of parliament behind him but with 25 years' experience of Leeds Town Hall as well:

1880: March 11, Thursday: Had our final French class at the Barrans ... We did nothing at French ... but talk about the Dissolution. All immensely excited.

March 27, Saturday: Received from good Uncle Jem a packet of yellow leaflets with our song ['The Despot! Lord B!' to the tune of Bonnie Dundee] printed thereon. Took them down to the Mercury Office to be used for the Cause! Went to see Millais' portrait of 'Our Chief of Men', which is truly grand.[47]

March 31, Wednesday: Went down to town, and got some gorgeous yellow ribband for favours tomorrow ... Came home, worked and made us each a rosette. Read a capital placard on my way home on the 'Strange Disappearance' of 'A Young Person named National Prosperity'...

April 1 Thursday: Ethel and I, largely decorated, started off for Headingley. Our favours drew forth various remarks, chiefly of approval, such as 'That's the Colour! Stick to it!' etc ... to Aunt Louie's to tea. Found the children all much excited, disporting themselves in yellow. Then went up to St. Ann's ... Had hoped Papa would take us to the Town Hall, to hear the Declaration of the Poll, but when we did not appear at Chapel, he imagined we must have gone with Mr Willans. All we c[ou]ld do was to 'tram it' home ... A little before 11 [Laurie] came in with the grand news:

1   Gladstone   24,600
2   Barran   23,600
3   Jackson
4   Wheelhouse.

We went to bed in a state of mighty exultation![48]

April 2 Friday: Drenching with rain. Heard from Louie Barran, regretfully
giving up the work-house. Wrote to her, sending our heartiest congratula-
tions.

April 3 Saturday: ... meeting the Scattergoods ... Gloated over the victory. Papa
and Mama called at the Barrans to congratulate them.

April 5 Monday: Drenched with rain and hail, also snow, thunder and lightning
... had to shelter for about half-an-hour in a little grocer's shop, had some
very amusing political discussions with the owner. Grand victories of Midlothian and our West Riding!

April 17, Saturday: .... down to see Mr Gladstone's portrait ... it rained.

That entry of 5 April reminds us that this is the world of Midlothian, Leeds
side up. In 1880, following established practice, Gladstone sensibly ran for
two constituencies, Leeds and Midlothian. On assuming office he surrendered both seats without the embarrassment, as he put it, of having to
opt for either just yet, and his fourth and youngest son, Herbert, in his late
twenties and a history don at Keble who had made a bravely unavailing
showing in Middlesex, stepped in at Leeds which was to be his for 30 years.

April 30, Friday: Lucky Laurie has got his ticket for the meeting at the Mechan-
ics, and is gone to hear Mr Herbert Gladstone...

May 1, Saturday: Laurie was delighted with Mr Herbert Gladstone last night. The
meeting was most enthusiastic. Maggie has been reading the account of it
aloud this morning. Mrs Gladstone spoke a few words! Papa has promised to
take us to the 'Mass Meeting' at the Coloured Cloth Hall Yard this afternoon!
They say that over 30,000 tickets have been issued for it. I do hope we shall
be able to get in ...

We went to the meeting and enjoyed it immensely, all agreeing it was one
of the greatest treats we have ever had ... Papa got some extra tickets from
Mr Willans ... The huge yard was already crowded near the stairs, though
we got there one and a quarter hours before the time. Mr W. most kindly got
us tickets for the barricaded area round the stairs, where we could see and
hear splendidly. A small balcony had been erected in front of the steps, with
chairs for Mrs Gladstone, Mr Herbert Gladstone and Mr Kitson.[49] The Barrans

had chairs just behind them: of course everyone else stood. Great Liberal pro-
cessions soon came pouring in, with bands and banners, and long before 4
o'clock the whole vast hall was densely crowded, except just in one furthest
corner. We were in a tremendous jam, but are not the least the worse for it
... Papa ... got a 'platform ticket'. At 19 minutes to 4 they arrived, being
greeted with tremendous enthusiasm. The cheers then, and at every mention
of the name of Gladstone were something to remember all one's life. Mr Herbert Gladstone is very good looking, and very clever-looking, with a most
intelligent, wide-awake expression, and a very lively pleasant smile. He made
a capital speech, without the slightest hesitation for one moment, and it
seemed wonderfully little exertion to him. He has a very nice voice and capital delivery, and forms all his words with beautiful distinction. There were
about 30,000 people there, and he seemed to be heard perfectly all over. It
was most amusing to hear the remarks of the people round us: 'Good lad!'
'Eh, he's a nice lad!' 'Stick to it, my lad!' etc. and the enthusiastic cries of 'No!
No!' when he said anything about his 'own unworthiness'. Once he spoke of
the 'far greater men who had stood upon that platform', and was interrupted
with loud shouts of 'No! No!' whereupon he seemed much amused, shook his
head, and said laughing 'No, No. You won't quite make <u>that</u> go down with
me'. After his speech, a good many questions were sent up in writing, which
Mr Kitson read, and the tact and readiness with which Mr Herbert Gladstone
answered them delighted everyone. In fact, he really has taken everyone by
storm, and has completely stolen our hearts!

Then Mr Kitson asked whether any one wished to propose any other candidate, whereupon, amidst tremendous hooting and howling and roars of
laughter, a dirty, toothless, disreputable-looking workman mounted the platform, and (after daring to drink out of Herbert's glass of water!) proposed
John de Morgan! The hooting and howling made it often quite impossible for
him to speak, though the horn was blown two or three times for silence, and
Mr Kitson besought the people to 'give this gentleman two little minutes.'
The man declared 'he was a good Liberal and' (waving his hand in Mr Gladstone's face) 'I've noothing to say against this 'ere yoong mon. I daresay he's
a very good yoong mon!' upon which Mr Gladstone raised his hat, and made
him a most polite bow! No one was forthcoming to second the amendment,
which of course fell through and the resolution adopting Mr Herbert Gladstone was carried with immense enthusiasm, only 3 out of the 30,000 hands
being held up against it. Then 'Archie Sear' started 'For he's a jolly good
fellow!' which was roared out by the whole crowd, all of us doing our little
best to swell the chorus. Mr E. Wilson, Mr L. Gain, Mr McCheane, Mr Barran
and Mr Kitson also spoke. Mr Carter made the one bad-taste speech, raking
up the disestablishment question, and receiving little sympathy.[50] Mrs Gladstone authorised Mr Kitson to say that 'Mr Gladstone was the youngest
member of his family and Herbert was the youngest of hers', and also 'that
young gentleman had taken upon himself to select Downing St. as the place

of his birth!' – remarks which were received with much laughter and applause, and considered as arguing that we are now electing our future Premier. When the meeting was over they made their way along a raised passage which had been erected all along the side of the yard, and as they did so, hundreds of not-over-clean hands were stretched up for a shake! Mrs Gladstone bore it for some time and then she had to leave off; but we thought Mr Herbert's hand would be pretty nearly wrung off, as it was grasped by about 8 or 10 hands at a time the whole way along, while he gave them all hearty shakes, laughing the whole time. All the road was thronged with an enthusiastic crowd, and every available window crammed with spectators.

We got home at about 7, perfectly wild with admiration of our new hero. I wrote a four-sheet description of it all to Grandmamma.[51] The weather yesterday and today has been all that could be desired – 'Gladstone weather', we call it.

May 3, Monday: Into town ... and bought a capital cabinet of Mr Herbert Gladstone, Lilly doing the same.[52]

May 4, Tuesday: Finished 'Waverley' ... read 'Modern Painters'.

May 5, Wednesday: Alice and Marian Butler came to tea, and we took them there [to the Jowitts'] in the evening and finding them enthusiastic Gladstonians raved about 'Herbert' (whom they had not yet seen) the whole time.[53]

May 6, Thursday: Read aloud Mr Reid's lecture on Mr Gladstone. Mamma went to the lunch at S. Ann's, taking Eddie to Aunt Louie's, in hopes of his seeing the young hero[54] ... Mamma came home almost as enthusiastic as we are about Herbert. Says, 'she fell in love with him at once', 'he's a dear boy', 'perfectly charming and fascinating', 'one of the sweetest faces she ever saw', etc! Three cheers for the worthy son of a noble sire!

May 7, Friday: We talked, and read a pamphlet on Lord Beaconsfield aloud by turns. What a contrast to our Heroes!

May 8, Saturday: A most lovely day. Armed ourselves with Tennyson, and went to Mr Jowitt's where we read 'Maud' ... At 2 o'clock, Mrs S[cattergood], Lilly, Nelly, Louie and I, presented ourselves at Rice's, where we had been promised seats opposite the plat-form from which Mr Gladstone was to address the crowd. He was nominated, and returned unopposed, to everyone's great joy. A huge crowd filled the square, and we were dreadfully afraid we should not be able to hear a word, but Mr Gladstone's splendid clear voice was heard all over without any difficulty. He looked as charming as ever, and spoke so nicely. The show of hands was a sight to remember. Mr Barran disgusted us with a horribly conceited, patronising speech, talking of himself and Herbert as 'one man'!!

Afterwards we went round to the back of the Town Hall in hopes of seeing Herbert drive away; but the crush was so great that we could only see the top of his hat waving, and the carriage ...

May 9, Sunday: Cold and dull. Walked down to E.P.C. with Miss Shaw, who told me that she was in the Great Northern hotel on the night of Mr Herbert Gladstone's first arrival, and that he shook hands with her, all of his own accord! She was in one of the windows near the Cloth Hall Yard that Saturday, and took an active share in showering down primroses on the carriage after the meeting. She also threw down a handful of hot-house flowers, which he caught, and drove away holding them in his hand. Everyone seems to have shaken hands with him except our unhappy selves! A poor woman in the crowd yesterday told us that she had – wretch! ...

Pyp preached a very original and striking sermon (I thought) this morning, from Job 11.10: 'Shall we receive good at the hand of God, and shall we not receive evil?'

May 10, Monday: ... met Rose Henderson and Emily Pollock, who said they sat opposite Mr Herbert Gladstone in Church yesterday. Being prejudiced and ignorant Tories, they did not admire him! ... Read 'Alton Locke', darned, and read aloud a 'Spectator' article on the Indian appointments. (Lords Ripon and Hartington).[55]

May 12, Wednesday: Received by post this morning our Hero's autograph! I started the idea of asking him for it, in fun: Nellie took it up in ernest [sic], and insisted on writing, enclosing stamped and addressed envelope. Then we concocted a note, signed with all our initials, saying that 'Four enthusiastic young Liberals' (we were afraid to say 'admirers') 'would consider it the greatest possible favour if Mr Herbert Gladstone would send them his autograph'. So now behold the reward of cheek – one for each of us! ...[56]

May 14, Friday: ... studied the papers, reading a very good speech of Mr Herbert Gladstone's at the Devonshire Club banquet. Then went to Chapeltown shopping and strolled by Gledhow avenue examining the trees, which are just perfection ...

With those Chapeltown trees we return to the Leeds chapel round of Sunday school classes and Whitsun treats for the children in Mr Jowitt's park and a Sunday school glory to beat them all on Whit Tuesday. This was the Quinquennial Sunday School Sing (given added bravura by the approaching Robert Raikes centenary) held for the chapel children of Halifax in the Halifax Piece Hall, with Katharine sitting there in glorious sunshine, armed with *Alton Locke* and an ample lunch basket furnished by Uncle

Edward Crossley's factotum, two hours before it all began but not a moment too soon.[57]

> *May 18, Tuesday*: ... The schools were already pouring in, each preceded by a band (mostly very good ones) playing some lively tune. When two came in at once – as happened not infrequently – each lustily playing some tune totally different from the other, the effect was somewhat dire! While waiting I finished 'Alton Locke'. By 12, all the 99 schools (over 30,000 children and teachers) had assembled in the great square. As each school carried some gorgeous banner, and all the children were arrayed in their best, the effect was very bright and pretty. Also the whole square was hung with flags, and draped with crimson cloth. All the bands united in the orchestra, and led splendidly. The effect of the singing was very grand; the volume of sound not so great as I had expected, but beautifully pure and true, and the time capital. Before each tune, the drums sounded a roll for silence, then the band played the tune over, and then the children struck up. The simple hymn tunes (St. Ann's, Bradford, Eisenach and the Old Hundredth especially) were very grand. They also sang the choruses – Beethoven's Halleluiah, Mozart's Gloria, and Handel's Halleluiah – admirably, the Gloria being especially fine. Almost every single thing was encored, which we thought very hard upon the poor children's legs (they were standing nearly all the time), not to mention voices. The performance lasted till almost 4. We finished with the 'National Anthem', which was as grand as anything, everyone singing.

These were the hustings of heaven: loyalty, popular religion, popular culture, mass excitement, warmed and moulded into collectivity and mutuality, none here excluded from the pale of the Christian constitution, each with a part to play, each standing firmly on his (or her) own ground.

> All being over, we walked up to Bermerside, where we were soon followed by Aunt Janie and the Scattergoods, and had dinner. I gave Lilly the autograph, to her grand delight.
> After dinner, we had some music, and then left by the 8:13 train. The station was so crammed that I do not think we should ever have got tickets, but for a benevolent official, who went into the office, and brought us them. Came home tired, and of course found the car crowded, so came up on the top (for the first time). My valiant example was quickly followed by 5 other distressed feminines, who had not ventured to lead the way!

Thus are women of the Sunday school dominating classes emancipated – though not from the claims of cousinhood:

> *June 4, Friday*: Papa, Mamma and I went to tea at Mr Willans's ... to meet the Manwarings, Talbots, Maggie Reed, and Maggie and Emmie Baines ... Had a

very pleasant evening of music. This morning came a most scrumptious lovely invitation from Aunt Elise for E. and myself to go there in July. Calloo, callay![58]

It is important to be reminded that life is seriously to be enjoyed, that responsibility can be assumed, matter of course, and not be burdensome, that politics is part of life, its froth and passion too, and that women are part of politics as of life. Newton Park had an oblique but real family investment in Gladstonianism. It was more than flavour of the month or spirit of the age. For Lilly, Nellie, Laurie, Eddie, Ethel, Papa, Mamma, Aunt Janie, Aunt Louie, Uncle Jem, Cousin Manwaring, and deaf grandpapa isolated at St Ann's, it was heart beat, or at least heart-throb. There is nothing in Katharine Conder's account that may not be more acutely or immediately found about Yorkshire elections in Lady Frederick Cavendish's diaries or Lady Amberley's journals, but Lucy Cavendish and Kate Amberley were noblewomen, Anglican by formation and in Lady Frederick's case by conviction, daily in political circles.[59] Katharine Conder, Dissenting by formation and by conviction, was also daily in political circles. She was no noblewoman and until marriage took her to London her life was entirely provincial, but her fragmentary diaries are the counterpoint to theirs. Kate Amberley's are those of the aristocratic intelligentsia moving into a post-aristocratic age. Katharine Conder's are those of a Puritan intelligentsia less ready than they thought for that age but quite capable of adapting. They too had their networks.[60] And there was a useful place in them for a Grand Old Man and his promising youngest son.

IV

Note the names in Katharine Conder's diary. Most of them are related or at least connected: Lupton, Rücker, Conder, Baines, Barran, Crossley, Willans, Scattergood, Jowitt, Crewdson, Reed, Batten, Winterbotham, Heaton, Marchetti, Whitley. Their value lies in the fact that they are not (or not yet) Grosvenor, Lyttelton, Leveson-Gower, Cavendish or Russell. They are Congregational, Baptist, Quaker, Unitarian. They are carpets, textiles, newsprint, rag trade, medicine, law, banking. They are Leeds, Manchester, Cheltenham, Stroud, Halifax and Huddersfield. Sheffield, Bradford, Liverpool, London, Norwich and Edinburgh swim easily in. They are shades of Liberal, for these are the election-platform, aldermanic-bench, back-bench classes, municipal wire-pullers, ambitious for seats, poised for parliament. Here is the *Leeds Mercury* world of the Bainesocracy, in its late Indian summer. Its grand old man is soon-to-be-Sir Edward Baines up at St Ann's, deaf and isolated since his ousting by the Barranage in 1874. Their big new man is soon-to-be-Sir John Barran up at Chapel Allerton. But the Baineses and the Barrans are the same sort, East Parade Chapel to South Parade Chapel, and Edward Baines's step-granddaughter's greatest friend, Lilly Scattergood, daughter of Leeds's leading physician and East Parade's senior deacon, is shortly to marry South Parade's Alfred Barran, brother of the Rowland Barran whose by-election victory in the new century will be the last victory of Bainesocracy and Barranage alike.[61]

The diary's pivot, and pivotal to the network too, is papa. He is Eustace Rogers Conder, minister of East Parade Chapel and old Edward Baines's son-in-law. The *gravitas* of such a man, whether concentrated on one local congregation or mediated through a national network into several such congregations each represented by a string of such men, is not now easily understood. Yet an understanding of men like Conder is the key to this Dissenting peculiar established within the pale of the constitution, this choice chapel garden walled around in the pleasure grounds of the Victorian political nation. Gladstone had his finger on that key and he came closest to turning it in the late 1870s, greatly helped by his temperamental fascination with the working of institutions, his reverence for procedure and the consequent necessity for its due exploitation not least through established interest groups, among whom Dissenters were the most suggestive. Gladstone was more adept than any other parliamentary hand at pouring new wine into old bottles.[62]

This can be traced in his diaries. It can be understood in the moving (and now famous) reflection which he allowed himself in these otherwise dense *aides-mémoire* of days given to the higher stewardship. It can be followed in the lists of letters sent and received. It can be demonstrated by the infrastructure of letters, notes and cards with which the Grand Old Man got within the skin of each visiting experience. It can be pursued subliminally. When Gladstone read about 'The Water Supply of London' in *Fraser's*, he was reading a piece by F. R. Conder, Eustace's civil engineer brother.[63] When he wrote on 30 December 1878 to the Episcopalian incumbent of Fraserburgh to acknowledge his *The Real Character of the Early Records of Genesis* (which he looked at before turning to Dean Hook and chopping down a beech tree), he was writing to an apostate cousin of Eustace Conder's first wife.[64] When, on 8 January 1879, he was formally invited to stand for Midlothian, the invitation came from the constituency chairman, John Cowan, the Penicuik papermaker.[65] Although that set in train the events which at once took W. E. Gladstone from Leeds and sent Herbert Gladstone to Leeds, it was all within the network. The Cowans were great Free Church of Scotland people in Edinburghshire. John Cowan's brothers, Charles and James, sat for Edinburgh itself, Charles from 1847 to 1859 and James from 1874 to 1882. They were Gladstone's generation and their grandfather had been a Liverpool merchant.[66] That was not their only English link. Charlotte Cowan, Charles's daughter, was married to H. J. Wilson, the precious metal smelter and future MP whose family increasingly ran Sheffield Liberalism.[67] The Wilsons came originally from Nottingham where their most useful family and commercial connections were with Samuel Morley, that Olympian impresario of Congregational philanthropy and sensible (which by 1880 meant Gladstonian) politics; and he, of course, though his fortune was Nottingham-born, was London- and Kent-based.[68] In Sheffield the Wilsons and their kinsmen, the Leaders and Pye-Smiths, were the very pattern of Congregationalism and Sheffield's Leadership was a distinct, if faint, reflection of the Leeds Bainesocracy to which the Leaders, Pye-Smiths, Wilsons and Morleys were all connected by marriage or descent.[69]

It is Sheffield, indeed, which illustrates the naturalness of this Gladstonian–Nonconformist convergence. When the Gladstones grudgingly left 11 Carlton House Terrace for 73 Harley Street, they encountered the locketed, ringleted and Pre-Raphaelite Mrs Birks of No. 71. Gladstone enjoyed her hospitality and was soon on dining terms with her. She quizzed him on fiscal policy and he wrote to her about the malt tax.[70] Whatever her allure, Judith Ann Birks was no Laura Thistlethwayte or Olga Novikoff. She was the widow of Thomas Birks, a Sheffield brewer and former mayor.[71] Samuel Plimsoll had been one of his clerks. Birks's family, the brewery notwithstanding, were active at two, perhaps three, Sheffield Congregational churches. A great-uncle of Katharine Conder had ministered at one of them. Thomas Rawson Birks, who left Dissent for a safer Anglican Evangelicalism and became Knightbridge Professor at Cambridge, was Thomas Birks's first cousin.[72] There were other connections. Mrs Birks's daughter was Mrs Louis Crossley of Moorside, Halifax, whom Katharine Conder visited and with whom Lady Frederick Cavendish, Mrs Gladstone's niece and wife of the North-West Riding's Liberal candidate, stayed for the 1880 election.[73] Louis Crossley was the brother of Mrs Marchetti and the first cousin of Edward Crossley, whose wife was Katharine Conder's Aunt Janie. His niece, Margarita Marchetti, married a future Speaker of the House of Commons, J. H. Whitley, son of the Nathan Whitley who is also mentioned in Katharine Conder's diaries.[74] This was the very purple of Yorkshire Congregationalism. As for Mrs Birks, her own Congregationalism had survived Sheffield at least to February 1876, since she was until then a member of Westminster Chapel where Samuel Martin drew crowded but discriminating congregations.[75] That might explain her Pre-Raphaelite air since Martin's hearers included the art-collecting Glasgow MP, William Graham.[76]

Whatever the state of Mrs Birks's churchmanship at the time of her dinners for Mr Gladstone, its context cannot have been wholly unknown to him. For example, on 22 March 1878, Gladstone 'Spent the forenoon at a breakfast of Nonconformists around Mrs Birks's table: much interesting conversation'.[77] Such links were natural, as well as gratifying for the hostess and useful for her chief guest. On such occasions the Dissenting thinking classes could chatter with the Westminster classes. Here was the first Prime Minister whom they could easily see and quite likely meet and come to feel that they knew, without ever having to dethrone him from his necessary pedestal.

Their convergence, as concentrated so memorably as this one was, so representative because so outsize, was unique. No other politician could have retained that response once elicited, been so interested in it, or indeed would have wished to or needed to. Gladstone's prime ministerial predecessors furnish only one serious candidate, Lord John Russell, and he is easily ruled out.[78] Gladstone's successors furnish several candidates, but only in theory. Asquith's formation was firmly in Katharine Conder's world, but he made little use of it after 1890, although he was not allowed to slip away from it quite as easily as his biographers have made out.[79] Though received in his teens into the membership of a Congregational church, and a chapel-goer for longer, Asquith was not a serious person. The form marked him and it always interested him. The reality was irrelevant to him. Besides, regardless of any temperamental or spiritual affinities, the political attractiveness of a Free Church-accented Liberalism was visibly diminishing and its intellectual allure was increasingly confined to specialists. Sectional interests need sophisticated handling in a system of universal suffrage, especially if their solidarity cannot be taken for granted. At the very moment when that artefact of the years after 1885, the 'Nonconformist Conscience', was forming in people's minds and beginning to trip from their lips, the reality behind it was more than ever in doubt. That conscience was itself a convergence of influences of almost bewildering diversity, the Gladstonian rapport among them; but they were influences only, increasingly more memory than reality.

Yet influences can be strong. Their most powerful and enduring property is diffusion. Take the Conder connection. Ethel Mary transmitted its values as headmistress first of a school in north Kent for ministers' daughters, proud of its links with the women at Cambridge, and then of a school of her own in Hampstead and later in Swanage.[80] Katharine married an ophthalmic surgeon, moved to Kensington and became a deacon (and thus one of its earlier female officeholders) of Allen Street Congregational Church where at various times her stepmother and sisters were also members.[81] Ethel's church in Hampstead and Katharine's in Kensington, like Mrs Birks's in Westminster, were popular resting places for Free Church MPs when in town, though their most consistently distinctive members were society's proliferating intermediaries, the mental artmen of earlier generations now upgrading into the educators, civil servants and professionals who enacted while the MPs merely acted. Laurie married a Cheltenham cousin and became an architect in Buenos Aires.[82] Little Eddie became an Anglican parson, latterly at Leamington Spa.[83] Uncle John Willans, who by 1890 was second proprietor at the *Leeds Mercury*, retired first to Harrogate and then to West Hampstead where he died on May Day 1910. He was the as-yet-childless uncle who in the 1860s had had most to do with the London schooling of the man who by 1910 was Prime Minister.[84]

And there was a gentle, almost peripheral, social convergence. Cousin Talbot of the *Mercury* married in 1891, *en second noces*, a niece of Lady

Frederick Cavendish. Though she was thus a great-niece by marriage of Mrs Gladstone, she was also at once a Tory MP's daughter and niece of the vicar of Leeds, a man determined to do for Anglicanism and Leeds what R. W. Dale had done for Congregationalism and Birmingham.[85] One of Talbot's sons became a bishop.[86] Though the *Leeds Mercury* still sounded a home rule and therefore Gladstonian note (it could do little else given the circumstances of that celebrated proto-leak, Herbert Gladstone's 'Hawarden Kite'), the last Baines to be associated with it, and the first to be brought by marriage within the Gladstonian circle, was a Liberal Unionist and Liberal Imperialist. As one of the Jowitts put it: 'he had lost faith in Mr Gladstone, and could not trust any party which had him for its leader'.[87]

All of which suggests less the failure of Nonconformist politics, theology or nerve than their success. It suggests values as much assimilated as overturned or jettisoned, the values of a representative churchmanship, broad but freely elected, which is to say elite; the values of order as opposed to anarchy; of trust more than democracy; of principle enabled by, rather than trimmed or tempered by, policy. They are the natural values of sound establishments, developed in counterpoint to those of kings or barons: counterpoint, not opposition, for these, though chapel-styled and pulpit-slanted, were also Gladstonian values.

Notes

1　This paper reworks and redirects, with additional material to emphasise the networks of family connection, a paper given in Edinburgh and published as '"I suppose You Are Not a Baptist or a Roman Catholic?" Nonconformity's True Conformity', in *Victorian Values*, ed. T. C. Smout, Proceedings of the British Academy, 78, Oxford UP, 1992, pp. 81–107; it is further contexted in C. Binfield, 'The Story of Button Hill: An Essay in Leeds Nonconformity', in *Religion in Leeds*, ed. A. Mason, Stroud, Alan Sutton, 1994, pp. 79–107.

2　S. G. Checkland, *The Gladstones: A Family Biography 1769–1851*, Cambridge, Cambridge UP, 1971.

3　The Gladstone–Hawarden links over subsequent generations are set out in A. G. Veysey, *Mr Gladstone and Hawarden*, Hawarden, Clwyd Record Office, 1982. Hawarden Castle had belonged to Catherine Gladstone's family, the Glynnes, since 1653. The Gladstone involvement increased after financial crisis hit the ninth baronet, Sir Stephen Glynne, in 1847, and it was effectively W. E. Gladstone's country house from the early 1850s. In 1867 he purchased the reversion of the estate, transferring ownership to his eldest son, W. H. Gladstone, after Sir Stephen's death in 1874. The appalling financial problems, though reduced, were not solved in Gladstone's lifetime.

4　John Neilson Gladstone (1807–63) lived at Bowden Park, Chippenham, Wilts; Henry Neville Gladstone (1852–1935) owned Burton Manor, Neston, from 1903 to 1921. Designed (1904) by Sir Charles Nicholson with gardens (from 1906) by T. H. Mawson, Burton is described in J. M. Robinson, *A Guide to the Country Houses of the North West*, London, Constable, 1991, p. 16.

5 John Neilson Gladstone, Capt., RN, on half-pay in 1835; Sir John Robert Gladstone (1852–1926), third baronet, was in the Coldstream Guards; William Glynne Charles Gladstone (1885–1915), Royal Welsh Fusiliers, was killed at Laventie, 15 April 1915; (Sir) Charles Andrew Gladstone (1888–1968), sixth baronet, was attached to the R. F. C and taken prisoner in 1915; his brother Stephen, attached to the 9th Gurkha Rifles, MC, and mentioned in despatches.

6 Stephen Gladstone (1844–1920) was rector of Hawarden, 1872–1904, and Barrowby, Lincs., 1904–11; his elder sister, Agnes Gladstone (1842–1931), married Edward Wickham, later Dean of Lincoln, and his younger sister, Mary Gladstone (1847–1927), married Henry Drew, vicar of Buckley, 1897–1905, and rector of Hawarden, 1905–10. Stephen's first cousin, Catherine Gladstone (d. 1919) of Bowden Park, married W. C. Lake, Dean of Durham.

7 In addition to W. E. Gladstone's double first, there was W.H.Gladstone's first in Classical Moderations (1860) and second in Classics (1862), and Herbert Gladstone's first in History (1876; also his third in Classical Moderations, 1874). W. E. Gladstone was president of the Union in 1830; W. G. C. Gladstone in 1907.

8 W. E. Gladstone became Lord Rector of Edinburgh in 1859 and 1862 and of Glasgow in 1877; Henry Neville Gladstone became President of the University College of North Wales, Bangor, in 1928; Herbert Gladstone was History Lecturer at Keble, Oxford, 1877–80.

9 Helen Gladstone (1849–1925) was Vice-Principal of Newnham, 1882–86, and Head of the University Settlement, Southwark, 1901–06. Mrs Gladstone's niece, Lady Frederick Cavendish, was a supporter of Lady Margaret Hall, Oxford, chiefly promoted by her brother-in-law (Mrs Gladstone's nephew-in-law), Edward Stuart Talbot, then Warden of Keble. Lady Frederick felt that Lady Margaret Hall sounded like a noblewoman fallen on hard times; what would she have made of her own late memorial, Lucy Cavendish College, Cambridge? Margaret Stewart Gladstone (Mrs Frank Pollard, 1903–96) was the Cambridge orientalist.

10 (Sir) Charles Andrew Gladstone was a master at Eton, 1912–46, as was his son Sir William Gladstone (seventh baronet, b. 1925), 1951–61, who was then headmaster of Lancing College, 1961–69. Edward Wickham, later Dean of Lincoln, was Master of Wellington.

11 The family firm was Ogilvy Gillanders and Co. Henry Neville Gladstone's concern for the Indian side of the business lasted from 1874 to 1889. (Sir) Albert Charles Gladstone (1886–1967), fifth baronet, was also with Ogilvy Gillanders and became a director of the Bank of England. For Robert Gladstone (b. 1833), great-nephew and grandson-in-law of Sir John Gladstone, first baronet (he married a daughter of Robertson Gladstone, Sir John's second son, mayor of Liverpool in 1842) see W.T.Pike (ed.), *Liverpool and Birkenhead in the Twentieth Century: Contemporary Biographies*, Brighton, W. T. Pike, 1911, pp. 137–38.

12 J. Bateman, *The Great Landowners of Great Britain and Ireland*, 4th edn, 1883, Leicester University Press reprint, ed. D. Spring, 1974, p. 184.

13 Herbert Gladstone became Viscount Gladstone of Lanark in 1910; his house in the country, Dane End, Ware, belonged to his wife's family; he also had a seaside house, Sandycroft, Littlestone, in a part of Kent peppered with Liberal houses. Henry Neville Gladstone became Baron Gladstone of Hawarden in 1932.

14 W. E. Gladstone married Catherine Glynne, daughter of Sir Stephen Glynne,

eighth baronet; J. N. Gladstone married Elizabeth Bateson, daughter of Sir Robert Bateson (1782–1863), first baronet, of Belvoir Park, Antrim, Conservative MP, Londonderry, 1830–42, and sister of Sir Thomas Bateson (1819–90), Conservative MP, Londonderry, 1844–57, and Devizes, 1864–85 (his Gladstone brother-in-law's old seat), created first Baron Deramore 1885. These potentially useful Irish (and Wiltshire) links were compounded when Elizabeth Gladstone (d. 1919), daughter of J. N. Gladstone, married the fourth Earl of Belmore (d. 1913). They extended Wales-wards when Thomas Bateson married a daughter of the fourth Lord Dynevor.

15 Robert Gladstone married Dorothy Paget, daughter of Sir Richard Horner Paget (1832–1908), first baronet, Conservative MP, E. Somerset, 1865–68, Mid Somerset, 1868–85, and Wells, 1885–95; Henry Neville Gladstone married Maud Rendel, daughter of Stuart Rendel (1834–1913), MP, Montgomery, 1880–94, first Baron Rendel 1894; William Henry Gladstone married Gertrude Stuart, daughter of twelfth and last Baron Blantyre (1818–1900) and granddaughter of second Duke of Sutherland. Sir John Evelyn Gladstone (1855–1945), fourth baronet, married Gertrude Miller, daughter of Sir Charles Miller, seventh baronet; his sisters Lucy (d. 1921) and Elizabeth (d. 1919) married Sir Reginald Hardy Bt (d. 1938) and the fourth Earl of Belmore respectively. Lord Belmore, a governor of New South Wales, was first cousin of Disraeli's secretary, Montagu Lowry Corry, first Baron Rowton.

16 The town addresses of Sir Thomas Gladstone (second baronet), J. N. Gladstone, W. H. and W. G. C. Gladstone, Herbert Gladstone and W. E. Gladstone respectively.

17 The Gladstone MPs were Sir John (first baronet), Lancaster, 1818–20, Woodstock, 1820–26; Berwick, 1826–27; Sir Thomas (second baronet), Queenborough, 1830–32, Portarlington, 1832–35, Leicester, 1835–37, Ipswich, 1842; W. E. Gladstone, Newark, 1832–45; Oxford University, 1847–65; S. Lancashire, 1865–68, Greenwich, 1868–80, and Midlothian, 1880–95; J. N. Gladstone, Walsall, 1841, Ipswich, 1842–47, and Devizes, 1852–57, 1859–63; W. H. Gladstone, Chester, 1865–68, Whitby, 1868–80, and E. Worcestershire, 1880–85; Herbert Gladstone, Leeds, 1880–85, and W. Leeds, 1885–1910; W. G. C. Gladstone, Kilmarnock Burghs, 1911–15. In addition to the seats which the seven failed to capture, two Tory Gladstones (Robert, for Lancaster 1857, and John Evelyn, for Spen Valley 1885) stood, failed and made no further attempt.

18 Lord Frederick Cavendish (1836–82), a younger son of the Duke of Devonshire, had married Mrs Gladstone's niece, the Hon. Lucy Lyttelton, in 1864.

19 Sir Stephen Glynne, W. E. Gladstone's brother-in-law, was MP for Flintshire, 1831–47.

20 Stuart Rendel. See above n. 15.

21 The main office holders were of course W. E. Gladstone and Herbert Gladstone; W. H. Gladstone was a Lord of the Treasury (1869–74) and W. G. C. Gladstone was a private secretary to Lord Aberdeen, Viceroy of Ireland, in 1909, and Honorary Attaché at Washington under James Bryce (1910–11): here indeed was a grave statesman in the making, last of the great and truly good Whigs.

22 The Tory Gladstone MPs were (Sir) John and (Sir) Thomas (unseated for Berwick, 1827, and Ipswich, 1842, respectively) and J. N. Gladstone. The Liberals were Herbert, William Henry and W. G. C. Gladstone. The Grand Old Man was, of course, both.

23 Robert Rainy (1826–1906) was the acknowledged statesman and thrice moderator of Scotland's second largest denomination, the Free (later the United Free) Church of Scotland. As principal of its New College from 1874 he was supreme among manse-placers. He followed Gladstone on home rule and his son, A. R. Rainy (1862–1911), was MP for Kilmarnock, 1906–11.

24 Enoch Gibbon Salisbury (1819–90), barrister and gasworks proprietor, was son-in-law and brother-in-law of Congregational ministers. He was Liberal MP for Chester, 1857–59, and candidate, 1859 and 1868.

25 M. Bentley, 'Gladstonian Liberals and Provincial Notables: Whitby Politics, 1868–80', *Historical Research*, Vol. 64, 1991, pp. 172–85, and 'Gladstone's Heir', *English Historical Review*, Vol. 107, 1992, pp. 901–24.

26 Arthur Pease (1837–98), son of the first Quaker MP, Joseph Pease (MP South Durham, 1832–34), was Liberal MP Whitby, 1880–85, and Liberal Unionist MP, Darlington, 1895–98.

27 Katharine Roubiliac Conder (1860–1948), a great-great-granddaughter of the sculptor L. F. Roubiliac (1695–1762). I am indebted to her grandson, Mr R. J. Simpson, for access to her diaries and permission to quote from them, and to Dr Emma Mason for first alerting me to them. I am indebted to Mr Jack Winterbotham, his cousin Mr John Winterbotham, and his daughter Mrs Melanie Cox, and to Mr Hew Stevenson for elucidation of the Winterbotham and Conder family trees.

28 Ethel Mary Conder (1859–1942), Girton, 1879–82.

29 William Bolton (1846–1921), Congregational minister at Newton, Leeds, 1874–79, subsequently in Hastings and London. Papa is Eustace Rogers Conder (1820–92), Congregational minister at Poole (1844–61), and East Parade, Leeds (1861–92), Chairman of Congregational Union of England and Wales, 1873.

30 Baby is Edward Baines Conder (1872–1936), son of E. R. Conder by his second wife, Anne Catherine Baines (1841–1924); Laurie is Eustace Lauriston Conder (1863–1935), son of E. R. Conder by his first wife, Mary Batten Winterbotham (1835–69).

31 Mamma is thus step-mamma, Anne Catherine Baines, daughter of (Sir) Edward Baines (1800–90). Min is perhaps Margaret Brend Conder (1862–1945), later Mrs Ernest Hill.

32 David Livingstone (1813–73), Scottish Congregationalist serving with the London Missionary Society 1840–57, had become a living legend. He was found dead in Ilala, 1 May 1873, and buried in Westminster Abbey, 18 April 1874.

33 St Ann's, Burley, was the home of (Sir) Edward Baines (Grandpapa B), proprietor of the *Leeds Mercury* and MP, Leeds, 1859–74, knighted December 1880. Aunt Jainie (sic) was his third daughter, Jane Eleanor Baines (1844–98), wife of Edward Crossley of Halifax (see n. 37). The Jubilee Singers were a choir of black American gospel singers, originally freed slaves.

34 *Diary of Mrs Kitty Trevylyan: A Story of the Times of Whitefield and the Wesleys*, By the Author of 'Chronicles of the Schonberg-Cotta Family' etc etc. (1865). *Chronicles* was a story of the times of Luther. Both were immensely popular and the *Schonberg-Cottas* were translated into Arabic. Their author was Elizabeth Rundle Charles (1828–96), whose immense published *oeuvre*, chiefly tales of Christian life, equalled her popularity. She is today best known for the hymn, 'Never Further than Thy Cross, Never Higher than Thy Feet'. In earlier life her

Tractarian-accented Anglicanism almost lapsed into Roman Catholicism but her Nonconformist readers were unwavering.

35 The Jowitts of Newton Grove and Harehills were originally a Quaker family, several times related to the Whitwells and Wilsons of Kendal and Middlesbrough and the Crewdsons of Manchester. Their Congregationalism (like that of several Whitwells, Wilsons and Crewdsons) dated from the Beaconite controversy and their active association with East Parade began in 1858. By the 1870s they were also several times related to the Baineses. John Jowitt was a deacon by 1858; Florence Jowitt (b. 1855), member from 1868, married Annie Conder's first cousin, A. P. Baines, (b. 1848). For the Barrans see below n. 40. Maggie Baines is probably Margaret (1856–1926), half-sister of A. P. Baines.

36 Medical men were often at the heart of a provincial city's literary culture. Dr Thomas Scattergood (1826–1900), of Park Square, was a leading Leeds physician, an early pillar of the Leeds School of Medicine and its dean when it united with Yorkshire College (ancestor of the present University of Leeds). His wife, Mary Haigh (d. 1892), helped compile the widely used *Leeds Hymn Book*. Dr Scattergood was a member of East Parade from 1853 and a deacon by 1858. His daughter, Lilly Maria Scattergood (d. 1885), joined East Parade in 1875 and married Alfred Barran (see below n. 61). Dr Heaton is John Deakin Heaton (1817–80). The Heatons were old friends of the Baineses and originally South Parade Baptists. J. D. Heaton, of Claremont, had become firmly Anglican and moderately Tory. Physician at Leeds General Infirmary from 1850, he too was active in the cultural, educational and philanthropic life of Leeds and was prime mover of the Yorkshire College of Science. He died 28 March 1880. The Little Owl, a society of twelve young women (not so much ladies who lunch as ladies who count, and think) which still exists, had been founded in November 1879 by Dr Heaton's daughter Helen. It seems to have been modelled on the male Conversation Club (founded 1849) whose members included Dr Heaton, two Baineses, two Jowitts and, it is thought, E. R. Conder. I am indebted to Miss Joan Newiss for this information

37 Dean Clough was the Crossley family's carpet factory in Halifax. An assertive man, Edward Crossley (1841–1905), husband of Jane Eleanor Baines, was a deacon of Square Congregational Chapel, Halifax, 1872–88; mayor of Halifax, 1874–76, 1883–85; MP, Sowerby, 1885–92. In October 1887 he laid a foundation stone of the grandly rebuilt Newton Park Union Church.

38 Broomfield had been the home of Edward Crossley's father, Joseph Crossley (1813–68). Mrs Marchetti was Anne Crossley (d. 1925), daughter of Joseph's brother, John Crossley (1812–79), of Manor Heath, MP, Halifax, 1874–77. She was the second wife of Giulio Marchetti (1843–1931), who had fought with Garibaldi, came to England in 1865, married first the daughter of a prominent London Congregational minister related to the Morleys of Nottingham, London, and Leeds (see below n. 68), and secondly, in 1871, Anne Crossley. He was a director of Crossleys from 1879. Nathan Whitley (1830–89), of Greenroyd, was mayor of Halifax, 1877, 1882–83, deacon of Park Congregational Church, Halifax, and cardmaker of John Whitley & Sons, and S. Whitley & Co.

39 Edward Crossley's Bermerside, like his cousin Louis Crossley's Moorside (see below n. 73), was famous for its observatory and its gadgets.

40 Chapel Allerton Hall was the home of (Sir) John Barran (1821–1905), first

baronet (1895), founder of John Barran & Sons which revolutionised the Leeds rag trade; mayor of Leeds, 1870–72; MP, Leeds, 1876–85, Otley, 1886–95; deacon of South Parade Baptist Church, treasurer of Rawdon Baptist College. He laid the foundation stone of the Newton Congregational Chapel in 1870 and (with Edward Crossley) that of its grand successor, the Newton Park Union Church, in 1887.

41 Papa's class did not train superior servants; it studied Joseph Butler of *Analogy* (1736) fame. Joseph Butler (1692–1752), Bishop of Durham, intended for the Presbyterian ministry, had been educated at a Dissenting academy.

42 Louie Barran (d. 1944), daughter of John Barran of Chapel Allerton, married Harry Manfield (1855–1923), the Northampton boot manufacturer, Liberal MP, Mid Northants, 1906–18, and son of Sir Philip Manfield (1819–99), MP, Northampton, 1891–95. The Manfields were Unitarians.

43 Alfred, Duke of Edinburgh, later of Saxe-Coburg (1844–1900), the Queen's second son, married the Grand Duchess Marie of Russia (1853–1920), who swiftly became the least fairy-tale (though probably the most intelligent) of the royal daughters-in-law.

44 Auntie Katie was perhaps Katharine's unmarried aunt Catherine Brend Winterbotham (1844–1931).

45 Arthur (1850–1942), the Queen's third, and by all accounts most straightforward son, was created Duke of Connaught that May. Beatrice (1857–1944), the Queen's youngest child, married Prince Henry of Battenberg in 1885.

46 Mrs Dent (d. 1900) was born Emma Brocklehurst, third daughter of a silk manufacturer, John Brocklehurst (1788–1870), Liberal MP, Macclesfield, 1832–68. In 1847 she married the Tory J. C. Dent (1819–85) of Sudeley Castle, whose family had restored the ruined castle in 1837. On Mrs Dent's death the Sudeley estate passed to a Brocklehurst nephew who in 1881 had married a Lascelles. Thus was an instant recreation of antique England legitimated. The Macclesfield Brocklehursts were of Unitarian stock. Katharine's *entrée* to Sudeley was through a family friend, Mrs Swinburne, as well as through her uncle and aunt, the Lauriston Winterbothams. The Winterbothams by 1874 were concentrated in Stroud, where they were solicitors, bankers and manufacturers; in Cheltenham, where they were solicitors; and in London, where they were also solicitors. They prospered in all three places.

47 Sir J. E. Millais (1829–96) 'was never more successful than in realising the grand head and keen expression of W. E. Gladstone, whom he painted in 1879, 1885, and 1890' (*DNB*); his was a Gladstone baronetcy (1885). Uncle Jem is probably the Cheltenham solicitor, Liberal and wirepuller, James Batten Winterbotham (1837–1914).

48 The full figures were: W. E. Gladstone (L) 24,622; W. L. Jackson (C) 13,331; J. Barran (L) 23,647; W. St. J. Wheelhouse (C) 11, 965. Leeds was a three-member seat 1868–85, so Wheelhouse, MP since 1868, was out. J. Vincent and M. Stenton (eds), *McCalmont's Parliamentary Poll Book: British Election Results 1832–1918*, 8th edn, Brighton, Harvester Press, 1971, p. 136. Mr Willans is John Wrigley Willans (1831–1910), wool merchant, carpet manufacturer and, from 1875, a partner in and proprietor of the *Leeds Mercury*; he married Charlotte Baines (1830–79), eldest daughter of (Sir) Edward Baines and sister of Mrs Eustace Conder; he was a member of East Parade,

1876–94.

49 (Sir) James Kitson (1835–1911), first baronet 1886, first Baron Airedale 1907; Lord Mayor of Leeds, 1896–97; MP, Colne Valley, 1892–1907; iron and steel manufacturer of Gledhow Hall; Unitarian.

50 Robert Meek Carter (1814–82), of Hope Well House, coal merchant, cloth finisher and Radical. MP, Leeds, 1868–76.

51 Mrs John Brend Winterbotham of Cheltenham, neé Mary Prowse Batten (d. 1881).

52 From the 1860s the calculated immediacy of photography created a mass celebrity trade in which the royal family, politicians and preachers vied with each other. The *carte-de-visite* (it was calling-card size) made famous faces collectible in countless homes. In the 1870s the cabinet size became the vogue. Larger and broader, it favoured head-and-shoulders portraits. At the turn of the 1880s came the promenade portrait, which was larger again. See A. Thomas, *The Expanding Eye: Photography and the Nineteenth-Century Mind*, London, Croom Helm, 1978, p. 84 and *passim*.

53 Perhaps daughters of Edward Butler (d. 1891), descendant of Oliver Cromwell, of Hampden Villa, Leeds, Chairman of Leeds School Board, 1882–88; co-compiler of *Leeds Hymn Book*, and member of East Parade from 1846.

54 Mr Reid was (Sir) Thomas Wemyss Reid (1842–1905), son, son-in-law, and father of Congregational ministers, connected with the *Leeds Mercury* from 1866 and its editor 1870–87, thus providing the wind for the Hawarden Kite; biographer *inter alia* of Dr J. D. Heaton (1883) and Gladstone (1899); knighted 1894; member of East Parade from 1870. Aunt Louie was Louisa Haigh (b. 1838), widow of J. W. Baines (1839–75), who was a founder and deacon of Headingley Hill Congregational Church, to which Reid transferred his membership.

55 The first Marquess of Ripon (1827–1923) had been MP, Hull, 1852–53, Huddersfield, 1853–57, West Riding, 1857–59. He was Viceroy of India, 1880–84. It was thought shocking that a Roman Catholic convert should hold that post. The Marquess of Hartington, later eighth Duke of Devonshire (1833–1908), Frederick Cavendish's elder brother, was MP, Lancashire, 1857–68, Radnor, 1869–80, North-East Lancashire 1880–85. He was Secretary of State for India, 1880–82.

56 Nellie was Helen Elizabeth Conder (1865–1946), Katharine's youngest sister, member of East Parade, 1881–1900.

57 The Quinquennial Sunday School Sings were held in the Halifax Piece Hall from 1831 to 1890. In 1881 (the Robert Raikes Jubilee), 13,801 children took part. In 1888 there were 30,985 with 3,593 teachers from 93 local Sunday schools, all of them Dissenters, ranging from 6,472 Congregationalists to 320 Unitarians: J. A. Hargreaves, 'Religion and Society in the Parish of Halifax, *c*. 1740–1914', unpublished Ph.D. thesis, Huddersfield Polytechnic, 1991, pp. 187, 315.

58 Edward Manwaring Baines (1842–97) and his half-brother Talbot Baines (1852–1923, see also n. 85), first cousins of Mrs E. R. Conder, had married Ulsterwomen, Maria and Margaret McCrone Greer, daughters of Samuel McCurdy Greer (1810–80), Presbyterian, barrister and Liberal MP, Co. Derry, 1857–59. Their sister, Elizabeth Greer, married Talbot Baines's cousin and closest friend Talbot Baines Reed (1852–93), the writer, and their brother, Thomas Macgregor Greer (1853–1928), Presbyterian, solicitor and Unionist, in 1880

married Reed's sister Margaret (Maggie) Reed, daughter of Sir Charles Reed (1819–81), Liberal MP, Hackney, 1868–74, and St Ives, 1880–81. Lady Reed was Margaret Baines (1817–91), sister of Sir Edward. Charles Reed's brother, Andrew Reed (1817–91), a Congregational minister, married Rachel Jowitt at East Parade in 1846. Emily Baines, Talbot's sister, married J. Henry Best (b. 1856), her first cousin, Congregational minister at Hopton, Yorkshire, 1883–92, then curate at Kirkstall, 1892–95, and vicar of Stanningley, 1895–1906. Aunt Elise was the recently married Mrs James B. Winterbotham (Eliza McLaren) of Cheltenham; in August she gave birth to her first child, Clara, who in 1921 became Cheltenham's first woman mayor.

59 See J. Bailey (ed.), *The Diary of Lady Frederick Cavendish*, 2 vols, London, John Murray, 1927; B. and P. Russell (eds), *The Amberley Papers*, 2 vols, London, L. & V. Woolf, 1937.

60 See, for their cultural outworking, for Quakers, C. Binfield, 'The Pleasures of Imagination: A Conundrum and its Context', *Durham University Journal*, Vol. 86, 1994, pp. 227–40; and, for Baptists, Marjorie Reeves, *Sheep Bell and Ploughshare*, London, Moonraker Press, 1978, and *Pursuing the Muses*, London, Leicester University Press, 1997; and June Lewis (ed.), *The Secret Diary of Sarah Thomas 1860–1865*, Moreton-in-Marsh, Windrush Press, 1994. Sarah Thomas's step-daughter became the second wife of J. W. Willans of Leeds.

61 Alfred Barran (1851–1927), of Moor House, Headingley, second son of Sir John Barran, clothier, sewing-machine dealer and director of Wall Paper Manufacturers Ltd; deacon of South Parade Baptist Church from 1885; president of Yorkshire Baptist Union, 1907. (Sir) Rowland Hirst Barran (1858–1949), of Beechwood, Roundhay, was sixth son of Sir John Barran, and MP, North Leeds (the Newton Park area), 1902–18; his was a famous victory attributed by Nonconformists and Passive Resisters to his stand against Balfour's Education Act. He was a Liberal Imperialist and later a Coalitionist; knighted 1917. When in London he worshipped at Allen Street Congregational Church (Kensington Chapel).

62 This argument is developed in A. Adonis, 'Byzantium and Liverpool: Marx's critique of Gladstone – and Gladstone's refutation by example', *Times Literary Supplement*, 9 February 1996, pp. 12–13.

63 GD, 6 March 1880. Francis Roubiliac Conder (1815–89), civil engineer, pupil of Brunel and Robert Stephenson; prolific writer best known for *Personal Recollections of English Engineers*, 1868.

64 GD, 30 December 1878. Rayner Winterbotham (1842–1924), canon of Edinburgh.

65 GD, 8 January 1879, n. (Sir) John Cowan (1814–1900), first baronet, (1894); paper manufacturer of Penicuik.

66 Charles Cowan (1801–89), paper manufacturer, MP, Edinburgh, 1847–1869; James Cowan (1816–95), paper manufacturer, Lord Provost of Edinburgh, 1872–74; MP, Edinburgh 1874–82. Their mother, Mrs Alex. Cowan, was daughter of George Hall, of Liverpool.

67 Charlotte Cowan (1833–1921) married Henry Joseph Wilson (1833–1914), Sheffield precious metal smelter and Congregationalist with strong Quaker tendencies; MP, Holmfirth, 1885–1912. Their son, Cecil Henry Wilson (1862–1945), Congregationalist turned Quaker, was Labour MP, Sheffield Attercliffe, 1922–31, 1935–44.

68 Samuel Morley (1809–86), Nottingham hosiery manufacturer, son-in-law of Samuel Hope, Liverpool banker, and member of King's Weigh House Congregational Church, London; MP, Nottingham, 1865, Bristol, 1868–85. H. J. Wilson's father was his first cousin (and brother-in-law). His grandson, Geoffrey Hope-Morley, second Baron Hollenden (1885–1977), married Muriel Gladstone (d. 1962), daughter of Sir J. E. Gladstone, fourth baronet.

69 Samuel Morley's first cousin, Richard Morley (1801–56), was a Leeds manufacturer and member of East Parade; Richard Morley's niece, Ada Smith, was the first wife of Giulio Marchetti (see above, n. 38). The Leaders ran the *Sheffield Independent* from 1829; Mrs Robert Leader, the founder's wife, and Mrs Edward Baines sr of Leeds were cousins. The Pye-Smiths, Congregationalists like the Leaders and Wilsons, furnished a civic dynasty of Sheffield solicitors, and several times intermarried with Leaders, Wilsons and Baineses. They replicated the Winterbothams, with whom there were close friendships as well as distant relationships.

70 *GD*, vol. 9, p. lxxx.

71 Thomas Birks (d. 1861), brewer, and mayor of Sheffield, 1849; associated with Queen Street Congregational Church; married secondly Judith Ann Elam.

72 Thomas Rawson Birks (1810–83), first cousin of Thomas Birks the brewer; educated at the Dissenting Mill Hill School; rector of Holy Trinity, Cambridge, 1866–77; Knightbridge Professor of Moral Philosophy, 1872–83; married into the formidably Evangelical Bickersteth family.

73 Hannah Rawson Birks (d. 1925), of 21 Gloucester Gardens, member of Westminster Chapel 1862–66, married Louis John Crossley (1842–91), of Moorside, Halifax, organist at Square Chapel and son of John Crossley (d. 1879). For Lady Frederick's visit to the Louis and Edward Crossleys see J. Bailey (ed.), *The Diary of Lady Frederick Cavendish*, vol. 2, p. 247.

74 John Henry Whitley (1866–1935), MP, Halifax, 1900–28, Speaker, 1921–28; married, first, Margarita Virginia Marchetti (1872–1925). Taught in Park Chapel's Sunday school.

75 Of 71 Harley Street; member of Westminster Chapel 1870—29 February 1876, when she withdrew. Samuel Martin (1817–78) ministered at the massive Westminster Chapel, 1842–78. Latterly his health failed.

76 William Graham (1817–85), MP, Glasgow, 1865–74; India merchant and father of Lady Horner, of Mells, for whose childhood memory of art and chapel intertwined see Frances Horner, *Time Remembered*, London, William Heinemann, 1933, p. 43.

77 *GD*, 22 March 1878.

78 But the networks were set in motion: Russell's son, Lord Amberley (1842–76), had an unsatisfactory candidature in Leeds in 1865 before stepping into Samuel Morley's shoes in Nottingham, 1866–68. Amberley was a constituent of H. S. P. Winterbotham (1837–73), MP, Stroud, 1867–73, Katharine Conder's first cousin once removed and mourned by many as the rising star of responsibly political Dissent. Certainly Gladstone took him sufficiently seriously to appoint him quickly to minor but promising office.

79 See C. Binfield, 'Asquith: The Formation of a Prime Minister', *Journal of the United Reformed Church History Society*, Vol 2, 1981, pp. 204–42, and *A Congregational Formation: An Edwardian Prime Minister's Victorian Education*, The Congregational Memorial Hall Trust, 1996, for extensive explorations of

Asquith's family connections. H. H. Asquith joined St Leonard's Congregational Church in 1867; its minister, Andrew Reed, had married a Leeds Jowitt (see above n. 35); Asquith's mother was then living at St Leonard's.

80 Ethel Mary Conder taught at Leeds High School, 1882–89; was headmistress of Milton Mount College, Gravesend, 1889–1905; and of Lansdowne House School Hampstead (later Swanage), 1905–c.1925.

81 Katharine Conder in 1888 married a second cousin, Dr Rayner Derry Batten (b. 1858), Old Millhillian and ophthalmic surgeon of 81 Harley Street and 82 Campden Hill Road. His consulting rooms were thus close to where Mrs Birks and the Gladstones had lived in the 1870s; from the early twentieth century another ophthalmic surgeon, Dr Nathaniel Bishop Harman (1869–1945), was at No. 108. With their Baptist, Congregational and Unitarian connections, the Harmans replicated the Conders: their politics, however, were more Chamberlainite than Gladstonian, for Mrs Harman was a niece of Joseph Chamberlain. Since their descendants include the Countess of Longford and Harriet Harman MP, the political and dynastic tendencies become unusually suggestive. Katharine (Conder) Batten was a member of Kensington Chapel from 1891, and became a deacon. She was especially active in the chapel's Notting Dale Mission, whose supporters included the Barrans, and she succeeded a cousin, Lady Winterbotham, as superintendent of its Mothers' Meeting.

82 Eustace Lauriston Conder married Mary Lauriston Winterbotham and settled in Buenos Aires. Their daughter, Helen Muriel (b. 1910), was educated at her aunt's school, Lansdowne House, then at Hayes Court (also founded by a woman from a Congregational family), then Cheltenham Ladies' College, and then Girton.

83 Although Edward Baines Conder (1872–1936) joined East Parade in November 1888, he became an Anglican (Wadham College intervening) and was a canon of Coventry from 1931.

84 His first wife had been a *Leeds Mercury* Baines; his second wife was a granddaughter of the Baptist missionary hero, William Knibb (1803–45). Willans was buried at Lawnswood, Leeds, in the midst of the parliament crisis. Asquith, who was one of the executors, came up for the funeral. Was Cousin Talbot, who had useful *Times* connections, responsible for the obituary which appeared, 3 May 1910?

85 Talbot Baines (Rugby and Cambridge) began with the *Leeds Mercury* in 1875, moved to London in 1897 and was secretary of the National Society, 1905–16. In 1891 he remarried; his second wife was Caroline Agnes Talbot, daughter of J. G. Talbot (1835–1910), MP, Oxford University, 1878–1910, and granddaughter of the fourth Lord Lyttelton; her uncle, Edward Stuart Talbot (1844–1934), Warden of Keble, 1869–88, was vicar of Leeds, 1888–95 and then successively Bishop of Rochester, Southwark and Winchester. In Leeds he described himself as 'a Conservative with a bad conscience' (*DNB*). R. W. Dale (1829–95), whom he admired, minister at Carrs Lane, Birmingham, 1854–95, had become famous for his civic gospel and his work on the atonement.

86 Henry Wolfe Baines (b. 1905), Bishop of Singapore.

87 Thus R. B. Jowitt, *Leeds Mercury*, 14 June 1887, quoted in A. W. Roberts, 'The Liberal Party in West Yorkshire 1885–1895', unpublished Ph.D. thesis, University of Leeds, 1979, p. 156.

Gladstone and Irish Nationalism: Achievement and Reputation

Alan O'Day

14 Gladstone in the House of Commons, drawing by Harry Furniss, 8 May 1882

He was the first major British statesman to consider seriously the implications of the parliamentary union between Great Britain and Ireland, and to realize that if Ireland were indeed an integral part of the United Kingdom, it must be governed on the same principles as the rest; and it was this realization that prepared him to accept the policy of home rule. His importance in the history of Anglo-Irish relations lies less in the measures that he actually carried, far-reaching though they were, than in the immense influence that his concern for Ireland had on British public opinion. It was he, more than anyone else, who made the state of Ireland an issue in British politics.[1]

I

J.C. BECKETT'S estimate of Gladstone in *The Making of Modern Ireland* probably offers the most succinct and compelling testament by a modern Irish historian of the G. O. M.'s impact on John Bull's Other Island. Beckett, who can scarcely be labelled a wild-eyed nationalist but rather reflects the values of northern Liberal Unionism, captures the essence of Gladstone's majestic appeal to the Irish national audience – the nobility of Gladstone's vision rather than his concrete accomplishments. This chapter has two aims. It describes and assesses what Gladstone actually achieved for Ireland, that is principally for Irish Catholics. The material for this evaluation is well known and merely requires reiteration here. Second and more unusually, this chapter considers his long-term reputation through an examination of how Gladstone has been treated by Irish, that is, mainly Irish-born historians. This second strand grows out of two influences – Herbert Butterfield's and others' stress upon the importance of discovering how historical ideas come into existence along with their transmission, and the recent debate on revisionism in Irish history spearheaded in academic circles by Fr Brendan Bradshaw.[2] A cameo of Irish historical references to Gladstone affords a useful addendum to Butterfield and Bradshaw while giving an indication of how historiography develops.

II

In 1868 Gladstone began the Hibernian enterprise that occupied so much of his remaining political career. In his words, 'my mission is to pacify Ireland', an aim that even his fondest admirers would not claim was fulfilled. More accurate was his profession that he was 'as fast bound to Ireland as Ulysses was to his mast'.[3] Gladstone's mast was erected in 1868 and it did not finally come down when he retired in March 1894. Generations of students and teachers equally have been chained to the task of explaining why Gladstone chose to champion the cause of Ireland's Catholics and what effect his various schemes had. No doubt Irish difficulties were sufficiently immense to deserve a good deal of attention, but Gladstone's obsession with Ireland fully warrants the close analysis it receives; no celebration of his life would be complete without considering his relationship with Ireland and the Irish.

Gladstone's Irish reforms are imposing in number and are, of course, thoroughly documented. During his first ministry (1868–74) he was chiefly responsible for the Irish Church Act, disestablishing the Church of Ireland. This legislation removed the state from the realm of religion in Ireland by also ending subsidies for Catholic and Presbyterian theological training. Less successfully, he grappled with the treacherous land question in the Land Act of 1870; less happily still, Gladstone responded to the demand of the Catholic Church for a state-funded university under its control in his abortive Irish University Bill in 1873. He released many of the imprisoned Fenians with the intent 'to draw a line between the Fenians & the people of Ireland, & to make the people of Ireland indisposed to cross it'.[4] His very exacting efforts were dogged by the opposition of Conservatives and a section of his own party, but excepting the instance of the University Bill, Gladstone enjoyed the support of Irish Liberals, the Catholic Church and the nascent home rule movement. Even at the start of his endeavour, Bishop Daniel Moriarty, best remembered for his stinging condemnation of Fenians for whom in his words 'eternity is not long enough, nor hell hot enough',[5] remarked, 'liberalism is the new religion and there is no seeking Justice except through its help'.[6] Following the electoral defeat in 1874 Gladstone resigned the leadership of the Liberal party and threw himself into writing tracts against the Vatican decrees of the Catholic Church. Nevertheless, despite the ill-feeling his writing engendered among Irish Catholics, he remained the most revered English politician. In 1877 Gladstone made his only substantial visit to Ireland (he returned to Dublin briefly in 1880), receiving the freedom of Dublin as a mark of respect for his Irish labours.

Gladstone's second government, extending from 1880 to 1885, was, if anything, even more immersed in Irish problems and he had to pursue these with less reliable support from Irishmen than he had during the first ministry. He attempted to mitigate the growing land agitation across the Irish Sea in 1880 with the Compensation for Disturbances Bill, a measure defeated in the House of Lords. The following year he piloted the Land Act of 1881, generally regarded as a seminal piece of legislation, and secured a further Land Act in 1882 as part of the bargain known as the Kilmainham Treaty. In 1883 the Liberals passed the Agricultural Labourers' Act, legislation close to the heart of the Irish party. In 1885 Gladstone was part of the cabinet minority who wanted to implement more extended local government in Ireland. Other legislation, though not directed exclusively at Ireland, had enormous effects there. The Corrupt and Illegal Practices Act of 1883 and the Franchise and Redistribution Acts of 1884 and 1885 are such instances. The effect of parliamentary reform without clauses to ensure the representation of the Protestant minority, especially in the southern provinces, was to turn the Catholic districts of Ireland into a Parnellite sea.

15 Gladstone welcomed to the Commons by Irish MPs, *The Graphic* c 1893

Gladstone specifically rejected special or 'fancy' franchises. This legislation defined the two Irelands geographically whereas previously the fault line had fallen more surely along confessional boundaries. The real losers were southern Protestants and the practical outcome was the partition of Ireland into its present-day shape. It would be an exaggeration to label Gladstone the 'father of partition', but he undoubtedly contributed to its coming and he certainly failed to foresee that his policies drove Ireland in that direction.

Most famously, he became Prime Minister for a third time in February 1886 in order 'to examine whether it is or is not practicable to comply with the desire ... for the establishment ... of a legislative body, to sit in Dublin, and to deal with Irish as distinguished from imperial affairs'.[7] His answer was in the affirmative; Gladstone's plan was encapsulated in the Government of Ireland Bill which he introduced on 8 April in a speech lasting three hours and twenty-five minutes that held the House of Commons spellbound throughout. Now often seen as a limited half-way house, it was a bill which the Chancellor of the Exchequer, Sir William Harcourt, when he first saw it in draft, thought qualified Gladstone as a 'criminal lunatic'.[8] Few on any side saw his scheme as anything less than a bold stroke for good or ill, a point sometimes lost in the modern literature. He promoted home rule at the cost of splitting his parliamentary ranks and party. Though the bill was defeated and the Liberals lost heavily at the general election of 1886, it provided the basis of the bills of 1893 and 1912. His impress was to be evident up to and beyond 1921. In what must be one of the great ironies of Anglo-Irish history, Gladstone's reasoning about the distinctive character of Ireland and the necessity of founding institutions to reflect this reality was assumed by Andrew Bonar Law, Austen Chamberlain and Walter Long between 1919 and 1921 when they along with Lloyd George were midwives to post-1921 Ireland.[9]

Defeated and with the Liberals out of office for perhaps as long as seven years, Gladstone might have gone into an honourable retirement. Following the election, the Tory front bencher, W. H. Smith, thought: 'the G. O. M. seems to me to have become something very like a dangerous lunatic. Of him probably there is an end.'[10] This, like so much about Gladstone, proved a false prophecy. Despite advanced age he stayed bound to the Irish mast. Had Gladstone retired in 1886, it is entirely probable that his party would have moderated its home rule commitment. Most of his important colleagues held reservations about the project. A rising young Liberal, Richard Haldane, in the late 1880s remarked that, while it was legitimate for Gladstone to 'regard the establishment of a Parliament in Dublin as the be-all and end-all of Liberal policy', it was also the case that 'his colleagues are hardly justi-fied in adopting substantially the same course'.[11] The violence engendered by the Plan of Campaign in Ireland and the infamous allegations by *The Times* of Parnellite complicity in crime took a heavy toll on many Liberals' faith in their Irish commitment, yet none of these things deterred Gladstone. During the crisis over the Parnell divorce Gladstone played an instrumental role, having perhaps the single greatest impact on Parnell's fall by insisting that if Parnell remained at the head of the Irish party his own leadership of the Liberals would be 'almost a nullity'.[12] In the crunch the majority of Irish party MPs and the preponderance of Ireland's Catholics opted for Gladstone. For Parnell Gladstone was now the 'Grand Old Spider' and it was he who was caught in his web.

In many ways the most demanding part of Gladstone's commitment still lay ahead in his final period of office from 1892 to March 1894. Following an electoral outcome that would have warranted postponing a Home Rule Bill, Gladstone soldiered on. He gave notice to the friends and opponents of home rule alike that 'the question of Ireland is almost, if not altogether, my sole link with public life'.[13] He did not ignore the threat posed by the House of Lords to home rule, warning later in the same speech that if the peers acted against the will of the House of Commons over home rule, it is 'impos-sible for such a [Liberal] government to regard the rejection of such a bill as terminating its duty'. His introduction of the second Home Rule Bill on 13

February 1893 lasted two and a quarter hours and, according to Henry Lucy, the doyen of lobby journalists, 'the explanation of the intricate measure was a model of lucidity; the opening passages of the speech soared on lofty heights of eloquence; the stately peroration that closed it will take rank with its most famous predecessors'.[14] The parliamentary struggle in 1886 was short and sharp; in 1893 it dragged on for months. After the Easter recess Lucy observed, 'both sides mean business, the business of the opposition being obstruction'.[15] He could not 'call to mind any epoch of obstruction exceeding in deliberation and pertinacity that which clogged the wheels of Parliament during the past eight weeks'. The bill finally passed in the House of Commons on 2 September. Individual divisions on clauses often had turnouts numbering more than 600. The physical endurance required was enormous. Throughout the episode Gladstone remained fastened to his Irish mast. After what can only be called a Herculean effort, Gladstone himself was prepared to revive the bill in the next session of the House of Commons. His colleagues desisted. A few months later in March 1894 Gladstone laid down his burden and no further Home Rule Bill came before the House of Commons until 1912.

By any measure Gladstone's input into Irish affairs down to his final days was huge. Paradoxically, the effort was not commensurate with the results. Of his several major exclusively Irish proposals, only the Irish Church Act can be counted an unambiguous success. Over the years 1885 to 1905 Conservatives and Unionists not only passed more legislation for Ireland but their acts had immeasurably larger long-term beneficial consequences. It was they who turned Irish tenants into owner occupiers, it was they who dealt with the democratisation of Irish local institutions and it was they who came closest to grappling with the religious dimension of Ireland in the education domain. Gladstone's land acts may have undermined the sanctity of property rights and set other important precedents but he was never more than lukewarm about tenant proprietorship, an issue to which he responded pragmatically as in 1886 rather than from high principle. F. S. L. Lyons suggests that the act of 1881 may have delayed the final solution though he also praises Gladstone's intent.[16] It is certainly the case that the act, particularly the creation of land courts which set rentals for 15 years, was the unwitting progenitor of the second phase of the land war, the Plan of Campaign which began in 1886. The two Home Rule Bills may have set back other more pertinent Irish reforms without advancing self-government. Moreover, the bills of 1886 and 1893 had a major and not always helpful effect on the bill of 1912. As George Boyce points out, not until 1920 was a Home Rule Bill skilfully drafted, and that came from the hands of Unionist politicians.[17] Gladstone's adoption of home rule, as Lyons notes, exacerbated polarisation of communities in Ireland, pushing, for instance, Presbyterian Radicals 'into a unionism which always went somewhat against the grain'.[18] Nor can it be overlooked that Gladstone, albeit reluctantly, implemented coercion in the

1870s and did so again twice in the first half of the 1880s. Though he initiated the release of Fenian prisoners, he was no soft-hearted sentimentalist where rebels were concerned. He treated the military prisoners, Fenians in the British army, without remorse and it was Benjamin Disraeli's government which set the last of these men free. None of these observations is original; none seriously impairs Gladstone's repute as Ireland's benefactor.

Despite a lengthy catalogue of Unionist measures and some reservations about what Gladstone actually did in Irish affairs, we are unlikely to be witness to historical revisionism placing any single Conservative or collective of Tories and Unionists on a plane with Gladstone. It is tempting to concur with the American historian who insists, 'toward Ireland the Conservative Party, in general, had displayed a consistently negative attitude'.[19] The same author suggests, 'compared with the Conservative interpretation of the Irish question, Gladstone's attitude was not only more courageous but farsighted as well. The Liberal leader saw beyond the "external symptoms" of the agitation in Ireland.'[20] This common view receives reinforcement from Roy Foster in his *History of Modern Ireland, 1600–1972*, where he states, 'the home rule crisis produced a Gladstonian conversion to home rule and a Conservative party driven back on die-hard rhetoric'.[21] But neither of these historians is exactly accurate. The Conservatives were anything but consistently negative;[22] it would not require overly demanding intellectual gymnastics to find that Arthur Balfour was at least as prescient as, if not more farsighted than, Gladstone. It was he along with others who recognised that uneven economic development between Ireland and Britain, and also within Ireland itself, lay at the heart of the country's problems. Balfour grasped the fundamental nature of the land question in a way that eluded Gladstone. It is difficult to see in what way Balfour was less courageous, for he often withstood the wrath of Irish landowners, senior Tories and rank-and-file Unionists to promote Irish legislation. Bonar Law, who is unlikely to be elevated to heroic status in nationalist mythology, at least comprehended the obstacle to an Irish settlement better than did Gladstone. Contrary to Foster's allegation, the Conservatives were not pushed back on an exclusive anti-Irish rhetoric in or after 1886 though one can certainly find an embarrassing abundance of such sentiments, something also flowing all too readily from the tongues and pens of Liberals. At present there is no comparative study of Conservative and Liberal rhetoric on Ireland; such an investigation might prove revealing. For the moment we can offer nothing better than Professor Beckett's insightful explanation of Gladstone's special place in Irish affections. For Gladstone's esteem in nationalist Ireland owes much less to his accomplishments, does not even hinge on his intentions, but rests on the intangible element of his generosity of spirit. What gives him a unique place in Irish historical memory may be best described by that overworked word, charisma. He possessed a charisma for nationalists that in the years between Daniel O'Connell's death and 1916 was second to none excepting perhaps

Parnell's and even the great Irish Chief himself could not match Gladstone's appeal when put to the acid test.

III

Unsurprisingly, Gladstone's contribution to Ireland, that is nationalist and predominantly Catholic Ireland, has received exhaustive treatment in histories written by the Irish and through a selection of these it is possible to examine his reputation and the extent this has been altered over time. The rationale for looking at these authors is three-fold: they may be presumed to have been influenced subconsciously at least by a received version of their national past; they are passing a historical legacy on to subsequent generations of their own people (and of course to others as well); and it is this group rather than outsiders who have provoked the wrath of Fr Bradshaw and the 'anti-revisionists'. Were sufficient space available there are, of course, other categories of historians – Americans, British, etc., or alternatively Liberal, Conservative or Marxist – which could be equally valuable for analysis but in the present context the 'Irish' prove to be a suitable and definable assemblage. So-called Irish 'revisionists' and 'anti-revisionists' establish common ground on one point: that beginning with new research-driven historical writing in the 1930s Irish historiography changed direction. Both sides describe this as an attempt at 'objective' or 'value-free' historical analysis. They disagree on the viability and outcome of this project. It is the third wave, the work of a generation of Irish historians who have been the leading force since the 1970s, that arouses exceptional hostility from 'anti-revisionists'. For present purposes attention is focused on a sample of writers representative of the various phases of historical writing since Gladstone's own day. This is not intended to be a complete list; it is one that contains a substantial number of historians of Protestant origin, an interesting factor in itself, given that many, like Professor Beckett, might not be expected to have much natural enthusiasm for Gladstone. The conclusion is that, whatever the implications of 'revisionism' for Irish history generally and in particular for the stature of nationalist figures, Gladstone has emerged with relatively modest scars. Perhaps the only comparable figure in post-famine Anglo-Irish affairs is Parnell. Eamon de Valera, as those who saw Neil Jordan's film, *Michael Collins*, realise, has enjoyed no such fate at the hands of the Irish intelligentsia in spite of being a national icon in his own time. In fact Gladstone's treatment at Irish hands differs sharply from and is demonstrably more generous than what had been meted out to him by many British scholars during the past three decades.

In 1957 Conor Cruise O'Brien noted that in the early 1880s, when the land war was at its height, none the less 'even among the Parnellites the great Liberal party already exercised powerful fascinations ... members of the Parnellite faction tended to become attached, not so much to the Liberal party as an institution, as to the person of Gladstone himself'.[23] Many of these same men shaped the Irish image of Gladstone. Justin McCarthy, a prominent member of Parnell's party and chairman of the majority section at the split, was a noted journalist who was closely identified with the Liberals. Predictably, his very popular and frequently reissued book, *A History of Our Own Times*, is laudatory about Gladstone. In 1898 McCarthy marked Gladstone's death with a volume entitled *The Story of Gladstone's Life* in which he proclaimed, 'I think I may take it for granted that Mr Gladstone is the greatest statesman who has appeared during the reign of Queen Victoria. This, indeed, seems to me a statement of fact and not a subject for criticism.'[24] The same position defines the voluminous writings of T. P. O'Connor, again an anti-Parnellite at the split, who had strong links to Liberalism. In 1908 he published a pamphlet summarising Gladstone's career. In O'Connor's words,

It is too soon to form an estimate of Mr Gladstone's final place in history. Much of the work he did will live after him; some of it must be put down as inconclusive and futile. Similarly it is impossible to say what posterity will think of him as an orator. The men of this generation will be agreed in ranking him as the greatest Member of Parliament that the House of Commons has ever seen.[25]

And, in O'Connor's evaluation,

Such then he was – a marvel and a portent in every one of his qualities; in his vast intellectual powers, in his indomitable courage, in his incessant energy, in his tremendous physical activity and strength, in the vehemence and fervour of his political passion, in the tenacity and tempest of his purpose he was more like an embodied cyclone rushing tempestuous, irresistible, merciless through his times, than a single and solitary human being. And every man who has seen and known him, whether in love or in hate, can say to himself that never in this world will we look upon his like again.[26]

McCarthy's son, Justin Huntly McCarthy, who in fact never lived in Ireland though he sat in the House of Commons as a member of the Irish party, in 1887 dedicated his tome *Ireland Since the Union* to Gladstone. Referring to Gladstone's immersion in Irish affairs in 1868, the younger McCarthy writes, 'Mr Gladstone was then, as he is now, the most advanced thinker and the most keen-sighted statesman in the English House of Commons.'[27] When coming to home rule in 1886 he observes, 'with the recognition by a great English Prime Minister of the justice of Ireland's appeal and the righteousness of her cause, the whole aspect of the longest political struggle in history changes'.[28] These three men were Irish party MPs and opposed Parnell's leadership in Committee Room 15 in December 1890. Perhaps their attitudes to Gladstone are predictable. But Gladstone's spell over even ardent Parnellites was not dissolved by the divorce crisis. R. Barry O'Brien's *Life of Charles Stewart Parnell*, published in 1898, is no less Gladstonian than the works of the two McCarthys. Indeed, O'Brien, who travelled with Parnell in 1891, records, 'in some of his speeches Parnell had made personal attacks on Mr Gladstone. I thought these attacks undeserved and told him so', noting also that he strongly disapproved of references to the 'Grand Old Spider'.[29] 'Upon another occasion I said that Mr Gladstone deserved well of Ireland, adding, "almost all that has been done for Ireland in my time has been done by Mr Gladstone – Gladstone *plus* Fenianism, and *plus* you".'[30] Curiously, O'Brien, even in his remarks to Parnell, awards Gladstone pole position. To this assemblage it is appropriate to add J. G. Swift MacNeill, another member of the Irish party who in 1890 rejected Parnell. At the close of his life in 1925 he published *What I Have Seen and Heard*, a volume of reminiscences and reflections rather than a proper history, though not less pertinent for all that. In it, as in his earlier account, *W. E. Gladstone: Anecdotes and Reminiscences*, published in 1898, Gladstone's genius and statesmanship are amply lauded. He was, according to MacNeill,

> an absolutely unique personality. His gestures, his astonishing dexterity in debate, his power of stirring the deepest emotions, the impression he conveyed of single-mindedness, of desire to do the right thing and to preserve a good conscience before God, to Whose direction he essayed to submit himself, all worked together to render him a great moral and intellectual influence in the House of Commons – a fact of which every member, irrespective of creed or party, was justly proud. I was then – and I am now – no worshipper of men, but the expression 'great man', so often applied to persons of very modest rank in conduct and in abilities, is, in my judgement, pre-eminently applicable to Mr Gladstone, whose claim to that title, while he was still with us, was acknowledged as unreservedly by his political opponents as by his supporters.[31]

None of the authors could be counted a professional historian in the present-day sense. They would not have thought that political commitment in historical writing ought to be eschewed; on the contrary they regarded history as the handmaiden of politics.

The Easter Rising, the Anglo-Irish Treaty in December 1921 and the division of Ireland inevitably had an impact on attitudes to Gladstone, though the pertinent question is the extent to which his reputation was reappraised. Possibly the foremost historian of the interwar years, Denis Gwynn, was an academic and for many years held the Chair of History at University College, Cork. Gwynn is now largely overlooked among the acclaimed pioneers of modern Irish historiography. A committed nationalist sympathetic to the home rulers, he relied upon manuscript sources and built up his picture in much the same fashion as the later recognised leaders of Irish historical research. Gwynn's writings exemplify the trend in Ireland to recognise

Gladstone's role but to give greatest weight to Irish and nationalist forces. In his fine biography of John Redmond, still the leading study of this neglected figure, Gwynn writes,

> by 1886 Gladstone had been compelled to make Home Rule one of the chief planks in the Liberal programme. The importance of Irish sympathies and of Irish propaganda in the Colonies, and still more in the United States, had not yet become widely recognised. But in England great progress had been made, with Gladstone's assistance, in converting public opinion to the necessity of granting the Irish demand for self-government. Such was the situation when the O'Shea divorce case produced a sudden crisis in English politics. Gladstone, as a patriarchal leader who could not expect to continue as Prime Minster [sic] for much longer, announced that his Non-conformist followers would desert him if Parnell did not resign the leadership of the Irish Party.[32]

Subsequently, in his attractive biography of The O'Gorman Mahon, Gwynn describes Gladstone's conversion to home rule: 'A whole year passed, and in the interval Gladstone had announced his own conversion to Home Rule and brought in his Home Rule Bill, during O'Gorman Mahon's absence from the House. Gladstone himself had grown extremely old, and Parnell saw the necessity of doing everything possible to reinforce his courage.'[33] He puts the blame for the split squarely on Parnell.

Dorothy Macardle's *The Irish Republic*, first published in 1937 as a tribute to de Valera and a paean to the republican ideal, adopts a line broadly similar to Gwynn's. Her largely bland references can be seen in two examples. She observes, 'Parnell died, at the age of forty-five, in the following year.' 'Ireland', she goes on, 'did not get his prize. Gladstone's second Home Rule Bill in 1893 passed the Commons but was rejected by the Lords. When in 1894, Gladstone retired, Home Rule for Ireland seemed almost a lost cause.'[34] Referring to the House of Lords, Macardle states, 'it was the veto which had frustrated Gladstone'.[35] To be sure, this is rather bland commentary which is best read in the context of her unsympathetic comments on other British, Unionist and home rule politicians. Discussing the home rule proposals in 1910, she observes, 'such was the modest measure of self-government which Redmond was demanding now. He was putting the Irish demand before the electorate in a manner calculated to allay Unionist fears rather than to express the hopes of Irish Nationalists.'[36] This she compared unfavourably with Parnell's stance, a now standard theme in the nationalist version of history.

Though P. S. O'Hegarty's *A History of Ireland Under the Union* was not published until 1952, it properly belongs to this earlier phase of the literature. O'Hegarty had been active in Sinn Fein and saw those who opposed Parnell's leadership as traitors. Thus it is instructive to look at his comments on Gladstone in some detail. He begins discussion of Gladstone's mission with the following description:

William Ewart Gladstone, the greatest of English Liberal Prime Ministers of the Nineteenth Century, was in his sixtieth year in 1869. He had been in Parliament since 1832, entering as a follower of Peel, and he had taken much of the same view of Ireland and the Irish situation as the rest of his colleagues, that she was to go on being governed by England, and that our tribulations were due to some sort of original sin. But Gladstone was a Christian, in actuality as well as in profession, and his political nature was generous and against all manner of oppression. He had moral principles and moral fervour and the courage to stand up for his beliefs even though he were one against all the rest. In a few words, he was a Christian, a Liberal, and a statesman, with ability and courage so far above the average that, in retrospect, he towers above nineteenth century England, towers above every other political leader of the day save Parnell. They two dominated the House of Commons while they lived, and they dominate the history of that period now that they are dead.

Being what he was Gladstone could not forever stand for a policy of injustice and repression in Ireland.[37]

O'Hegarty's opinion of Gladstone's determination in 1886 is equally illustrative. He writes:

He was now 76 years of age, an age at which he might reasonably have expected to be able to lay down the cares of public life, and pass his remaining years in peace and meditation under his own fig tree. But this task had been laid on him, and he did not shirk. He knew that he was risking his peace of mind, his health, his Party, but only he and Parnell, only they two in Parliament, only they two in the two islands, knew that that moment was pregnant with the fate of Nations, that the 'Irish Question' had been brought to the point where it had to be resolved or worse would befall.[38]

Later he observes, 'Gladstone died in 1898. The greatest Englishman of his day, he was a man in whom moral fervour, moral courage, moral integrity were marked, and with his passing these qualities went out of English public life.'[39] In a free Ireland, O'Hegarty pleads, 'let her remember Gladstone also, with gratitude. A great man, though an Englishman, a great man, none the less great because he was good.'[40] Gladstone's part in the split of the Irish party presented O'Hegarty with a difficulty which he ingeniously resolved by declaring that Gladstone's letter containing the phrase indicating that his leadership would be 'almost a nullity', was merely a semantic misunderstanding. This group of authors provided the staple histories of the new Irish national state.

The new university-based history pioneered in Ireland in the 1930s avoided the comparatively recent past and was therefore slow to make an impress on our topic. An exception is Nicholas Mansergh, who though an Irish Protestant attended Cambridge. His *Ireland in the Age of Reform and*

Revolution, 1840–1921, first appeared in 1940 and from the mid-1960s in a slightly revised form it was often republished under the title, *The Irish Question, 1840–1921*. Mansergh is the first author examined who was a professional academic in the modern sense of purporting to write 'value-free' history. Did this academic detachment affect his treatment? His comments, retained in subsequent editions, are consistent with those of Justin Huntly McCarthy or O'Hegarty. He states, 'Mr Gladstone was the only English statesman of this epoch who made a positive contribution, so ambitious in character as to aim at a final settlement of the Irish Question.'[41] In another revealing passage, Mansergh observes:

> in the long unhappy history of Anglo-Irish relations only one event is more truly tragic than the rejection of Home Rule in 1886. The opportunity of settlement had come, perhaps the greatest of English statesmen was ready to grasp it and yet the unique chance was destroyed by a failure in perception whose consequences not even time can wholly repair.[42]

We cannot pass without consideration of another historian of this first wave, T. W. Moody. Moody was a founder member of the group who imported into Irish historiography scholarly standards from the Institute of Historical Research at the University of London. The remarks quoted here were not published until 1967. The text formed part of an annual radio series in Ireland. In his section of a volume that continues to have a major place in Ireland, *The Course of Irish History*, Moody writes regarding the Fenian revolt in 1867:

> in Britain it reacted decisively on the mind of W. E. Gladstone, the greatest British statesman of the age, impelling him to embark upon a programme of 'justice for Ireland' to which he continued to give his best efforts for the rest of his life. His conscience had long been troubled on the subject of Ireland, but he confessed that it was the Fenian rising that had awakened him to a sense of 'the vast importance of the Irish question'. His first administration marked a new era in the history of the union both by the spirit in which he sought to solve Irish problems and by two great measures of reform.[43]

Of the home rule proposal in 1886 Moody declares, 'the British Liberal party under the leadership of Gladstone acknowledged the justice and the necessity of giving Ireland self-government'.[44] Referring to the electoral defeat in 1886, he states, 'it resulted in a heavy defeat for Gladstone, which he accepted with magnificent courage and with no thought of abandoning the struggle'.[45] His comment on Gladstone's part in the break-up of the Irish party also deserves notice. For Moody responsibility rested primarily with the attitude of the Irish leader not Gladstone: 'it was this political fact [meaning the Nonconformist response] and not any moral judgement on Parnell that caused Gladstone to demand his temporary retirement from the leadership. Parnell's ferocious refusal to do so produced a bitter and demoralising split in the party he had largely created.'[46] Beckett, whose work we have noticed at the outset, belongs to the initial academic group, as does R. B. McDowell, the latter being a bridge between the first and second wave of university academics trained in 'value-free' techniques. McDowell, for example, refers to 'Gladstone's first great ministry'.[47] The words 'great', 'greatest', 'courageous' and the like are not less in evidence when Gladstone is mentioned in these academic accounts than in earlier journalistic histories. So-called 'value-free' or 'objective' history bears remarkable similarities to the old history.

Conor Cruise O'Brien, F. S. L. Lyons and Oliver MacDonagh, the former two being students of T. W. Moody, represent a second phase of Irish academically trained historians. The views of the first have been sampled briefly above. He has been an exceptionally influential commentator on Irish affairs. His major historical study, *Parnell and his Party, 1880–90*, retains its stature in the field. Examining Gladstone's adoption of home rule as the corollary to the outcome of the general election of 1885, O'Brien suggests:

> Yet, if the eighty-six Irish votes represented a parliamentary temptation – to purchase power by assenting to home rule – did they not also, to the liberal mind, represent a moral force, the deliberate voice of the majority of the Irish people, for the first time unequivocally expressed, in favour of home rule? This idea also was present to Gladstone's mind, as a hypothesis, before the general election; he asked his chief associates in that autumn of 1885: should not the liberals be prepared to act, if Ireland both declares for home rule and stands by her declaration? Once the results, in their main outline, were known, Gladstone prepared, in his majestic way, to draw the necessary conclusion.[48]

Of the Home Rule Bill itself, he observes 'there were convincing signs that Gladstone's gesture, and the eloquence with which it was accompanied, had captured the imagination of the Irish people generally'.[49] O'Brien, like O'Hegarty, deplores the state of Gladstone's status in nationalist circles, arguing 'on the Irish side, in the tradition which formed in the minds of the young, it was Gladstone who suffered injustice, in being remembered, not for devoting his last years to the cause of home rule for Ireland but as the vaguely malevolent "Grand Old Spider" who figured with the "English Wolves" in the zoology of Parnellite invective'.[50]

Lyons's numerous writings show the continuing impress of the Gladstone mystique.[51] His most widely read book, *Ireland since the Famine*, did not appear until 1971, but its references to Gladstone fairly sum up more than twenty years of his writing. As in the case of O'Hegarty, it is appropriate to examine him more closely. On Gladstone's entry into the Irish arena in the 1860s, Lyons comments that he was younger, sensitive not just to criticisms of Europe but to the more insistent prompting of his own conscience, moving steadily after Palmerston's death in 1865 to a dominant position amongst that medley of Whigs and Radicals, churchmen and non-conformists, bourgeoisie and working men, of which a great Liberal party was to be fashioned, he could turn at last to 'look in the face and work through' the problems Ireland still presented.

For such a man it was possible to see the Fenian outbreak not just as a series of acts of terrorism, but as a symptom of a deeper malaise and ... only a few days after the Clerkenwell explosion, he tried to pass on to his English audience his own conviction – antedating Fenianism by many years – that Irish violence was the product of Irish grievance.[52]

For Lyons, Gladstone's decision to disestablish the Church of Ireland, 'though a long way short of revolutionary, had a symbolic significance far beyond its immediate effects. It signalled a fresh way of looking at Irish problems ... Above all, it gave notice that the Protestant Ascendancy was no longer immutable and invulnerable.'[53] Though more restrained in tone and sophisticated in analysis, the language still seems remarkably familiar. However, Lyons, as seen above, did acknowledge that not all of Gladstone's actions had beneficial effects, something not so evident in much of the previous literature.[54]

MacDonagh, educated at University College, Dublin, and Cambridge in the later 1960s, when commenting on the Land Act of 1870, observes:

> Gladstone, the very pivot of mid-Victorian politics, the principal heir of both Cobdenite and Peelite political traditions, and the destined captain of reform for two decades still had been moved to act, not by direct pressure, but by conviction that he was correcting an original and historical injustice. This meant that whatever was said in Parliament at its introduction, the 1870 Act was not a final settlement but the start of a new process of amelioration, once time had shown that the Act had altered nothing. It also heralded a dynamic and self-consciously experimental approach to Irish social problems, one of the fruits of which was, of course, Gladstone's own conversion to Home Rule.[55]

Yet his perspective was in certain respects more distinctly nationalist at the same time. Gladstone's investment in dealing with Ireland was not exclusively the result of 'high-mindness' but also the consequence of nationalist pressure, specifically organised and focused by Parnell. In MacDonagh's account, conversion to home rule in 1886 is attributed to the fact that

> from 1878 on, his [Parnell's] power was growing fast; by 1882, no ordinary challenge was likely to disturb him; by 1885, he had acquired an almost Louis XIV-like domination. This combination, the very concentration of all nationalist, separatist and Catholic forces upon a single leader, and the electoral demonstrations of the impregnability of his leadership, were probably the decisive

factors in inducing Gladstone and later the bulk of his cabinet and party to commit themselves to Home Rule.[56]

Thus far there is not much of a whiff of 'revisionism'. The literature produced by a third cycle of academically trained historians beginning in the mid-1960s is more varied, but though Gladstone does not emerge unblemished, on the whole he is less tarnished than Irish leaders, especially republican figures. Possibly the chief characteristic of the new research-driven approach is to treat historical verities with a greater degree of scepticism, to challenge received opinions. Thus, it may be said that excepting the Irish Church Act, every other major piece of Irish legislation proposed by Gladstone has been subjected to close and critical scrutiny. Gladstone's motives, too, have been assessed in a more critical light, though this tendency is considerably more marked in the work of British historians, especially those using the so-called 'high politics' approach associated with Peterhouse, Cambridge. Nevertheless, it is inevitable that this new perspective would find its way into Irish accounts. Five recent historians, Paul Bew, James Loughlin, Roy Foster, Margaret O'Callaghan and D. George Boyce, are examined as representative examples. Bew, who teaches at The Queen's University of Belfast, has made numerous stimulating contributions to the field. In his influential biography of Parnell he places Gladstone's Land Bill in 1881 within a modern critical framework, writing,

> the British premier continued to feel that Ireland was on the edge of social dissolution – or, to put it another way, was about to enter a crisis which contained incalculable risks for British policy. The obvious alternative was to attempt to split the agitation by buying off a significant section of its adherents. In April 1881 he therefore introduced a bill which provided for a fixed period of tenure at fair rents and for free sale of the tenants' interest in the farms. Parnell immediately recognised privately that Gladstone had done enough. It was indeed a major reform.[57]

Bew's handling of the divorce episode is also revealing. He puts blame on Justin McCarthy for the confusion and presents a favourable account of Gladstone's position during the crisis.[58] Another northerner, James Loughlin, in contrast, casts doubt on Gladstone's home rule schemes, arguing 'the defeat of his Home Rule plans also ensured Gladstone's reputation as one of the few British politicians who possessed a correct understanding of Irish nationalism and who proposed enlightened legislation to deal with it'.[59] In his assessment 'Gladstone's insight into Irish nationalism ... was highly flawed.' Yet Loughlin does not contest Gladstone's intentions as such and a significant aspect of his study shows how notions of the past and the reputation of politicians are converted into common currency.

The pointed edge of 'revisionism' is found most completely in Roy Foster's

Modern Ireland, a book much maligned by 'anti-revisionists'. Brendan Bradshaw, in particular, objects to Foster's iconoclasm, a view that cannot be lightly brushed aside. Foster's book more than any other falls into the 'high politics' mode. Summing up Gladstone's failed attempt to pass an Irish University Bill, Foster observes: 'When, after an abortive attempt to seize the nettle of Irish university education, Gladstone left office in 1874, he had made, at least, a decisive gesture. Perhaps because of this, he turned with relief to anti-Romanist polemic in the controversy over the Vatican decrees.'[60] It is such juxtapositioning that gives one sympathy with Fr Bradshaw's concerns. Referring to the home rule contest in 1886, Foster maintains, 'Politics were polarised round Ireland, conveniently for both Gladstone and Salisbury',[61] which is a one-sentence synthesis of *The Governing Passion* and *The Discipline of Popular Government*.[62] Also, writing about the same episode, Foster declares, 'It was none the less Gladstone's finest hour: in full moral cry, he projected a rather unconvincing retrospective continuity, presenting his "mission to pacify Ireland" as consistent since the 1860s. In fact, he had moved through a series of energetic but short-term reactions to immediate political problems.'[63] And, of Gladstone's part in the Parnell divorce incident, he notes, 'Gladstone had little strategic choice in his response to party pressure, but he showed curious unhelpfulness towards delegations from the Parliamentary Party during the internecine horrors of the split.'[64]

The influence of 'revisionism' with Peterhouse overtones can be found in Margaret O'Callaghan's recent book on the 1880s. A graduate of University College, Dublin, she originally prepared her study for a doctorate at the University of Cambridge. She argues that in the early 1880s,

> while Foster continued to inhabit a mental world of the [Land] League as ruffians, Gladstone though perhaps also considering them to be ruffians, seemed appraised of the magnitude of the step that he had taken. Gladstone's strength as a politician was partly derived from his ability, after careful, tortuous and exhaustive mulling, to make a decision. Slower colleagues assumed that the nature of the material mulled over determined the nature of the decision. The material perused usually related to the decision arrived at, but really his leaps were intuitive.[65]

Referring to the same crisis, she suggests that his view of Ireland was 'purely academic'. 'True', she writes,

> he had spent some three weeks touring country houses in the east in 1877 and was, late in 1880, to make a bizarre visit to the Sunday congregation of Christ Church in the course of a cruise. But the prevailing sense that emerges ... is that he viewed Ireland, when forced to turn his attention to it by virtue of its persistence, as an intellectual conundrum to which he had merely to apply his intellect to 'solve'.[66]

Words such as 'great' and 'courageous' are replaced by Foster and O'Callaghan with 'unhelpfulness' and 'bizarre' and can, for instance, be contrasted with the moderation of another Irish scholar, Frank Callanan.[67]

Modern academic interpretations are varied, but more typical is the work of George Boyce, who cannot be accused of sentimentality towards Irish nationalism. His studies reflect modern sober critical historical analysis. In *Nineteenth-Century Ireland* he contends, 'Gladstone was motivated as much by British or English as by Irish considerations. Ireland was a weakness, a problem, an irritant for Britain, "a preoccupation, not an interest".'[68] In a short account for the Historical Association aimed at students, *Ireland 1828–1923: From Ascendancy to Democracy*, he points out that during his first ministry, 'Gladstone was obliged to sanction coercion in order to maintain law and order, but he had an unswerving faith in the power of public opinion properly organised and given moral leadership. He set himself to tap this resource in Ireland and offer it the voice it could not find for itself.'[69] Boyce's discussion of home rule urges,

> Gladstone's move towards home rule was no sudden, binding conversion, but neither was it a kind of linear progression, with home rule following inevitably from disestablishment of the Church of Ireland and land reform. Gladstone, like any politician, had many preoccupations; Ireland was but one among many imperial and domestic affairs. But two perceptions drove him towards home rule; he believed in the power of moral judgement in politics (although he was not above squaring it with political necessities as well) and he believed that public opinion must be the stuff of political life – public opinion properly led, possessing a strong affection for the law and public institutions. Ireland was a moral problem; coercion was not, ultimately, the answer. Moreover, Irish public opinion lacked what Scottish opinion enjoyed: a close association with governing structures and the law. Gladstone assumed too that the British Parliament was a place where political conflicts could be resolved. The resolution of the Irish conflict through home rule was, he came to believe, essential, and he could cite precedents in both the empire and Europe: Canada and Norway pointed the way. The general election of 1885 convinced him that 'Ireland has now spoken; and that an effort ought to be made *by the Government* without delay to meet her demands for the management of an Irish legislative body of Irish as distinct from Imperial affairs'.[70]

Boyce, who provides the best one-paragraph explanation of the home rule proposal, also gives a cold-eyed assessment of its limitations, recognising the introduction of the bill as 'one of the greatest and most moving performances of his career'.[71] Elsewhere in a commentary that makes a fitting finale to this discussion he writes,

> His passionate oratory still obscures the flaws, constitutional and financial, in his Home Rule bill. But he was frustrated by the fact that, even if Ireland, or

most of it, was ready for Home Rule in 1886, England was not. Gladstone hoped that his bill would be one of those political departures, which, taken at the flood, would combine political and public opinion in an irresistible movement towards his political goal. But it turned out to be a boat bobbing about on an uncertain political sea. The next twenty years were to see almost unbroken Conservative (or as it was now called, Unionist) rule, with a brief Liberal interlude.[72]

IV

This short analysis of an Irish historiography of Gladstone concludes in a similar manner to that in which it began, with the quotation from Professor Beckett. Gladstone has not emerged totally unscathed at the hands of the new generation of Irish scholars, but on the whole and with notable exceptions he has been treated more generously by them than he has been treated by a segment of their British counterparts. What impresses most is that Gladstone's mystique continues to exert an appeal second to none to Ireland's historians, with the exception of a handful of cynics, underlining the observation of T. P. O'Connor cited above: he was 'a marvel and a portent'.[73]

Notes

1   J. C. Beckett, *The Making of Modern Ireland, 1603–1923*, London, Faber & Faber, 1989, p. 412.
2   See H. Butterfield, *Man on his Past*, Cambridge, Cambridge UP, 1955; C. Brady (ed.), *Interpreting Irish History: The Debate on Historical Revisionism*, Dublin, Irish Academic Press, 1994, which in addition to the editor's important introduction also contains the article by Bradshaw first published in *Irish Historical Studies*; D. G. Boyce and A. O'Day (eds), *The Making of Modern Irish History: Revisionism and the Revisionist Controversy*, London, Routledge, 1996, pp. 1–14.
3   Quoted in E. D. Steele, 'Gladstone and Ireland', *Irish Historical Studies*, Vol. 17, 1970, p. 58.
4   H. C. G. Matthew, *Gladstone, 1809–1874*, Oxford, Clarendon Press, 1986, p. 192.
5   Quoted in F. S. L. Lyons, *Ireland since the Famine*, London, Fontana, 1976, p. 130.
6   Quoted in Patrick Corish, 'Cardinal Cullen and the National Association of Ireland', *Reportorium Novum*, Vol. 3, 1961–62, p. 57; article reprinted in A. O'Day (ed.), *Reactions to Irish Nationalism, 1865–1914*, London, Hambledon Press, 1987.
7   Quoted in J. Morley, *The Life of William Ewart Gladstone*, London, Macmillan, 1903, vol. 3, p. 292.
8   Lewis Harcourt's Journal, 8 March 1886, Harcourt Papers, Bodleian Library, Oxford, MS 377.
9   A. O'Day, *Irish Home Rule, 1867–1921*, Manchester, Manchester University Press, 1998, pp. 294–304.
10 Quoted in A. B. Cooke and A. P. W. Malcolmson, *The Ashbourne Papers, 1869–1918*, Belfast, Public Record Office of Northern Ireland, 1974, p. 174.
11 Quoted in H. C. G. Matthew, *The Liberal Imperialists*, Oxford, Oxford UP, 1973, p. 266.

12 Quoted in Morley (1903), vol. 3, p. 437.

13 *Hansard's Parliamentary Debates*, 4th series, vol. 7, cols 210–14.

14 H. W. Lucy, *A Diary of the Home Rule Parliament, 1892–1895*, London, Cassell, 1896, p. 55.

15 Ibid., p. 93.

16 Lyons (1976), p. 172.

17 D. G. Boyce, *The Irish Question and British Politics, 1868–1986*, London, Macmillan, 1988, p. 62.

18 F. S. L. Lyons, *Culture and Anarchy in Ireland, 1890–1939*, Oxford, Clarendon Press, 1979, p. 135.

19 L. P. Curtis, Jr, *Coercion and Conciliation in Ireland, 1880–1892: A Study in Conservative Unionism*, Princeton, NJ, Princeton UP, 1963, p. 27.

20 Ibid., p. 428.

21 R. F. Foster, *Modern Ireland, 1600–1972*, London, Penguin, 1989, p. 422.

22 See A. O'Day, *Parnell and the First Home Rule Episode, 1884–87*, Dublin, Gill & Macmillan, 1986, pp. 178–227; O'Day (1998), pp. 107–311.

23 C. C. O'Brien, *Parnell and his Party, 1880–90*, 2nd edn, Oxford, Clarendon Press, 1964, p. 49–50.

24 J. McCarthy, *The Story of Gladstone's Life*, London, Adam & Charles Black, 1898, p. 1.

25 T. P. O'Connor, *W. E. Gladstone, Statesman, Orator, Scholar & Theologian*, London, T. P.'s Weekly, 1908, p. 5.

26 Ibid., p. 16.

27 J. H. McCarthy, *Ireland since the Union*, London, Chatto & Windus, 1887, p. 194.

28 Ibid., pp. 353–54.

29 R. B. O'Brien, *The Life of Charles Stewart Parnell, 1846–1891*, London, Smith, Elder, 1989, vol. 2, p. 335.

30 Ibid., p. 336.

31 J. G. Swift MacNeill, *What I Have Seen and Heard*, London, Arrowsmith, 1925, p. 244–45; see *W. E. Gladstone: Anecdotes and Reminiscences*, London, Swan Sonnenschein, 1898, p. 63.

32 D. Gwynn, *The Life of John Redmond*, London, George G. Harrap, 1932, p. 16.

33 D. Gwynn, *The O'Gorman Mahon: Duellist, Adventurer and Politician*, London, Jarrolds, 1934, pp. 272–73.

34 D. Macardle, *The Irish Republic*, 1st edn 1937; London, Corgi, 1968, p. 54.

35 Ibid., p. 66.

36 Ibid.

37 P. S. O'Hegarty, *A History of Ireland Under the Union, 1801 to 1922*, London, Methuen, 1952, p. 458.

38 Ibid., p. 546.

39 Ibid., p. 601.

40 Ibid., p. 602.

41 N. Mansergh, *Ireland in the Age of Reform and Revolution, 1840–1921*, London, George Allen & Unwin, 1940, p. 100.

42 Ibid., p. 150.

43 T. W. Moody, 'Fenianism, Home Rule and the Land War (1850–91)', in *The Course of Irish History*, ed. T. W. Moody and F. X. Martin, Dublin, Mercier Press, 1967, pp. 280–81.

44 Ibid., p. 275.
45 Ibid., p. 291.
46 Ibid., p. 292.
47 R. B. McDowell, *The Irish Administration, 1801–1914*, London, Routledge & Kegan Paul, 1964, p. 58.
48 O'Brien (1964), p. 160.
49 Ibid., p. 187.
50 Ibid., p. 352.
51 Lyons's writings are treated most fully in A. O'Day, 'F. S. L. Lyons: Historian of Modern Ireland', in *Recent Historians of Great Britain: Essays on the Post-1945 Generation*, ed. W. L. Arnstein, Ames, Iowa, Iowa State University Press, 1990, pp. 172–91.
52 Lyons (1976), p. 142.
53 Ibid., p. 146.
54 Ibid., p. 172.
55 O. MacDonagh, *Ireland: The Union and its Aftermath*, London, George Allen & Unwin, 1977, p. 48.
56 Ibid., pp. 63–64.
57 P. Bew, *C. S. Parnell*, Dublin, Gill & Macmillan, 1980, p. 52.
58 Ibid., pp. 114–15.
59 J. Loughlin, *Gladstone, Home Rule and the Ulster Question, 1882–93*, Dublin, Gill & Macmillan, 1986, p. 289.
60 Foster (1989), p. 397.
61 Ibid., p. 422.
62 A. B. Cooke and J. Vincent, *The Governing Passion: Cabinet Government and Party Politics in Britain, 1885–86*, Brighton, Harvester Press, 1974; P. Marsh, *The Discipline of Popular Government: Lord Salisbury's Domestic Statecraft, 1881–1902*, Hassocks, Sussex, Harvester Press, 1978.
63 Foster (1989), p. 423.
64 Ibid., p. 424.
65 M. O'Callaghan, *British High Politics and a Nationalist Ireland: Criminality, Land and the Law under Forster and Balfour*, Cork, Cork UP, 1994, p. 90.
66 Ibid., p. 25.
67 Frank Callanan, *The Parnell Split, 1890–91*, Cork, Cork UP, 1992; Frank Callanan, *T. M. Healy*, Cork, Cork UP, 1996.
68 D. G. Boyce, *Nineteenth-Century Ireland: The Search for Stability*, Dublin, Gill & Macmillan, 1990, p. 149; his observation has its origins in Matthew (1986), p. 192.
69 D. G. Boyce, *Ireland, 1828–1923: From Ascendancy to Democracy*, Oxford, Blackwell, 1992, p. 43.
70 Ibid., p. 52.
71 Ibid., p, 57.
72 Boyce (1989), p. 34.
73 See n. 26.

In the Front Rank of the Nation: Gladstone and the Unionists of Ireland, 1868–1893

D. George Boyce

STRANGE BEDFELLOWS.
" Fortune makes us acquainted with strange bedfellows."

16 'Strange Bedfellows', *The Union*, 11 February 1888

A ny discussion of Gladstone and Irish Unionists takes place against the background of Irish history and politics since 1886. This is because the first home rule bid is measured against the cataclysmic years of 1912–22 when the conflict of nationality in Ireland resulted in the partition of the island into two states, a predominantly nationalist Irish Free State and a predominantly Unionist Northern Ireland; and the 'troubles' of the past 25 years only enhance this perspective, raising yet again reflections on what might have been had Gladstone achieved his home rule settlement. These considerations invite further ruminations on that home rule plan: it might be seen as the 'Irish settlement that never was', the one hope of achieving a stable constitution for Ireland; or, on the other hand, as a wilful blindness to the facts of Irish political life, and in particular to the deep-seated mistrust, even hatred, between Catholic/nationalists and Protestant/Unionists, which could not be overcome in a unitary Irish state.

Neither of these interpretations does justice to the complexity of Gladstone's approach to the problem of Ireland, and to his concept of where Irish Unionists would fit in his home rule constitution. On the face of it, Gladstone ought to have understood better than anyone the Protestant dread of a Catholic majority, and its domination of an Irish parliament. His own deep-seated mistrust of the temporal claims of the Pope was forcefully expressed in his *Vaticanism* pamphlet in 1874: few Irish Protestants would have quarrelled with his rebuttal of the 'Pope of Rome's power to make any claim upon those who adhered to his communion of such a nature as to impair the integrity of the civil allegiance', and his call for any such claim to be 'repelled and rejected'.[1] He renewed his dispute with Rome in July 1890 when speaking on the question of mixed marriages in Malta.[2] This must have been soothing balm to Irish Protestants; but some of them found Gladstone's *Vaticanism* conclusions unacceptable. The Belfast Liberal newspaper, *The Northern Whig*, criticised Gladstone's 1874 pamphlet: 'does anyone really and seriously question the loyalty of the great body of our Roman Catholic countrymen whether in England or in Ireland?' The *Whig* pointed out that even the home rule movement was not exclusively Catholic, and agreed with Cardinal Newman that Rome could only bind Rome. Statesmen, it concluded, should confine themselves to practical questions of the day and allow all theories of infallibility 'to pass by them as the idle wind'.[3]

Irish Protestants always denied that their dispute with nationalists was a religious one; it was a political one, of loyal men against disloyal men.[4] Gladstone saw the religious divisions in Ireland in a political context but drew different conclusions. In 1890, when he questioned the papacy's pretensions in mixed marriages, he also criticised the Vatican for interfering in the politics of Ireland; when the Pope issued a papal rescript against the 'Plan of Campaign' agrarian agitation in 1888, he 'at great cost to his own influence within the legitimate sphere of purely spiritual authority – at very great cost, damage, and detriment to himself, undoubtedly did his utmost to prop up a labouring and failing cause – namely, that of the anti-Irish party in this country.'[5]

The significance of that phrase, 'the anti-Irish party', must be stressed, for by that Gladstone meant the Irish Unionists. Gladstone's project was to win back the Protestants of Ireland to their true allegiance, as an integral part of the Irish nation. Gladstone identified, not the Irish Protestant gentry, nor indeed their church, as the problem; what was wrong was the special nature of that gentry's relations with the bulk of the Irish people, a relationship characterised by the term 'Anglo-Irish ascendancy', with all its implications of a privileged caste unreasonably dominating the nation.[6] One example of the dire impact of that predicament was the anomaly of a state church, the Church of Ireland, representing only a minority of the population, and yet enjoying all the privileges of the Church of England. This ascendancy position, not the Irish gentry as such, was the 'Upas tree' whose roots poisoned all around it[7] – poisoning also the possibility of the gentry enjoying a fruitful relationship with the Irish tenantry. Thus, when Gladstone pondered on the impact of Turkish rule in the Balkans, he compared that unhappy region with Ireland. Ireland was 'a far slighter case ... a vastly milder instance'. But he accepted the comparison. Turkey's domination was 'incurable', as was the Protestant ascendancy's position in Ireland. But neither case was in principle hopeless: 'The thing is incurable, but not the men who have to do with the thing. To make them curable, you have to take them out of a position which is false, and leave them in a position which is true, sound and normal.'[8]

These were vital words: the Irish gentry could be eased into a 'true, sound and normal' role; that is, a proper role as the leaven of Irish society, as the class that could mediate between what Gladstone called, on the one hand, the 'Orangemen', and on the other, the 'law haters'.[9] When Gladstone made his first and only significant visit to Ireland in 1877, receiving the freedom of the city of Dublin, he mused on the difference between Ireland and England, particularly in relations between landlord and tenant. In England it was essential that the land should be owned by one set of men and tilled by another. But in Ireland it would be desirable to create at least a 'class of small propriety' because of that sharp division between the interests of the cultivators and those of the proprietors. To make some of the cultivators proprietors as well would teach the cultivator/proprietor to look at the whole case, and realise that there was no necessary conflict between the two classes, but that they ought 'mutually to assist and support one another'.[10]

Gladstone did not proceed with his land strategy which he outlined in Dublin in 1877; but the principle, that there could be a reconciliation between gentry and people, was central to his Irish thinking. His Land Act of 1881 was based, not upon the creation of a peasant propriety, but upon establishing institutions through which tenants could obtain a reduction in their rents. But within a few years he returned to the policy he had adumbrated in 1877, and introduced legislation facilitating land purchase, and as part of a wider Irish settlement plan: that of home rule for Ireland.[11]

Gladstone's approach to the problem of Irish Protestants, or specifically, the Irish Protestant gentry, was based upon the belief that the Irish home rule party undoubtedly after 1884 represented Ireland, that a reconciliation between England and Ireland was possible, and that it would end the quarrel of centuries. A second major consideration now fitted into this: that the policy of home rule, in achieving the settlement of Ireland, would also save the Irish gentry, and secure their essential role in the politics and society of Ireland. And both these principles derived their persuasive power from Gladstone's analysis of the political structure of the United Kingdom.

Gladstone recognised that there was no such thing as a 'British nation', but that there were in the United Kingdom distinct historical nations. Ireland was 'inhabited by Irishmen, as was England by Englishmen and Scotland by Scotchmen'.[12] On other occasions he included the Welsh nation,[13] and this concept of the historic nations gave rise in 1887 to a controversy in the letters column of *The Times*, where James Bryce defended Gladstone's views. Bryce denied that by 'nationality' Gladstone meant race:

> the point of Mr Gladstone's remarks seem [*sic*] to me to be, that in a question involving national sentiment the opinion of each of the nationalities surviving in our islands is worth regarding; and that the people of Scotland and Wales, still cherishing a distinct national feeling of their own, though one happily compatible with attachment to the greater nationality of the United Kingdom, have shown that they can extend their sympathy to the sentiment of nationality among the Irish, and that they do not deem it dangerous to Imperial unity.[14]

Bryce's use of the word 'nationality' is itself significant; for Gladstone preferred this to 'nationalism',[15] with its more radical and dangerous ideological connotations. Within the nationality of Ireland the Protestant gentry were rooted. Bryce denied that Gladstone had ever claimed that 'Ireland is at present a cohesive whole'; what he did say was that there existed a 'passionate feeling of nationality among the great bulk of the Irish people' which was 'not a matter of race or religion only, for it is now shared by many Protestants and many descendants of Englishmen and Scotchmen'.[16]

This claim that 'many Protestants' shared a feeling of nationality was central to the Gladstonian home rule project. And it was based upon Gladstone's reading of Irish history, especially the history of the last decade and a half of the eighteenth century. It is debatable whether Gladstone's reading of Irish history inspired his Irish policy, or whether, as a practical, executive-minded politician, he merely used history to bolster up what he believed to be a political imperative, the policy of home rule. The question is probably wrongly posed: once Gladstone embarked upon his Irish venture, his collapsing of politics and history was immediate; but his reading of Irish history

preceded his embracing of the home rule agenda, and was easily incorporated into the politics of home rule.

Whatever the relationship between history and politics, Gladstone
brought history to the bar of politics, and used it as the chief witness on
behalf of home rule. Gladstone ransacked some of the chief historians and
political observers of Ireland, especially Edmund Burke[17] and W. E. H. Lecky.
These were the sources of his most telling quotations and arguments. The
Union, he held, was immoral and invalid. It was a Union 'resolutely carried
by means which I will not stop short to describe, but which I think were the
foulest and the wickedest that ever were put in action, as far as I know ...'.[18]
This Union, then, involved voting for 'coercive measures in Ireland'; indeed,
so relentlessly did coercion accompany it that even Gladstone's favourite
Irish leader of the late eighteenth century, Henry Grattan, Protestant and
patriot, voted for coercive measures in the Union parliament; for which Gladstone did not blame him, for the Union itself 'entailed coercion against the
Irish people, as it entailed neglect of Irish interests, as it entailed the destruction of almost all care for Ireland on the part of nearly the whole upper class
of the Irish community'.[19]

This reference to the destruction of the Irish gentry's care for the community is deeply significant; for here, again, Gladstone revealed a central
part of his home rule policy, that of recovering, or enabling the gentry to
recover, their role in Irish political society that they had, because of the
Union, forfeited. Gladstone harked back to the days when that gentry was
truly Irish in its politics, and that was a time when Ireland possessed her
own legislative assembly. The lesson from history was plain: create a moderate home rule parliament, possessing moderate powers of self-government
(which was not the policy of repeal of the Union once demanded by Irish
Catholics in the 1830s and 1840s)[20] and the Irish gentry would find their
positive, eighteenth-century role restored, and their future life in Ireland stabilised. In the eighteenth century the 'Protestants, and the upper classes
generally ... were then almost to a man true Irishmen in the first rank of the
nation'.[21] Even the revolutionary United Irishmen revealed this fact. The
'spirit of nationality' (that word again) supplied to the entire nation a
common source of life, fusing them into a mass; the spirit of sectarian bigotry 'draws them off from that in which they agree, and inflames them in
what they differ'.[22]

This proposition rested on the assumption that Parnell's home rule
movement represented the nation in political terms, and that it would be reconciled, through home rule, to the Union. Gladstone had no doubt that the
home rule party did represent Ireland: in 1888 he referred to the 'Eighty-six
members from Ireland out of 103, or rather out of 101, because to call the
two representatives of Dublin University representatives of Ireland is an
absolute mockery.'[23] As to morality, Gladstone was convinced that this Irish
party was not separatist, not narrowly nationalist, but stood for a new spirit

THE NEW SAMSON AGONISTES;
OR.
GLADSTONE PULLING DOWN THE PILLARS OF THE EMPIRE.

17 'The New Samson Agonistes', *The Union*, 18 February 1888

of nationality. Ireland was now fighting her battle, 'not with the threat of sectarianism, not with Fenian outbreaks', not with 'the extension of secret societies': she was 'fighting the contest with the weapons of confidence and affection – of confidence in the powerful party by whose irrevocable decision she knows she is supported, and of affection towards the people of England'.[24] This contest was aimed, not at destroying the Union, but at saving it. For the Union, though indeed carried 'by means so indescribably foul and vile that it can have no moral title for existence whatever ... was a very great Act. It produced enormous results.'[25] The Irish themselves ceased to demand repeal of the Union, but wanted instead a local parliament in Dublin invested with the authority to deal with the whole of Ireland's internal concerns, leaving imperial matters to Westminster. The alternative policy, that of the Unionist party, was immoral, placing as it did Ireland in the hands of 'three powers – the Army, the Constabulary, and inferior tribunals of justice'.[26] There was 'one nation' in Ireland against whom coercion was being employed by 'the other nation or nations which inhabit Great Britain'.[27]

The moral dimension to Gladstone's reading of the Irish question, together with his plans for its resolution, helps explain his dismissal of any opposition from the Protestants of Ireland. They were standing in the way of progress, of reconciliation, of peace. This moral dimension endured until the end. In June 1892, campaigning in Edinburgh, Gladstone urged the people to

> go forward in the good work we have in hand and let us put our trust not in squires and peers – and not in titles nor in acres. I will go further and say not in man as such, but in the Almighty God, who is the God of justice, and who has ordained the principle of right, of equity, and of freedom to be the guides and the masters of our life.[28]

It followed that anyone who stood in the way of this great work was immoral, motivated by the basest desires. Gladstone dismissed the anti-home rule Nonconformists of the north of Ireland as a handful. He claimed that he understood the reluctance of pro-home rule Protestants to state their real views because of the hostile and intimidatory atmosphere in which they lived.[29] The Protestants of Ireland, he told a Liberal Unionist delegation in March 1891, were the cause of 'disunion' in Ireland, the 'real obstacle' to social and economic progress: 'your opinions constitute the disunion'.[30] The 'Irish Liberals', he said to R. B. O'Brien in November 1885,

> with an expression of sublime scorn which I shall never forget, 'the Irish Liberals. Are there any Liberals in Ireland? Where are they? I must confess (with a magnificent roll of the voice) that I feel a good deal of difficulty in recognising these Irish Liberals you talk about: and (in delightfully scoffing accents) I think Ireland would have a good deal of difficulty in recognising them either.'[31]

Gladstone reserved his special scorn for the anti-home rule Nonconformists of Ireland because they could not see that their best interests, too, lay in the making of an Ireland based on English Liberal principles of government – which a home-rule Ireland was longing to embrace. When Gladstone welcomed the 3,535 pro-home rule Presbyterians (one per cent) who had not bowed the knee to Toryism, the *Irish Ecclesiastical Gazette* responded that 'drowning men clutch at a straw'.[32] Worse was to follow. In 1888 Gladstone dismissed the claim of Irish Nonconformists that they had a special knowledge of 'the state of affairs in Ireland'. These gentlemen, Gladstone asserted, 'many of them of Scotch extraction', were denying that English Nonconformists were to be considered as competent judges. The 'vast majority of Irishmen' had as much local experience as the Nonconformist ministers, and were convinced friends of home rule. The Irish Nonconformists appealed to English Nonconformists for solidarity; but they did so on religious grounds, and thus 'our friends' were 'going back to the worst principles of the old Protestant ascendancy'.[33] In 1892 990 Irish Nonconformist ministers again wrote directly to Nonconformists in England, and again Gladstone became embroiled in controversy, doubting if there were that many who were involved in this appeal, and calling their action a 'secret underground appeal to religious bigotry'.[34]

But Gladstone stood on easier ground when he considered the specific case of the Anglo-Irish gentry; for here he had some evidence, on the face of it at least, that there was indeed a spirit of nationality that could be fanned once again into life. There was in the Anglo-Irish tradition an enduring trait of Irish patriotic feeling (and indeed in his day, all Irish Unionists, including Ulster Unionists, insisted that they were indeed Irish, Irish in thought and feeling).[35] The *Dublin University Magazine* exhibited powerful Irish patriotic sentiments; the idea that Celtic Ireland was a sort of Protestant Ireland in embryo was commonly held, especially by the Church of Ireland, which liked to claim that it was the original Celtic church, whose authority was overthrown by Rome.[36] And then there was the Irish historian, W. E. H. Lecky, who provided the perfect case for Gladstone's belief that Protestants could become patriots again. Lecky was a luminary of Irish intellectual and political life.[37] His great *History of England in the Eighteenth Century* stands as but one monument to his historical scholarship, and the Irish section, which he published separately as his *History of Ireland* in that period, still remains as the starting point for any serious student of eighteenth-century Ireland. His *Leaders of Public Opinion in Ireland* likewise stands out, not least because he felt obliged to alter it in the light of political developments in Ireland;[38] and the chief of these developments was Gladstonian Irish policy in the 1880s.

Lecky conformed, at first sight, to the character of the Irish Unionists whom Gladstone sought to use and mobilise in the interests of Ireland and the Anglo-Irish relationship. He was a profoundly patriotic Irishman; he was deeply conservative in instinct; he was in early days a home ruler; indeed in 1871, shortly after Isaac Butt's Home Government Association was founded, Lecky was a supporter because he was a federalist, and home rule was presented by Butt as a federal solution, one based on the secret ballot and restricted franchise of his day. Lecky believed that if the mistake of the Union had been avoided – and it was an error – then the choice of the Irish public of the day would have been federalism. He also supported Gladstone's Land Act of 1870 because it gave the tenants security and therefore must, in time, cure the division of classes in Ireland (which Lecky thought more serious than that of sects). This act, if it did not extinguish the desire of the people for national institutions, 'will greatly increase the probability of their obtaining them'.[39] Lecky, like Gladstone, believed in justice for Ireland. He hoped for an Irish parliament made up of gentry. Irish nationality must be recognised, but there was an ambiguity here – Gladstone's reforms would create a situation in which self-government would be conceded, or would wipe out the demand for it altogether.[40] Lecky spoke for a certain strand of Irish Conservatism, exemplified in the *Dublin University Magazine*. But revolutionary movements in Ireland after 1879, the Land League, the rise of Parnellism, pushed him in a more conservative, less national direction. Now he led the Unionist-landlord protest against Gladstonianism, against the new Gladstonianism that threatened the gentry, social stability and order in Ireland. Yet he remained a patriot, resenting the imputations of historians such as Froude who insisted that the Irish were so backward and feckless that they must be governed by England. But Parnellism was different; it had 'killed home rule by demonstrating in the clearest manner that classes who possess political power in Ireland are radically and profoundly unfit for self-government'.[41] How horrible, then, that Gladstone (like Irish nationalists) should quote Lecky against himself – should take his great work, his search for a new Henry Grattan who would inspire the true patriotism of those fit to rule, and turn this weapon against Unionism! The point was that Lecky and other Irish Unionists, notably Edward Carson, were patriots, not nationalists, and perhaps Lecky had always been such an article; yet Gladstone and Lecky were at one in believing that land and home rule were inseparable: the problem was that Lecky believed that the conjunction of the two showed that nationalism was not to be trusted, was anarchic, was aimed at destroying social peace in Ireland. By 1880 Lecky was a determined foe of home rule, Gladstone was soon to embrace it and link it with land reform, and thus the two men drew the opposite conclusions from their reading of Irish history.[42]

Lecky still looked to Grattan's parliament, but it was a golden age, never to be recovered; whereas for Gladstone it was a golden age recoverable. In 1881 Lecky broke with Gladstone over the Land Act, seeing it as tending towards socialism and democracy in Ireland, his two great enemies.[43] Gladstone, in invading the rights of private property, was creating not one, but two 'predatory bodies' in Ireland: the Land League and the land courts; the act was an instrument of dishonesty and confiscation.[44] The home rulers were motivated by a desire to plunder landlords and separate Ireland from England.[45] Gladstonian home rule policy would take power from those most attached to the Union.[46]

Lecky now championed the Unionist cause. In a public letter in *The Times*, on 4 February 1886, he accused Gladstone of pandering to the dissolution of the Union and dismemberment of the empire, striking a blow that he hoped would drive apart Gladstone and those Liberals who were worried about home rule.[47] He contrasted the Protestant, loyal and propertied nationalists of Grattan's time with the Catholic, disaffected, democratic agitators of Parnell's.[48] But Lecky was still suffering from his earlier writings on the golden age. Gladstone, fighting his way back to office, quoted Lecky against Lecky.[49] When Gladstone reviewed Lecky's *Eighteenth Century* in the *Nineteenth Century* in 1887, he noted Lecky's claim that the United Irish Society was 'well and wisely instituted with a reform of Parliament for its object, and the union of Protestants with Catholics for the means'. Lecky, he went on, stated that 'The Society of United Irishmen was at first constituted for the simple purpose of forming a union of Protestants and Catholics, and thus obtaining a liberal measure of parliamentary reform.' But Lecky then 'proceeds to describe, very truly, the contrast between the policy of Grattan and the ideas of Tone' (the United Irish leader); and with Grattan in his view he says:

> The spirit of the United Irishmen was from the beginning wholly different. They believed, in opposition to Grattan, that it was possible for Ireland to subsist and flourish as a separate state, and their attitude to Great Britain, when it was not one of disaffection and hostility, was at least one of alienation and indifference.

Gladstone concluded, with no little satisfaction, 'I am wholly unable to reconcile these statements.'[50] The war of quotes went on. Gladstone agreed with Lecky that the north of Ireland was in the eighteenth century the centre of active citizenship, wealth and progress,[51] but Lecky saw it as therefore the best bulwark against home rule. Gladstone was wrong in thinking that the strong Puritan element underlying the resolution of Ulster would evaporate into mere words.

The Lecky–Gladstone relationship, once close, was now an exercise in cross purposes. Gladstone had what seemed on the face of it good reasons for thinking he could revive the spirit of 1782, and indeed for believing that Irish Protestants were part of the Irish nation. He was wrong in thinking that this spirit could be revived. But it seemed at least a possibility: was not Lecky a perfect example of that Irish nationality, that patriotism, that conservative landlord admiration that Gladstone believed was the key to an Irish settlement? Of course he was. It was, then, ever Lecky's fate to be quoted against himself, as he moved from moderate home rule to Liberal Unionism. It would be absurd to say that without Lecky there would be no Gladstonian case for home rule; but with Lecky the case was, in Gladstone's eyes, even stronger, and certainly more moral. Lecky was convinced that, if it had not been for Gladstone, home rule would not have had as many as 50 supporters among British MPs; home rule rested largely upon a single life. Both men were political moralists, and both were possessed of a deep sense of righteousness.[52] This short summary of their relationship helps explain Gladstone and the Unionists more clearly; for Gladstone was convinced that he, and he alone, knew where their true interests lay. Lecky, after all, helped point him towards this, or at least provided the best arguments for the policy of home rule. Gladstone, while not quoting Lecky directly, recognised, as did Lecky, that laws must be not only good, but native as well.[53]

As McCartney writes, when John Morley denied that it was he who had converted Gladstone to the idea of historical justice for Ireland, Lord Acton then staked his claim. But if any single man did so (a doubtful proposition) Lecky would have the right to be considered; and if any book more than another influenced Gladstone in this matter, a case could be made for Lecky's *Leaders of Public Opinion*. At any rate, once Gladstone had made up his mind that the time was ripe and the case was irrefutable, Lecky's history offered a rich fund of material to help convince Gladstone of what he knew was true. Gladstone could claim that he brought to his side as witness the greatest living authority on eighteenth-century Ireland; the best textbook, as Harcourt called it, of home rule that he knew.[54] This enabled Gladstone to claim that sectarian bigotry was in what he called a period of 'decadence' in the last decade of the eighteenth century, but was fanned into flames by official government policy.[55] In 1795, he noted, religious animosities were at their nadir, because the spirit of nationality was at its zenith.[56] This was central to the Liberal case. John Morley put it succinctly: the problem was, not that there were Protestants in Ulster, but that 'the Protestants were anti-national'.[57] The abatement of the struggle would open the way for the Catholics to fall into the two natural dimensions of Clerical and Liberal. 'What we may be quite sure of is that the feud will never die so long as sectarian pretensions are taken as good reason for bad government.'[58] This brought the argument back to history. Gladstone read into the history of the later eighteenth century the lesson that the Protestants, even of the north – especially of the north – could also be reconciled to the Irish nation and to home rule. There was, he wrote,

> an occasion when Belfast was visited by the deputies which the Roman Catholics had collectively appointed to maintain and plead their interests, and the protestant populace took their horses from their carriages and drew them through the town amidst intense enthusiasm. The torch of religious bigotry was thrown by the British Government among them, and the Orange Lodges were instituted in the year 1795 for the purpose of calling in the bad and evil principle, for the purpose of dividing Ireland.[59]

This was demonstrated in the violations of public peace in Ireland in recent years, which were not Catholic violence. The Belfast riots that accompanied the home rule crisis were 'far more shocking and destructive and guilty', and were evidence of a 'perilous state of mind', more frightful than 'any manifestations, even including those that have been culpable, and have taken place within a recent period, than has appeared from the quarter of Irish Nationalism'.[60]

Given this acknowledgement of the reality of the Belfast disturbances, the question arises, finally, of Gladstone's attitude to the specific problem of the Ulster Protestants. Much speculation has arisen over what might have happened, not only in 1886 and 1893, but in Ireland since then, had Gladstone taken special measures to deal with the Ulster Protestant minority. The Gladstonian response, in approaching this problem, was to consider, but dismiss, any idea that they formed a separate nationality. Gladstone believed that Ireland possessed what he called the elements of nationality: 'collective or corporate individuality tested by reason, and sufficiently confirmed by history'.

He held that the 'map of Europe shows us that in cases like those of Hungary or Norway, a vigorous sense of nationality is compatible with effective organic union tempered by autonomy' – in other words, home rule.[61] As for the Protestants of Ulster, they might 'at first glance, be mistaken for signs of an historic nationality', such as that possessed by the Basques. But he placed them on the same footing as Scottish highlanders 'before the assimilating measures of the reign of George III'. The highlanders had a separate language, traditions, usages and social habits; with these distinctions they 'joined a marked military superiority over their neighbours; yet the candid observer will feel that they did not possess the constituent conditions of a true historic nationality; and they have learnt recently, but fully, familiarly, and freely, to feel that they belong to the integral nationality of Scotland'.[62] Thus, in introducing his Home Rule Bill, Gladstone in May 1886 claimed that 'the North was more opposed to the Union probably than the South', and 'Irish national patriotic sentiment' was 'more vivid in the North of Ireland than in any other quarter'.[63]

But Gladstone was an executive politician as well as a student of Irish history, and he claimed, in defending the policy of home rule, that one of the 'essential conditions' for the establishment of a parliament in Dublin was 'the protection of minorities'.[64] When he considered the position of the Ulster Protestants in the autumn of 1885, he thought that their concern was confined to matters of education, but he consoled himself with the reflection that Ulster could 'take care of itself in respect of education'.[65] In December 1885 and March 1886 James Bryce, an Ulsterman and his only colleague with first-hand knowledge of the province, gave Gladstone a paper on the Ulster question which, J. L. Hammond claimed, was unfortunately lost.[66] Gladstone wondered in 1885 what protection the Protestants of Ulster wanted, 'apart from the Land of the four provinces', by which he meant that, if Ulster Protestants did not accept home rule, they could not participate in the Land Reform Bill that would accompany it.[67] He thought when drafting his Home Rule Bill, in March 1886, of providing for the consideration during the progress of the bill through parliament of excepting from it 'any particular portion of Ireland'. But if Ulster were omitted, it was hard to see how that province could enjoy the benefits of the Land Purchase Bill.[68] Here again there was evidence from Ireland sufficient to add certainty to Gladstone's conviction that he was right in his assessment of the significance of the land question in Ulster – sufficient, at any rate, to persuade further a politician who was already persuaded of the rightness of his diagnosis. S. C. McElroy, a leading tenant right campaigner, explained at a meeting held on 27 May 1886 how the Co. Antrim Route Tenants' Defence Association (founded in Ballymoney in 1869) 'sympathised' with Gladstone in his bid to settle the question of Irish self-government and 'hailed with satisfaction' the possibility of the Liberal government compromising on the issue of Irish representation at Westminster, which Gladstone intended to remove altogether in his

Home Rule Bill. In 1887 the 'Plan of Campaign' organisers, seeking a reduction in rents, spared 'no effort', wrote the Liberal Unionist journalist Thomas MacKnight, to advance their cause; he noted that there was 'undoubtedly some hesitation even among the tenant farmers who, as Unionists, had no sympathy with Irish nationalism'. In the early 1890s the land question still surfaced to disturb landlord–tenant relations in Ulster. But Gladstone's optimism was badly founded. Land reform was of course attractive to tenant farmers in the north as much as anywhere else; but what they regarded as a radical change in the constitution was quite another question, and even Ulster Presbyterian tenant farmers could not see the issue, as did nationalists, as one of evicting an 'alien ascendancy' of Protestant landlords.[69]

On 8 April 1886 Gladstone acknowledged the existence of that 'wealthy, intelligent, and energetic portion of the Irish community, which ... predominates in a certain portion of Ulster'. They must receive the 'utmost consideration'. But Ireland had spoken, and Ulster could not rule the 'question at large for Ireland'.[70] In introducing his Home Rule Bill, Gladstone enumerated the options for Ulster. One scheme was to exclude Ulster itself, 'or, perhaps with more appearance of reason, a portion of Ulster', from home rule. Another was that Ulster might have separate autonomy. Another was that specific subjects, such as education, should be reserved and placed, to a certain extent, under the control of provincial councils. These had been suggested to Gladstone, but

> there is no one of them which has appeared to us to be so completely justified, either upon its merits or by the weight of opinion supporting and recommending it, as to warrant our including it in the Bill and proposing it to Parliament upon our responsibility.

Yet any of these, or other proposals, might well be given a practicable form; some such plan 'may be found to be recommended by a general or predominating approval. If it should be so, it will, at our hands, have the most favourable consideration, with every disposition to do what equity may appear to recommend'. That was what 'I have to say on the subject of Ulster'.[71]

Gladstone had little fear that any such proposal would be made, for the objective of all Irish Unionists, like that of British Unionists, was to defeat the whole Home Rule Bill, to destroy the entire enterprise. Ironically, an attempt was made to use Gladstone's own tactics against home rule in June 1913, during the debates on the third such bill; Mr Cave, a Unionist, reminded the House that Gladstone in 1893 admitted that

> we did state that if the inhabitants of the North east corner of Ireland, only a very small and very limited portion indeed of the general community, were resolutely desirous of being exempted from the operation of that Act, we should

have been prepared to entertain a proposal to that effect, and I believe we made that declaration with the general concurrence of those who are returned by the Nationalist party.[72]

But these words only further confirm that Gladstone was intent on evading the issue, not confronting, let alone, resolving it, for in 1886 and 1893 (unlike 1913) all Unionists sought to defeat home rule for all Ireland. Gladstone probably hoped that, by seizing the moment, by getting the bill through parliament, he would thereby surmount the Ulster difficulty; and, after all, the Protestants of Ireland as a whole had died in the last ditch in 1869 when he disestablished the Church of Ireland, and yet, in the event, had accepted the measure. The complicated nature of the home rule legislation was undeniable, but it could be got through by an appeal to the moral conscience of the British people, and thus, in this great achievement, this moral crusade, the Ulster problem would play but a minor part and be resolved. The failure of the first Home Rule Bill to pass the House of Commons in June 1886 did not fundamentally alter Gladstone's strategy; he still waited to be convinced that Ulster wanted separate treatment, but no realistic scheme had as yet been proposed. In October 1887 he claimed that opposition to home rule would be undermined by maintaining Irish representation in Westminster, which his 1886 bill had proposed abolishing.[73] By 1890 he was convinced that the Ulster Unionists were numerous enough to 'hold their own'.[74]

And their opposition could be faced down. In March 1893 Gladstone noted that, while 'ferment' was 'increasing in Belfast', and there was a fear that the 'Orange leaders may be unable as the Bill proceeds to restrain their followers', there was 'no fear of "an organised rising"'; the military commanders, Sir Redvers Buller and Sir Garnet Wolseley, were 'in good heart'.[75] On 12 April, on the occasion of the decision of Lord Wolverton to resign 'on Ulster grounds', Gladstone assured his Postmaster General that he would if need be contradict Wolverton, stating that the 'pretensions of Ulster to rebel were fully announced 6 or 7 years ago'.[76]

But it would not be true to say that Gladstone was wholly unmindful of the minority problem in Ireland. His policy was shaped by his overall purpose, to restore the Irish gentry to their rightful place in Irish politics, and thus address the nub of the Irish problem: that 'social order is not broken in Ireland', but 'it is undermined, it is sapped, and by general and universal confession it imperatively requires to be dealt with'.[77] Restoring this order was at the core of Gladstonian political and land policies. In the proposed Irish constitution there was the 'first order' in the Irish legislature, consisting of 75 members elected by a constituency of rated occupiers of £25 and upwards (which the Ulster Liberal Unionist Thomas MacKnight denied would secure the rights of the Irish minority).[78] John Morley, in his *Life of Gladstone*, referred specifically to the protection of minorities. In this, he wrote, there was 'no novelty in the device adopted'. The two orders, with the first consisting of 28 representative peers and 75 elected members, was a device, and so was the gradual transition of executive functions. The viceroy would remain, and that was a safeguard. So was the viceroy's power to refer *ultra vires* laws to the judicial committee of the Privy Council in London. So was making judges independent of government, moveable only by an address of both orders. So was the fact that the viceroy would retain control of the Royal Irish Constabulary.[79] These were what might be called traditional English-style safeguards, harking back to the Glorious Revolution of 1688, with its securing of individual liberties by checks and balances, by independent judges, and with the protection of a class – the Anglo-Irish gentry rather than the ethnic-religious community in Ulster. And this was all part of that central purpose of Gladstone's policy: the restoring to their central place of 'the Protestants and the upper class generally' who in the late eighteenth century 'were ... almost to a man, true Irishmen ... in the front rank of the nation'.[80] Morley echoed Gladstone's thoughts of 1877, when Gladstone compared Turkish rule with that of Ireland under the Union: 'the real bitterness of the feud arose from the fact that Protestantism was associated with an exclusive and hostile ascendancy, which would now be brought to an end'.[81]

Gladstone never lost sight of this great aim. On 1 October 1892 he wrote to James Bryce, advising him that, 'in considering the question of the formation of Chambers, and especially of a second Chamber or Order for Ireland', he should 'please bear in mind a point which is not on the surface but yet I think important':

> The Irish Peers are deservedly unpopular. They are anti-national. They are an inferior set of men. But it is desirable if we can bring them back to nationality, to love of country, to popularity; for they are the natural heads of Irish Society, and in the 18 Cent. [sic] they were true Irishmen and were of a higher intellectual level than now.
>
> I have a yearning to recognise them in some way, to favour their moral repatriation, which they need so much.[82]

The Anglo-Irish gentry would, then, save themselves by Gladstone's exertions and Ireland by their example. But the home rule crisis of 1912–14, the struggle for national independence of 1916–21, and the partition of Ireland, all demonstrated, not only that Gladstone's project failed, but that the set of people who Gladstone hoped would stand between the 'Orangemen' and the 'law haters' not only failed to do so, but opposed Irish self-government, and in the end were politically ruined. But all this cannot set aside the fact that the Unionists of Ireland were not marginal to Gladstone's search for an Irish settlement, but, on the contrary, were central to it.

Notes

1 V. A. McClelland, 'Gladstone and Manning: A Question of Authority', in *Gladstone, Politics and Religion*, ed. P. J. Jagger, London, Macmillan, 1985, pp. 148–70, at p. 163. Irish Unionists, for their part, were not unaware of the connections; see *Irish Unionist Alliance Publications*, Vol. 2, Dublin, Belfast and London, Irish Unionist Alliance Publications, n.d. [1893?], pp. 8–9, 'Speech of Mr John Atkinson at Enniskillen, 12 January 1893', and Vol. 3, Dublin, n.d. [1893?], pp. 287–88, 'Mr Gladstone on the Church of Rome and Civil Authority'.

2 *The Speeches of the Rt. Hon. W. E. Gladstone on Home Rule, Criminal Law, National Debt and the Queen's Reign*, ed. A. W. Hutton and H. J. Cohen, London, Methuen, 1902, pp. 218–22.

3 Quoted in D. McConnell, 'The Protestant Churches and the Origins of the Northern Ireland State', unpublished Ph.D. thesis, Queen's University, Belfast, 1998, p. 94.

4 See, for example, the report of the great Unionist demonstration in Belfast in 1892: *The Ulster Unionist Convention*, 17 June 1892, Belfast, Belfast Newsletter Publications, n.d. [1892?], pp. 20–21, 29, 30, 34, 36, 40.

5 Gladstone, *Speeches* (1902), p. 224.

6 For a discussion of the etymology of the term see Jacqueline Hill, 'The Meaning and Significance of "Protestant Ascendancy", 1787–1840', in *Ireland after the Union: Proceedings of the Second Joint Meeting of the British Academy and the Royal Irish Academy, London, 1986*, ed. Lord Blake, Oxford, Oxford UP, 1989, pp. 1–22.

7 H. C. G. Matthew, *Gladstone, 1809–1874*, Oxford, Clarendon Press, 1986, p. 147.

8 H. C. G. Matthew, *Gladstone, 1875–1898*, Oxford, Clarendon Press, 1995, p. 29.

9 Ibid., p. 199.

10 *Dublin Daily Express*, 8 November 1877.

11 Matthew (1995), pp. 244–48.

12 Ibid., p. 213.

13 R. Shannon, *Mr. Gladstone in Swansea, 1887*, Swansea, Swansea University Inaugural Lecture Publications, 1982, p. 10; Gladstone described Wales as a 'nationality' with 'grievances'.

14 Sir J. Lubbock, *Mr. Gladstone and the Nationalities of the United Kingdom: a series of letters to the 'Times', with rejoinders by Mr. J. Bryce, M.P. and letters in support by the Duke of Argyll, Dr. John Beddoe etc ...*, London, Bernard Quaritch, 1887, pp. 13–15. Bryce's letter was published on 19 March 1887.

15 J. Loughlin, *Gladstone, Home Rule and the Ulster Question, 1882–93*, Dublin, Gill & Macmillan, 1986, p. 184; James Bryce explained the distinction between 'nationality' and 'race', emphasising that Gladstone preferred 'the former': Lubbock (1887), p. 23.

16 Bryce, in Lubbock (1887), p. 25.

17 Loughlin (1986), p. 179. Gladstone noted (*GD*, 18 December 1885) that he had 'Read Burke. What a magazine of wisdom on Ireland & America!'

18 Gladstone, *Speeches* (1902), p. 82.

19 Ibid., p. 83.

20 Ibid., pp. 242–43.

21 W. E. Gladstone, 'Notes and Queries on the Irish Dilemma', *Nineteenth Century*, Vol. 21, 1887, pp. 165–90, at p. 167.

22 W. E. Gladstone, 'Lecky's *History of England in the Eighteenth Century*', *Nineteenth Century*, Vol. 21, 1887, pp. 919–36, at pp. 929–30.
23 Gladstone, *Speeches* (1902), p. 84.
24 Ibid., p. 96.
25 Ibid., pp. 242–43.
26 Ibid., pp. 10, 21.
27 Ibid., p. 84.
28 D. McCartney, *W. E. H. Lecky: Historian and Politician, 1838–1903*, Dublin, Lilliput Press, 1994, p. 125.
29 McConnell (1998), pp. 95–96.
30 Loughlin (1986), p. 279.
31 Ibid., p. 138.
32 McConnell (1998), p. 96.
33 Gladstone, *Speeches* (1902), pp. 92–93.
34 McConnell (1998), p. 158.
35 See, for example, the sentiments expressed at the Unionist demonstration of 1892, *Ulster Unionist Convention*, 17 June 1892, p. 90. For Southern Unionists, see R. B. McDowell, *Crisis and Decline: The Fate of the Southern Unionists*, Dublin, Lilliput Press, 1997, pp. 16–19.
36 D. G. Boyce, 'Trembling Solicitude: Irish Conservatism, Nationality and Public Opinion, 1833–86', in *Political Thought in Ireland since the Seventeenth Century*, ed. D. G. Boyce, R. Eccleshall and V. Geoghegan, London, Routledge, 1993, pp. 124–45.
37 D. McCartney's *Lecky* (1994) is the best study; see also J. J. Auchmuty, *Lecky: A Biographical and Critical Essay*, Dublin and London, Hodges, Figgis & Co., 1945.
38 D. McCartney, 'Lecky's *Leaders of Public Opinion in Ireland*', *Irish Historical Studies*, Vol. 14, 1964, pp. 119–41.
39 McCartney (1994), p. 60.
40 Ibid., p. 61.
41 Ibid., p. 95.
42 Ibid., p. 96.
43 Ibid., pp. 99–100.
44 Ibid., p. 100.
45 Ibid., p. 115.
46 Ibid., p. 116.
47 Ibid., p. 118.
48 Ibid., p. 119.
49 Ibid., p. 121.
50 Gladstone, 'Lecky's *History of England*', p. 929.
51 McCartney (1994), p. 126.
52 Ibid., p. 127.
53 McCartney (1964), p. 137.
54 McCartney (1994), p. 143.
55 Gladstone, 'Lecky's *History of England*', p. 929.
56 W. E. Gladstone, 'Notes and Queries on the Irish Demand', *Nineteenth Century*, Vol. 21, 1887, p.167.
57 J. Morley, 'The Government of Ireland: A Reply, II', *Nineteenth Century*, Vol. 21, 1887, pp. 301–20, at p. 317.

58 Ibid., p. 317.
59 Gladstone, *Speeches* (1902), pp. 88–91.
60 Ibid., p. 231. For other examples of Gladstone's historical reading see his 'Plain Speaking on the Irish Union', and 'Mr. Ingram's History of the Irish Union', *Nineteenth Century*, Vol. 21, 1887, pp. 1–20, 445–69.
61 D. G. Boyce, *The Irish Question and British Politics, 1868–1986*, London, Macmillan, 1988, p. 33.
62 Ibid., pp. 35–36.
63 Gladstone, speech on the first Home Rule Bill, *Hansard's Parliamentary Debates*, 3rd series, vol. 305, cols. 584–85.
64 *Hansard*, 3rd series, vol. 305, col. 587. See also his draft in November 1885 for his Home Rule Bill, which included a reference to the need to secure 'for the minority a proportionate representation' (Matthew (1995), p. 229), and his consideration in November 1892 of provisions for the minority (*GD*, vol. 13, pp. 143–51).
65 Loughlin (1986), p. 139.
66 J. L. Hammond, *Gladstone and the Irish Nation*, London, Longmans Green, 1938, p. 515.
67 Matthew (1995), p. 235.
68 Ibid., p. 236n.
69 D. G. Boyce, *Nineteenth Century Ireland: The Search for Stability*, Dublin, Gill & Macmillan, 1990, pp. 206, 208; see also p. 187 for examples of how the land question divided Protestant Conservative supporters in Ulster.
70 Matthew (1995), pp. 235–36.
71 Hammond (1994), pp. 516–17. See also his speech at Farringdon Street, 30 July 1887, in ibid., p. 569 n.1.
72 Loughlin (1986), pp. 139–40; *Hansard*, 5th series, vol. 53, col. 1321. I am grateful to Professor Paul Bew of The Queen's University of Belfast, for drawing my attention to this reference.
73 Loughlin (1986), p. 236.
74 Ibid., p. 241.
75 *GD*, vol. 13, p. 213. Gladstone's notes of a cabinet meeting, 9 March 1893.
76 Gladstone to A. Morley, 12 April 1893. *GD*, vol. 13, p. 224.
77 Gladstone, speech on the first Home Rule Bill, *Hansard*, 3rd series, vol. 305, col. 596.
78 T. MacKnight, *Ulster as It Is, or Twenty Eight Years' Experience as an Irish Editor* London, Macmillan, 1896, vol. 2, pp. 128–29.
79 *Select Documents on the Constitutional History of the British Empire and Commonwealth*, Vol. V, *The Dependent Empire and Ireland*, ed. F. Madden and D. Fieldhouse, London and New York, Greenwood, 1991, pp. 781–82.
80 Gladstone, 'Notes and Queries on the Irish Demand', p. 167.
81 Morley (1887), p. 317.
82 *GD*, Vol. 13, p. 98.

Exporting 'Western & Beneficent Institutions': Gladstone and Empire, 1880–1885

Eugenio Biagini

18 Intervention in Egypt: Europeans leaving Alexandria before the bombardment, *Illustrated London News*, 8 July 1882

'WHAT ... is the real relationship between *ethics* and *politics*? Have they nothing at all to do with one another ...? Or is the opposite true, namely that political action is subject to "the same" ethic as every other form of activity?'[1] This question, raised by Max Weber in his *Politik als Beruf*, summarises one of the inescapable dilemmas of practical politics. On the one hand there is the 'ethic of principled conviction', which is not concerned with consequences; on the other, there is the 'ethic of responsibility'. As Weber put it,

> It is not that the ethic of conviction is identical with irresponsibility, nor that the ethic of responsibility means the absence of principled conviction ... But there is profound opposition between acting by the maxim of the ethic of conviction (putting it in religious terms: 'The Christian does what is right and places the outcome in God's hands'), and acting by the maxim of the ethic of responsibility, which means that one must answer for the (foreseeable) *consequences* of one's actions.[2]

Thus, while logically the only position consistent with Christian ethics 'is to *reject* any action which employs morally dangerous means',

> [i]n the real world we repeatedly see the proponent of the 'ethics of conviction' suddenly turning into a chiliastic prophet. Those who have been preaching 'love against force' one minute, for example, issue a call to force the next; they call for the *last* act of force to create the situation in which all violence will have been destroyed for ever ...[3]

A good testing ground for Weber's hypothesis is offered by the imperial policy of the 1880–85 Liberal government. As a statesman inspired by Christian ethics, Gladstone knew the difficulty of reconciling what Weber described as 'the absolute ethics of the Gospel' with the responsibilities of office. Contemporaries and historians alike have often been baffled by the ambiguities and apparent (or actual) inconsistencies in Gladstone's attitudes towards the empire and colonial expansion. As Edward Hamilton wrote in 1885, '[t]he prevalent view is that Mr G. won't trouble himself about foreign matters like Egypt; whereas it is Egypt, and nothing but Egypt, which occupies his thoughts.'[4]

Paradoxically, precisely because Gladstone had the reputation of being hostile to imperial expansion, in practice at crucial times he had to bow to the demands of the imperialists within and without his party. As Hamilton noted in his diary in 1892,

> The question is full of difficulties; but, no matter how great they are as regards our remaining somehow or another in Uganda, I am convinced that Mr. G. cannot evacuate the country without greatly damaging himself: – where John Bull has once been, he hates going out of it. Lord Salisbury might have carried

out the evacuation in the same way as he gave up Heligoland; but Mr. G. can not, any more than he could have given up Heligoland.[5]

In some ways, therefore, Gladstone could be taken as an example of the weaknesses inherent in an idealistic approach to international affairs. However, his imperial policies were not really idealistic in any simple sense of the word. It is true that he advocated morality in politics, including a commitment to the general principles of civil and political liberty and national self-government. Yet, he accepted what he saw as the lessons of history and the limitations of a fallen world, both of which qualified the way in which abstract principles could be applied constructively to specific realities.

In this chapter I shall propose an interpretation of how Gladstone could harmonise principles with pragmatism by focusing, first, on his intellectual indebtedness to Edmund Burke; second, on the importance of financial and fiscal stability as components of the Liberal understanding of what self-government really meant; and finally, on self-government as an imperial strategy, whose aim was to reconcile indigenous opinion to continued British rule.

I

Let me start by providing a short survey of the controversial imperial achievements of the 1880–85 administration. When Gladstone returned to power in the spring of 1880 at the head of a large Liberal majority, his priority was to restore financial 'good government'. It was quite obvious that this would not be an easy task, partly because of the trade and agricultural crisis, and partly because of Beaconsfield's imperial 'adventures' – which, in themselves, were supposed to be largely responsible for the trade difficulties. Purging the country of 'the short fit of delirious Jingoism'[6] and restoring prosperity were the two sides of the same coin. With typical zeal and energy, and combining the positions of Prime Minister and Chancellor of the Exchequer, Gladstone set out to deal with these difficulties. At first it seemed that he would succeed: his 1880 budget achieved the repeal of the much hated malt tax as a first instalment of revived fiscal virtue. However, already at the beginning of 1881 the restorative thrust of his government was running into major difficulties. As he told a junior minister: 'It is not possible for me at this time to anticipate what may be our financial position in March. Events like those in South Africa ... are affecting it unfavourably.'[7] What was happening?

As in the 'bad old days' of Palmerston's premiership, *foreign* policy was once again determining *financial* policy. The difference was that in 1880–81 foreign policy choices seemed to be dictated by events which were out of the government's control. As a consequence, and despite the fact that at the time Gladstone was Chancellor of the Exchequer, his diaries contain comparatively few references to the Treasury. Instead, they are dominated by the events in South Africa, Ireland, Egypt and the Sudan. At first Gladstone could delude himself that he was still dealing with the heritage of Beaconsfieldism. However, the reality was that Gladstone's strategy of controlling imperial expansion by imposing a 'fiscal constitution' on the government had become obsolete. It would have been inapplicable even in 1874, had Gladstone won the election; but by the 1880s it was eminently unsuitable for the defence of Britain's global interests.

Granted that 'true economy' was hardly feasible, the question was how to contain any further increase in imperial expenditure. In Midlothian Gladstone had proposed two strategies: avoidance of new commitments and extension of self-government. However, in 1880 he missed the first opportunity for a magnanimous application of his new policy in the case of the South African Boers. When they took up arms, Gladstone was faced with the alternatives of enforcing large-scale repression or conceding something like independence; he opted for the latter course, even at the cost of the implication that he was capitulating to them. This move 'from coercion to conciliation'[8] was the prelude to a similar change in Irish policy from 1886.

In India too there was an important move towards a more liberal regime with the appointment of Lord Ripon as viceroy. The establishment of forms of representative government at the provincial level, the repeal of the restrictive Vernacular Press Act, and the passing of the Ilbert Act, which gave Indian magistrates jurisdiction over Europeans, were highly controversial among the British community in India. Gladstone, however, firmly supported Ripon all the way along.[9] This was the context in which the first Indian National Congress (1883–85) was established as an organisation basically inspired by the ideals of Gladstonian Liberalism.[10]

Rather different was the outcome of Liberal policy in Egypt. British involvement in the Suez Canal Company, together with Anglo-French financial control of the country and the imposition of a British-friendly khedive, generated growing discontent and hastened the formation of a nationalist movement spearheaded by Egyptian army officers. Gladstone initially regarded this movement as a further instance of 'a people rightly struggling to be free', but in the course of 1882 local British officials, fiercely hostile to the nationalists, managed to convince him that the situation was degenerating into anarchy and military despotism.[11] When most Liberal ministers demanded the forcible restoration of the status quo, Gladstone was apparently reluctant to act. However, once he had embarked upon a policy of intervention, he pursued it without vacillation or misgivings. Militarily effective, in the short term the initiative was highly successful: as Professor Hopkins has put it, 'Britain's economic interests had been upheld; the Liberal party had been united; and the Conservatives had been rendered at least temporarily speechless.'[12] However, it soon emerged that the operation had opened a veritable Pandora's box of troubles for the Liberal government: the British found that their 'police' operation had to be prolonged indefinitely in order to fill the power and legitimacy vacuum that their intervention had created.

Yet, by mid-1883 it seemed that the Egyptian crisis would soon be over. 'Law and order' and the khedive's authority had been restored. Under British administration Egyptian finance was on its way back to 'rectitude'.[13] The British expeditionary force was being progressively withdrawn: by August 1883 only 5,000 troops were still in Egypt, down from 35,000 a few months before. Final withdrawal seemed only weeks away.[14] However, right at that time something happened which finally undermined Gladstone's hope of restoring mid-Victorian standards of retrenchment, either in Egypt or at home. At Kashgal, a large part of the newly created Egyptian army, led by General Hicks, was destroyed by the militant Muslims of the Ansar Sunni sect (the so-called dervishes). A whole set of new problems was thus introduced.[15] From then on the dimensions and cost of British commitment in northern Africa continued to increase, reaching a climax in February 1885, with the Gordon disaster. Yet, on the wave of success in home politics – with the passing of electoral reform (1884–85), the single greatest step towards democracy in Victorian Britain – the government managed to recover credibility. Another colonial crisis, this time on the Indian frontier, was handled with much greater ability and success: a war with the Russian empire was averted and the status quo consolidated.

II

[Y]ou claim the policy of non intervention 'to be an unworthy and ignoble doctrine.' This is a doctrine held by Washington, & to which Civilization and Christianity are evidently tending. You speak of the 'honour and interest of England' as justifying intervention ... Are not your words of the stock arguments of the Jingo school? ... They are the words of Palmerston throughout his mischievous career...[16]

Thus wrote John Bright to Joseph Chamberlain, who defended the Liberal government's decision to invade Egypt. In Bright's words we find a clear contemporary statement of the dilemma between 'the absolute ethic of the Gospel' and the ethic of political responsibility. Though Bright decided 'to treat the Egyptian incident rather as a diplomatic blunder than as a crime',[17] his case was, in a sense, irrefutable. Elaborating on it, the historian Robert Harrison has argued that the British intervention was 'blatantly aggressive, and hypocritical'.[18] Though such a clear moral judgement would seem to suit the spirit of Midlothian, we should not accept it without first examining the issue in the broader context of Gladstone's attitudes to empire and imperial expansion.

We must of course bear in mind that, as Colin Matthew has pointed out, in principle Gladstone was not hostile to imperial expansion, and in practice he was always a great defender of the British empire.[19] Furthermore his Midlothian principle of the 'sisterhood of nations' applied specifically only to 'Christendom':[20] as for the rest, general humanitarian considerations applied, such as respect for human life and avoidance of unnecessary bloodshed. But, unlike John Bright, he did not necessarily feel on the horns of a dilemma between principle and pragmatism whenever military action or repression was contemplated.

In Schreuder's words, Gladstone's imperial policy represented 'an *extension* of the liberal creed with its inherent beliefs in reform, *laissez-faire*, financial economy, Hellenism, and Christianity: a singularly strange yet powerful gospel of power and trusteeship'.[21] The intellectual background of this approach was obviously complex. In constitutional and historical terms, Gladstone was inspired by the ancient Greek and Roman empires:[22] from the classics he sought to extract teachings and models which he then applied to contemporary political planning, according to Bishop Butler's principle of analogy.[23]

However, above all, Gladstone's outlook was informed by Edmund Burke, from whom he derived both a sensitivity to national differences, and a historicist approach to constitutional conservation through change and reform[24] – or, if we prefer, a historicist approach to 'organic growth as permanent change'.[25] Gladstone had come to know and admire Burke's thought at a very early stage, in September 1826.[26] He was immediately captivated by the writings of the great Anglo-Irish political philosopher, who both inspired and qualified Gladstone's fervent Tory views.[27] In later life he changed his mind about Toryism, but not about Burke,[28] especially in matters of imperial affairs.[29] In a sense, there was nothing atypical in the mature Gladstone's Liberal reading of Burke: indeed, as Burrow has shown, late Victorian interpreters turned Burke into one of the lights of Liberalism,[30] as much as he had been a Tory guru for an earlier generation.

During the years of his second and third administrations Gladstone even went so far as to try to emulate Burke's rhetorical style.[31] More generally he searched Burke's writings for inspiration and 'analogies', especially in times of crisis. Thus, in defending his policy of home rule for Ireland in 1886, Gladstone wrote to the editor of *The Spectator*:

> For opponents I generally have four prescriptions. 1. Study the abominable, the almost incredible history of the Union ... 2. *Soak & drench yourselves with the writings of Mr Burke on Ireland* ... most of all with his writings on the American War. 3. Look a little at the effects of Home Rule (a) in Europe (b) in the colonies ... 4. Consider a little what is representation & what does it mean.[32]

The broader implications of these four prescriptions are not difficult to perceive: statesmen should learn both from history and from their own personal experience, paying attention to analogies and precedents drawn from both

Europe and the colonies. In this context they should consider the importance of representation for the mediation of ethnic and regional conflicts and the preservation of imperial unity; and, more generally, they should 'soak & drench' themselves with the writings of Edmund Burke. Implicit in this approach was a vision of what the British empire ought to be. In particular, 'home rule' in all its regional incarnations was an attempt to implement such 'prescriptions' and legislate in such a way as to provide a constitutional framework for peaceful and orderly progress.

This view had evolved gradually since 1837, well before Gladstone's conversion to Liberalism. In his speeches on the 1840 Government of Canada Bill, on the 1849 Australian Colonies Bill and on the 1852 New Zealand Government Bill, Gladstone had laid out what he described as the principle of 'local freedom'. The latter was not the first step towards severing the connection between Britain and its colonies, but, on the contrary, the safest bond of imperial unity and strength.[33] The 'error' which Britain ought to avoid was that of trying 'to hold the colonies by the mere exercise of power'.[34] To this doctrine he gave fullest expression in a speech delivered at Chester, on 12 November 1855:

> Experience has proved that if you want to strengthen the connection between the colonies and this country – if you want to see British law held in respect and British institutions adopted and beloved in the colonies, never associate with them the hated name of force and coercion exercised by us, at a distance, over their rising fortunes. Govern them upon a principle of freedom. Defend them against aggression from without. Regulate their foreign relations. These things belong to the colonial connection. But of the duration of that connection let them be the judges, and I predict that if you leave them the freedom of judgement it is hard to say when the day will come when they will wish to separate from the great name of England. Depend upon it, they covet a share in that great name. You will find in that feeling of theirs the greatest security for the connection ... Their natural disposition is to love and revere the name of England, and this reverence is by far the best security you can have for their continuing, not only to be subjects of the crown, not only to render it allegiance, but to render it that allegiance which is the most precious of all – the allegiance which proceeds from the depths of the heart of man.[35]

This vision continued to inspire Gladstone's approach to colonial policy for the rest of his career. Coupled with the principles of the famous 'Third Midlothian Speech' (1879),[36] such a vision could be mistaken for an endorsement of national aspirations, though, as Deryck Schreuder has pointed out, it was 'concerned ... with both liberal reform (devolution, autonomy, freedom, voluntaryism) and imperial conservation (reserved powers, delineated responsibility, circumscribed status, and qualified home rule in colonial societies)'.[37] In fact it embodied Gladstone's enormous confidence in the superiority of the British empire over any alternative arrangement which colonial societies might consider.

It has been argued that Gladstone took a different approach to colonies which, like India, were not, and could not become, colonies of 'white settlement'. I shall discuss this question in the last part of this chapter. However, if we accept that Burke influenced Gladstone's attitudes to the empire,[38] then we should bear in mind that Burke did not see India as radically different from either the British Isles or Europe. Indeed, according to Conor Cruise O'Brien, Burke perceived certain significant parallels between India and his own native Ireland,[39] a perception which was to be shared by later generations of imperial reformers, as has been pointed out by S. B. Cook and others in recent studies.[40] Furthermore, Burke made no secret of his admiration for the Indian people, who had been 'for ages civilised and cultivated; cultivated by all the arts of polished life, whilst we were yet in the woods'; a people with their 'antient and venerable priesthood, depository of their laws, learning and history', their 'nobility of great antiquity and renown', and their 'merchants and bankers, individual houses of whom have once vied in capital with the Bank of England'.[41] In terms of policies, he insisted that – in India as much as in America – conciliation was an essential component of sound imperial government.[42] The latter should be about the well-being of the local population and the spreading of what Marxist historians would have called the institutions and values of bourgeois civilisation, including private property and personal security.

However, this philosophy did not rule out the possibility that coercion might sometimes be necessary as a short-term restraint for evil tendencies and irrational behaviour. After all, the apostle Paul (Romans 13:3–4) had made it clear that coercion was one of the chief purposes for which government had been instituted. From Gladstone's Christian point of view *both* coercion *and* conciliation might involve the Weberian dilemma between an 'ethic of conviction' and an ethic of 'political responsibility'. Therefore the choice between coercion and conciliation did not necessarily involve either upholding or betraying any general moral principle. Liberal imperial policy consisted in determining how to move from occasional and limited coercion back to conciliation as the general rule. Granted that conciliation was the rule and self-government the method, coercion might be applied whenever the circumstances required it. Indeed, Edmund Burke had pointed out that '[c]ircumstances ... give in reality to every political principle its distinguishing colour and discriminating effect. The circumstances are what render every civil and political scheme beneficial or noxious to mankind.'[43] Almost paraphrasing Burke, Gladstone noted towards the end of his life:

> I am by no means sure ... that Providence has endowed me with anything which can be called a striking gift. But if there be such a thing entrusted to me, it has

been shown, at certain political junctures, in what may be termed appreciation of the general situation and its result ...[44]

In the 'circumstances' of the Transvaal crisis, Gladstone thought that coercion was likely to precipitate a permanent imperial crisis – 'another Ireland in South Africa'.[45] Moreover, in a Burkean perspective, conciliation and the retention of British control were not mutually exclusive, as was shown by the settlement of the national question in Canada. After the 1837 rebellion, the French Canadians had been appeased and integrated through confederation and self-government; if such a policy had pacified Canada, its application to South Africa was 'all-important'.[46] From Gladstone's point of view the Pretoria Convention was, as Deryck Schreuder has put it, 'the British North America Act on the highvelds'.[47]

While the Transvaal crisis was being solved, the imperial dilemma of choosing between coercion and conciliation presented itself again in Egypt. Which approach would commend itself to a statesman 'drenched and soaked' in Burke? While the latter did not write on Egypt, his letters and essays on the French Revolution addressed a situation analogous in many ways to the 1882 Egyptian crisis:[48] a people desperately struggling to be free, and yet obviously unfit for self-government and dangerously misguided by demagogues; a bankrupt state and a discredited prince, prisoner in his own capital. In a letter to the Earl of Charlemont, in August 1789, Burke had commented:

> England gazing with astonishment at a French struggle for Liberty and not knowing whether to blame or to applaud! ... The spirit it is impossible not to admire; but the old Parisian ferocity has broken out in a shocking manner. It is true, that this may be no more than a sudden explosion: If so, no indication could be taken from it. But if it should be character rather than accident, then that people are not fit for Liberty, and must have a Strong hand like that of their former masters to coerce them ... To form a solid constitution requires Wisdom as well as spirit ...[49]

If one replaces the words 'France' and 'Parisian' with the words 'Egypt' and 'Muslim', a tempting analogy emerges. In Gladstone's view the situation in Egypt in 1882 was at least as bad as that in France in 1789 according to Burke. As Gladstone wrote to Bright on a curiously appropriate date, 14 July:

> The general situation in Egypt had latterly become one in which everything was governed by sheer military violence. Every legitimate authority – the Khedive, the Sultan, the Notables & best men of the country ... had been put down and a situation of *force* had been created, which could only be put down by force.[50]

Only coercion offered hope of restoring 'wisdom' and 'virtue' among the Egyptians: '[t]hese madmen, to be cured, must first, like other madmen, be subdued'.[51] The Egyptians had to be 'cured' of their 'irresponsible spirit' by familiarising them with British financial administration and rule of law. For '[i]t is most true as Mr Burke says that the right to govern lies in wisdom and virtue', and '[i]t is not less true that irresponsible power is a dangerous thing unless curbed by wisdom and virtue'.[52] The Egyptians needed to be coerced in order to be both free and virtuous.[53]

It should not be supposed that Gladstone had been diverted from his own more Liberal instincts by imperialist pressures from both within and without his party. He had always been ambiguous as to the extent to which he was prepared to stand by the Radicals' demand of 'Egypt for the Egyptians'.[54] To Gladstone the people's right of self-government was not an 'absolute' or abstract theory, a notion which, ever faithful to Burke, he explicitly rejected:

> But as to those abstract doctrines about the indefeasible right of some portion of an oppressed people to exercise all the full-blown privileges of a high Constitution at a moment's notice, I disclaim this abstract proposition. Mr. Burke, among ten thousand things he said which should be eternally remembered, said that 'in politics the space afforded to abstract reasoning is extremely limited.' We must learn to look at the facts as they are; and, looking at them as they are, I say the duty of a Government situated as we are is to decline assenting to this abstract and unlimited demand which proceeds in contempt of all existing and prior circumstances; but, on the other hand, never forget the genuine interests of practical freedom, and using every legitimate and fair opportunity of bringing the people forward so far as they are fit for it, and so far as the circumstances permit to the enjoyment of its privileges.[55]

In the specific 'circumstances', Egypt's self-government could only be restored 'by degrees'[56] and 'with due regard to international and other existing rights'.[57] Thus, as Robinson and Gallagher have pointed out, '[t]here appeared to be no invincible difficulty about combining Egyptian self-government with guarantees that Egypt would fulfil her financial obligations'.[58]

III

By the 1880s establishing self-government or 'home rule' in the settlement colonies was no longer a controversial policy. However, applying the same principles to other parts of the empire and to non-British or non-European subjects was quite another question. For example, in both India and Egypt it involved, among other issues, what Gladstone described as the problem of 'how to plant solidly western & beneficent [sic] institutions in the soil of a Mahomedan community'.[59]

In 1882 the Suez Canal was the only reason for British intervention in Egypt,[60] though behind it were two distinct sets of concerns – namely, the strategic interest in retaining full control of the shortest route to India, and

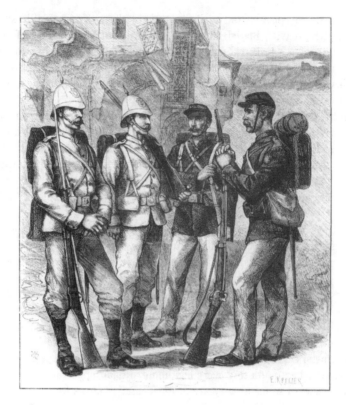

19 The Anglo-American partnership: British and American Marines in Alexandria,
Illustrated London News, 29 July 1882

the financial concerns of the European bondholders (many of them British,[61] including Gladstone himself).[62] Historians have traditionally focused on either the strategic or the economic concerns;[63] nevertheless, the *political* implications of the financial dimension deserve further attention in the present context because of the light they throw on Gladstone's understanding of what 'self-government' meant and ought to mean.

As Robinson and Gallagher have pointed out, Gladstone's preferred solution for the Egyptian trouble, both before and after the invasion, would have been to '"neutralise" the country on Belgian lines'.[64] This, however, would have presupposed the existence of a 'reliable' Egyptian elite: 'reliable' in the sense of being perceived by the European powers as sharing western capitalist notions of financial rectitude and respect for treaty obligations. Despite the emphasis on neutralisation, perhaps the best example here is not Belgium, as suggested by Robinson and Gallagher, but Italy between 1861 and 1876. After the unification, Italian governments struggled with a heavy national debt, and for years tried in vain to balance the budget and thus earn international financial respectability. The latter was perceived as necessary to the real completion of the Risorgimento not only by the French and British financiers who sponsored the new state, but also by the Italian political elite, and indeed by Gladstone himself. In his occasional meetings with Italian statesmen and diplomats, he urged them to reduce military expenditure and think about the financial viability of the new state.[65] Financial viability meant independence, while bankruptcy meant foreign control: this was the stark alternative which the Italian government had to consider between 1861 and 1876. Egypt was held up to them as the prime example of a country whose national progress had been hindered by financial irresponsibility which – well before the British invasion – had led to loss of independence in the shape of international financial control.[66] Duly warned, the governments of the *Destra storica* were able to tread the narrow path of Gladstonian rectitude.[67] They stabilised the new country by a severe fiscal diet, which they imposed with Peelite resolve until 1876, when the revenue balanced the expenses. The international financial community was reassured, the Italian bourgeoisie sighed with relief, and the government fell. Things were back to normal, at last.

The *Destra storica* had done the job which in Egypt was ineffectively attempted first by the khedive, then by the Dual Financial Control, and finally, with greater success, by the British on their own. Unilateral British action was resorted to only when all other options appeared to be unworkable. From the point of view of the British Liberal government this happened when even Gladstone and Chamberlain agreed with their more belligerent colleagues that Arabi's revolutionary movement could not be 'guided', and should therefore be repressed.[68] By the summer of 1882 Egypt seemed devoid of any degree of stability – financial or otherwise – and Arabi could be construed as a military adventurer who benefited from the ruin of his own country.

One of the differences between the Italian and Egyptian cases was the weakness of the middle classes in Egypt.[69] Even more important than their *numerical* weakness was the fact that they were predominantly neither 'bourgeois' in economic attitude, nor 'national' in political sentiment: rather, they formed a cosmopolitan collection of social groups, each with differing interests and ethnic and religious backgrounds, ranging from the native Copts (10 per cent of the population), to the Jews, the Greeks and the western Europeans, who were very numerous in Alexandria and Cairo.[70] It has been argued that, before the British intervened, the spread of European-style education and the reaction against European financial exploitation were in the process of unifying some of these groups and bringing them together with politicised farmers and soldiers into a new 'national' movement.[71] Nevertheless, in 1882 Egypt was not ready for its 'Risorgimento' without foreign help, any more than Italy would have been ready in 1859 without French help. Instead of help the Egyptians received foreign occupation, which, as Cain and Hopkins have put it, destroyed the proto-nationalist movement in the name of the 'Holy Alliance' of gentlemanly capitalism and its best 'security organisation', the British empire.[72] As might be expected national rights were to be subordinated 'to the maintenance of international right'.[73] Bourgeois criteria of political legitimacy, more than 'Orientalism' or racism, influenced the British government as it took the final decision to intervene, even though 'Orientalism' and racism coloured both the interventionist propaganda of the time and the responses of the European community in Egypt.[74]

Yet it is true that there was an important cultural component in Gladstone's approach to Egypt: namely, his dislike of Islam. Both in the *Bulgarian Horrors*[75] and in his 1877 article 'Aggression on Egypt and Freedom in the East', republished as a pamphlet in 1884,[76] the Liberal leader had expressed strong reservations as to the possibility of Islam ever establishing 'a good or tolerable government over civilised and Christian races', though in given circumstances it could conceivably lead to decent rule over Muslim 'races'.[77] In July 1882 he expressed the hope that

> when ... a reign of law is substituted for that of military violence, something may be founded there [in Egypt] which ... may tend to show that the desire for free institutions is not wholly confined to Christian races, but that even in a Mohammedan people, whose circumstances are certainly less favourable to the development of free institutions, a noble thirst may arise for the attainment of those blessings of civilised life which they see ... achieved in so many countries of Europe. ... Our purpose will be to put down tyranny and to favour law and freedom ...[78]

Having devoted so much time and eloquence to defending the Liberal legitimacy of the British invasion, Gladstone insisted, somewhat inconsistently, that Britain had no duty to remain in Egypt until the newly established 'western & beneficent institutions' had been given time to consolidate themselves.[79] He thought that indirect rule and 'a political link such as functioned well in India between the Raj and the princely states'[80] would work much better than direct rule. Britain required 'all the power necessary for efficiency; but ... no more'.[81] Quite apart from his concern to avoid any unnecessary affront to the sensibilities of Islamic clerics and fanatical crowds, Gladstone believed that the Egyptians would always prefer a native administration,

> which ... they love far more than foreign domination. Few, indeed, are the peoples so degraded and so lost to every noble sentiment, that it shall be a matter of indifference to them whether they are governed by persons who belong to the same political Constitution with themselves, or whether they are governed by those who come from a remote quarter, with foreign instincts, foreign sympathies and foreign objects.[82]

Therefore, in contrast to what Edward Said has written, Gladstone's imperial policy involved no denial that the Egyptians had national aspirations and instincts as much as the Greeks or the Italians:[83] rather, the aspirations and instincts which they did possess were to be subordinated to British imperial interests, as much as the aspirations and interests of both the Italians and Greeks had been in the past,[84] and would continue to be in the future.[85]

Indeed, in some respects the Egyptian nationalist leaders of 1882 were ideologically very similar to their Italian and Greek counterparts: many of them, far from being Islamic fundamentalists, were freemasons, liberal in politics and freethinkers in religion. Some of them, such as the founders of *La Jeune Egypte*, were predominantly Jewish or 'Levantine' Christians.[86] As for Arabi himself, though neither sophisticated nor well educated, he was influenced by American democratic ideas, with which he had become acquainted through the American Civil War veterans who served with him in the Egyptian army in the 1870s.[87] In general, the Egyptian nationalist elites were hostile to France and Britain only in so far as they needed to challenge the influence of these two powers, in the same way as the Italians had needed to challenge the Austrians between 1848 and 1866: it was an issue of *economic and political* independence, not of *cultural or ideological* antagonism. As the 'Arabist' leader Ahmad Rif'at argued, the Egyptian nationalists 'all desire[d] to share in the benefits conferred by such political institutions as Europe possesses'.[88] If they used a religious rhetoric, it was because they tried to manipulate Islam and turn it into an ideology of modernisation,[89] more or less as Vincenzo Gioberti had tried to manipulate Italian Roman Catholicism in the 1840s, when he invented 'neo-Guelph' liberalism.

In so far as he decided to ignore such 'analogies', Gladstone's analysis of the ideology of the Arabi movement was certainly not correct. This mistake was reminiscent of his 1876 failure to identify the reform potentials of the Ottoman government, which, as Ann Pottinger Saab has argued, was influenced by 'Liberal' elites and was genuinely struggling to modernise the state.[90] The effects of Gladstone's aversion to Islam were compounded by the attitude to Egypt of Hartington and the other Whigs in the government: traditionally less hostile to the Ottomans, in 1882 they clamoured for military intervention. It is possible, as al-Sayyid has suggested, that their attitude to revolutionary nationalism was hardened by the death of Hartington's brother, Lord Frederick Cavendish, who had been assassinated only a few months before, on 6 May 1882.[91] Furthermore, in the aftermath of the Phoenix Park murders, the government as a whole needed to demonstrate its ability to defend British lives and property and uphold 'law and order' – even at the cost of coercion in Ireland and intervention in Egypt. Finally, despite their protests and John Bright's resignation, it is remarkable that even the Radicals failed to challenge the government's policy either before[92] or after the invasion,[93] chiefly, it would seem, because of their disgust for both military rule and financial profligacy.

Having failed to sympathise with secularised Islamic reformers, Gladstone managed to manufacture an ideology of imperial domination which presented Britain's new Egyptian policies as consistent with Liberal pledges. From this point of view he was very successful. It is remarkable that most of the traditional opponents of jingoism, both in parliament and in the country, seemed to be persuaded,[94] while in the mass-circulated weeklies Arabi was represented as an adventurer rather than a liberal,[95] another Louis Napoleon rather than another Garibaldi. Later, when the Radicals began to feel uneasy about the prospect of a prolonged military occupation,[96] Gladstone could still argue that the transition to British control in Egypt was at least an improvement on Turkish rule. Furthermore, a commitment to 'home rule' as a long-term settlement was firmly retained and explicitly affirmed on more than one occasion.[97]

Accordingly, in February 1883 the special commissioner, Lord Dufferin, proposed the creation of new representative assemblies, starting at a provincial level. These assemblies had only consultative powers, 'except for the general assembly's right of assent to taxation; the membership was indirectly elected and, at the national level, diluted by nomination'.[98] Constitutional reforms were to be accompanied by extensive improvements to the fiscal system, as well as to land tenure, education and taxation, all to be reformed 'on the best Indian lines'.[99] As Robinson and Gallagher have concluded,

> Dufferin had recommended stability before liberty, administrative reform in preparation for constitutional advance. It was a scheme for implanting British influence more radical than Palmerston's plans for regenerating Turkey. Where he had relied on free trade and private enterprise ... it was clear by the Eighteen eighties that commerce and ideas alone were not enough. Success in India had shown what could be done through administration; hence Dufferin's method was administrative rather than commercial.[100]

IV

Egypt was being 'Indianised' at the very time when India was being 'liberalised.' As a consequence of the reforms of 1882–83, both Gladstone and his viceroy, Lord Ripon ('Ripon the Righteous'),[101] were long regarded as heroes by the Indian National Congress, as well as by the Indian National Liberal Federation. By contrast, modern historians have usually taken a less sympathetic view. Thus Anil Seal, Hugh Tinker and Thomas Metcalf have emphasised the administrative functionalism behind the Ripon reforms: '[l]ocal bodies could raise local taxes, and so increase government revenue while defusing popular animosity'.[102] Furthermore, following Eldridge and Knaplund, Metcalf has postulated a fundamental difference in approach to imperial reform: Gladstone's model 'for colonies of non-white settlement ... whether Jamaica or India, was the empire of Rome', rather than the 'Greek model' of self-governing colonies, to be reserved for the 'white settlements'.[103] Such a position was clearly held by some members of the Liberal government, including the Radical Chamberlain, who had strong misgivings about any further extension of Indian self-government.[104]

However, we may wonder to what extent such a sharp distinction is really helpful or realistic. As Metcalf himself points out, the Raj began to move towards forms of self-government soon after the 1857 'Mutiny'. 'The Councils Act of 1861 first announced the principle that Indians ought to be members of India's highest legislative body, and with it of provincial legislative councils.'[105] Moreover, as far as Gladstone himself was concerned, Metcalf is prepared to accept that there was a quality change when, with the Prime Minister's support,[106] 'Ripon introduced for the first time into Indian local-government the objective of training Indians for self-rule', and 'was prepared even to sacrifice administrative efficiency for this purpose'.[107] He 'set Indian controlled district and municipal boards in place across British India'. Thus, in 1882, another Gladstonian Councils Act 'further extended Indian membership in the provincial and imperial legislative bodies, and recognized election as the normal and appropriate means of securing Indian representatives'.[108]

Perhaps, as Metcalf suggests, this was an attempt to 'cope with the contradictions' between liberalism and the imperialist ideology of 'difference'.[109] However, there was nothing new in the approach to Indian reforms chosen by Gladstone and Ripon, as they sought 'at once to accommodate Indian participation in a public arena, and yet secure power firmly in British hands'.[110] The Canadians, Australians and New Zealanders were all contentedly accustomed to this strategy.[111] So, for a while, were the Indian elites. The difference was that India was more similar to Ireland than to Canada.[112] In particular, between the loyalist elites and the non-politicised masses there was a huge and yawning gap, which would have eventually provided a later generation of nationalists with their historical opportunity.

Ripon's aims and rhetoric were reminiscent of those which had characterised generations of reformers in Britain from the 1830s, and which were characterising Liberal attitudes to Ireland in the 1880s. In Ripon's words, local government in India was 'chiefly designed as an instrument of political and popular education'.[113] One of his lieutenants put it even more clearly:

> It may not seem a lofty employment to teach the people … of country towns how to manage local conservancy, primary schools and dispensaries, but it is the underlying growth of social organization which is really important, and I think it is not unworthy of the best abilities and the highest ambitions to build up in one's people with unpretentiousness and patient assiduity, the first foundations of a national spirit.[114]

More or less in the same period, at the other end of the empire, writing to the Irish Secretary, Gladstone defended the expediency of establishing provincial councils in the Emerald Isle, and argued:

> Until we have seriously responsible bodies to deal with us in Ireland, every plan we frame comes to Irishmen, say what we may, as an English plan. As such it is probably condemned. At best it is a one-sided bargain, which binds us, not them ... If we say we must postpone the question till the state of the country is more fit for it, I should answer that the least danger is going forward at once. It is liberty alone, which fits men for liberty. This proposition like every other in politics has its bounds; but it is far safer than the counter-doctrine, wait till they are fit.[115]

Of course, none of the reforms introduced or proposed by either Gladstone or Ripon was – or was supposed to be – 'democratic': rather, each was Whig and Liberal in the spirit of the 1835 Municipal Corporations Act. In the subcontinent they were accompanied by what Indian historians have rightly stigmatised as 'condescending paternalism',[116] involving an emphasis on racial distinctions and a hierarchy of races, and the deliberate attempt to consolidate imperial rule. However irritating this may be from an Indian nationalist point of view, the European scholar can hardly miss the similarities between Ripon's reform rhetoric in 1882 and the traditional Whig/ Liberal approach to reform in the United Kingdom. Such similarities can best be discerned when we compare India with Ireland. In each case the approach chosen by both Gladstone and Ripon combined considerations of administrative and fiscal efficiency and responsibility with concerns for civil and political liberties.[117] While Ripon was reforming Indian local government, Gladstone was trying to do the same – along similar lines and for similar reasons – in Ireland. From this perspective, the language of 'Orientalism' and the language of 'class' and intercommunal strife become reciprocally interchangeable:[118] different terminologies denoted the same political strategy, which in both cases was based on the familiar staple of Victorian reform – an emphasis on social and political peace, retrenchment, responsibility, moral improvement and civic virtue.

The aims of Gladstone's policy in India, and indeed in Egypt or Jamaica,[119] were not fundamentally dissimilar to those of his policy in the British Isles. Political rights and self-government went hand in hand with financial integrity. If the latter was 'the sum of all ... virtues and more'[120] for the bankers who sponsored Egypt in the 1870s, it was also one of the traditional prerequisites for the franchise and full political citizenship in the United Kingdom – an essential component of that famous 'moral fitness' on which Gladstone had been preaching in 1864 and in 1866–67, when he endeavoured to bring the self-reliant worker 'within the pale of the constitution'.[121] In the empire, as much as in British internal affairs, Gladstone's ultimate end was the creation of a culture of those modern bourgeois values which were necessary both for the modernisation of the British empire, and for economic and social development in a capitalist, free-trade world economy. These were to Gladstone both ends in themselves and means to an end – the means whereby an 'ethic of conviction' could be reconciled with an 'ethic of political responsibility'.

Notes

1 M. Weber, 'The Profession and Vocation of Politics', in *Weber: Political Writings*, Cambridge, 1994, p. 357.

2 Ibid., pp. 359–60. Emphasis in the original.

3 Ibid., p. 361. Emphasis in the original.

4 D. W. R. Bahlman (ed.), *The Diary of Sir Edward Walter Hamilton*, vol. 2, Oxford, Clarendon Press, 1972, p. 763 (entry for 5 January 1885).

5 D. W. R.Bahlman (ed.), *The Diary of Sir Edward Walter Hamilton 1885–1896*, Hull, University of Hull Press, 1993, vol. 3, pp. 174–75 (entry for 3 October 1892).

6 Leading article, 'The Liberal Answer to the Beaconsfield Challenge', *Weekly Times*, 4 April 1880, p. 4.

7 W. E. Gladstone to Sir Charles Dilke, Foreign Under-Secretary, 1 January 1881, *GD*, vol. 10, p. 1.

8 D. M. Schreuder, *Gladstone and Kruger: Liberal Government and Colonial 'Home Rule', 1880–85*, London, Routledge & Kegan Paul, 1969, p. 160.

9 W. E. Gladstone to Lord Ripon, 1 June 1883, *GD*, vol. 10, p. 456; H. C. G. Matthew, *Gladstone, 1875–1898*, Oxford, Clarendon Press, 1995, p. 126; A. Denholm, *Lord Ripon, 1827–1909: A Political Biography*, London, Croom Helm, 1982, pp. 157–59.

10 See O. Ralph, *Naoroji: The First Asian MP*, Antigua, WI, Hansib Caribbean,1997, pp. 92–94.

11 Matthew (1995), p. 132.

12 A. G. Hopkins, 'The Victorians and Africa: A Reconsideration of the Occupation of Egypt, 1882', *Journal of African History*, Vol. 27, 1986, p. 385.

13 Eventually achieved under Lord Cromer's management: P. Mansfield, *The British in Egypt*, London, Weidenfeld & Nicholson, 1971, pp. 96, 102–03.

14 Notes of a cabinet meeting, 8 August 1883, in *GD*, vol. 11, p. 14.

15 Notes of a cabinet meeting, 22 November 1883, in ibid., p. 62.

16 J. Bright to J. Chamberlain, 4 January 1883, in Joseph Chamberlain Papers, 5/7/30, Birmingham University Library. I wish to express my thanks to the archivist of the Chamberlain Papers for permission to quote from this collection.

17 Ibid.

18 R. T. Harrison, *Gladstone's Imperialism in Egypt: Techniques of Domination*, Westport, Connecticut, Greenwood, 1995, p. 7.

19 Matthew, 'Introduction', *GD*, vol. 10, p. xc.

20 Ibid., p. lxii.

21 Schreuder (1969), p. 41. Emphasis added.

22 T. R. Metcalf, *Ideologies of the Raj: The New Cambridge History of India*, vol. III, part 4, Cambridge, Cambridge UP, 1995, p. 54; W. E. Gladstone, 'Our Colonies' (1855), in P. Knaplund, *Gladstone and Britain's Imperial Policy*, London, 1927, p. 204.

23 D. W. Bebbington, *William Ewart Gladstone*, Grand Rapids, Michigan, Eerdmans, 1993, pp. 236–38.

24 H. C. G. Matthew, *Gladstone, 1809–1874*, Oxford, Clarendon Press, 1986, p. 199.

25 D. Schreuder, 'The Making of Mr Gladstone's Posthumous Career: The Role of Morley and Knaplund as "Monumental Masons"', 1903–27', in *The Gladstonian Turn of Mind*, ed. B. L. Kinzer, Toronto, University of Toronto Press, 1985, p. 203.

26 *GD*, vol. 14, p. 321.

27 J. Brooke and M. Sorenson (eds), *The Prime Minister's Papers: W. E. Gladstone*, 4 vols, London, HMSO, 1971–81, vol. 1, *Autobiographica* (1971), p. 36; cf. *GD*, 16 October 1832.

28 'I venerate & almost worship him': Gladstone to G. W. Russell, 13 October 1884, *GD*, vol. 11, p. 225; entry for 9 January 1886, in ibid., p. 476; and Gladstone to Sir H. Ponsonby, 27 May 1886, in ibid., p. 562: 'Mr Burke said with great truth that the only ultimate titles to govern were in wisdom & virtue. I do not think this can be much mended.'

29 Gladstone, 'Our Colonies', p. 209.

30 J. W. Burrow, *Whigs and Liberals: Continuity and Change in English Political Thought*, Oxford, Clarendon Press, 1988, pp. 14–16, 134.

31 *GD*, vol. 10, p. 103.

32 Gladstone to R. H. Hutton, editor of *The Spectator*, 2 July 1886, in *GD*, vol. 11, p. 580. Emphasis added.

33 Schreuder (1985), p. 229.

34 J. Morley, *The Life of William Ewart Gladstone*, 3 vols, London, Macmillan, 1903, vol. 1, p. 361.

35 Ibid., p. 363.

36 Particularly 'to acknowledge the equal rights of all nations' (p. 115) and to ensure that 'the foreign policy of England should always be inspired by the love of freedom' (p. 117): in W. E. Gladstone, *Midlothian Speeches 1879*, with an introduction by M. R. D. Foot, Leicester, Leicester UP, 1971.

37 Schreuder, (1985), p. 230.

38 For an explicit reference to Burke's influence on Gladstone's attitude to India see 'Morley/Gladstone Dialogues at Biarritz', in *Gladstone's Boswell: Late Victorian Conversations by Lionel A. Tollemache and Other Documents*, ed. A. Briggs, Brighton, Harvester Press, 1984, p. 197.

39 C. C. O'Brien, *The Great Melody*, London, Sinclair-Stevenson, 1992, p. 309.

40 S. B. Cook, *Imperial Affinities: Nineteenth Century Analogies and Exchanges between India and Ireland*, New Delhi, Sage, 1993, pp. 29, 31, 36–37. The most famous example is J. S. Mill (L. Zastoupil, *John Stuart Mill and India*, Stanford, California, Stanford UP, 1994, pp. 183–86). Though Zastoupil has suggested parallels between Mill's recommendations and Gladstone's 1882 Indian policies (ibid., pp. 204–05), the *GD* offer little or no evidence that the Liberal leader was influenced by the ideas of either John Stuart or his father.

41 E. Burke in 1783, cited in O'Brien (1992), p. 322.

42 Metcalf (1995), pp. 19–20; cf. P. J. Marshall (ed.), *The Writings and Speeches of Edmund Burke*, vol. 5, *India: 1774–1785*, Oxford, Clarendon Press, 1987. In a similar spirit Gladstone argued: 'Our title to be in India depends on a first condition that our being there is profitable to the Indian nations, and on a second

condition that we can make them see and understand it to be profitable.' (Cited in Denholm (1982), p. 139.

43 Cited in C. O'Brien, 'New Introduction', in E. Burke, *Irish Affairs*, ed. M. Arnold, London, 1988, p. xiii; cf. E. Burke, 'A Letter from Mr Burke to a Member of the National Assembly' (1791), in *Reflections on the French Revolution and Other Essays*, London, Everyman's edn, 1943, pp. 276–78.

44 Morley (1903), vol. 2, p. 240.

45 R. E. Robinson, 'Imperial Problems in British Politics, 1880–1895', in *The Cambridge History of the British Empire*, ed. E. A. Benians, J. Butler and C. E. Carrington, 3 vols, Cambridge, Cambridge UP, 1959, vol. 3 p. 136.

46 Gladstone, in *Hansard's Parliamentary Debates*, 3rd series, vol. 252, col. 461, 25 May 1880; cf. Robinson (1959), p. 134.

47 Schreuder (1985), p. 231.

48 For this analogy and the next two quotations (notes 49 and 50, below) I am indebted to my former student J. L. Davis (Princeton University, class of '95), and his unpublished paper 'Gladstone, Burke and Organic Change: Towards Self-Government in the British Empire', pp. 24–25.

49 Burke, cited in O'Brien (1992), p. 387.

50 To John Bright, 14 July 1882, *GD*, vol. 10, p. 298.

51 Burke, 'Letter ... to a Member of the National Assembly', in *Reflections* (1943), p. 255.

52 Gladstone to Lady Tennyson, 6 July 1884, *GD*, vol. 11, p. 171; cf. Burke (1943), p. 241.

53 There are interesting analogies here with the revolutionary mandate of Italian bureaucrats in the newly unified southern part of the peninsula, in 1861–1901, as analysed by R. Romanelli, *Il comando impossibile: Stato e società nell'Italia liberale*, Bologna, il Mulino, 1995.

54 'I suppose we are entitled to hold the present position so far as it is necessary to guarantee the pecuniary interests ... "Egypt for the Egyptians" is the sentiment to which I would like to give scope: and could it prevail, it would I think be the best, the only good solution of the "Egyptian question".' Gladstone, *GD*, vol. 10, p. lxviii.

55 *Hansard*, 3rd series, vol. 273, col. 1951, 16 August 1882.

56 *Hansard*, 3rd series, vol. 273, col. 1950, 16 August 1882.

57 *Hansard*, 3rd series, vol. 273, col. 1836, 15 August 1882.

58 R. Robinson and J. Gallagher with A. Denny, *Africa and the Victorians: The Official Mind of Imperialism*, London, Macmillan, 1965, p. 125.

59 Gladstone to Lord Rosebery, 15 November 1883, in *GD*, vol. 11, p. 59.

60 Gladstone to Lord Ripon, 6 September 1882, *GD*, vol. 10, p. 327; cf. Robinson et al. (1965), p. 123.

61 Cf. M. Swartz, *The Politics of British Foreign Policy in the Era of Disraeli and Gladstone*, Houndmills, Basingstoke, Macmillan, 1985, pp. 125, 129.

62 P. J. Cain and A. G. Hopkins, *British Imperialism, Innovation and Expansion, 1688–1914*, London, Longman, 1993, pp. 365–66.

63 For an effective survey of the debate cf. Hopkins (1986), pp. 363–91; see especially p. 385 for Hopkins's emphasis on 'Britain's economic interests'.

64 Robinson et al. (1965), p. 122.

65 F. Chabod, *Italian Foreign Policy: The Statecraft of the Founders*, Princeton, New

Jersey, Princeton UP, 1996, p. 410. Cf. W. E. Gladstone, 'Italy in 1888–89', *Nineteenth Century*, Vol. 25, May 1889, pp. 763–80.

66 Chabod (1996), p. 413.

67 D. Mack Smith, *Modern Italy: A Political History*, New Haven, Connecticut, Yale UP, 1997, pp. 78–83, 100; R. Romanelli, *L'Italia liberale, 1861–1900*, Bologna, il Mulino, 1979, pp. 63–86.

68 J. L. Garvin, *The Life of Joseph Chamberlain*, 3 vols, London, Macmillan, 1932, vol. 1, pp. 447–48.

69 The semi-colonial status of Egypt, and the 'capriciously authoritarian' personal government to which it was subjected, were, of course, part of a broader context within which the conditions for financial disaster matured: D. Landes, *Bankers and Pashas: International Finance and Economic Imperialism in Egypt*, London, Heinemann, 1958, pp. 97, 317.

70 Harrison (1995), pp. 40–41, 47; A. Schoelch, *Egypt for the Egyptians! The Socio-Political Crisis in Egypt, 1878–1882*, Oxford, St Anthony's Middle East Monographs, 1981, pp. 33–39.

71 M. J. Reimer, 'Colonial Bridgehead: Social and Spatial Change in Alexandria, 1850–1882', *International Journal of Middle East Studies*, Vol. 20, 1988, pp. 546–47.

72 Cain and Hopkins (1993), p. 368.

73 In Gladstone's words, *Hansard*, 3rd series, vol. 262, col. 1589, 24 July 1882.

74 Landes (1958), pp. 322–23. For examples of 'Orientalist' language used by Gladstone to *justify* the invasion after it had taken place, see the penny pamphlet edition of his speech on the vote of censure of February 1884: *Egypt and the Soudan*, printed for the Liberal Central Association, London, n.d. [1884], p. 25.

75 W. E. Gladstone, *Bulgarian Horrors and the Question of the East*, London, Murray, 1876, pp. 12–15.

76 W. E. Gladstone, *Aggression on Egypt and Freedom in the East, article contributed by the Right Hon. W. E. Gladstone to the Nineteenth Century, in 1877*, London, National Press Agency, 1884, p. 18.

77 Ibid., p. 18. Gladstone's attitude to 'race' would deserve a longer discussion than is possible here. However, we should remember that his notion of race seemed to be defined culturally and ideologically, rather than biologically. He frequently referred to 'the Christian races' (for another example see Gladstone to Gordon, 9 January 1877, in 'W. E. Gladstone-A. Hamilton Gordon Correspondence', ed. P. Knaplund, *Transactions of the American Philosophical Society*, new series, Vol. 51, Part 4, 1961, p. 71), and at least once described Disraeli as someone who belonged to the Jewish 'race' (a feature which constituted 'the most real, & so far respectable, portion of his profoundly falsified nature': Gladstone to Gordon, 16 May 1877, ibid., p. 75). From a political point of view, in his attitude to the empire he was concerned about stability and finding reliable partners, and did not really care too much whether the latter were European, Afghan, Christian or Muslim (Matthew, 'Introduction', *GD*, vol. 10, pp. lxv, lxvi).

78 *Hansard*, 3rd series, vol. 272, col. 1590, 24 July 1882.

79 Gladstone to Lord Rosebery, 15 November 1883, '*Private*', *GD*, vol. 11, p. 59.

80 D. Steele, 'Britain and Egypt 1882–1914: The Containment of Islamic Nationalism', in *Imperialism and Nationalism in the Middle-East: The Anglo-Egyptian Experience, 1882–1982*, ed. K. M. Wilson, New York, Mansell, 1983, p. 4.

81 *Hansard*, 3rd series, vol. 284, col. 712, 12 February 1884.

82 Ibid. This speech was also published as a penny pamphlet by the Liberal Central Association, under the title of *Egypt and the Soudan* (London, n.d. but probably 1884).

83 E. Said, *Culture and Imperialism*, London, Chatto & Windus, 1994, pp. 205–06.

84 Landes (1958), pp. 46–47.

85 Hopkins (1986), p. 390. From 1832 till the end of the nineteenth century, Greece, like Egypt, was under the financial tutelage of the European powers (including Russia); following effective bankruptcy, after 1897 an International Financial Commission assumed control of part of the Greek revenue for the purposes of repaying the loans contracted by various Greek governments. R. Clogg, *A Concise History of Greece*, Cambridge, Cambridge UP, 1992, pp. 64–65 n.18. These arrangements were similar to the Dual Control imposed on Egypt 20 years earlier.

86 Schoelch (1981), pp. 118–19.

87 Harrison (1995), p. 84.

88 Schoelch (1981), p. 127.

89 Steele (1983), pp. 8–9; Afaf Lutfi al-Sayyid, *Egypt and Cromer*, London, Murray, 1968, pp. 6–9; cf. E. Kedourie, *Afghani and 'Abduh: An Essay on Religious Unbelief and Political Activism in Modern Islam*, London, Cass, 1966. 'Islamic liberalism' included something like 'the rule of law': Schoelch (1981), p. 7.

90 A. P. Saab, *Reluctant Icon*, Cambridge, Massachusetts, Harvard UP, 1991, pp. 6, 22–24, 39–40.

91 Al-Sayyid (1968), p. 22; cf. P. Jackson, *The Last of the Whigs: A Political Biography of Lord Hartington*, London, Associated University Presses, 1993, p. 140.

92 MS Memo, June 1882, 7/1/3/1, Joseph Chamberlain Papers: it summarises the Liberals' dilemma over the Egyptian crisis before the British invasion took place.

93 MS Memo, 18 October 1882, 7/1/3/3, Joseph Chamberlain Papers.

94 A. J. P. Taylor, *The Trouble Makers*, London, Oxford UP, 1985, pp. 88–90; despite Chamberlain's misgivings: MS Memo, 18 October 1882, 7/1/3/3, Joseph Chamberlain Papers.

95 See for example 'Our Egyptian Patchwork', leading article in *Lloyd's Weekly*, 21 May 1882, p. 6.

96 'Nothing is done to "develop the institutions" to "promote the liberties" to give "Egypt to the Egyptians" – in fact to carry out a single word of the fine phrases with which we went to war.' J. Chamberlain to C. Dilke, 22 October 1882, Joseph Chamberlain Papers, 5/24/327.

97 'The Egyptian Settlement', *GD*, vol. 10, pp. 332–33.

98 Steele (1983), pp. 6–7; Robinson et al. (1965), p. 128.

99 Robinson et al. (1965), p. 128; see R. Tignor, 'The Indianization of the Egyptian Administration under British Rule', *American Historical Review*, Vol. 68, 1963, pp. 636–61.

100 Robinson et al. (1965), p. 129.

101 Ralph (1997), p. 75.

102 Metcalf (1995), p. 200; see also A. Seal, 'Imperialism and Nationalism in India', *Modern Asian Studies*, Mansell, vol. 7, 1973, pp. 12–13; H. Tinker, *The Foundations of Local Self-Government in India, Pakistan and Burma*, London, Pall Mall Press, 1968.

103 Metcalf (1995), p. 54.
104 J. Chamberlain to C. P. Albert, legal Member of the Council of India, 19 December 1884, 9/1/2/1, Joseph Chamberlain Papers.
105 Metcalf (1995), p. 190.
106 W. E. Gladstone to Lord Ripon, 1 December 1882, *GD*, vol. 10, p. 373.
107 Metcalf (1995), p. 200; cf. Denholm (1982), p. 150.
108 Metcalf (1995), p. 200.
109 Ibid., p. 234.
110 Ibid., p. 185. Cf. p. 150: 'Ripon's success here, as in so many other ways, lay ... in the greater and more substantial achievement of reconciling native opinion to continued British rule after Lytton. He endeared himself to Indians by his sincere efforts to redeem the pledges of Midlothian and ... the educated Indians never blamed him for his limited success in particular measures.'
111 J. B. Hirst, *The Strange Birth of Colonial Democracy*, Boston, Allen & Unwin, 1988, pp. 60–77.
112 Cook (1993), pp. 9–38.
113 Cited in Metcalf (1995), p. 201.
114 J. B. Peile, cited in Metcalf (1995), p. 201.
115 Memo to W. E. Forster, Irish Secretary, 12 April 1882, *GD*, vol. 10, p. 238.
116 Metcalf (1995), p. 201.
117 'Resolution of the Viceroy the Marquess of Ripon-in-Council, 18 May 1882', edited by F. Madden with D. Fieldhouse, *The Dependent Empire and Ireland, 1840–1900: Select Documents on the Constitutional History of the British Empire and Commonwealth*, vol. V, New York, Greenwood, 1991, p. 104.
118 Indeed the divide between the language of 'Orientalism' and that of 'class' was not always clear cut: Gladstonian colonial proconsuls did sometimes apply British categories to non-European natives. See for example the following assessment of the people of Fiji, sent by A. Hamilton Gordon to Gladstone, 12 October 1876: 'The people at large ... are in much the same state of civilization that our Scotch rural ancestors were four hundred years ago. – Like those Scotch, they are eminently improvable, and the problem is ... how to get them from the 15th century to the 19th.' 'W. E. Gladstone–A. Hamilton Gordon Correspondence', ed. P. Knaplund, p. 69. Note that Gordon was a Scot himself, and the son of Gladstone's mentor, the Earl of Aberdeen.
119 For interesting parallels between Jamaica and Ireland in terms of ethnic conflict and the problems involved in granting self-government, see Gordon to Gladstone, 21 January 1882, ibid., p. 84. For the general methodological and historical context see C. A. Bayly's masterly *Imperial Meridian: The British Empire and the World, 1780–1830*, London, Longman, 1989.
120 Landes (1958), p. 35.
121 Cf. E. F. Biagini, *Liberty, Retrenchment and Reform*, Cambridge, Cambridge UP, 1992, chapter v.

Gladstone's Fourth Administration, 1892–1894

David Brooks

WILLIAM THE WHEELMAN.

"'I CAN ONLY EMPHASISE THE FACT THAT I CONSIDER THAT PHYSICALLY, MORALLY, AND SOCIALLY, THE BENEFITS THAT CYCLING CONFERS ON THE MEN OF THE PRESENT DAY ARE ALMOST UNBOUNDED.' (*Aside.*) *WISH I WERE ON A 'SAFETY'!!*"

20 'William the Wheelman', *Punch*, 30 July 1892

'IT is a situation which would have suited the game of Palmerston or of Dizzy – whether it can be handled by sublimer spirits remains to be seen.'[1] This was the view of Sir William Harcourt, effectively Gladstone's second-in-command in the House of Commons, and for much of his life a candid friend to other leading Liberals. It was expressed in a letter to John Morley on 10 July 1892, just as the – for the Liberals – less than satisfactory results of the general election were starting to become apparent. In modern parlance, a hung parliament was in the offing. Harcourt here put his finger on the Liberals' predicament during what would prove to be the eighteen months of Gladstone's final administration. How much could they hope to achieve in unpromising parliamentary circumstances, maintained in office by a heterogeneous and insufficiently substantial majority? More to the point, perhaps, what indeed could Gladstone himself expect to accomplish on behalf of Ireland, whose cause he described as his only 'tie in honour left to public life'?[2] Would he be able to regard his fourth administration as in any meaningful sense his own government at all?

Gladstone had been sanguine as to his expectations of the outcome of the 1892 general election. As he wrote to Earl Spencer on 13 July 1892,

> The argument from the by-elections and the computations of our skilled and sober-minded friends at headquarters appeared to justify the expectation of a minimum majority of 80 or 90, probably rising into three figures. With such a majority we should have been very strong, and we could have carried Home Rule into the House of Lords with a voice and impetus somewhat imperative. Our majority is now placed by Marjoribanks at 30, and though I do not abandon the hope of its coming near 40, yet it is not homogeneous throughout and much reduces the scale of our immediate powers as compared to our hopes ten days ago.[3]

Writing to John Morley, Gladstone put the blame squarely on the division in the ranks of the Irish parliamentary party consequent upon the O'Shea divorce case in late 1890.

> Until the Schism arose, we had every prospect of a majority approaching those of 1868 and 1880. With the death of Mr Parnell it was supposed that it must perforce be close. But this expectation has been disappointed. The existence and working of it have to no small extent puzzled and bewildered the English people. They cannot comprehend how a quarrel to them utterly unintelligible (some even claim it discreditable) should be allowed to divide the host in the face of the enemy: and their unity and zeal have been deadened in proportion. Herein we see the main cause why our majority is not more than double what it actually numbers and the difference between these two scales of majority represents as I apprehend, the difference between power to carry the Bill as the Church and Land Bills were carried into law and the default of such power.[4]

The final tally, at the end of the 1892 general election, gave Gladstone a majority of 42, including, as Harcourt's son caustically put it, 'the labour members, Parnellites, Anti-Parnellites, and Dilke'.[5] What had gone wrong with the Liberals' protracted general election campaign, which in a sense stretched back to 1886? How far was Gladstone's diagnosis correct? That is a large question, and the confines of the present chapter preclude any thoroughgoing examination. But with regard to the Liberals' possible future strategy, a number of considerations need to be borne in mind. Clearly the Liberals in July 1892 had failed to realise their potential electoral strength. They had counted on getting back to something like the level of 1885, when, with the adhesion of the Irish nationalists, they could expect to have 400 or more supporters in the House of Commons. To accomplish this, they hoped to make another virtual clean sweep of the English county constituencies, and to eliminate more or less the Dissentient Liberals or Liberal Unionists. Neither of these objectives had been achieved. Though the Liberals gained 80 seats at the general election, they also lost 26 of those which they had held at the dissolution. In terms of English county seats, they won 32 fewer than in 1885. The Liberal Unionists were diminished somewhat in numbers, but remained a formidable presence in the House of Commons. Indeed in the west Midlands, Chamberlain's influence was credited with increasing their representation. The Liberals also performed disappointingly in Scotland. Gladstone suffered a drastic reduction in his own majority in Midlothian. Though, for once, the Liberals did rather well in London, they recorded only partial successes in the other major towns and cities. An 'urban cow', to recall Labouchere's picturesque comment in 1885, failed to materialise in 1892, just as it had failed to do on the previous occasion. Independent labour candidates were a thorn in the Liberals' side, and third-party intervention cost them a number of seats by splitting the anti-Unionist vote.

What was to be done in these less than auspicious circumstances? Should the Liberals even challenge for power at all? Salisbury did not resign at the conclusion of the general election, and was evidently intent on meeting parliament. Would the Liberals be able to dislodge him? Irish support in the House of Commons, which was in any case divided, could not be guaranteed, especially if there were any doubts about home rule retaining its place in the forefront of the Liberal programme. And doubts there were in July 1892, under the impact of electoral disappointment. Even Gladstone's nerve failed him for a time. As he admitted, 'if we had thrown British questions into the shade we should have had no majority at all'. He pondered what could now be done for Ireland 'in a situation, which forbids simple postponement of the main Irish issue, and also forbids carrying it'. He had a 'hankering after legislation which shall be at once concise and decisive, to help the *British* part of the bill of fare'.[6] Harcourt of course was much stronger in this sense. He hoped that the Irish MPs would be satisfied for the time being with the simple abandonment of coercion, and already he had his eyes set on introducing a wide-ranging budget, of the dimensions of that which would later take shape in 1894.[7] Such a major financial reform, envisaged for 1893, would fulfil key radical objectives, and, if coupled with democratising measures such as one man one vote, could make possible a Liberal triumph at the hustings if the government was forced into an early dissolution of parliament. Harcourt's rather vigorous canvassing of Liberal backbenchers on these lines in late July 1892 provoked a reaction from the Irish ranks. Morley and Spencer helped to stiffen Gladstone's resolve to give unquestioned priority to home rule. Without Irish support, the Liberals had no real prospect of regaining power; and they had committed themselves so wholeheartedly to home rule since 1886 that to relegate it now would look like political cowardice.

All the same, the formation of Gladstone's fourth administration was in certain ways a close run thing. At the start of August 1892, it was by no means clear that he would be fit enough again to assume the reins of office. Colleagues noted how he seemed to have aged even since the dissolution of parliament in June 1892. The election campaign had tired and demoralised him, and his eyesight had worsened as a result of an injury sustained at an election meeting in Chester. There were rumours of his having contracted bronchitis at the end of July, which threatened to bring his career to an abrupt and final end. Politically his touch in any case seemed lacking. Harcourt despaired at the draft of a no-confidence motion – a 'most feeble product'[8] as he called it – with which Gladstone proposed to turn out the Unionist government. Harcourt and his son also blamed Gladstone's want of tact for threatening to deprive the government of the services of Rosebery, much as had happened with Chamberlain in 1886. The Unionist government was at last turned out of office in mid-August 1892, but a degree of bad blood was created in the allocation of offices in Gladstone's incoming administration. Only after considerable pressure from Harcourt was Gladstone prevailed upon to include in the cabinet young and rising stars in the Liberal party such as Acland and Asquith, the latter being appointed Home Secretary without any previous ministerial experience. Gladstone retained his predilection in favour of aristocracy in government; Cobden, Bright and Chamberlain, he declared, were the only middle-class statesmen to have emerged since 1832. Gladstone's prejudices appear to have been reinforced by the experience of his second administration, when he blamed the middle-class element for the leaking of cabinet secrets. In August 1892, he attempted, without obvious justification, to resist Fowler's return to ministerial office on the grounds that 'the ideas of cabinet loyalty of an able Wolverhampton solicitor were not quite the same as those of a highly cultivated statesman of an elder stamp'; and he added that 'a man like Sir Henry Fowler, with the pronounced servility of a certain kind of provincial attorney, was bad for the Queen, though infinitely less so than Disraeli'.[9]

As John Morley put it, in constructing his cabinet, Gladstone's 'old-fashioned ideas about length of service came into play'.[10] This was particularly apparent in his insistence on appointing a significant number of peers to high office, including the Admiralty (a major spending department) and three secretaryships of state; and all this despite the minimal Liberal representation in the upper house. Gladstone got his way here, though not without opposition from Morley, and especially from Harcourt, who warned against 'carrying the claims of the Lords to such extremities'.[11] Altogether, his experience of cabinet proceedings during his fourth administration does not seem to have been a very happy one. At the end of his life, he rated it as 'the least good' over which he had presided. Partly this was a consequence of his greater age and physical incapacity, especially his deafness; but it also reflected the combustible mix of personalities within cabinet ranks. 'Never before', he declared, 'had he had such personal difficulties as those with Harcourt, Rosebery and John Morley in this government.' They were, he asserted, 'three very queer people'; and of Rosebery and Harcourt he stated that 'in all his experience of seventy colleagues in cabinet office' he knew 'no two men at once so clever and so difficult to deal with as colleagues'. Rosebery 'wanted judgement, plain good sense, and courageous consistency', whereas Harcourt was 'half statesman, half impostor'.[12] Clearly Gladstone missed the mediating role of Lord Granville, a kind of William Whitelaw figure, who had died in 1891.

Gladstone tried to deal with what John Morley called his 'invincible aversion to cabinets'[13] by endeavouring to hold as few as possible. In the 18 months of his fourth administration, Gladstone contrived to summon the cabinet together 47 times, as compared, for example, with 36 occasions during the last six months of his second administration. Gladstone's unhappy experience of cabinet meetings during his final period in government began in the early autumn of 1892 with stormy encounters over Rosebery's forward policy in Uganda. Foreign and imperial affairs will not be a principal theme of this chapter; its concern will remain the affairs of the United Kingdom, and here the pattern was set at a cabinet meeting on 11 November 1892 when Gladstone, most reluctantly, was prevailed upon at least to include the forthcoming Home Rule Bill on the cabinet agenda. In the words of Lewis Harcourt, Gladstone 'read out certain heads of a bill to be given to the draftsman, most of them being alternative and contradictory', and added that 'he did not intend that they should be discussed, not even the broad principles on which the bill was to be founded', as 'there would be sufficient time for that when the cabinet met in January a few days before parliament reopened'. The explosive reaction from ministers was perhaps understandable. Harcourt described it as 'a worse cabinet even than any of those during 1886'.[14] Angry colleagues insisted that Gladstone begin the detailed drafting of a Home Rule Bill at once. And Gladstone had to consent to hold more regular cabinets, and to appoint a special cabinet committee which would concern itself exclusively with preparation of the measure.

Finance was the first major hurdle facing home rule. To Gladstone, it all seemed straightforward enough. He saw no reason to reconsider his own cherished scheme of 1886, involving the device of the quota whereby Ireland would pay a fixed regular sum to the imperial Exchequer and would be free to dispose of the remainder as it thought fit. Consequently he had given minimal thought during the years in opposition to the financial side of the next Home Rule Bill, despite the warnings of his close advisers. For Gladstone it was sufficient that finance should comply with the general purpose of home rule as he conceived it. And fundamentally this was to diminish the role of government, or, in more modern parlance, to roll back the frontiers of the state. In his view the expansion of government was automatically attended with dire consequences, most obviously in terms of financial extravagance. He had criticised the Unionists' policies as much as anything because they had involved reckless expenditure in Ireland in the effort to kill home rule with kindness, and he had condemned their land purchase scheme as 'a precedent for rankest socialism'.[15] Home rule would give the British Treasury the chance to cut its spending in Ireland and return to stricter standards of public economy. Thus Gladstone urged that Ireland's administrative autonomy should be as complete as possible so as to relieve the British government of its more irksome and costly responsibilities. 'Will they not like to do their own Meteorology?' he demanded. 'Our sentiment was that wherever the Irish duties to be performed are exceedingly small, it may be well to get rid of the interference.'[16] And he added that 'we should make a great mistake in the interests of Great Britain were we to undertake any levy of internal monies in Ireland'.[17]

British Liberalism in general was little inclined to financial generosity to Ireland. Its leaders saw themselves as the paladins of Treasury orthodoxy, who were certainly not going to sacrifice their tenets on such dubious grounds as those of political favouritism. No doubt they recalled John Bright's aphorism that 'Ireland is never unanimous but on one thing – getting something from the Imperial Exchequer.'[18] But it was also true, as Parnell had once said, that 'the G.O.M. was the hardest taskmaster Ireland ever had'.[19] In 1893 Gladstone staunchly resisted the view that 'we ought not to take from Ireland as imperial contribution more than what is now the residue of her taxes after defraying the enormous civil charges at the present rate', for that would mean that, 'besides making a clear income for her of £400m per annum at Imperial cost, we are to abjure the whole benefit (so I think it would come out) of the very large economies which will almost spontaneously be made'.[20] Where Treasury matters were concerned Gladstone invariably took up the 'British cudgels'. He regarded home rule not least as a means of checking the gross financial extravagances which he held to have characterised Unionist policies in Ireland over the preceding years.

21 'Writing the Queen's Speech', *Punch*, 28 January 1893

Gladstone of course had no monopoly of British fiscal chauvinism. In particular the views of Harcourt, the cabinet's other main financial authority, were rapidly assuming an importance early in 1893. Harcourt's own susceptibilities were twofold. He had a highly orthodox sense of his departmental responsibilities as Chancellor of the Exchequer. But he also saw himself as the spokesman of rank-and-file Liberalism, especially in its more Radical inclinations. In his own mind there was no incompatibility between these two identities. Harcourt was a home ruler by necessity. He foresaw no hope for Radical progress in England until it was rid of the Irish incubus. But he harboured, along with many of his fellow Liberals, an underlying distrust of Irish good faith bred of hard experience before 1886, and he feared that Ireland might retreat from its obligations. He therefore considered the most serious problems as proceeding from 'the ethical and patriotic temperament of the men with whom we have to deal'. In particular what would happen in the event of war or special emergency? How could additional revenue be raised from Ireland if its contribution were fixed at a certain quota by law? In mid-January 1893, only a fortnight before the recall of parliament, Harcourt proposed an alternative scheme. Ireland should not be given an autonomous power of levying taxation. Instead it would simply be granted an annual dole, to enable it to meet its own requirements, of £600,000 by the imperial Exchequer, which would itself still retain responsibility for the collection of all Irish revenues. The British Chancellor would thus keep his freedom of action. But the plan offered political, as well as financial, advantages. It would, as Harcourt said, 'savour as little as possible of separation', and it would allay the fears of Ulster Protestants with regard to possibly vindictive taxation by a Dublin parliament, fears which had prompted a certain sympathy amongst the Nonconformist sections of English Radical opinion.[21]

Surprisingly, this was far from being the end of the story. Gladstone at first welcomed Harcourt's plan for its simplicity. Then he had second thoughts. The plan, he pointed out, contained 'no forcible motive for economy'.[22] It allowed the Irish government to spend freely up to a given amount, knowing that the British taxpayer would always foot the bill, and this despite the likelihood of considerable savings in Irish social expenditure as a consequence of reduced social tensions and fewer problems of law and order. The Treasury mandarin, Edward Hamilton, now came forward with yet another possible solution. Calculating that the expenses of civil government in Ireland roughly equalled the proceeds of all Irish revenues excluding customs, he proposed to reserve the latter only for imperial purposes and to place all other sources of income in Ireland (excise, stamp duties, income tax, etc.) at the disposal of the new parliament in Dublin. Like its predecessors, this deceptively simple plan contained one serious snag. What would happen when a British Chancellor of the Exchequer, perhaps faced with a national emergency, found himself obliged to raise rates of taxation across the United Kingdom? This was of particular concern to Harcourt, who had to deal with a large deficit of one and three quarter million pounds, and who had in mind a major reforming budget. Gladstone and Morley together agreed on an adjustment to Hamilton's plan without consulting Harcourt. The result was a predictable explosion from the latter, who angrily fired off a letter to Gladstone. 'I plainly foresee', he declared, 'that either the budget will kill the Irish finance, or the Irish finance will kill the budget.'[23]

Here another stressful episode in the career of Gladstone's last government took place. Harcourt's son, Lewis, has left in his journal a vivid account, which is worth quoting at length for the flavour which it gives us of so many of the cabinet's proceedings at this time. He records on 13 February 1893 that John Morley

> Has written very angrily to Chex [i.e. the Chancellor of the Exchequer] to say that he can think of no one but Lord Brougham who would have written such a letter to Mr Gladstone as Chex had done and have sent it on such a day [the day of the introduction of the Home Rule Bill in the House of Commons] ... Chex replied that he was much too old to quarrel with anyone over anything; that J.M. knew so much more history than he did that perhaps he would point out the incident in Lord Brougham's life to which he referred but that personally he could not remember the case which would have been if the Irish Secretary of those days had gone without the permission or knowledge of Lord Brougham into his Court of Chancery and delivered judgement in opposition to that of Brougham.

16 February. Mr G. wrote to Chex this morning to say that he had called a Cabinet at 2.30 today in consequence of his alarming letter ... The Cabinet sat from 2.30 to 3.30 in Downing Street but came to no conclusion and was adjourned to 6.30 at the House of Commons. Rosebery tried to reintroduce his scheme for the collection of Irish Excise but Mr G. snubbed him at once saying that his plan had been considered on Tuesday and rejected and they could not look at it again. Rosebery was furious and left Downing Street swearing that he would never attend a Cabinet again and as matter of fact he did not appear at Mr G's room at the House of Commons at 6.30 when the Cabinet was returned. Neither did Mr G. attend the greater part of it as he was sitting on the Treasury Bench listening to Randolph Churchill's speech against the H.R. Bill ... The whole Cabinet (except John Morley) agreed with Chex and even Fowler – who is absolutely mute when Mr G. is present – spoke out strongly in that sense. J.M. was in a state of furious excitement, nervousness and irritation; he was constantly jumping up with rather incoherent ejaculations and ultimately announced that 'he was no longer Irish Secretary'. The other members of the Cabinet were much disturbed and perplexed and did not know from one moment to another whether Chex or J.M. had resigned or both ... Chex also complained that a vital financial point like this should not have been decided without any communication with the minister of finance (the Ch. of Exchequer). J.M. replied that he had the authority of the First Lord of the Treasury whom he considered a sufficient financial authority but Chex pointed out that the responsibility for finance rested absolutely with the Ch. of Ex. and that the First Lord had no authority in the matter which seemed to be an absolutely new idea to J.M. Mr G. entered the Cabinet at this point, smiling cheerfully and asked if the matter had been settled! On this there was a fresh outburst by J.M. who said that if the words in the Bill were altered he would not communicate the fact to the Nationalists ...[24]

Matters continued in this vein for some months. Only in June 1893, four months after the Home Rule Bill had been introduced in the House of Commons, were its critical financial clauses agreed upon in cabinet. Ministers now reverted more or less to Harcourt's plan of the previous January. Collection of all Irish revenues would remain in imperial hands, but the Irish government would be granted two-thirds of the proceeds for its own purposes. Somewhat surprisingly the plan found favour with the Irish nationalists, no doubt because of its provisional nature. Ireland was promised a Royal Commission to examine the whole question of fiscal relations between Ireland and the rest of the United Kingdom, and to ascertain whether, as the Irish members claimed, their country had been over-taxed since the Union in 1800. By this stage, in the protracted parliamentary proceedings of the Home Rule Bill, a rather different problem was engrossing ministerial attention. This concerned the retention of Irish MPs at Westminster once Ireland again had a parliament of its own restored to it in Dublin. The question had been at the back of the minds of leading Liberals for some considerable time, and by the summer of 1893 its settlement could no longer be postponed. Its background requires some explanation. As is well known, the first Home Rule Bill in 1886 made no provision for continued Irish representation at Westminster, but out of office in 1887 the Liberals decided to reverse this line. They arrived at this decision for a number of reasons. Partly it was hoped to win back to the Liberal fold those who on this ground alone had voted with Chamberlain against the second reading of the Home Rule Bill in 1886. Also a growing number of Scottish Liberals were looking to the possibility of wider devolution in the United Kingdom, of 'Home Rule All Round' as it was popularly called, and saw in continued Irish representation at Westminster a necessary precedent. Lastly Harcourt pressed strongly for retention, as he saw Irish members as a vital reinforcement to the Liberals in the Westminster arena. Only in 1880, he asserted, had the Liberals won a majority independent of Irish support. Gladstone accepted the change of policy in 1887 with reluctance. In his view retention of Irish MPs at Westminster doubled the difficulties of successfully enacting home rule. For this reason, among others, he made little attempt in opposition to grapple with the detailed problems involved in maintaining an Irish presence in the imperial parliament. (Today, over a century later, we would now recognise this as the West Lothian question.) Should Irish MPs, following home rule, continue to sit at Westminster, but in reduced numbers, or perhaps under a restriction as to the subjects on which they could vote; or should both these limitations apply? As the future Lord Chancellor, Herschell, put it, should it be a matter of All for All, All for Some, or Some for All?[25] No firm decision had been reached in this regard by the time the Home Rule Bill was presented to the House of Commons in mid-February 1893, though, probably under Spencer's influence, Gladstone appeared to favour what was quaintly called the In and Out scheme, whereby Irish members at Westminster would be permitted to vote on certain subjects but not on others. By mid-summer, however, his opinion had hardened in a different sense, abetted by the great majority of Liberals, who were loath to part with the full-time services of a full complement of Irish MPs, whom they counted on as being their allies at Westminster for the foreseeable future. The formula now adopted was therefore All for All, or, perhaps more precisely, Almost All for All; as there would be a slight reduction in the number of Irish MPs from 103 to 80 in line with Ireland's declining population. Gladstone found himself greatly relieved by the revised formula. 'As regards the division of questions into imperial and domestic, he did not believe that to be possible, not so much because of the difficulty of category as from the impossibility of having a government in a majority on one kind of legislation and in a minority on another kind.' 'The highest function of the House of Commons lay in choosing the executive, and could the Irish properly be excluded from that?'[26]

Even so, a number of Liberal voices, at least on the backbenches, were still raised against the retention of Irish members in any form at Westminster.

Though by now in a small minority, these objections are worth some consideration, partly perhaps because of their renewed relevance today, but more especially because they emphasise something of the dilemma at the heart of the Liberal conception of home rule. For instance Dr G. B. Clark, the MP for Caithness, though a protagonist of eventual home rule for Scotland, disagreed with the other Scottish federalists in this respect, and considered that Scotland's interests would best be served by restricting the votes of her future delegates at Westminster to purely imperial issues. 'The scheme in the bill', he declared was 'neither federal nor incorporating, and was in part tributary, and it had all the evils of the three without the good of any one of them.'[27] Dr Robert Wallace, another Scottish Liberal MP, with a 'reputation as the most vigorously original speaker in the present Parliament',[28] went further and contended that Irish home rule, with all-purpose retention at Westminster, would actually prove prejudicial to Scottish interests. Home Rule All Round, he pointed out, had hardly yet got off the ground, and in the meantime Irish MPs would be free to interfere with Scotland's most cherished concerns, regarding education and the land. Thus 'under this coming Irish Home Rule Bill, unlucky Scotland, so long snubbed by England, is next going to be oppressed by Ireland'.[29] Wallace felt strongly enough about the inclusion of Irish MPs to pursue his battle in the pages of learned journals, and even to deny his vote to the government on the final reading of the Home Rule Bill. Supported by older Liberals such as William Rathbone, he embodied a long-standing Liberal distrust of Irishmen, fed by memories of their behaviour in the early 1880s. It was, he contended, misconceived as well as dishonest to keep Irish members with full voting rights at Westminster in the belief that they would always vote in the Liberal lobby, and thus 'to pass off government of the British people by the Irish people as Radical Democracy'. Indeed what could it profit a Radical 'if he shall gain the whole Irish vote and lose his own Parliamentary soul'?[30] In any case 'a nation of small landlords (like the Irish) was more likely to be a nation of great Tories'. The Irish at Westminster would be mere interlopers or '*adveni* ... responsible to no constituency for what they did in British affairs'. In short 'if Irish Members were to be hanging about this House with no other business to do, they would be put under the inevitable temptation of employing their powers to impede legislation in order to force fresh concessions from this Parliament'.[31] 'They will want ... control of some of the reserved subjects, of legislation – or money, whether in grant or loan – or Catholic rights asserted in Uganda – or Imperial interference against some accidental and distasteful majority in the Dublin Legislature, and if we refuse out we must go.'[32]

Here speaks a voice representative of a certain kind of British Radicalism. Gladstone, on the other hand, conceived of home rule as a work, not of Radicalism, but of restoration, 'a measure which acknowledges and consecrates the traditions of the country that calls for its application'. It would assist 'the restoration of the national life by reviving, in Ireland's ancient capital, the management of Irish affairs'.[33] Of Chamberlain, Gladstone wrote that if he 'is still at bottom the ultra-radical he used to be, he will be able to boast that he has never served Radicalism half so effectively as he has done by his able though rabid opposition to the conservative measure of Home Rule'.[34] Gladstone generally resisted attempts to smuggle elements of the wider Radical agenda, for instance female suffrage, into the Home Rule Bill: though he did agree to the suppression of university representation in the new Irish parliament. Somewhat puzzlingly, he asserted that university representation had originated 'in the very worst and most reactionary period of our history for six hundred years'.[35] The clearest instance of Gladstone's essentially conservative understanding of home rule is shown by his concern to provide the new Irish parliament with an upper chamber, in its way modelled on the House of Lords at Westminster. British Radicals were horrified; to one of them it was 'like introducing a fox into the hen-roost',[36] and the government managed to carry the clause by only 15 votes. For Gladstone, an Irish upper chamber was central to his conception of Home Rule as a great work of restoration. 'When the leisured class', he wrote, 'is deposed, as it is now to a very large extent deposed in Ireland, that fact indicates that a rot has found its way into the structure of society.'[37] But 'from the moment when a statutory parliament shall have been established in Dublin, the position held by the leisured and landed class of Ireland, as towards the people, will be entirely changed'. An upper chamber would provide a particular forum for this class who were 'the natural heads of Irish society'. It would 'bring them back to nationality, to love of country, to popularity', and 'further their moral repatriation which they need so much'.[38]

The successful passage of the second Home Rule Bill through the House of Commons did, in its way, represent a triumph for the government. Despite numerous predictions to the contrary, the heterogeneous government majority maintained its discipline and cohesion throughout the long, hot summer of 1893, in what would prove a record-breaking parliamentary session. The Great Reform Act, as it later became, had consumed 47 days of debate in 1831. The Land Act of 1881 had required 46 days to pass, and the Coercion Act of 1887, 42. The Home Rule Bill of 1893 was at length carried on its third reading in the House of Commons by a majority of 34, after no fewer than 82 days of debate. It was Gladstone's last great parliamentary tour de force. The long and exhausting session indeed seemed partly to rejuvenate him. 'The moment Mr G. gets into the House', recorded Hamilton in his diary, 'he seems to breathe an air which reinvigorates him.' 'His spars with Chamberlain are, I am sure, a real delight to him; they positively infuse fresh life into him.'[39] Gladstone was under no illusions as to the likely fate of home rule in the House of Lords, which duly rejected the bill by 419 votes to 41 in early September 1893. But he still regarded the work of the session as a triumph, and following the bill's passage on the third reading in the Commons, he expressed himself buoyantly:

The distance which has been actually travelled over between the physical misery and political depression that marked the early years of the century, and the victory recorded last night, is immeasurable; and the distance between that recorded victory and the final investment of Ireland with full self-governing control of her domestic affairs is not only measurable but short ... When at the close of next week the Bill will be rejected by a large majority of the House of Lords, we shall know, the people of Ireland will know, the world at large will know, that this rejection will mean no more than a dilatory vote and that there now remains but a single step into the promised land.[40]

Gladstone's last government would not remain barren of actual legislative achievement. Despite the unprecedented exertions of the spring and summer of 1893, parliament was recalled in the autumn in order to push forward bills dealing with employers' liability and the reform of local government; and of these two the Local Government Act reached the statute book just prior to Gladstone's resignation as Prime Minister early in March 1894. Why, amid the many and varied items in the Newcastle programme, adopted by the party in that city in 1891, did this particular subject assume pride of place? It was not one in which Gladstone displayed much passionate involvement, but Liberals in general understood that politically much was at stake in the English countryside, with which local government reform essentially proposed to deal. Since 1885, the two main parties had competed vigorously for the new voters enfranchised by the Third Reform Act. Sweeping Liberal successes in 1885 had been reversed in 1886, and, though the tide had turned fairly strongly in the Liberals' favour in 1892, it had in part been checked by the Unionists' flaunting of recent benefits which they had conferred on the agricultural labourer, such as free education, allotments and small holdings. By 1893, the renewal of serious agricultural depression gave an additional edge to the party battle in the English countryside. Local government reform also had the advantage of appealing to most sections of Liberal opinion. Essentially the Liberals proposed to add to the system of county councils, established in 1888, a nationwide network of parish councils, reinforcing the principles of democratic accountability and control at an even more local level. This would represent a blow on behalf of enfranchisement, and a blow also against the parochial pretensions of parson and squire; and this latter aspect would in particular find favour with English Nonconformists and with Welsh Liberals disappointed at the postponement of legislation to disestablish the Anglican church in Wales. Thus it was proposed to undermine some of the privileges of the Church of England, for instance by placing non-ecclesiastical charities in the hands of the new parish councils rather than the churchwardens. Also the new councils would have the right to use Church of England schoolrooms for their deliberations; the only alternative was likely to be the local public house, and no good Liberal could countenance that. Reform of local government would also carry significant implications for social policy. Among other things, it was proposed to democratise the management of the Poor Law, partly by abolishing most ex-officio guardians and ensuring that new representatives were no longer elected on a system of plural voting weighted in favour of propertied interests. Lastly the Local Government Bill proposed to tackle the contentious subject of land reform. Thus responsibility for village allotments would pass from ad hoc authorities to the parish councils, which would in addition receive novel powers of compulsory purchase.

Gladstone, as has been noted, took little interest in the local government measure, but none the less it carried some instructive lessons for his last administration. Most of the parliamentary work was managed by Harcourt, and by Fowler, the President of the Local Government Board. In line with his views expressed at the start of this chapter, Harcourt discerned an element of advantage for the Liberals in the existing parliamentary situation. He understood that the Unionists, unhappy though they might be with threats to the local dominance of parson and squire, yet dared not too obviously affront the agricultural labourers, whose votes might prove crucial at the next general election. Consequently the Unionists did not try to debate to death the local government measure, as they had previously sought to do with home rule, nor did they use the House of Lords to forestall it completely. This was the case, not least, because the Liberal Unionists in the upper house, led by the Duke of Devonshire, were particularly loath to alienate an important rural constituency.

The Local Government Act of 1894 represented the only substantial piece of legislation actually carried into law by the Liberals in a parliamentary session of unprecedented length. It was undoubtedly the measure in which the party as a whole felt most interest, and for a short while the Liberals basked in a sense of legislative accomplishment. Thus Harcourt expressed his conviction that the act would 'prove by far the most important and beneficial agrarian revolution of our time'. 'We shall', he continued,

in fact, as far as the rural districts are concerned, get a miniature general election throughout the country in November next. At that election the prominent topic will be what we proposed to give and what the Lords, the squires and the parsons have refused. A better electioneering position it is impossible to conceive ... whatever failure or disappointment may ensue will be attributable and attributed to the Lords, and will bear bitter fruit for the Tories at the general election ... When you get a complete reform done out of hand, like Free Education, people forget all about it, but in this case we shall get the main thing viz. the council and we shall keep the grievance in the practical demonstration of the desire of the Tories to destroy its action.[41]

The act of 1894 thus represented the high point in the Liberal programme for the rehabilitation of the countryside and the securing of the rural vote.

But Harcourt's prognostications were to be grievously disappointed. In the general election of 1895, the Liberals would perform disastrously in the rural constituencies. It seemed, after all, that the countryside preferred not so much allotments and opportunities for village debate, but instead hard cash in the form of rate-relief and Treasury subventions. And these were boons which only the Tories had indicated a willingness to provide.

All this lay some while in the future. At the start of 1894, the political world, as Gladstone saw it, was subsumed in his bitter conflict with the cabinet over naval rearmament. Here it really did seem to be a case of *Athanasius contra mundum*. Naval scares, usually intensified by the recurrent bogey of foreign invasion, afflicted Britain regularly enough throughout the Victorian and Edwardian periods, and one such notable example occurred towards the end of 1893. A number of factors were responsible, not least the increasingly close relationship between France and Russia, Britain's two principal imperial, and indeed potential naval, adversaries. What is important at this juncture is that the members of the Board of Admiralty indicated that they could not continue in office without large-scale increases in naval expenditure, and that, except for Gladstone, the whole cabinet agreed with them, including even Harcourt. Gladstone's views, however, rapidly assumed a hardened form. Those who supported the naval proposals, he declared, were either mad or drunk, or else prey to irrational and discreditable panics. No statesman that ever lived, with the possible exception of Palmerston, would have given way.[42]

Finance was naturally one crucial consideration for Gladstone at this point, but so also were constitutional propriety and the threat to European peace. Naval rearmament, he declared, would commit the government to expenditure over a term of years, and thus subvert 'the principle of annual account, annual proposition, annual approval by the House of Commons, which ... is the only way of maintaining regularity, and that regularity is the only talisman which will secure Parliamentary control'.[43] Worse still, rearmament represented 'a complete surrender to the professional element', whose increasing influence Gladstone discerned as a grave constitutional menace. 'It is the first time', he observed, 'that the admirals have dictated terms to the executive government of the day.'[44] Finally, and this Gladstone avowed to be his dominant consideration, the naval scheme involved 'directly challenging Europe in the race of armaments'. 'It is', he insisted, 'not the largest piece of militarism in Europe, but it is one of the most virulent.'[45] Gladstone depicted the likely consequences in apocalyptic terms. It would be taken as a long step towards the Triple Alliance; it would stimulate naval shipbuilding and preparations in France and Russia; it would not improbably cause a league, as had been the case before, of all the naval powers against Britain's intolerable pretensions; it might rouse dormant jealousies and cause the United States to construct a naval fleet; but above all it was a great stimulus to that accursed militarism which was the bane of the world. Britain should do nothing to 'accelerate, exasperate ... the controversies of blood which we all fear and seem to see are hanging over Europe'.[46]

At this point the question of Gladstone's health becomes especially intriguing. Adopting an uncompromising line on the navy, he seemed careless as to whether he continued in office or not. We have earlier referred to the effects of old age and cognate infirmities on Gladstone's political capacity. Failing eyesight had been a particular handicap, and significantly it worsened considerably in the second half of 1893. The severity of his condition became apparent when a cataract was diagnosed in one eye, though it was forming too slowly to allow of an early operation. Only Gladstone's family, anxious as always to keep him in office, dissuaded him from making the facts known publicly. In a letter to his Chief Whip at the end of January 1894, Gladstone spoke of 'the reality and sufficiency of those impediments (except to writing) which are connected with the senses', and hinted strongly at retirement.[47] It seemed that the naval controversy might provide the dramatic occasion for a resignation in practice forced on Gladstone by visual incapacity.

To a large extent, this was how things happened. The question of Gladstone's health served, conveniently in its way, to break his fall. 'It is', he wrote at the end of February, 'indeed a real solace, and a much needed one, that the case of my defective and declining senses is such a solid case.'[48] Still, and characteristically, even at the age of 84, Gladstone did not relinquish power without a struggle. The battle with his cabinet over naval rearmament seemed for a time to revitalise him, much as had the home rule debates in parliament during 1893. For nearly two months he fought a determined rearguard action, and even came up with the idea of calling a snap general election, ostensibly on the grounds of the House of Lords' obstruction of employers' liability and local government reform. Ministers reacted furiously. Harcourt described the proposal, in fact emanating from Gladstone's winter retreat at Biarritz, as 'absolutely insane', 'the act of a selfish lunatic'.[49] It seemed that the nadir of cabinet government during Gladstone's fourth administration had finally been reached. Gladstone now at last understood the extent of his isolation from his colleagues, which had become increasingly marked during his last 18 months in office. Maybe also he reflected that it was fitting to make his bow on a matter of principle that had been of recurrent concern to him in the course of his long political career.

What verdict can one, in conclusion, pass on Gladstone's fourth administration? As has been seen, it pointed up significant weaknesses in Liberalism, to be seen not least in the differences of emphasis that divided an octogenarian leader from many of his colleagues and followers. On the other hand, the fourth ministry also underlined Liberalism's strengths. Gladstone himself still proved an inspirational presence in parliamentary terms in 1893, and his last government had a unique record in that, unlike its predecessors, it remained undefeated in the House of Commons. Against all the odds, it survived from mid-August 1892 until Gladstone's resignation in early March 1894, at which point the leadership of the Liberal party in effect skipped two generations. The long and seemingly fruitless battle for home rule in 1893 at least paid dividends in that it enabled the heterogeneous government majority to hold together until mid-1895, though in the process it probably put paid to any lingering hopes of Liberal reunion in the aftermath of 1886. The landmark budget of 1894, passed several months after Gladstone's resignation, was therefore not the least of the legacies of his last ministry, though it was probably not one that he would have happily endorsed. But that is another story.

Notes

1   Harcourt to J. Morley, 10 July 1892, MS Harcourt dep. 706, Bodleian Library, Oxford.
2   Gladstone to Harcourt, 14 July 1892, MS Harcourt dep. 12.
3   *GD*, vol. 13, p. 41.
4   Gladstone to J. Morley, 26 November 1892, GP 44549.
5   Lewis Harcourt Journal, 19 July 1892, MS Harcourt dep. 383, f. 1.
6   Gladstone to Lord Spencer, 13 July 1892, and to Harcourt, 14 July 1892, *GD*, vol. 13, pp. 41–42.
7   Harcourt to Gladstone, 19 July 1892, GP 44202.
8   Lewis Harcourt Journal, 2 August 1893, MS Harcourt dep. 384, f. 24.
9   'Conversations with Gladstone', 7–15 February and 31 October–1 November 1897, Rendel MSS, National Library of Wales, Aberystwyth.
10 D. W. R. Bahlman (ed.), *The Diary of Sir Edward Walter Hamilton, 1885–1906*, Hull, Hull UP, 1993, p. 162.
11 Harcourt to Gladstone, 14 August 1892, GP 44202.
12 F. E. Hamer (ed.), *The Personal Papers of Lord Rendel*, London, Ernest Benn, 1932, pp. 135–38; 'Conversations with Gladstone', 2 February and 22 December 1897, Rendel MSS.
13 J. Morley to Spencer, 10 December 1892, Althorp MSS.
14 Lewis Harcourt Journal, 11 November 1892, MS Harcourt dep. 387, ff. 67–68.
15 'Conversations with Gladstone', 27 January 1892, Rendel MSS.
16 Gladstone to Sir R. E. Welby, 27 November 1892, GP 44549.
17 Gladstone to Harcourt, 21 January 1893, GP 44549.
18 J. Vincent, *The Formation of the British Liberal Party, 1857–1868*, London, Constable, 1966, p. 13.
19 R.B.McDowell, *The Irish Convention, 1917–1918*, London, Routledge & Kegan Paul, 1970, p. 9.
20 Gladstone to J. Morley, 2 January 1893, GP 44257.
21 Memorandum, 21 January 1893, MS Harcourt dep. 160; Harcourt to Lord Ripon, 19 January 1893, MS Harcourt dep. 724.
22 Memorandum, GP 44775, f. 35.
23 Harcourt to Gladstone, 15 February 1893, GP 44203.
24 Lewis Harcourt Journal, 13 and 16 February 1893, MS Harcourt dep. 391.
25 Memorandum, 8 February 1890, Rosebery MSS, National Library of Scotland, Edinburgh.

26 Memorandum, 7 July 1890, Rosebery MSS; Gladstone to Lord Kimberley, 12 November 1892, GP 44549.

27 *Hansard's Parliamentary Debates*, 4th series, vol. 14, cols 1534–35, 13 July 1893.

28 H. W. Lucy, *Diary of the Home Rule Parliament, 1892–95*, London, Cassell & Co., 1896, p. 191.

29 R. Wallace, 'Scotland's Revolt against Home Rule', *New Review*, 1893.

30 R. Wallace, 'The Ninth Clause (to my Fellow Gladstonians)', *Nineteenth Century*, vol. 34, 1893.

31 *Hansard*, 4th series, vol. 14, cols 1485–95, 13 July 1893; cols 1425–27, 12 July 1893.

32 Wallace, 'Ninth Clause'.

33 W.E. Gladstone, 'Notes and Queries on the Irish Demand', *Nineteenth Century*, Vol. 21, 1887; Gladstone, 'Further Notes and Queries on the Irish Demand', *Contemporary Review*, Vol. 53, 1888.

34 Gladstone to Admiral Geston, 23 May 1893, GP 44549.

35 *Hansard*, 4th series, vol. 14, cols 1390–93, 11 July 1893.

36 *Hansard*, 4th series, vol. 16, col. 307, 15 August 1893.

37 Gladstone, 'Notes and Queries'.

38 Gladstone to J. Bryce, 1 October 1892, GP 44549.

39 Hamilton Diary, 16 November 1893, BL Add. MS 48661.

40 Gladstone to Edward Blake, 2 September 1893, GP 44549.

41 Harcourt to Fowler, 8 February 1894, MS Harcourt dep. 721.

42 Gladstone to J. Morley, 14 December 1893, *GD*, vol. 13, pp. 338–39; Bahlman (1993), pp. 237–38.

43 *Hansard*, 4th series, vol. 19, cols 1789 ff., 19 December 1893.

44 Bahlman (1993), p. 237.

45 Gladstone to J. Morley, 7 January 1894, *GD*, vol. 13, pp. 353–54.

46 *GD*, vol. 13, pp. 354–57 (notes for cabinet, 9 January 1894); p. 374 (to Lord Acton, 8 February 1894).

47 Gladstone to E. Marjoribanks, 29 January 1894, *GD*, vol. 13, p. 367.

48 Gladstone to Rosebery, 25 February 1894, GP 44290.

49 Bahlman (1993), p. 233.

'Carving the Last Few Columns out of the Gladstonian Quarry': The Liberal Leaders and the Mantle of Gladstone, 1898–1929

Chris Wrigley

22 Gladstone's statue, Westminster Abbey, 1903

Writing in his *Napoleon: For and Against*, Pieter Geyl commented, 'And all the time the historical presentation turns out to be closely connected with French political and cultural life as a whole.'[1] Something of the kind can be said of the invocation of Gladstone's name in Liberal politics during the 30 years after his death.

For a period after 1898 Gladstone was revered with little equivocation by Liberals as the great Christian statesman who towered morally over his contemporaries.[2] After the Liberal Unionist split of 1886, the Liberal party had had a greater cohesion around the person of Gladstone and the issue of home rule. For some years after May 1898 the appeal to his name was often an appeal for Liberal unity and concentration on great Liberal issues. In time, while there were growing qualifications to the GOM's record, the appeal to the memory of Gladstone by Asquithians after 1918 could be to old established principles, while Lloyd George and his supporters were more ambivalent between 1918 and 1922, using his name for justification where it suited them but otherwise intimating that it represented a clinging to now outdated policies.

In Gladstone's lifetime Hawarden had been a place of pilgrimage for the faithful. J. H. Morgan, writing in 1924, observed when commenting on a feature of Gladstone's career covered in Morley's *The Life of William Ewart Gladstone* (1903),

> Lord Morley ... was writing the life of a man for a generation which had known and revered him, and an enormous proportion of whom took an insatiable interest in everything he did and everything he said. Crowds of pilgrims visited Hawarden like a shrine, collected the chips whittled by his axe as though they were sacred relics, clamoured for a speech as though it were manna from heaven. Never was there such political idolatry before; never will there be such again. To-day these transports of public enthusiasm are reserved for the transatlantic heroes of the film and the boxing-ring; or the protagonists of the cup-tie and the golf championship.

Morgan added an explanation for this: 'The Victorians venerated character, as the one thing needful, and in Mr. Gladstone with a sure instinct they found it.'[3]

This assessment combined historical understanding with then current or recent political concerns. After 1916, especially after 1918, Asquithian Liberals had little difficulty in contrasting the character of Gladstone or his Liberal values with that of Lloyd George and his alleged lack of principles.

Before the First World War there was a period of eulogy followed by some doubts being expressed about Gladstone's legacy. After a short interlude following his death (when there was insufficient enthusiasm for the Manchester Liberal Federation to commemorate Gladstone in 1898[4]) several memorials were commissioned. These included a statue in Albert Square, Manchester, in October 1901, a memorial in Westminster Abbey in March

1903, a statue at Temple Bar in London in November 1905, a tablet in Westminster Hall in March 1906, the monument to Mr and Mrs Gladstone in the chapel at Hawarden church in July 1906, and a later statue in Edinburgh in December 1916, as well as the three volumes of Morley's *Life* in 1903.[5]

John Morley spoke at the unveiling of the bronze statue in Albert Square, Manchester, on 23 October 1901 and afterwards at a public meeting in the Town Hall. These were occasions appropriate for eulogies, and Morley did not stint in his efforts. By this time the Jingo mood, which had rewarded the Conservatives with another general election victory in 1900, was waning. Morley himself had made some relatively slight efforts to emulate Gladstone's condemnations of Beaconsfieldism in opposing the Boer War and was immersed in his large biography. When speaking beside the statue he declared Gladstone was

> one of the truest patriots that this country has ever boasted ... a man who was not only a great statesman but a transcendent orator and a great scholar, and, more than a statesman, patriot or scholar, was a great teacher of the noblest lessons that nations can ever learn of those who rule over them ... It is enough to say that no more splendid gifts have ever been devoted to the noble exercise of public duty. Nobody in our time, no man in our day and generation has shown a more resounding example of the great thing that a great man may make of a great life.

This was something of a 'warm-up' for his eulogy in Manchester Town Hall. At this he commented of Gladstone:

> The thought with which he rose in the morning and went to rest at night was of the universe as a sublime moral theatre, on which an omnipotent Dramaturgist used kingdoms and rulers, laws and policies, to exhibit a sovereign purpose for good, to light up what I may call the prose of politics with a ray from the Divine Mind. This exalted his ephemeral discourses into a sort of visible relation to the counsels of all time ... He at all events, in the face of all the demands of practical politics, did his best to bring those considerations of truth and justice into the minds and hearts of his countrymen. (Cheers). He was a great teacher. Besides being a statesman, besides being a patriot, besides being a magnificent orator, besides being a scholar, he was a great moral teacher. His language would not be mine but I do say that Mr Gladstone, when he saw the nations going on the wrong path, saw high in the heavens the flash of the uplifted sword and the gleam of the avenging angel.[6]

Morley's three-volume *Life* went further in helping to turn William Gladstone, the human being and politician, into an embodiment of Good and, in particular, of Liberal goodness. Michael Bentley has written of this biography, 'The image placed personal character at the centre of explanation of

Gladstone's politics ... At the outset one feels that Mr Gladstone is not merely on the side of the angels but occasionally flies with them.'[7] The portrait of Gladstone by Morley in his *Life* was not only a personal tribute but what seemed needed in the chaotic world of the Liberals in the period after the retirement of Gladstone in 1894. As the *Manchester Guardian* put it in late 1900, 'Liberalism was disorganised by the loss of Mr Gladstone ... The forces on which the Liberalism of the sixties could rely are no longer at its disposal'.[8]

After the 1900 general election, the Liberals revived with the failure of the Balfour government to achieve a speedy conclusion to the Boer War and with the enthusiasm engendered by opposition to both the Education Bill, 1902, and the threat of protection. Faced with educational proposals which they believed to be hostile to their interests, the Nonconformists rallied again, as they had done in 1868 and 1880, now turning not to Gladstone but to their own leaders, including David Lloyd George. After a large by-election swing in 1902 against the Conservatives, the Rev. Walter Wynn wrote to the *Daily News*, thanking God for the result and adding, 'Though Gladstone is dead, John Clifford lives.'[9] By the unveiling of the London Gladstone statue, the Duke of Devonshire was perhaps four or five years behind the changing political mood when he commented, with particular reference to empire and home rule for Ireland, that 'the partial obscuration of his memory' after his death 'must be due to the fact that he placed himself in antagonism to the true current of his era'.[10]

During the Liberal ascendancy between December 1905 and the First World War, Gladstone's name was invoked by Liberals as something of a political gold standard. This was notably so with regard to budgets and, from 1910 onwards, Ireland. Thus, for example, Herbert Samuel, responding to Austen Chamberlain during the 1912 debates on home rule, observed, 'It is true ... that we do not have the eloquence or fervour of Mr Gladstone. Who can be expected to attain that matchless precedent?'[11]

However, there were more equivocal views expressed. According to John Morgan in an account of a conversation between Lord Morley, Lord Haldane and himself in 1912, Morley was himself bringing Gladstone down to earth (in contrast to his earlier speeches). When Morgan observed that Disraeli did not have the honesty of Gladstone, Morley responded,

LORD MORLEY: Well, but was Mr. G. always honest?

J.H.M.:   I admit his casuistry. But wasn't it an intellectual rather than a moral fault? Didn't he convince himself that the course he sought was the right one? Whereas Disraeli only sought to convince himself that it was a profitable one.

LORD MORLEY: That won't do. The Bessborough Commission on Irish Land Tenure reported in favour of the three F.'s. What did Mr. G. do? He denounced it in private as monstrously inequitable, and two months later he introduced a bill to that effect.[12]

In the period before the First World War Lloyd George was expressing the view that Gladstonian politics – both Gladstone and the Liberalism of the last phase of Gladstone's career – was all but exhausted. In 1913 he observed that the Liberals were then 'carving the last few columns out of the Gladstonian quarry'.[13] Soon after becoming Prime Minister in 1916, he told C. P. Scott, the editor of the *Manchester Guardian*, 'Old hidebound Liberalism was played out; the Newcastle programme [of 1891] had been realized. The task now was to build up the country.'[14]

Lloyd George, however, had always had reservations about Gladstone. He had been attracted to Joseph Chamberlain's 'Home Rule All Round' suggestions and there was an element of Orange in his sentiments towards Ireland; indeed in the 1890s he sometimes expressed fairly strong anti-Catholic sentiments. Quite possibly he was hostile to Gladstone's High Anglicanism. When making his name in the House of Commons, he had clashed with Gladstone over a bill concerning the disciplining of errant clergymen. Many years later he recalled with relish that when, on his return to Wales, '[t]he more proper folk reproached him for his attack on Gladstone, he said: "I give you the same reply that Cromwell gave, 'If I meet the King in battle, I will fire my pistol at him'"'.[15]

Yet Lloyd George combined his dislike of Gladstone, the High Anglican, with admiration for Gladstone, the combative politician. According to Lord Riddell, in 1915 Lloyd George commented,

Gladstone was the man for long sentences, but his voice and presence carried them off. What a man he was! Head and shoulders above anyone else I have ever seen in the House of Commons.

I did not like him much. He hated Nonconformists and Welsh Nonconformists in particular, and he had no real sympathy with the working-classes. But he was far and away the best Parliamentary speaker I have ever heard. He was not so good in exposition. He was very long and often bored you, but in debate, when he was attacked, he was superb. He had all the arts – gesture, language, fire and latterly, curiously enough, he developed a very pretty wit. That was when he was over seventy.[16]

After the First World War, when Lloyd George and his Coalition Liberals were under attack as traitors to 'pure Liberalism' by Asquith and, even more so, his followers, he was to use Gladstone's name in his defence. The particularly savage attacks came more from Asquith's supporters (including Margot, his second wife) than from Henry Asquith himself. In later life Lloyd George would reminisce warmly of Asquith, setting him 'miles ahead' of 'the Eton–Balliol gang' as 'a human fellow ... and with an understanding of people'.[17]

Asquith's wife and his followers saw Asquith as pope-like in a near holy line of succession from Gladstone. Lloyd George, in this view, was a sacrilegious

THE IRREPRESSIBLE.

MR. ASQUITH (*waiting for the "patter" to finish*). "THIS IS THE PART THAT MAKES ME NERVOUS!"

23 Asquith and Lloyd George, *Punch*, 29 October 1913

pretender, supping with the devil. In her *Autobiography* (1920) and its successor volumes, *More Memories* (1933) and *Off the Record* (1943), Margot Asquith
even suggested not only that her husband was in true succession to Gladstone
but also that in a way so was she. She wrote of a dinner party held at the
home of Sir Henry Campbell-Bannerman and his wife on 22 February 1894,
soon after her engagement to Asquith.

> While the women were talking and the men drinking, dear old Mrs Gladstone
> and other political wives took me on as to the duties of the spouse of a possible
> Prime Minister; they were so eloquent and severe that at the end my nerves
> were racing round like a squirrel in a cage. When Mr Gladstone came into the
> drawing room ... I ... said I feared the ladies took me for a jockey or a ballet-girl,
> as I had been adjured to give up, among other things, dancing, riding and
> acting. He patted my hand, said he knew no-one better fitted to be the wife of
> a great politician than myself and ended by saying that, while I was entitled to
> discard exaggeration in rebuke, it was a great mistake not to take criticism
> wisely and in a spirit which might turn it to good account.[18]

As for Gladstone, he wrote perceptively of her to Earl Spencer, 'She has very fine qualities and capabilities. I should be glad were she to add to them more of humility and dependence.'[19]

Leading Asquithian Liberals in public, like Margot Asquith in private, contrasted Asquith's attachment to the politics of principle and integrity with the highly changeable politics of Lloyd George ('Dr Lloyd and Mr George' as Sir Donald MacLean put it in April 1922[20]). The issue of character was expressed bluntly by Sir John Simon in July 1921:

> I would venture to say of the Prime Minister, with great respect, that he incurs Liberal criticism because he sometimes acts like an unprincipled and like an undependable person. What is an unprincipled person? An unprincipled person is a person whose action today bears no relation to what he said yesterday. What is an undependable person? An undependable person is a person whose words today are no guarantee as to what he will do tomorrow.

He went on to speak of Lloyd George's recent record, notably of his government's policy in Ireland.

> Cleverness, ingenuity, adroitness! There has been nothing like it in human history. But, after all, character is more than cleverness. Sticking to principle is more than adroitly shifting from one position to another. And, in the view of the Liberals, Mr Lloyd George has shown himself a faithless trustee of their tradition and beliefs.[21]

The Liberal *Daily News*, in welcoming the return to active politics of Lord Grey, commented:

> It is impossible to imagine him angling for power and influence with the petty arts of the demagogue or the courtier as it is to imagine Mr Gladstone resorting to such shifts. Sincerity, simplicity even, is the key-note of his character; and if we are to be delivered from the foul vapours of vacillation and distrust which infect the air of our politics today like a disease, it can only be by the reassertion in the lives and conversation of our leading statesmen of the old standards of honour and integrity.[22]

While the Asquithian attacks on Lloyd George stressed the need for character, with Gladstone as the usual contrast, there were also several issues in which the GOM was invoked. These were most notably the continuing relevance of traditional Liberal values in the post-war world; the virtues of 'sound finance'; the desirability of peaceful policies in international relations; the treatment of Ireland; and the continuation of coalition government into the post-war years.

The relevance, or lack of relevance, of traditional Liberal values after the Great War was one area in which Gladstone was much mentioned.

Asquith's first major speech after he and his leading colleagues had lost their seats in the 1918 general election was on the theme that younger Liberal supporters should not despair and turn to Labour and in it he gave an outline of Liberal ideals and aims. In it he argued for the continuing relevance of the old Liberal principles, commenting,

> That is the purpose and the spirit of Liberalism, as I learned it as a student in my young days, as I was taught it both by the precept and the example of the great Liberal statesman Mr Gladstone, and the others it was my pride and privilege to be associated with in the earlier days of my political life. That remains the same today. Do not forsake for temporary expediencies, for short-lived compromises, for brittle and precarious bridges – do not forsake the great heritage of the Liberal tradition of the past. It is not superstition; it is not a legend; it is founded upon faith and experience, and justified at every stage in our political history, and in my judgement, if only you would keep your heads clear, your courage firm and unperturbed by the passing vicissitudes of political fortune, it will be in the future, as it has been in the past, the inspiration of the liberties of this country.[23]

Lloyd George's view of the changed political circumstances of the post-Great War world has much about it that could have been aired as 'New Times' by the revisionist section of the Communist Party of Great Britain or as 'New Labour' by Tony Blair and his close associates in the 1990s. When speaking at the Constitutional Club, the social hub of national Conservative politics, on 3 December 1920, Lloyd George stated,

> I am here, not because I have changed; you have invited me here, not because you have changed, but because times have changed. The problems have changed and the methods of dealing with them must be changed as well, and the men who do not realise that are not fit for responsibility in a great epoch ... The instinct of the nation is that unity is essential until we get to smoother waters.[24]

Similarly, his fellow Coalitionist, the Liberal Unionist Austen Chamberlain, observed, 'But Mr Asquith today lives in a world that is past. The great wave of the war has passed over his head, and left him stranded on barren sands, trying to salve a cargo which even the underwriters have abandoned. It is not likely to repay salvage.'[25]

Asquith and his colleagues attacked the Lloyd George coalition government's financial policies, both during the reconstruction period of the postwar boom (1919–20) and the period of severe retrenchment (1921–22). They were very much in tune with the middle-class tax-payers' revolt against 'waste' (by which they meant high public expenditure on social welfare and foreign adventures) and in condemning such 'waste' they repeatedly called for a return to Gladstonian prudence in finance. Thus, for example, a report of Asquith speaking in Islington in November 1920 noted, 'Here Mr Asquith quoted twice from Gladstone to point to both the failure of the coalition government and the only way to escape from the financial morass towards which the government are heading.'[26]

Gladstonian finance was but one part of his inheritance that was promoted as the better way after the war. Sir John Simon, speaking in Nottingham on 21 February 1922, observed, 'Coalition in time of peace means government without principle and without conviction.' He continued,

> It is no accident that the Liberal tradition, inherited from Mr Gladstone and pre- served by all who are faithful to Liberal principles ever since, should have com- bined a policy of sound finance at home with a policy of peace and non-intervention abroad. The ideals of Liberal foreign policy are the counterpart of thrifty administration at home.[27]

Asquith and Grey condemned interference in 'the domestic and internal affairs of Russia' and muddle in Mesopotamia. There was vigorous condem- nation over possible war with Turkey arising from the Chanak crisis in Sep- tember 1922, though interestingly Grey was critical of Gladstone's invasion of Egypt in 1882 when arguing that the government should learn from that example of independent action: 'the result, however materially beneficial to Europe, was bad blood between France and ourselves which poisoned inter- national relations for twenty-two years'.[28]

Lloyd George responded with vigour to another Asquithian Liberal's crit- icism of his Chanak policy, that of Lord Gladstone, the son of William Ewart Gladstone. At Manchester Reform Club on 14 October 1922 he savaged the son by invoking the father:

> It was rather a shock to me to see a Gladstone denouncing us because we were trying to protect Christian minorities against the Turk ... I am told, I think by a Liberal newspaper, that I must not invoke the name of Gladstone. I can well understand the reluctance to call the great spirit from the vasty deep to witness the spectacle of Liberal leaders and Liberal newspapers attacking a government because it is doing its best to prevent the Turks from crossing into Europe and committing atrocities upon the Christian population.
>
> [Lord Gladstone] has actually excommunicated us from the Liberal Party. Well, the papacy is not a hereditary office, and Mr Gladstone in his most powerful moments never excommunicated Liberals who dared to disagree, but invited them back with all his great powers of persuasion. But Lord Gladstone excom- municated us. What service has he rendered Liberalism? I know of no service except one. He is the best living embodiment of the Liberal doctrine that quality is not hereditary ... There is no more ridiculous spectacle on the stage than a dwarf strutting before the footlights in garments he has inherited from a giant.[29]

Lloyd George was also to use Gladstone as a weapon against another Asquithian he came to hate – Lord Grey. He began the first volume of his *War Memoirs* (1933) with anecdotes of meetings with Lord Rosebery and earlier with Gladstone, the point of which was to show the Radical and pro-French sympathies of Gladstone. Lloyd George argued that on the whole Gladstone's views 'more or less represented the Radical attitude towards the French Republic and its citizens at the time when I came into active politics'. In contrast, he argued that in the period up to 1914 Sir Edward Grey (as he was then) as Foreign Secretary was found wanting: 'he lacked the knowledge of foreign countries and the vision, imagination, breadth of mind and that high courage, bordering on audacity, which his immense task demanded'.[30]

However, Lloyd George was much more exposed to attack over Ireland before the settlement of December 1921. Asquith in March 1920 praised the pre-war Home Rule Bills, commenting that then 'an undivided Liberal Party, after years of struggle, carrying on the traditions and following in the footsteps of our illustrious leader, Mr Gladstone, succeeded after infinite struggle and conflict in putting the Home Rule Bill upon the statute book'. In contrast, Lloyd George's coalition government substituted 'for the Home Rule Act the most fantastic and impracticable scheme of the greatest travesty and mockery of real self-government that was ever offered to a nation'.[31]

Later that year Asquith vigorously condemned government-backed violence in Ireland. At the National Liberal Club he commented:

> We have denounced in days gone by the Neapolitan oppressions of Bomba, no one doing so with more eloquence than our great, illustrious leader Mr Gladstone. We have denounced again and again the atrocities of the Turk in Bulgaria and Armenia, wherever his devastating rule has blighted the Christian population. Are we going to content ourselves with protesting against the misdoings of other people while we ourselves ... are here in Ireland doing things ... which would take a fitting place in the blackest annals of the lowest despotism of the European world?[32]

In attempting to rebut such attacks, Lloyd George took particular pains to use Gladstone's name. In response to similar criticisms by Asquith and his colleagues over reprisals by the Black and Tans and others in Ireland, he observed:

> Mr Gladstone, once upon a time, roused great indignation in this country over the atrocities of the Turks in Bulgaria ... These little imitation Gladstones are going about the country delivering speeches to rouse the same indignation by a denunciation of gallant men who fought bravely for us as if they were Bashi Bazouks. They have neither the genius of Gladstone nor have they his cause.[33]

Lloyd George also referred to Gladstone's use of coercive measures in Ireland when defending his Restoration of Order in Ireland Bill of 1920. It was also even suggested by supporters of the coalition government, following comments by Lord Morley, that Gladstone himself had desired a coalition in order to settle the Irish question. The editor of *Liberal News* went to some length to use Morley's own *Life*, vol. 2, pp. 351–75, to argue that 'Mr Gladstone never did, for any purpose, desire or attempt to secure a coalition in the sense in which that word is understood today.'[34]

More generally, Asquith and his followers invoked Gladstone in attacking the continuance of coalition government beyond the end of the war. Lloyd George and his allies made much of the threat of socialism to private enterprise and of a public desire for continued co-operation in politics until there was a full recovery from the war. At Glasgow, in the heart of 'Red Clydeside', in March 1920 Lloyd George spoke of the growing socialist movement in Britain.

> Where do Liberals stand on that? This is the party which would have a majority at the elections if the Liberals and Conservatives were to fight each other. It [socialism] is not the doctrine of Liberalism. The doctrine of Liberalism is a doctrine that believes that private property, as an incentive, as a means, as a reward, is the most potent agent not merely for the wealth, but for the well-being of the community. That is the doctrine not merely of Peel, of Disraeli, of Salisbury, and Chamberlain; it is the doctrine of Gladstone; it is the doctrine of Cobden; it is the doctrine of Bright; and it is the doctrine of Campbell Bannerman. It is the doctrine of the great leaders of both parties ... It is the doctrine of all the great Liberal leaders of the past and present.[35]

A year later, in April 1921, in two speeches, Lord Derby, a leading Conservative, welcomed Lloyd George as 'the newest recruit to our party'. Derby commented that the war had transformed the political landscape and that 'there was no doubt in the future the fight was going to be between the forces of law and order and the forces of revolution, between those who supported the Constitution and those who wished to upset it'. This reasonable interpretation of Lloyd George's anti-Red rhetoric and his apparent political trajectory forced Lloyd George to issue a statement through Frances Stevenson to the effect that coalition was necessary to face the serious post-war problems: 'No man, by doing so, will sacrifice his convictions. It is not a matter of conversion, but of co-operation.'[36]

Asquith replied to Lloyd George's Glasgow speech of March 1920 a month later at a dinner held at the National Liberal Club to mark his victory in the Paisley by-election:

> We are in a region of small, petty expediencies, improvisions, accommodations, compromises, which are unworthy of self-respecting men. My counsel to you is

... to keep faithful to your old traditions; to safeguard and vivify your organisation, and never to lose sight of that saving quality which alone makes politics a reputable profession for honourable men, for the Liberal Party exists not to keep power, not to acquire power but for the protection of a great and worthy ideal. Think, in a situation such as this, and with appeals such as those which have been made to our fellow Liberals outside, what would have been the attitude of Mr Gladstone. Do you think they would have allowed themselves to be scared by the bogey of Bolshevism, to furl the old flag and march with bowed heads and reversed arms, horse, foot and artillery, into the camp of the enemy?[37]

Asquith's rhetoric on this as on other occasions was notably old-fashioned and his appeals often appeared directed at an educated elite. Working people inclined to transfer their allegiance to Labour (or, for that matter, to the Conservatives) were unlikely to be persuaded otherwise by talk of furled old flags and lengthy appeals to eternal verities of Liberalism and roll-calls of its champions of long ago.

There were problems with Gladstonian Liberalism in the years immediately after the GOM's retirement, let alone in the 1920s. Peter Clarke has observed,

The unique personal ascendancy of Gladstone went far towards masking many of the shortcomings and internal tensions of the party he led for so long and in so distinctively personal style. It was, then, inevitable, that the legacy of Gladstonian Liberalism should be the post-Gladstonian Liberal party. It was exceedingly difficult in the 1890s to strike a resoundingly positive note about Liberal virtues.[38]

After the Great War there was little enough rethinking of policies for new circumstances by many of Asquith's older colleagues. There is much truth in John Campbell's critique of Lord Gladstone and his associates. Campbell commented that he was one 'who put reverence for Asquith and the Gladstonian tradition above the pressing contemporary need for a policy to meet the Labour challenge. Their attitude to Liberalism was rather that of high priests of some exclusive sect towards their doctrine than that of political propagandists to a party dependent on popular support.'[39]

Nevertheless, when Lloyd George eventually became the leader of the Liberal party in 1926, on suitable occasions he was sensitive to the political wisdom of pleasing many old Liberals, especially Asquithians, by referring warmly to Gladstone. After Lord Gladstone and his brother successfully vindicated their father's name in a celebrated libel case in 1926–27, Lloyd George concluded a major speech in Middlesbrough by congratulating them. *The Times* reported Lloyd George laying on praise of Gladstone with the proverbial trowel:

'He was one of our greatest inheritances as Liberals', he said amid cheers. 'But he is more than that. You cannot go abroad without realizing that he has added to the fame of Britain. His record is part of the achievements of his native land, and you cannot deface his name without tarnishing the fair name of Great Britain.'[40]

Liberal reunion, in the face of the renewed Conservative challenge of tariffs in 1923, brought more innovative former independent Liberals back into contact with Lloyd George. People as diverse as John Maynard Keynes and Charles Masterman recognised, in spite of their reservations about Lloyd George's political integrity, that he was far more receptive to new ideas than Asquith and his colleagues. Ramsay Muir, Professor of History at Manchester University, wrote in early 1923 before this reunion:

> The thing I care about is to set on foot an active process of criticism and discussion – an intellectual activity independent of formal associations ... I believe we have thought too much about leaders and organization and enquired too little; this has been the malady of the Liberal Party for a long time. I put it down to the tremendous personal ascendancy of Gladstone, which was mischievous in the long run.[41]

With Lloyd George's active support for the series of Liberal new policy statements during the 1920s, there was generally much less talk of Gladstone at the highest levels of the party. Yet Gladstone remained a major focus of admiration for some grassroots supporters long after. Indeed, one Liberal activist in Lowdham, Nottinghamshire, in the 1966 general election when canvassing a gardener in his seventies, was brusquely informed, 'I'm a Gladstone [Liberal] and a Primitive Methodist.'[42]

Curiously, after the great revisionist endeavours of the 1920s culminating in the well-respected and influential *We Can Conquer Unemployment* (1929), Lloyd George himself was judged to be living in outdated nostalgia by some. The editor of the *Manchester Guardian*, W. P. Crozier, noted comments made in 1935 by Leslie Hore-Belisha, a National Liberal and Minister of Transport, after talking with Lloyd George: 'he was assuming the existence of a "Nonconformist role" of the old kind. He had talked a great deal of what had happened in the days of Gladstone ... and seemed to think things had not changed.'[43]

Lloyd George, indeed, liked to reminisce and generally talk of Gladstone as he got older. In 1940, for instance, he commented to his private secretary, 'All the things that Gladstone stood for are things that will triumph in the end, whatever happens in this war. It does not depend on victory or defeat. The other thing lasts.'[44] Yet, in some ways Hore-Belisha's attitude to Gladstone and Liberal verities as a member of a coalition government had some similarities to Lloyd George's in 1918–22 in his coalition government.

Gladstone's name was long a potent force in Liberal politics. What had been living flesh – Gladstone, like Disraeli, Keir Hardie or Churchill – became mummified legend, whereby a 'Gladstone' or a 'Disraeli' epitomised desirable political qualities. 'Gladstone' became a gold standard by which later Liberal politicians could measure opponents or even colleagues and usually find them wanting. Gladstone and the others became key figures in later periods, each in an intellectual mausoleum, rather than a physical one as in the instance of Lenin in Red Square.

Gladstone for the Asquithian Liberals represented a dominant figure from the Liberals' halcyon days. It was not easy to put on a pedestal the GOM's immediate successors: Rosebery, Harcourt or Campbell Bannerman. For some, Asquith had seemed a possible candidate for such elevation, but the First World War and the Liberal party's decline after it made this unfeasible for any but his most eager supporters. For Asquith, the line of succession was a key matter. He, like Lloyd George, expressed the view that the past statesman he most admired was Peel, not Gladstone.[45] But his own legitimacy seems in his and his associates' eyes to have rested in good measure on his apostolic succession from Gladstone, not the succession sinister of Lloyd George, an illegitimate succession to a noble inheritance. In addition to the social, racial and character critiques of Lloyd George – 'the little Welsh attorney', 'the bounder from Wales' and such like – there was what was deemed to be highly damaging, the contrast with Gladstone, the man of character and the Christian statesman.

Yet there were dangers in the heavy use of Gladstone's name. The man of sternly controlled public finance was a doubtful hero in a period of expanding social welfare and naval expenditure, as in 1908–12. It is interesting, however, that in reporting to his orthodox Liberal wife his attempts to cut naval estimates in January 1914, Lloyd George expressed his dilemma as having to take 'an important decision – the same decision that Gladstone and Bright had to take'.[46] In the post-Great War world there was a major danger of appearing archaic and inflexible. Moreover, with Ireland seemingly settled in late 1921, Nonconformity declining as a powerful political force and, a decade later, the gold standard and even free trade crumbling, Gladstone's concerns and the world he operated in were fading away. Indeed, with the spread of attitudes epitomised by Lytton Strachey's *Eminent Victorians* (1918), Victorian high seriousness and its notable practitioners, of which Gladstone was a prime example, were treated with less reverence.[47] By the 1930s 'Gladstone' was not even being used as a code-word for criticisms of colleagues in the way that 'Disraeli' was used by Conservative dissenters during Margaret Thatcher's premiership (1979–90).

Notes

1   P. Geyl, *Napoleon: For and Against*, London, Cape, 1949, p. 11.
2   H. C. G. Matthew, 'Gladstone's Death and Funeral', *The Historian*, Vol. 57, 1998, p. 20; reprinted in *Journal of Liberal Democrat History*, Vol. 20, 1998, pp. 38–42.
3   J. H. Morgan, *John, Viscount Morley: An Appreciation and Some Reminiscences*, London, Murray, 1924, p. 129. For an example of the highly reverential attitude to Gladstone and Hawarden Castle before his death, see Archibald Cromwell, 'Hawarden, the Home of the Gladstones', *The Windsor Magazine*, Vol. 5, 1897, pp. 192–99.
4   P. Clarke, *Lancashire and the New Liberalism*, Cambridge, Cambridge UP, 1971, p. 348.
5   *The Times*, 24 October 1901, 30 March 1903, 6 November 1905, 24 March 1906, 20 April 1906 and 2 December 1916. Rosebery's speech at the unveiling in Edinburgh in December 1916 led to much local controversy as he speculated that Gladstone's attitude to Britain's involvement in the Great War would not have been favourable.
6   *The Times*, 24 October 1901, p. 9. An adjusted version of part of his speech in the Town Hall is in Lord Morley, *Recollections*, 2 vols, London, Macmillan, 1917, vol. 2, p. 93.
7   M. Bentley, *The Climax of Liberal Politics*, London, Arnold, 1987, p. 129.
8   *Manchester Guardian*, 17 October 1900; quoted in Clarke (1971), p. 4.
9   The by-election was North Leeds, August 1902. Quoted in M. Watts, 'John Clifford and Radical Nonconformity 1836–1923', unpublished D.Phil. thesis, University of Oxford, 1966, p. 334.
10   *The Times*, 6 November 1905.
11   H. H. Asquith (introduction), *Home Rule from the Treasury Bench*, London, Fisher Unwin, 1912, p. 228. For other examples, see Winston Churchill, p. 114, and Sir Edward Grey, pp. 185–86; and Asquith, *Speeches by the Earl of Oxford and Asquith, K.G.*, London, Hutchinson, 1927, pp. 84, 155, 164.
12   Morgan (1924), p. 103. According to Edwin Montagu, Morley, when comparing Gladstone and John Bright as orators, commented that Gladstone was better 'but on the Day of Judgement I would rather be Bright – that is if there is a Day of Judgement'. Diary entry, 13 January 1920. *Lord Riddell's Intimate Diary of the Peace Conference and After, 1918–1923*, London, Gollancz, 1933, p. 160.
13   C. J. Wrigley, *Lloyd George*, Oxford, Blackwell, 1992, p. 121.
14   T. Wilson (ed.), *The Political Diaries of C. P. Scott, 1914–1928*, London, Collins, 1979, p. 257.
15   A. J. P. Taylor (ed.), *Lloyd George: A Diary by Frances Stevenson*, London, Hutchinson, 1971, p. 291. For other examples of his criticism of Gladstone, see Lucy Masterman, *C. F. G. Masterman: A Biography*, London, Cass, 1939, pp. 142–44 (on 1909).
16   Lord Riddell, *Lord Riddell's War Diary, 1914–1918*, London, Ivor Nicholson & Watson, 1933, pp. 66–67 (7 March 1915).
17   T. Clarke, *My Lloyd George Diary*, London, Methuen, 1939, p. 191 (27 January 1933).
18   Margot Asquith, *Autobiography*, London, Thornton Butterworth, 1920, pp. 266–67.

19 Letter of 27 March 1894, *GD*, vol. 13, p. 379.
20 In a debate in the House of Commons, 3 April 1922. *Hansard's Parliamentary Debates*, 5th Series, vol. 152, col. 1933.
21 Speech at Keighley, 16 July 1921. *Liberal Magazine*, 29 August 1921, pp. 415–16.
22 *Daily News*, 11 October 1921.
23 At Newcastle-upon-Tyne, 16 May 1919. *Liberal Magazine*, 27 June 1919, p. 288. Asquith aired very similar sentiments after the count in the Paisley by-election, 25 February 1920. *Liberal Magazine*, 29 March 1920, p. 71.
24 *Liberal Magazine*, 28 January 1921, p. 764.
25 At Birmingham, 10 June 1920. *Liberal Magazine*, 28 July 1920, p. 361. See also *The Times*, 10 and 11 June 1920.
26 On 13 November 1920. *Liberal Magazine*, 28 December 1920, p. 647. Sound finance was a theme of Asquith's Paisley campaign. H. H. Asquith, *The Paisley Policy*, London, Cassell, 1920, pp. 20–29, 48–51, 77–81.
27 *Liberal Magazine*, 30 March 1922, pp. 113–14.
28 H. H. Asquith (1920), p. 51. Given at Berwick-on-Tweed, 9 October 1921, *Liberal Magazine*, 29 November 1921, p. 615, and in a letter to the *The Times*, 21 September 1922.
29 *The Times*, 16 October 1922, quoted in P. Rowland, *Lloyd George*, London, Barrie & Jenkins, 1975, p. 581.
30 D. Lloyd George, *War Memoirs*, 6 vols, London, Nicolson & Watson, 1933, vol. 1, pp. 5, 99.
31 At the National Liberal Club, 24 March 1920. *Liberal Magazine*, 28 April 1920, p. 166.
32 At the National Liberal Club, 19 November 1920. *Liberal Magazine*, 28 December 1920, p. 654.
33 At the Constitutional Club, 3 December 1920. See note 24.
34 *Liberal Magazine*, 29 January 1922, pp. 716–19.
35 *Glasgow Herald*, 17 March 1920.
36 Derby's speeches of 17 and 25 April 1921 and Frances Stevenson's letter are reprinted in *Liberal Magazine*, 29 May 1921, pp. 251–53.
37 On 14 April 1920. *Liberal Magazine*, 28 May 1920, p. 205. For a similar, vigorous denunciation of the use of the Red Bogey, see Sir John Simon denouncing Winston Churchill in Churchill's Dundee constituency, *Dundee Advertiser*, 19 April 1922.
38 Clarke (1971), p. 3.
39 J. Campbell, *Lloyd George: The Goat in the Wilderness*, London, Cape, 1978, p. 55.
40 At Middlesbrough, 5 February 1927. *The Times*, 7 February 1927.
41 Ramsay Muir to H. A. L. Fisher, 9 February 1923; quoted in Campbell (1978), p. 188.
42 Michael Watts, the historian of Nonconformity, to the author, 29 April 1998.
43 Diary entry, 19 July 1935. W. P. Crozier, *Off The Record: Political Interviews, 1933–1943*, ed. A. J. P. Taylor, London, Hutchinson, 1973, p. 49.
44 Diary entry, 24 April 1940. A. J. Sylvester, *Life With Lloyd George*, ed. C. Cross, London, Macmillan, 1975, p. 258.
45 According to Lloyd George. Diary entry, October 1910. Lord Riddell, *More Pages From My Diary, 1908–1914*, London, Country Life, 1934, p. 18.

46 Letter of 15 January 1914. K. O. Morgan (ed.), *Lloyd George Family Letters, 1885–1936*, Cardiff, University of Wales Press, 1973, p. 166.

47 My mother growing up in an army household (a Devonshire regiment) at home and in India in the 1920s remembers her father (a soldier from 1897) and his friends using the phrase 'Mr Gladstone says' (followed by a banality) as a jeer at Liberals. This may have stemmed from music hall, where 'Mr Gladstone said in 1864 ...' (or variants) was a catch-phrase. One person I have met recalls it being used in music hall at the Chiswick Empire. It was even used on radio comedy programmes, but seems to have died out in the 1940s. (The radio points I owe to Eric Jenkins and others in the discussion at the Gladstone Centenary International Conference at University College Chester, 6–9 July 1998. I am grateful to Mrs Joan Hooker of the Beckenham branch of the Historical Association for the Chiswick Empire point. I am also grateful for comments made by David Bebbington, Stewart Brown and Patrick Jackson.)

William Ewart Gladstone: A Select Bibliography

Roger Swift

Primary Sources

Gladstone's Diaries

The Gladstone Diaries, 14 vols (Oxford, 1968–94), ed. M. R. D. Foot (vols 1–2); ed. M. R. D. Foot and H. C. G. Matthew (vols 3–4); ed. H. C. G. Matthew (vols 5–14). The *Diaries* have been acclaimed critically and reviewed extensively, but see especially the reviews of the complete series by Agatha Ramm in the *English Historical Review*, Vols 85 (1970), 91 (1976), 94 (1979), 99 (1984), 102 (1987), 106 (1991), 110 (1995).

The Gladstone Papers

The 750 volumes of the Gladstone Papers in The British Library form the largest collection of papers of a British Prime Minister held there. They are described in A. T. Bassett's anonymous volume *The Gladstone Papers* (London, 1930) and catalogued in *British Museum Catalogue of Additions to the Manuscripts: The Gladstone Papers* (London, 1953).

The Glynne–Gladstone Manuscripts

These comprise over 25,000 items, including family letters, estate, household and business papers. For further details, see especially C. J. Williams (ed.), *Handlist of the Glynne–Gladstone MSS in St Deiniol's Library* (Richmond, 1990).

Edited Collections: Papers, Speeches and Correspondence

The most comprehensive published collection of Gladstone's correspondence, drawn from the Gladstone Collection at The British Library and St Deiniol's Library, is now available in microform, edited by H. C. G. Matthew as *The Papers of William Ewart Gladstone* (Papers of the Prime Ministers of Great Britain Series Eight, Primary Source Media, Reading, 1998). This ten-part series comprises printed speeches and newspaper cuttings from St Deiniol's Library and notes for speeches from The British Library (part 1); special correspondence, with appropriate Aberdeen Papers and Bright Papers from The

British Library (part 2); special correspondence from The British Library, including letters from eminent contemporaries (parts 3–6); Letter Books, in which Gladstone recorded and transcribed some 15,000 'out' letters (part 7); and general correspondence from The British Library (parts 8–10). Each part of this collection is accompanied by a printed bibliography, offering item-level listings.

Other collections include:

Bassett, A. Tilney (ed.), *Gladstone's Speeches: Descriptive Index and Bibliography* (London, 1916).
——, *Gladstone to his Wife* (London, 1936).
Brooke, J. and Sorensen, M. (eds), *The Prime Ministers' Papers: W. E. Gladstone* (4 vols, London, 1971–81), especially vol 1, *Autobiographica* (1971).
Foot, M. R. D. (ed.), *Midlothian Speeches 1879* (Leicester, 1971).
Guedalla, P. (ed.), *Gladstone and Palmerston: Being the Correspondence of Lord Palmerston with Mr Gladstone, 1851–1865* (London, 1928).
——, *The Queen and Mr Gladstone* (2 vols, London, 1933).
Hutton, A. W. and Cohen, H. J. (eds), *The Speeches and Public Addresses of the Rt. Hon. W. E. Gladstone, M.P.*, 2 vols (London, 1894).
Lathbury, D. C. (ed.), *Letters on Church and Religion of William Ewart Gladstone* (2 vols, London, 1910).
Ramm, A. (ed.), *Political Correspondence of Mr Gladstone and Lord Granville* (4 vols: vols 1 and 2, London, 1952; vols 3 and 4, Oxford, 1962); reprinted as *The Gladstone–Granville Correspondence* (2 vols, Cambridge, 1999).

Chief Books by Gladstone

A list of books and articles by Gladstone will be found under 'publications' in the subject index in volume 14 of *The Gladstone Diaries*.

The State in its Relations with the Church (London, 1838; 4th edn, 2 vols, London, 1841).
Church Principles Considered in their Results (London, 1840).
Prayers for Family Use (London, 1845).
(Trans.), Farini, L.C., *Lo Stato Romano* (4 vols, London, 1851–54).
On the Place of Homer in Classical Education and in Historical Inquiry (London, 1857).
Studies on Homer and the Homeric Age (3 vols, Oxford, 1858).
A Chapter of Autobiography (London, 1868).
Juventus Mundi: The Gods and Men of the Heroic Age (London, 1869).
The Vatican Decrees and their Bearing on Civil Allegiance: A Political Expostulation (London, 1874).
Vaticanism: An Answer to Replies and Reproofs (London, 1875).

The Church of England and Ritualism (London, 1875).
Rome and the Newest Fashions in Religion (London, 1875).
The Bulgarian Horrors and the Question of the East (London, 1876).
Homeric Synchronism: An Enquiry into the Time and Place of Homer (London, 1876).
Homer (London, 1878).
Gleanings of Past Years, 1843–79 (7 vols, London, 1879).
Political Speeches in Scotland, November and December 1879 (Edinburgh, 1880).
Political Speeches in Scotland, Second Series (London, 1880).
Landmarks of Homeric Study (London, 1890).
The Impregnable Rock of Holy Scripture (London, 1890).
The Odes of Horace (London, 1894).
The Psalter with a Concordance and Other Auxiliary Matter (London, 1895).
Studies Subsidiary to the Works of Bishop Butler (London, 1896).
(Ed.), *The Works of Joseph Butler, D.C.L.* (2 vols, London, 1897).
Later Gleanings (London, 1897).

Secondary Sources

There is a vast body of secondary material relating to Gladstone's life and career. Some of this is referred to in *Gladstoniana: A Bibliography of Material Relating to W. E. Gladstone at St Deiniol's Library*, edited by Caroline J. Dobson (Hawarden, 1981), although a more comprehensive bibliography is provided in *Gladstone: A Bibliography of Material held at St Deiniol's Library*, compiled by Lucy M. Adcock (Hawarden, 1998). Material from these two seminal bibliographies is contained in Nicholas Adams (ed.), *William Ewart Gladstone: A Bibliography* (Westport, Connecticut, 1994). A useful bibliographical essay, which offers a thematic treatment of the subject, is also provided by David Bebbington in *William Ewart Gladstone: Faith and Politics in Victorian Britain* (Grand Rapids, Michigan, 1993). The bibliography presented below is far from exhaustive and consists largely of works published in English since 1945.

Collected Essays on Gladstone

Jagger, P. J. (ed.), *Gladstone, Politics and Religion* (London, 1985).
——, *Gladstone* (London, 1998).
Kinzer, B. L. (ed.), *The Gladstonian Turn of Mind: Essays Presented to J. B. Conacher* (Toronto, 1985).

Biographical Studies of Gladstone

Books

Biagini, E. F., *Gladstone* (London, 2000).

Birrell, F., *Gladstone* (London, 1933).

Crosby, T. L., *The Two Mr Gladstones: A Study in Psychology and History* (New Haven, Connecticut, 1997).

Douglas-Home, A., 'Mr Gladstone', in *Gladstone, Politics and Religion* ed. P. J. Jagger (London, 1985), pp. 21–27.

Feuchtwanger, E. J., *Gladstone* (London, 1975).

Hammond, J. L. and Foot, M. R. D., *Gladstone and Liberalism* (London, 1952).

Jenkins, R., *Gladstone* (London, 1995).

Magnus, P., *Gladstone: A Biography* (London, 1954).

Matthew, H. C. G., *Gladstone, 1809–1898* (Oxford, 1997). [This was previously published as two separate volumes: *Gladstone, 1809–1874* (Oxford, 1986) and *Gladstone, 1875–1898* (Oxford, 1995).]

Morley, J., *The Life of William Ewart Gladstone* (3 vols, London, 1903).

Ramm, A., *William Ewart Gladstone* (Cardiff, 1989).

Reid, W. T. (ed.), *Life of William Ewart Gladstone* (London, 1899).

Schreuder, D. M., 'The Making of Mr Gladstone's Posthumous Career: The Role of Morley and Knaplund as "Monumental Masons", 1903–27', in *The Gladstonian Turn of Mind*, ed. B. L. Kinzer, (Toronto, 1985), pp. 197–243.

Shannon, R., *Gladstone* (2 vols, London, 1982 and 1999).

Stansky, P., *Gladstone: A Progress in Politics* (New York, 1979).

Stead, W. T., *Gladstone, 1809–1898: A Character Sketch* (London, 1898).

Young, G. M., *Mr. Gladstone* (Oxford, 1944).

Articles

Checkland, S. G., 'The Making of Mr Gladstone', *Victorian Studies*, Vol. 12 (1969), pp. 399–409.

Foot, M. R. D., 'Morley's Gladstone: A Reappraisal', *Bulletin of the John Rylands Library*, Vol. 51 (1969), pp. 368–80.

Knaplund, P., 'William Ewart Gladstone, the Christian Statesman', *Church Quarterly Review*, Vol. 162 (1961), pp. 467–75.

Malament, B. C., 'W. E. Gladstone: An Other Victorian?', *British Studies Monitor*, Vol. 8 (1978), pp. 22–38.

Murray, G., 'Gladstone, 1898–1948', *Contemporary Review*, Vol. 174 (1948), pp. 134–38.

Stephen, M. D., '"After Thirty Years": A Note on Gladstone Scholarship', *Journal of Religious History*, Vol. 15 (1989), pp. 488–95.

Gladstone in Private

Books

Battiscombe, G., *Mrs Gladstone: The Portrait of a Marriage* (London, 1956).

Briggs, A., 'Victorian Images of Gladstone', in *Gladstone*, ed. P. J. Jagger (London, 1998), pp. 33–50.

Checkland, S. G., *The Gladstones: A Family Biography, 1764–1851* (Cambridge, 1971).

——, 'Mr Gladstone, his Parents and his Siblings', in *Gladstone, Politics and Religion*, ed. P. J. Jagger (London, 1985), pp. 40–48.

Deacon, R., *The Private Life of Mr Gladstone* (London, 1965).

Drew, M., 'Mr Gladstone's Books', in *Acton, Gladstone and Others* (London, 1924).

——, *Catherine Gladstone* (London, 1930).

Esslemont, P., *To the Fifth Generation: A Hundred Minutes with Gladstone* (Aberdeen, 1941).

Fletcher, C. R. L., *Mr Gladstone at Oxford* (London, 1908).

Fletcher, S., *Victorian Girls: Lord Lyttelton's Daughters* (London, 1997).

Foot, M. R. D., 'The Gladstone Diaries', in *Gladstone, Politics and Religion*, ed. P. J. Jagger (London, 1985), pp. 28–39.

Garratt, G. T., *The Two Mr Gladstones* (London, 1936).

Gilliland, J., *Gladstone's 'Dear Spirit': Laura Thistlethwayte* (London, 1994).

Gladstone, H., *After Thirty Years* (London, 1928).

Gladstone, P., *Portrait of a Family: The Gladstones, 1839–1889* (Ormskirk, 1989).

Gower, Sir G. Leveson, *Some Memories of Gladstone* (n.p., 1938).

Jagger, P. J. (ed.), 'Gladstone and his Library', in *Gladstone*, ed. P. J. Jagger (London, 1998), pp. 235–54.

Jalland, P., 'Mr Gladstone's Daughters', in *The Gladstonian Turn of Mind: Essays Presented to J. B. Canacher*, ed. B. L. Kinzer (Toronto, 1985), pp. 97–122.

——, *Women, Marriage and Politics, 1860–1914* (Oxford, 1986).

——, *Death in the Victorian Family* (Oxford, 1996), chapter 8.

Lloyd-Jones, Sir H., 'Gladstone on Homer', *The Times Literary Supplement*, 3 January 1975, pp. 15–17; reprinted in his *Blood for the Ghosts* (London, 1982).

Mallet, C., *Herbert Gladstone: A Memoir* (London, 1932).

Marlow, J., *The Oak and the Ivy: An Intimate Biography of William and Catherine Gladstone* (New York, 1977).

Masterman, L. (ed.), *Mary Gladstone: Her Diaries and Letters* (London, 1930).

Ratcliffe, F. W., 'Mr Gladstone, the Librarian, and St Deiniol's Library, Hawarden', in *Gladstone, Politics and Religion*, ed. P. J. Jagger (London, 1985), pp. 46–67.

Ritchie, J. E., *The Real Gladstone: An Anecdotal Biography* (London, 1898).

Robson, A. P., 'A Bird's Eye View of Gladstone', in *The Gladstonian Turn of Mind: Essays Presented to J. B. Conacher*, ed. B. L. Kinzer (Toronto, 1985), pp. 63–96.

Tollemache, L. A., *Gladstone's Boswell: Late Victorian Conversations*, ed. A. Briggs (Brighton, 1984).

Turner, F. M., *The Greek Heritage in Victorian Britain* (New Haven, Connecticut, 1981).

Wickham, G., 'Gladstone, Oratory and the Theatre', in *Gladstone*, ed. P. J. Jagger (1998), pp. 1–32.

Articles

Beales, D., 'Gladstone and his Diary: "Myself, the Worst of All Interlocutors"', *Historical Journal*, Vol. 25 (1982), pp. 463–69.

Bentley, M., 'Gladstone's Heir', *English Historical Review*, Vol. 107 (1992), pp. 901–24.

Conacher, J. P., 'A Visit to the Gladstones in 1891', *Victorian Studies*, Vol. 2 (1958), pp. 155–60.

Jackson, A., 'A View from the Summit: The Gladstone Diaries Completed', *Irish Historical Studies*, Vol. 30 (1996), pp. 255–63.

Jenkins, R., 'Writing about Gladstone', *Journal of Liberal Democrat History*, Vol. 20 (1998), pp. 36–37.

Matthew, H. C. G., 'Gladstone's Death and Funeral', *The Historian*, vol. 57, 1998, pp. 20–24; reprinted in *Journal of Liberal Democrat History*, Vol. 20 (1998), pp. 38–42.

Meisel, J. S., 'The Importance of Being Serious: The Unexplored Connection between Gladstone and Humour', *History*, Vol. 84 (1999), pp. 278–300.

Nolan, D., 'Gladstone and Liverpool', *Journal of Liberal Democrat History*, Vol. 20 (1998), pp. 17–22.

Parker, W. M., 'Gladstone as a *Quarterly Review* Contributor', *Quarterly Review*, Vol. 293 (1955), pp. 464–76.

Pointon, M., 'Gladstone as Art Patron and Collector', *Victorian Studies*, Vol. 19 (1975), pp. 73–98.

Powell, J., 'Tollemache's Talks with Mr Gladstone', *Nineteenth-Century Prose*, Vol. 17 (1989), pp. 31–46.

——, 'Small Marks and Instructional Responses: A Study in the Uses of Gladstone's Marginalia', *Nineteenth-Century Prose*, Vol. 19 (1992), pp. 1–17.

Pritchard, T. W., 'The Revd. S. E. Gladstone, 1844–1920', *Flintshire Historical Society Journal*, Vol. 35 (1999), pp. 191–241.

Webb, C., 'Some Personal Reminiscences of Mr Gladstone', *Church Quarterly Review*, Vol. 153 (1952), pp. 320–34.

Gladstone and Religion

Books

Arnstein, W. L., *The Bradlaugh Case: Atheism, Sex and Politics among the Late Victorians* (Oxford, 1965).

Bebbington, D. W., 'Gladstone and the Nonconformists: A Religious Affinity in Politics', in *Church, Society and Politics*, ed. D. Baker, Studies in Church History, Vol. 12 (Oxford, 1975), pp. 369–82.

——, *William Ewart Gladstone: Faith and Politics in Victorian Britain* (Grand Rapids, Michigan, 1993).

Butler, P., *Gladstone: Church, State and Tractarianism: A Study of his Religious Ideas and Attitudes, 1809–1859* (Oxford, 1982).

Ellens, J. P., *Religious Routes to Gladstonian Liberalism: The Church Rate Conflict in England and Wales* (University Park, Pennsylvania, 1994).

Helmstadter, R. J., 'Conscience and Politics: Gladstone's First Book', in *The Gladstonian Turn of Mind: Essays Presented to J. B. Conacher*, ed. B. L. Kinzer (Toronto, 1985), pp. 3–42.

Hilton, B., 'Gladstone's Theological Politics', in *High and Low Politics in Modern Britain*, ed. M. Bentley and J Stevenson (Oxford, 1983), pp. 28–57.

Jagger, P. J., *Gladstone: The Making of a Christian Politician: The Personal Religious Life and Development of William Ewart Gladstone, 1809–1832* (Allison Park, Pennsylvania, 1991).

Kenyon, J., 'Gladstone and the Anglican High Churchmen, 1845–52', in *The Gladstonian Turn of Mind: Essays Presented to J. B. Conacher*, ed. B. L. Kinzer (Toronto, 1985), pp. 43–62.

Lathbury, D. C., *Mr Gladstone* (London, 1907).

Matthew, H. C. G., 'Gladstone, Vaticanism and the Question of the East', in *Religious Motivation: Biographical and Sociological Problems for the Church Historian*, ed. D. Baker, Studies in Church History, Vol. 15 (Oxford, 1978), pp. 417–42.

——, 'Gladstone, Evangelicalism and "The Engagement"', in *Revival and Religion since 1700: Essays for John Walsh*, ed. J. Garnett and H. C. G. Matthew (London, 1993).

Russell, G. W. E., *Mr Gladstone's Religious Development* (London, 1899).

Shannon, R., 'Gladstone, the Roman Church and Italy', in *Public and Private Doctrine*, ed. M. Bentley (London, 1993), pp. 108–26.

Vidler, A. R., *The Orb and the Cross: A Normative Study in the Relations of Church and State with Reference to Gladstone's Early Writings* (London, 1945).

Ward, W. R., 'Oxford and the Origins of Liberal Catholicism in the Church of England', in *Studies in Church History*, ed. C. W. Dugmore and C. Duggan, Vol. 1 (1964), pp. 233–52.

Articles

Addison, W. G. C., 'Church, State and Mr Gladstone', *Theology*, Vol. 39 (1939).

Altholz, J. L., 'The Vatican Decrees Controversy, 1874–5', *Catholic Historical Review*, Vol. 57 (1972), pp. 593–605.

Altholz, J. L. and Powell, J., 'Gladstone, Lord Ripon and the Vatican Decrees, 1874', *Albion*, Vol. 22 (1990), pp. 449–59.

Anderson, O., 'Gladstone's Abolition of Church Rates: A Minor Political Myth and its Historiographical Career', *Journal of Ecclesiastical History*, Vol. 25 (1974), pp. 185–98.

Bahlman, D. W. R., 'The Queen, Mr Gladstone and Church Patronage', *Victorian Studies*, Vol. 3 (1960), pp. 349–80.

Bebbington, D. W., 'Gladstone and the Baptists', *Baptist Quarterly*, Vol. 26 (1976), pp. 224–39.

Erb, P. C., 'Gladstone and German Liberal Catholicism', *Recusant History*, Vol. 23 (1997), pp. 450–69.

Fagan, E. F., 'The Religious Life of Mr Gladstone', *Church Quarterly Review*, Vol. 155 (1954), pp. 16–21.

Gray, W. Forbes, 'Chalmers and Gladstone: An Unrecorded Episode', *Records of the Scottish Church History Society*, Vol. 10 (1948), pp. 9–17.

Lynch, M. J., 'Was Gladstone a Tractarian? W. E. Gladstone and the Oxford Movement, 1833–45', *Journal of Religious History*, Vol. 8 (1975), pp. 364–89.

Machin, G. I. T., 'Gladstone and Nonconformity in the 1860s: The Formation of an Alliance', *Historical Journal*, Vol. 17 (1974), pp. 347–64.

Marsh, P. T., 'The Primate and the Prime Minister: Archbishop Tait, Gladstone and the National Church', *Victorian Studies*, Vol. 9 (1965), pp. 113–40.

Moberly, W. H., 'Gladstone on Church and State', *Theology*, Vol. 49 (1946), pp. 104–10.

Parry, J. P., 'Religion and the Collapse of Gladstone's First Government, 1870–74', *Historical Journal*, Vol. 25 (1982), pp. 71–101.

Petersen, W. S., 'Gladstone's Review of "Robert Elsmere": Some Unpublished Correspondence', *Review of English Studies*, Vol. 21 (1970).

Ramm, A., 'Gladstone's Religion', *Historical Journal*, Vol. 28 (1985), pp. 327–40.

Ruston, A., 'The Unitarian Correspondents of W. E. Gladstone: The British Library MSS', *Transactions of the Unitarian Historical Society*, Vol. 18 (1986), pp. 219–24.

Stephen, M. D., 'Gladstone's Ecclesiastical Patronage, 1868–1874', *Historical Studies: Australia and New Zealand*, Vol. 11 (1964).

——, 'Gladstone and the Composition of the Final Court in Ecclesiastical Causes', *Historical Journal*, Vol. 9 (1966), pp. 191–200.

Gladstone and General Politics

Books

Adelman, P., *Gladstone, Disraeli and Later Victorian Politics* (London, 1970).

Barker, M., *Gladstone and Radicalism: The Reconstruction of Liberal Policy in Britain, 1885–94* (Hassocks, Sussex, 1975).

Biagini, E. F., *Liberty, Retrenchment and Reform: Popular Liberalism in the Age of Gladstone, 1860–1880* (Cambridge, 1992).

Blake, R., *Gladstone, Disraeli and Queen Victoria: The Centenary Romanes Lecture* (Oxford, 1993).

Brown, S., 'One Last Campaign from the G.O.M.: Gladstone and the House of Lords in 1894', in *The Gladstonian Turn of Mind: Essays Presented to J. B. Conacher*, ed. B. L. Kinzer (Toronto, 1985), pp. 154–76.

Clarke, P., *A Question of Leadership: British Rulers – Gladstone to Thatcher* (London, 1991).

Cooke, A. B. and Vincent, J. R., *The Governing Passion: Cabinet Government and Party Politics in Britain, 1885–86* (Brighton, 1974).

Cowling, M., *1867. Disraeli, Gladstone and Revolution: The Passing of the Second Reform Bill* (Cambridge, 1967).

Hamer, D. A., *Liberal Politics in the Age of Gladstone and Rosebery: A Study in Leadership and Policy* (Oxford, 1972).

Hanham, H. J., *Elections and Party Management: Politics in the Time of Gladstone and Disraeli* (London, 1959).

Harvie, C., 'Gladstonianism, the Provinces, and Popular Political Culture, 1860–1906', in *Victorian Liberalism: Nineteenth-Century Political Thought and Practice*, ed. R. Bellamy (London, 1990), pp. 152–74.

Jenkins, T. A., *Gladstone, Whiggery and the Liberal Party, 1874–1886* (Oxford, 1988).

——, *The Liberal Ascendancy, 1830–1886* (London, 1994).

Jones, A., *The Politics of Reform, 1884* (Cambridge, 1972).

Matthew, H. C. G., 'Rhetoric and Politics in Great Britain, 1860–1950', in *Politics and Social Change in Modern Britain: Essays Presented to A. F. Thompson*, ed. P. J. Waller (Brighton, 1987), pp. 34–58.

——, 'Gladstone, Rhetoric and Politics', in Jagger, P.J. (ed.), *Gladstone* (London, 1998), pp. 213–234.

Morgan, K. O., 'Gladstone, Wales and the New Radicalism', in *Gladstone*, ed. P. J. Jagger (London, 1998), pp. 123–136.

Parry, J. P., *Democracy and Religion: Gladstone and the Liberal Party, 1867–1875* (Cambridge, 1986).

——, *The Rise and Fall of Liberal Government in Victorian Britain* (New Haven, Connecticut, 1993).

Peaple, S. and Vincent, J., 'Gladstone and the Working Man', in *Gladstone*, ed. P. J. Jagger (London, 1998), pp. 71–84.

Ramm, A., 'Gladstone as Politician', in *Gladstone, Politics and Religion*, ed. P.

J. Jagger (London, 1985), pp. 104–116.

Schreuder, D. M., 'Gladstone and the Conscience of the State', in *The Conscience of the Victorian State*, ed. P. T. Marsh (New York, 1979), pp. 73–134.

Searle, G. R., *The Liberal Party: Triumph and Disintegration, 1886–1929* (London, 1992).

Shannon, R. T., 'Midlothian: One Hundred Years After', in *Gladstone, Politics and Religion*, ed. P. J. Jagger (London, 1985), pp. 88–103.

Steele, E. D., *Palmerston and Liberalism, 1855–1865* (Cambridge, 1991).

Taylor, M., *The Decline of British Radicalism, 1847–60* (Oxford, 1995).

Vincent, J. R., *The Formation of the British Liberal Party, 1857–1868* (London, 1966).

Williams, W. E., *The Rise of Gladstone to the Leadership of the Liberal Party, 1859–1868* (Cambridge, 1934).

Winstanley, M. J., *Gladstone and the Liberal Party* (London, 1990).

Articles

Adelman, P., 'Gladstone and Education', *History Today*, Vol. 20 (1970), pp. 496–503.

Armitage, W. H. G., 'The Railway Rates Question and the Fall of the Third Gladstone Ministry', *English Historical Review*, Vol. 65 (1950).

Arnstein, W. L., 'Gladstone and the Bradlaugh Case', *Victorian Studies*, Vol. 5 (1962), pp. 303–30.

Beales, D., 'Gladstone and his First Ministry', *Historical Journal*, Vol. 26 (1983), pp. 987–98.

Brooks, D., 'Gladstone and Midlothian: The Background to the First Campaign', *Scottish Historical Review*, Vol. 64 (1985), pp. 42–67.

Cooke, A. B., 'Gladstone's Election for the Leith District of Burghs, July 1886', *Scottish Historical Review*, Vol. 49 (1970), pp. 172–94.

Goodlad, G. D., 'The Liberal Party and Gladstone's Land Purchase Bill of 1886', *Historical Journal*, Vol. 32 (1989), pp. 627–41.

Hamer, D. A., 'Gladstone: The Making of a Political Myth', *Victorian Studies*, Vol. 22 (1978), pp. 29–50.

James, R. R., 'Gladstone and the Greenwich Seat: The Dissolution of January 26th 1874', *History Today*, Vol. 9 (1959), pp. 344–51.

Jenkins, R., 'From Gladstone to Asquith: The Late-Victorian Pattern of Liberal Leadership', *History Today*, Vol. 14 (1964), pp. 445–52.

Jenkins, T. A., 'Gladstone, the Whigs and the Leadership of the Liberal Party, 1879–1880', *Historical Journal*, Vol. 27 (1984), pp. 337–60.

Jones, J. R., 'The Conservatives and Gladstone in 1855', *English Historical Review*, Vol. 77 (1962), pp. 96–98.

Mael, W. H., 'Gladstone, the Liberals and the Election of 1874', *Bulletin of the Institute of Historical Research*, Vol. 36 (1963), pp. 53–69.

Morgan, K. O., 'Gladstone and Wales', *Welsh History Review*, Vol. 1 (1960), pp. 65–82.

Nicholls, D., 'Gladstone on Liberty and Democracy', *Review of Politics* (1961), pp. 401–09.

Parry, J.P., 'Gladstone and the Disintegration of the Liberal Party', *Parliamentary History*, Vol. 10 (1991), pp. 392–404.

Primrose, A. P., 'Mr Gladstone's Last Cabinet', *History Today*, Vol. 1 (1951), pp. 31–41; Vol. 2 (1952), pp. 17–22.

Ramm, A., 'The Parliamentary Context of of Cabinet Government, 1868–1874', *English Historical Review*, Vol. 99 (1984), pp. 739–69.

Rossi, J. P., 'The Nestor of his Party: Gladstone, Hartington and the Liberal Leadership Crisis, November 1879–January 1880', *Canadian Journal of History*, Vol. 11 (1976), pp. 189–99.

Russell, C., 'Liberalism and Liberty from Gladstone to Ashdown', *Journal of Liberal Democrat History*, Vol. 20 (1998), pp. 4–10.

Searby, P., 'Gladstone in West Derby Hundred: The Liberal Campaign in South-West Lancashire in 1868', *Transactions of the Historic Society of Lancashire and Cheshire*, Vol. 111 (1960), pp. 139–66.

Temmel, M. R., 'Gladstone's Resignation of the Liberal Leadership, 1875–1880', *Journal of British Studies*, Vol. 16 (1976), pp. 153–77.

Thompson, A. F., 'Gladstone's Whips and the General Election of 1868', *English Historical Review*, Vol. 63 (1948), pp. 189–200.

Gladstone and Economic Policy

Books

Anderson, O., *A Liberal State at War: English Politics and Economics during the Crimean War* (London, 1967).

Biagini, E. F., 'Popular Liberals, Gladstonian Finance and the Debate on Taxation, 1860–1874', in *Currents of Radicalism*, ed. E. F. Biagini and A. J. Reid (Cambridge, 1991), pp. 134–62.

Buxton, S., *Mr Gladstone as Chancellor of the Exchequer* (London, 1901).

Hilton, B., *The Age of Atonement: The Influence of Evangelicalism on Social and Economic Thought, 1785–1865* (Oxford, 1988).

Hirst, F. W., *Gladstone as Financier and Economist* (London, 1931).

Howe, A., *Free Trade and Liberal England, 1846–1946* (Oxford, 1997).

Hyde, F. E., *Mr Gladstone at the Board of Trade* (London, 1934).

Maloney, J., 'Gladstone, Peel and the Corn Laws', in *Free Trade and its Reception*, ed. A. Marrison (London, 1998), pp. 28–47.

Matthew, H. C. G., 'Gladstonian Finance', in *Victorian Values: Personalities and Perspectives in Nineteenth-Century Society*, ed. G. Marsden (London, 1990), pp. 111–20.

Prest, J., 'Gladstone and the Railways', in *Gladstone*, ed. P. J. Jagger (London, 1998), pp. 197–212.

Searle, G. R., *Entrepreneurial Politics in Mid-Victorian Britain* (Oxford, 1993).

Articles

Baysinger, B. and Tollison, R., 'Chaining Leviathan: The Case of Gladstonian Finance', *History of Political Economy*, Vol. 12 (1980), pp. 206–13.

Ghosh, P. R., 'Disraelian Conservatism: A Financial Approach', *English Historical Review*, Vol. 99 (1984), pp. 268–96.

Hawkins, A. B., 'A Forgotten Crisis: Gladstone and the Politics of Finance during the 1850s', *Victorian Studies*, Vol. 26 (1983), pp. 287–320.

Maloney, J., 'Gladstone as Chancellor', *Journal of Liberal Democrat History*, Vol. 20 (1998), pp. 12–16.

Matthew, H. C. G., 'Disraeli, Gladstone and the Politics of Mid-Victorian Budgets', *Historical Journal*, Vol. 22 (1979), pp. 615–43.

——, 'Gladstonian Finance', *History Today*, Vol. 37 (1987), pp. 41–45.

Zimmeck, M., 'Gladstone Holds His Own: The Origins of Income Tax Relief for Life Insurance Policies', *Bulletin of the Institute of Historical Research*, Vol. 58 (1985), pp. 167–88.

Gladstone and Ireland

Books

Bell, P. M. H., *Disestablishment in Ireland and Wales* (London, 1969).

Boyce, D. G., *Nineteenth Century Ireland: The Search for Stability* (Dublin, 1990).

——, 'Gladstone and Ireland', in *Gladstone*, ed. P. J. Jagger (London, 1998), pp. 105–122.

——, *The Irish Question and British Politics, 1868–1986* (London, 1988).

Comerford, R. V., 'Gladstone's First Irish Enterprise, 1864–1870', in *A New History of Ireland, 5, Ireland under the Union, I: 1801–1870*, ed. W. E. Vaughan (Oxford, 1989), pp. 431–50.

Hammond, J. L., *Gladstone and the Irish Nation* (London, 1938).

Kee, R., *The Laurel and the Ivy: The Story of Charles Stewart Parnell and Irish Nationalism* (London, 1993).

Loughlin, J., *Gladstone, Home Rule and the Ulster Question, 1882–93* (Dublin, 1986).

Lubenow, W. C., *Parliamentary Politics and the Home Rule Crisis: The British House of Commons in 1886* (Oxford, 1988).

McDowell, R. B., *Crisis and Decline: The Fate of the Southern Unionists* (Dublin, 1997).

O'Callaghan, M., *British High Politics and a Nationalist Ireland: Criminality, Land and Law under Forster and Balfour* (Cork, 1994).

O'Day, A., *The English Face of Irish Nationalism: Parnellite Involvement in British Politics, 1880–86* (Dublin, 1977).

——, 'The Irish Problem', in *Late Victorian Britain, 1867–1900*, ed. T. R. Gourvish and A. O'Day (London, 1988), pp. 229–50.

——, *Irish Home Rule, 1867–1921* (Manchester, 1998).

Shannon, R. T., 'Gladstone and Home Rule, 1886', in *Ireland after the Union: Proceedings of the Second Joint Meeting of the Royal Irish Academy and the British Academy, London 1986* (Oxford, 1989), pp. 45–59.

Steele, E. D., *Irish Land and British Politics: Tenant Right and Nationality, 1865–1870* (Cambridge, 1974).

——, 'Gladstone, Irish Violence, and Conciliation', in *Studies in Irish History presented to R. Dudley Edwards*, ed. A. Cosgrove and D. McCartney (Dublin, 1979), pp. 257–78.

Articles

Beckett, J. C., 'Gladstone, Queen Victoria, and the Disestablishment of the Irish Church, 1868–9', *Irish Historical Studies*, Vol. 13 (1962), pp. 38–47.

Cosgrove, R. A., 'The Relevance of Irish History: The Gladstone-Dicey Debate about Home Rule, 1886–87', *Eire-Ireland*, Vol. 13 (1978), pp. 6–21.

Feuchtwanger, E. J., 'Gladstone's Irish Policy: Expediency or High Principle?', *Modern History Review*, Vol. 3 (1991), pp. 21–23.

Foot, M. R. D., 'The Hawarden Kite', *Journal of Liberal Democrat History*, Vol. 20 (1998), pp. 26–322.

Hamer, D. A., 'The Irish Question and Liberal Politics, 1886–1894', *Historical Journal*, Vol. 12 (1969), pp. 511–32.

Hawkins, R., 'Gladstone, Forster, and the Release of Parnell, 1882–8', *Irish Historical Studies*, Vol. 16 (1969), pp. 417–45.

Herrick, F. H., 'Gladstone, Newman and Ireland in 1881', *Catholic Historical Review*, Vol. 47 (1961), pp. 342–50.

Heyck, T. W., 'Home Rule, Radicalism and the Liberal Party, 1886–95', *Journal of British Studies*, Vol. 13 (1974), pp. 66–91.

Lubenow, W. C., 'Irish Home Rule and the Great Separation of the Liberal Party in 1886: The Dimensions of Parliamentary Liberalism', *Victorian Studies*, Vol. 26 (1983), pp. 161–80.

Matthew, H. C. G., 'Gladstone and Ireland', *Journal of Liberal Democrat History*, Vol. 20 (1998), pp. 23–25.

Steele, E. D., 'Ireland and the Empire in the 1860s: Imperial Precedents for Gladstone's First Irish Land Act', *Historical Journal*, Vol. 11 (1968), pp. 64–83.

——, 'Gladstone and Ireland', *Irish Historical Studies*, Vol. 17 (1970), pp. 58–88.

Vincent, J., 'Gladstone and Ireland', *Proceedings of the British Academy*, Vol. 63 (1977), pp. 193–238.

Warren, A., 'Gladstone, Land and Social Reconstruction in Ireland, 1881–87', *Parliamentary History*, Vol. 2 (1983), pp. 153–73.

——, 'W. E. Forster, the Liberals and New Directions in Irish Policy, 1880–82', *Parliamentary History*, Vol. 6 (1987).

Gladstone and Foreign Affairs

Books

Beales, D., *England and Italy, 1859–60* (London, 1961).

——, 'Gladstone and Garibaldi', in *Gladstone*, ed. P. J. Jagger (London, 1998), pp. 137–56.

Chadwick, O., 'Young Gladstone and Italy', *Journal of Ecclesiastical History*, Vol. 30 (1979), pp. 243–59; reprinted in P. J. Jagger (ed.), *Gladstone, Politics and Religion*, (London, 1985), pp. 68–87.

Davies, W. W., *Gladstone and the Unification of Italy* (London, 1913).

Eldridge, C. C., *England's Mission: The Imperial Idea in the Age of Gladstone and Disraeli, 1868–1880* (London, 1973).

Farnsworth, S., *The Evolution of British Imperial Policy in the Mid-Nineteenth Century: A Study of the Peelite Contribution, 1846–1874* (1992).

Hammond, J. L., 'Gladstone and the League of Nations Mind', in *Essays in Honour of Gilbert Murray*, ed. J. A. K. Thomson and A. J. Toynbee (London, 1936).

Harrison, R.T., *Gladstone's Imperialism in Egypt: Techniques of Domination* (Westport, Connecticut, 1995).

Knaplund, P., *Gladstone and Britain's Imperial Policy* (London, 1927).

——, *Gladstone's Foreign Policy* (New York, 1935).

——, *The Gladstone–Gordon Correspondence, 1851–1891: A Selection from the Private Correspondence of a British Prime Minister and a Colonial Governor*, (Philadelphia, 1961).

McIntyre, W. D., *The Imperial Frontier in the Tropics, 1865–1875: A Study of British Colonial Policy in West Africa, Malaya and the South Pacific in the Age of Gladstone and Disraeli* (London, 1975).

Martel, G., *Imperial Diplomacy: Rosebery and the Failure of Foreign Policy* (Kingston and Montreal, 1986).

Medlicott, W. N., *Bismarck, Gladstone and the Concert of Europe* (1956).

Parish, P. J., 'Gladstone and America', in *Gladstone*, ed. P. J. Jagger (London, 1998), pp. 85–104.

Saab, A. Pottinger, *Reluctant Icon: Gladstone, Bulgaria and the Working Classes* (Cambridge, Massachusetts, 1991).

Sandiford, K. A. P., 'Gladstone and Europe', in *The Gladstonian Turn of Mind: Essays Presented to J. B. Conacher*, ed. B. L. Kinzer (Toronto, 1985), pp. 177–96.

Schreuder, D. M., *Gladstone and Kruger: Liberal Government and Colonial 'Home Rule', 1880–85* (London, 1969).

Seton-Watson, R. W., *Disraeli, Gladstone and the Eastern Question: A Study in Diplomacy and Party Politics* (London, 1935).

Shannon, R. T., *Gladstone and the Bulgarian Agitation, 1876* (London, 1963).

——, 'Midlothian: One Hundred Years After', in *Gladstone, Politics and Religion*, ed. P. J. Jagger (London, 1985), pp. 88–103.

Shaw, A. G. L., *Gladstone at the Colonial Office* (London, 1986).

Swartz, M., *The Politics of British Foreign Policy in the Era of Disraeli and Gladstone* (London, 1985).

Taylor, A. J. P., *The Troublemakers: Dissent over Foreign Policy, 1792–1939*, (London, 1957), chapter 3.

Articles

Biagini, E., 'Gladstone and Britain's Imperial Role', *Journal of Liberal Democrat History*, Vol. 20 (1998), pp. 33–35.

Gopal, S., 'Gladstone and the Italian Question', *History*, Vol. 41 (1956), pp. 113–21.

Harcourt, F., 'Gladstone, Monarchism and the "New" Imperialism', *Journal of Imperial and Commonwealth History*, Vol. 14 (1985), pp. 20–51.

Herrick, F. H., 'Gladstone and the Concept of the "English-speaking Peoples"', *Journal of British Studies*, Vol. 12 (1972), pp. 150–56.

Hopkins, A. G., 'The Victorians and Africa: A Reconsideration of the Occupation of Egypt, 1882', *Journal of African History*, Vol. 27 (1986), pp. 363–91.

Kelly, R., 'Midlothian: A Study in Politics and Ideas', *Victorian Studies*, Vol. 4 (1960), p. 119–40.

Knox, B., 'British Policy and the Ionian Islands, 1847–1864: Nationalism and Imperial Administration', *English Historical Review*, Vol. 99 (1984), pp. 503–29.

Lambert, S., 'The influence of Parliament upon the Foreign Policy of the Gladstone Government, 1868–74', *Bulletin of the Institute of Historical Research*, Vol. 23 (1950), pp. 94–96.

Medlicott, W. N., 'Gladstone and the Turks', *History*, Vol. 13 (1928), pp. 136–37.

Sandiford, K., 'Gladstone and Liberal-Nationalist Movements', *Albion*, Vol. 13 (1981), pp. 27–42.

Schreuder, D. M., 'Gladstone and Italian Unification: The Making of a Liberal?', *English Historical Review*, Vol. 85 (1970), pp. 475–501.

——, 'Gladstone as "Trouble-Maker": Liberal Foreign Policy and the German Annexation of Alsace-Lorraine, 1870–1871', *Journal of British Studies*, Vol. 17 (1978), pp. 106–35.

——, 'The Gladstone–Max Müller debate on Nationality and German Unification: Examining a Victorian "Controversy"', *Historical Studies: Australia and New Zealand*, Vol. 18 (1979), pp. 561–81.

Steiner, K. von den, 'The Harmless Papers: Granville, Gladstone and the Censorship of the Madagascar Blue Books of 1884', *Victorian Studies*, Vol. 14 (1970), pp. 165–76.

Whitridge, A., 'British Liberals and the American Civil War', *History Today*, Vol. 12 (1962), pp. 688–95.

Gladstone and his Contemporaries

Books
Abbott, B. H., *Gladstone and Disraeli* (London, 1972).
Bastable, J. D., *Newman and Gladstone Centennial Essays* (Dublin, 1978).
Bebbington, D. W., 'Gladstone and Grote', in *Gladstone*, ed. P. J. Jagger (London, 1998), pp. 157–176.
Blake, R., 'Gladstone and Disraeli', in *Gladstone*, ed. P. J. Jagger (London, 1998), pp. 51–70.
Chadwick, O., *Acton and Gladstone* (London, 1976).
Dessain, C. S. and Gornall, T. (eds), *The Letters and Diaries of John Henry Newman, 27: The Controversy with Gladstone, January 1874 to December 1875* (Oxford, 1975).
Drew, M., *Acton, Gladstone and Others* (London, 1924).
Goodlad, G. D., 'Gladstone and his Rivals: Popular Liberal Perceptions of the Party Leadership in the Political Crisis of 1885–86', in *Currents of Radicalism*, ed. E. F. Biagini and A. J. Reid (Cambridge, 1991), pp. 163–83.
Kerr, F., 'Did Newman answer Gladstone?', in *John Henry Newman: Reason, Rhetoric and Romanticism*, ed. D. Nicholls and F. Kerr (London and Bristol, 1991), pp. 135–52.
McClelland, V. A., 'Gladstone and Manning: A Question of Authority', in *Gladstone, Politics and Religion*, ed. P. J. Jagger (London, 1985), pp. 148–70.
Rooke, P. J., *Gladstone and Disraeli* (London, 1970).
Steele, E. D., 'Gladstone and Palmerston, 1855–65', in *Gladstone, Politics and Religion*, ed. P. J. Jagger (London, 1985), pp. 117–47.
Wheeler, M., 'Gladstone and Ruskin', in *Gladstone*, ed. P. J. Jagger (London, 1998), pp. 177–196.

Articles
Blyth, J. A., 'Gladstone and Disraeli: "Images" in Victorian Politics', *Dalhousie Review*, Vol. 49 (1969), pp. 388–98.
Foot, M. R. D., 'Gladstone and Panizzi', *British Library Journal*, Vol. 5 (1979), pp. 48–56.
Holmes, D., 'Gladstone and Newman', *Dublin Review*, Vol. 241 (1967), pp. 141–53.
Joseph, G., 'The Homeric Competitions of Tennyson and Gladstone', *Browning Institute Studies*, Vol. 10 (1982), pp. 105–15.
Prest, J., 'Gladstone and Russell', *Transactions of the Royal Historical Society*, 5th series, Vol. 16 (1966), pp. 43–63.
Reynolds, B., 'W. E. Gladstone and Alessandro Manzoni', *Italian Studies*, Vol. 6 (1951), pp. 63–69.
Stephen, M. D., 'Liberty, Church and State: Gladstone's Relations with Manning and Acton, 1832–70', *Journal of Religious History*, Vol. 1 (1961), pp. 217–32.

Index

Page numbers printed in **bold** type refer to illustrations; a letter n following a page number denotes note number(s) on that page.